D0897620

# DUBLIN CASTLE AND THE FIRST HOME RULE CRISIS: THE POLITICAL JOURNAL OF SIR GEORGE FOTTRELL, 1884–1887

# DUBLIN CASTLE AND THE FIRST HOME RULE CRISIS: THE POLITICAL JOURNAL OF SIR GEORGE FOTTRELL, 1884–1887

edited by
STEPHEN BALL

CAMDEN FIFTH SERIES
Volume 33

## CAMBRIDGE
### UNIVERSITY PRESS

FOR THE ROYAL HISTORICAL SOCIETY
University College London, Gower Street, London WC1 6BT
2008

Published by the Press Syndicate of the University of Cambridge
The Edinburgh Building, Cambridge CB2 8RU, United Kingdom
32 Avenue of the Americas, New York, NY 10013-2473, USA
477 Williamstown Road, Port Melbourne, VIC 3207, Australia
Ruiz de Alarcón 13, 28014 Madrid, Spain
Dock House, The Waterfront, Cape Town 8001, South Africa

First published 2008

*A catalogue record for this book is available from the British Library*

ISBN 9780 521 519212 hardback

SUBSCRIPTIONS. The serial publications of the Royal Historical Society, *Royal Historical Society Transactions* (ISSN 0080–4401) and Camden Fifth Series (ISSN 0960–1163) volumes, may be purchased together on annual subscription. The 2008 subscription price, which includes print and electronic access (but not VAT), is £101 (US $166 in the USA, Canada, and Mexico) and includes Camden Fifth Series, volumes 32 and 33 (published in July and December) and Transactions Sixth Series, volume 18 (published in December). Japanese prices are available from Kinokuniya Company Ltd, P.O. Box 55, Chitose, Tokyo 156, Japan. EU subscribers (outside the UK) who are not registered for VAT should add VAT at their country's rate. VAT registered subscribers should provide their VAT registration number. Prices include delivery by air.

Subscription orders, which must be accompanied by payment, may be sent to a bookseller, subscription agent or direct to the publisher: Cambridge University Press, The Edinburgh Building, Shaftesbury Road, Cambridge CB2 8RU, UK; or in the USA, Canada, and Mexico: Cambridge University Press, Journals Fulfillment Department, 100 Brook Hill Drive, West Nyack, New York, 10994–2133, USA.

SINGLE VOLUMES AND BACK VOLUMES. A list of Royal Historical Society volumes available from Cambridge University Press may be obtained from the Humanities Marketing Department at the address above.

*Printed and bound in the United Kingdom at the University Press, Cambridge*

# CONTENTS

# ACKNOWLEDGEMENTS

I should like to thank the National Library of Ireland, the British Library, the National Archives, Kew, the National Archives of Ireland, the National Library of Scotland, and Birmingham University Library for permission to publish the documents reproduced in this volume.

I am grateful to Dr Aled Jones and Dr Jon Lawrence, who have been, throughout, most helpful and enthusiastic Literary Editors; and to my copy-editor, Dr Hester Higton. I am grateful to Dr Owen Magee for his comments on aspects of this work and to Mr Roger Sweetman, SC for information on the provenance of Sir George Fottrell's journal. I would also like to thank Dr Maki Ikeda for her kind understanding and support over a number of years.

It has been possible for me to prepare this edition through the support of the University of the West of England and I would like to thank Professor Diana Jeater for providing me with sufficient time to complete this work.

## ACKNOWLEDGEMENTS

# ABBREVIATIONS

| | |
|---|---|
| AP | British Library, Althorp Papers |
| BL | British Library |
| CAB | The National Archives: Public Record Office, Cabinet Papers |
| Con. | Conservative |
| CI | County Inspector (Royal Irish Constabulary) |
| CO | Commonwealth Office |
| CP | British Library, Carnarvon Papers |
| CP/TNA | The National Archives: Public Record Office, Carnarvon Papers |
| CSO RP | National Archives of Ireland, Chief Secretary's Office, Registered Paper |
| DICS | District Inspector, Crime Special (Royal Irish Constabulary) |
| DM | Divisional Magistrate |
| DMP | National Archives of Ireland, Dublin Metropolitan Police Reports |
| E Div. | Eastern Division |
| EHP | British Library, Edward Hamilton Papers |
| FCR | Fortnightly Confidential Report |
| *FJ* | *Freeman's Journal and Daily Commercial Advertiser* |
| FO | Foreign Office |
| *GD* | H.C.G. Matthew (ed.), *The Gladstone Diaries, with Cabinet minutes and prime ministerial correspondence*, vols X and XI (Oxford, 1990) |
| GP | British Library, Gladstone Papers |
| *Hansard* | *Hansard's Parliamentary Debates*, 3rd series |
| HMC | The National Archives, Historical Manuscripts Commission |
| HO | Home Office |
| HP | Bodleian Library, William Harcourt Papers |
| IG | Inspector-General, Royal Irish Constabulary |
| *IHS* | *Irish Historical Studies* |
| ILL & INL | National Archives of Ireland, Irish Land League and Irish National League |
| INLP | National Archives of Ireland, Irish National League Proceedings |
| IRB | Irish Republican Brotherhood |
| JCP | Birmingham University Library, Joseph Chamberlain Papers |

| | |
|---|---|
| Lib. | Liberal |
| Lib. U. | Liberal Unionist |
| MCR | Monthly Confidential Report |
| | (IG) – Inspector-General |
| | (M) – Midland Division |
| | (SE) – South-Eastern Division |
| | (SW) – South-Western Division |
| | (W) – Western Division |
| MEPO | The National Archives: Public Record Office, Records of the Metropolitan Police Office |
| NAI | National Archives of Ireland |
| Nat. | Nationalist |
| NLI | National Library of Ireland |
| NLS | National Library of Scotland |
| *PMG* | *Pall Mall Gazette* |
| *PP* | *Parliamentary Papers* |
| PRONI | Public Record Office of Northern Ireland |
| RCHL | Churchill Archives Centre, Randolph Churchill Letters (microfilm) |
| *RE* | Peter Gordon (ed.), *The Red Earl: the papers of the fifth Earl Spencer 1835–1910*, 2 vols (Northamptonshire Record Society, 1981 and 1986) |
| repr. | reproduced in |
| RIC | Royal Irish Constabulary |
| RM | Resident Magistrate |
| SAP | Gloucestershire Records Office, St Aldwyn Papers |
| SRM | Special Resident Magistrate |
| TCD | Trinity College, Dublin |
| TNA | The National Archives: Public Record Office |
| *TRHS* | *Transactions of the Royal Historical Society* |

# INTRODUCTION

The most interesting man at Gray's was Fottrell, the man whose memoirs ought to be interesting, for he had acted as intermediary between the Castle (that is, Hamilton) and Parnell at the time when secret communications were passing between them, although openly they were at war.[1]

It has been observed that generations of historians 'have been chained to the task of explaining why Gladstone chose in 1885 to champion Irish claims'.[2] Chief amongst these claims was that for national self-determination, an issue that was to determine the course of Anglo-Irish relations for the next forty years. It was, as one contemporary politician observed, 'the pivot on which the political future turned'.[3] This volume re-examines why, late in 1885, the leader of the Liberal Party embraced the idea of Irish home rule without securing the support of his party for this radical departure. In his recent biography of Gladstone, Richard Shannon admits that his subject's conviction that Irish home rule had become a matter of absolute urgency by mid-December 1885 'has always been something of a puzzle', and he claims that 'there is nothing in the records' to indicate that Irish nationalism then threatened any 'critical degree of violent action' against the British government of Ireland.[4] This book therefore examines the advice and information that Gladstone received about Ireland at this critical time. It casts light on communications and transactions that are only partly known in order to provide a fuller chronology of the first home rule episode, and so to help solve this puzzle.

The idea that Gladstone's promotion of Irish home rule was an act of magnanimity that sprang from his sense of fair play was first articulated by the liberal historians John Morley and J.L. Hammond. More recent study, which has drawn attention to Gladstone's reading of histories that emphasized the injustices of

[1] Stephen Gwynn and Gertrude M. Tuckwell, *The Life of the Rt. Hon. Sir Charles W. Dilke*, 2 vols (London, 1917), II, p. 140.

[2] Alan O'Day, *History Sixth* (March 1990).

[3] A. Hawkins and J. Powell (eds), *The Journal of John Wodehouse, First Earl of Kimberley for 1862–1902* (London, 1997), p. 35.

[4] Richard Shannon, *Gladstone: heroic minister, 1865–1898* (London, 2000), pp. 394–395.

British rule in Ireland, lends support to this interpretation.[5] Historians less enamoured by Gladstone have argued that political opportunism played a large part in his adoption of home rule. His conversion to this policy has been minutely examined within the particular contexts of Westminster politics and the internal dynamics of the Liberal Party, the conclusion being that home rule was the means by which Gladstone sought to maintain his ascendancy over a fractious following and actually had little to do with Ireland. The Irish policies pursued by successive British ministries, it is asserted, 'cannot be explained in terms of Irish circumstance' but should be understood solely 'in terms of parliamentary combinations'.[6] Even scholars sympathetic to Gladstone have pointed out that, during his first administration of 1868–1874, he regarded Ireland as 'a preoccupation, not an interest, an embarrassment, not an intellectual attraction', his Irish policy aiming simply 'to draw a line between the Fenians & the people of Ireland, & to make the people of Ireland indisposed to cross it'.[7]

The view that decisions about Irish home rule were taken in isolation from events occurring in Ireland has been challenged and should be further considered in the light of the documentary evidence contained in this volume.[8] It is now recognized that Irish contingencies and the relative balance of forces in Irish politics crucially influenced calculations made by British politicians and civil servants.[9] For this reason, the machinery of the responsible departments of government and the role played by civil servants merit closer attention. One authority on the home rule question has admitted an 'inability to trace the way in which cabinet discussion was embodied in the work of government departments'. The rarity of contact between politicians and administrators is cited as one reason why the former 'lost interest in questions once they had turned from matters of cabinet antagonisms in to administrative grind'.[10] But this is hardly the case for Irish policy, as huge numbers of administrative papers generated in Dublin Castle at this time have survived, while the papers of the viceroys, Earls

[5] John Morley, *The Life of William Ewart Gladstone*, 3 vols (London, 1908); J.L. Hammond, *Gladstone and the Irish Nation* (London, 1938); H.C.G. Matthew, *Gladstone, 1809–98* (Oxford, 1997); R.F. Foster, 'History and the Irish Question', *TRHS*, 5th series, 33 (1983), pp. 169–192.

[6] A.B. Cooke and John Vincent, *The Governing Passion: Cabinet government and party politics in Britain, 1885–86* (Brighton, 1974), p. 17.

[7] Matthew, *Gladstone*, p. 194, quoting Gladstone to General C. Grey, the Queen's Secretary.

[8] Margaret O'Callaghan, 'Parnellism and crime: constructing a conservative strategy of containment 1887–91', in Donal McCartney (ed.), *Parnell: the politics of power* (Dublin, 1991), p. 103.

[9] See J.L. Loughlin, *Gladstone, Home Rule and the Ulster Question 1882–1893* (Dublin, 1986) and Alan O'Day, *Parnell and the First Home Rule Episode* (Dublin, 1986).

[10] Cooke and Vincent, *Governing Passion*, pp. xiii–xiv.

Spencer and Carnarvon, are testament to the close interest that they, and at least some of their colleagues, took in administrative matters. This volume therefore examines the information supplied to those in power by men who possessed 'a more worm's-eye view' of Irish affairs, and were therefore best informed about the fragile nature of the social and political fabric of Ireland during 1884–1886.[11]

Gladstone always denied that there was any question of his experiencing a *conversion* to home rule. He claimed to regard the issue as a political one that had evolved from the experience of government, and argued that his policy was shaped by the recognition of particular contingencies. Its gestation was a complex process that integrated long-, medium-, and short-term influences, and required not a single moment of decision but 'an assessment of opportunity and "ripeness"'. An adequate understanding of Gladstone's views on Ireland therefore requires that the precise context of their development should be established.[12] Drawing upon previously neglected sources, this volume reveals some of the interchanges of information and ideas that lay behind shifts in Irish policy in the mid-1880s. The political journal kept by George Fottrell establishes that important officials within Dublin Castle favoured home rule, an aspect of the question too often ignored in historical accounts of this subject, and supporting documents demonstrate that Gladstone's adoption of home rule was significantly influenced by advice he received from Irish officials. Because he only visited Ireland twice (in 1877 and, briefly, in 1880), Gladstone's knowledge of Ireland was derived from informants and advisers. Regarding the accuracy of the reports he received, particularly those relating to clandestine organizations, it can only be said that they represent the best information that was available to his correspondents at the time and, perhaps, that they reflect the imperfect nature of the information available to policy makers when decisions are required of them.[13] Notwithstanding this, during the last months of 1885, Gladstone was persuaded by those with first-hand experience of Irish affairs that the devolution of political power was urgently required to forestall the growth of Irish separatism and to reach an accommodation that took into account Charles Stewart Parnell's enormous popular support in Ireland.

[11] Roy Jenkins, *Gladstone* (London, 1995), pp. 536–537.
[12] Matthew, *Gladstone*, pp. 464–466.
[13] For useful critiques of Irish police intelligence in this period, see Owen Magee, *The IRB: the Irish Republican Brotherhood from the Land League to Sinn Fein* (Dublin, 2005), and Margaret O'Callaghan, 'New ways of looking at the state apparatus and the state archive in nineteenth-century Ireland: "Curiosities from that phonetic museum" – Royal Irish Constabulary reports and their political uses, 1879–91', *Proceedings of the Royal Irish Academy*, 104C, no. 2 (2004), pp. 37–56.

Close examination of the first home rule episode from the perspective of the Irish administration requires re-thinking the commonly held view that Dublin Castle was the exclusive province of reactionary and autocratic bureaucrats. Some historians have observed that the real strength of the Liberal approach to Irish government lay in this official sphere, where the management of affairs resided in the hands of liberal-minded administrators. While the political and administrative relationship between Dublin and Whitehall in this period is a matter of current investigation, much has remained inaccessible to historical inquiry, owing to a lack of memoirs by senior officials and, as has been pointed out, 'unpublicized achievements are easily forgotten'.[14] Nevertheless, the views articulated by the Irish Under-Secretary, Sir Robert Hamilton, and Edward Jenkinson, the Assistant Under-Secretary for Police and Crime, are striking reminders of the fact that, while Irish government was both over-centralized and unrepresentative, and its vice-regal form of government inconsistent with the principle of parliamentary accountability, the idea that Dublin Castle was simply a sinister, secret, and closed bureaucracy requires careful revision. The views of Hamilton and Jenkinson on Irish government did carry significant weight in 1885–1886 and therefore deserve to be more fully considered and widely known than hitherto.

Dublin Castle was a unique apparatus of state, which wielded extensive executive powers. It contained twelve of the more than forty boards, offices, and departments connected with the administration of Ireland, of which the Chief Secretary's Office was the most important. This was the controlling department of most of the branches of Irish government and the mainspring of its administration. As Under-Secretary for Ireland, Hamilton was the permanent head of the Irish executive and was responsible to the Chief Secretary for the routine working of government. He supervised the administration of nearly every public department in Ireland, in accordance with the general policy of the British government. In addition to liaising with the major English departments, the Chief Secretary's Office was above all responsible for law and order and the co-ordination of criminal intelligence.[15] In August 1882, this pressing task was assumed

---

[14] A.B. Cooke and John Vincent, 'Lord Spencer and the Phoenix Park murders', *IHS*, 18, no. 72 (September 1973), p. 583, and see Allen Warren, 'Dublin Castle, Whitehall, and the formation of Irish policy, 1879–92', *IHS*, 34, no. 136 (November 2005), pp. 401–430, which breaks new ground yet neglects the voluminous collections of Irish administrative papers in the National Archives, Dublin.

[15] Kieran Flanagan, 'The Chief Secretary's Office, 1853–1914: a bureaucratic enigma', *IHS*, 24, no. 94 (November 1984), p. 210; R.B. McDowell, *The Irish Administration, 1836–1922* (London, 1964), pp. 71–72.

by Edward Jenkinson, who, like Hamilton, was unfamiliar with the rigours of Irish government when he arrived in Dublin. Yet both men were persuaded by subsequent experiences that it was vital to persuade British politicians to adopt a conciliatory approach to nationalist demands. Their story remains an important yet neglected aspect of the first home rule crisis.

Contemporaries were aware that, during his service in Ireland, Hamilton slowly became convinced of the advisability of home rule from an administrative point of view, and was 'said to have had some share in influencing both his chief, Earl Spencer, and W.G. Gladstone in the same direction'.[16] Yet this fact has received scant attention in recent historical treatments of the subject. The conversion of Sir Robert Hamilton to home rule is a major feature of the primary manuscript in this volume, the journal kept by George Fottrell during three years of his service as Clerk of the Crown for Dublin (administering to the court of assize). In it he describes his relationship with the Irish Under-Secretary and his role as an agent for the Liberal administration in its confidential dealings with nationalist politicians during the first home rule episode. Fottrell's journal sheds new light on the political crisis of 1885–1886 and the inner nature of Irish politics in this period. It presents the unique perspective of a man who was, at the same time, a devoted supporter of Charles Stewart Parnell and a crown official with unique access to the Chief Secretary's Office. Fottrell, like others characterized as 'Castle Catholic' fixers, has never been given credit for facilitating discussion of the most contentious political question of the day.

The official documents and private correspondence reproduced in this volume present the perceptions of British officials working in Ireland and shed light upon the efforts that they made to influence the decisions of senior politicians. A close examination of the sequence and substance of contemporary events, as revealed in these papers, provides a fresh perspective on the high-politics conundrum of Irish home rule. Sir Robert Hamilton and Edward Jenkinson each made a persuasive case that, by the end of 1885, the concession of an Irish parliament was necessary in order to avert a revolutionary crisis in Ireland. The evidence presented here suggests that Gladstone's stance on Ireland was heavily influenced by prevailing doubts about the practicability of persisting with existing constitutional arrangements. This volume therefore offers a fresh perspective on the home rule crisis and places the greatest upheaval in British political alignments between 1846 and 1922 within both an administrative and an Irish context.

---

[16] *Dictionary of National Biography: second supplement* (London, 1912–1913), II, p. 358.

## The Manuscripts

Sir George Fottrell's journal was acquired by the National Library of Ireland in 1986.[17] The soft-bound notebook measures 16 cm × 20 cm and is composed of eighty plain white, paper leaves, of which 153 sides have been written upon in a reasonably legible hand. It is bound in black leather with gold trim, the outside front cover bearing a fragment of a label and the inside Fottrell's book plate. The manuscript is 50,220 words in length and was compiled between 13 January 1885 and 24 January 1887, with each entry being clearly dated. The entries were generally made at regular intervals, although there are some temporal gaps that are provided for by Fottrell's summaries of foregoing events. The journal deals almost exclusively with public affairs and social events at which politics were the main topic of conversation. Of Fottrell's family and professional life relatively little has been recorded.

It has been argued that the world of the Victorian politician was a closed and insular one, in which decision making was not confined to Cabinet discussions but was complemented by an informal process of discussion and intrigue. It was to this private institutional world that Fottrell managed to gain access.[18] His accounts of meeting with members of this inner circle, which included Joseph Chamberlain, John Morley, Sir Charles Dilke, and Randolph Churchill, are characterized by clarity of presentation and pungency of detail and display the qualities of first-hand reportage. The impression Fottrell gives of himself is that of an honest broker – earnest, well-informed, and guileless – although his role as an intermediary between antagonists did arouse a certain amount of distrust. His journal contains a number of interesting diversions and anecdotes, and its narrative passages give the reader a sense of the uncertain and rapidly changing political climate of Dublin in this period. Fottrell penetrated different circles of political influence in both Ireland and Great Britain and records the interplay between Irish Nationalist, Liberal, and Unionist politicians. His services were prized because, in 1885, Liberal politicians and administrators had to embark upon a steep learning curve about Ireland as they tried belatedly to establish an information network akin to Lord Randolph Churchill's 'Howth symposium' of Irish Tories. Fottrell's journal re-opens the subject of Joseph Chamberlain and Ireland, and his accounts of conversations with Chamberlain and Lord Randolph Churchill tend to emphasize

---

[17] NLI, MS 33,670. The journal was presented to the National Library of Ireland by Mrs Rose Sweetman, widow of Gerald Sweetman, TD, who was a descendent of Sir George Fottrell.

[18] Cooke and Vincent, *Governing Passion*, pp. xi, 21–22.

the former's relative ignorance of the subject. Both men, however, recognized Parnell as a powerful and potentially conservative force in Irish politics and Fottrell noted that there was 'remarkably little difference' in their political opinions at that time. While political opportunism played a part in their involvement in Irish affairs, they each displayed, for a time at least, a genuine desire to find a credible settlement of the national question, short of granting home rule. Fottrell's account also challenges the idea that Chamberlain deliberately wrecked a Liberal consensus on Ireland by engineering the central board scheme.[19] He casts further light on other relevant issues, such as Gladstone's once reactionary attitude towards Ireland in contrast to Disraeli's more considered approach, and the relevance to Ireland of parallel cases of self-government in Europe and the British Dominions. Overall, he provides a fascinating record of the ways in which both Liberals and Conservatives tried to deal with nationalist aspirations at a time of severe crisis in Anglo-Irish relations.

The other documents reproduced in the present volume refer directly to the matters described and to the issues raised by Fottrell in his journal. The letters and memoranda, many of them produced by Hamilton, Jenkinson, and Fottrell himself, provide insights into how the Irish question was dealt with in the closed worlds of Dublin Castle and Westminster; and they demonstrate that influential figures within this highly specialized community pondered the question of home rule in the light of information that they received from Ireland. The documents are mainly drawn from the Althorp, Carnarvon, Chamberlain, and Gladstone collections held in the British Library, the National Archives, Kew, Birmingham University Library, and the Chief Secretary's Office registered papers in the National Archives of Ireland. Although they represent only a small portion of the huge volume of correspondence and papers generated during the home rule controversy, they shed valuable light on the way that information on Irish affairs was transmitted to both the Conservative and Liberal leaderships.

The idea that English politicians knew little of Ireland and the administrative problems encountered at Dublin Castle was one that was shared by many Irish administrators. At the same time, it cannot be said that Ireland was merely a factor in party alignments and that Irish affairs were hardly reported or discussed.[20] Lord Spencer's correspondence attests to the close interest that he and his colleagues took in Irish affairs, whether in or out of office, and offers an interesting perspective on their changing attitudes towards Irish governance.

[19] **Journal (19 June 1885)**; Cooke and Vincent, *Governing Passion*, pp. 34, 39.
[20] Cooke and Vincent, *Governing Passion*, pp. 17–18.

This aspect of the home rule question has largely been neglected by historians. A comprehensive biography of Lord Spencer has yet to be written and Peter Gordon's valuable work on his life and correspondence has never received the circulation and attention that it deserves.[21] The documents presented here reveal much about Spencer's not-ungenerous attitude towards Ireland and help to revise the unsympathetic view of Spencer's second term as viceroy. They shed further light on the political in-fighting that came to overshadow his earlier achievements, when the decisive action he took at the time of the Phoenix Park murders in 1882 saw him emerge as a major political figure. They correct the view that he was 'reactionary, uncreative and inflexible' and reveal him to have been a devoted and tireless administrator who, as John Morley recalled, 'sought the best practical advisors and listened to them'.[22] The period leading up to the home rule episode was a particular ordeal for this deeply reticent man, as his talents as a governor and his capacity for solving difficult administrative problems were frustrated and compromised by political manoeuvring for which he had little talent. Although Spencer went on to hold high office in later Liberal administrations, he paid a heavy social price for supporting home rule and was regarded in aristocratic circles 'as an especial traitor'.[23]

## The Liberals and Ireland, 1880–1884

Gladstone's journey on the path to home rule began when he inherited the Irish Land War upon returning to office in May 1880. The Land League's campaign, which has been described 'as near a revolutionary movement as anything seen in the United Kingdom between 1800 and 1914' was met first with repression and then by the concession of the Land Act in April 1881.[24] The conflict was largely resolved a year later when, after violence had escalated in the countryside following the suppression of the Land League, a compromise was reached with the League's leadership in the so-called Kilmainham Treaty. This settlement was almost immediately overturned by the assassination of the Irish Chief Secretary and Under-Secretary in Dublin, an event

---

[21] Peter Gordon (ed.), *The Red Earl: the papers of the fifth Earl Spencer 1835–1910*, 2 vols (Northamptonshire Record Society, 1981 and 1986).

[22] Cooke and Vincent, 'Lord Spencer', p. 584; John Morley, *Recollections*, 2 vols (London, 1923), I, p. 220.

[23] George Askwith, *Lord James of Hereford* (London, 1930), p. 189; Charles Spencer, *The Spencer Family* (London, 1999), pp. 278–280.

[24] Matthew, *Gladstone*, p. 442, and see Allen Warren, 'Forster, the Liberals and new directions in Irish policy, 1880–1882', *Parliamentary History*, 6 (1987), pp. 95–126.

which ushered in three years of less severe repression, characterized by the measured use of the Prevention of Crime Act, and the concession of further reforms. During this period, conflict in Ireland was largely confined to the political arena and was characterized by the bitter criticism of the Liberal administration made by Parnell's followers in Westminster, on the public platform, and in the Irish press.

During the Land War, elements within the Irish home rule party had been severely compromised by their apparent association with agrarian crime. Therefore, when the immediate crisis that followed the Phoenix Park murders subsided, the Chief Secretary for Ireland, George Trevelyan, announced that the administration intended to 'draw a deep line between what is criminal and what is political'. He declared that lawful political activity would not be the concern of government but promised to use emergency executive powers to wage 'an undying and unrelenting war' against subversion and crime and so 'guard the operation' of the recent land reforms.[25] However, the simple juxtaposition of moral force and physical force in Ireland was always a gross oversimplification because, at times of social strife, the relation between the two was largely symbiotic.[26] In the absence of a satisfactory land settlement, such conditions were never far away. Gladstone's desire to maintain the social role of an overwhelmingly Protestant landowning class as an element of order in Ireland had retarded the development of an effective land purchase scheme. The idea of joint proprietorship embodied in the 1881 Land Act had been tactically successful but soon became the 'salient point of friction' between landowner and tenant. Rent disputes continued to be a frequent cause of disorder and the National League, established from the ashes of the Land League in October 1882, made the establishment of peasant proprietorship their primary objective. The continuation of land agitation placed a prolonged burden on Dublin Castle and ensured that Irish social and political life continued to be closely regulated. Intensified policing inevitably created friction both in Ireland and at Westminster, where the actions of the authorities were challenged by an ever more tightly organized Irish nationalist party. As Matthew has concluded, the use of coercion to uphold Irish landowners 'guaranteed the demise of Liberalism in Ireland' and became 'the treadmill on which the Liberal party ran from 1880 to 1885'.[27]

---

[25] *The Times*, 24 August 1882, p. 4.

[26] Matthew, *Gladstone*, p. 456.

[27] Ibid., pp. 444, 446, 450–451; Allen Warren, 'Gladstone, land and social reconstruction in Ireland, 1881–1887', *Parliamentary History*, 2 (1983), pp. 153–173.

By the spring of 1884, the attempt to distinguish clearly between politics and crime already appeared to be failing. As a consequence, at least one Irish official was warming to the idea of home rule and recognized that Irish nationalism had become integrated into the fabric of British politics, just as its representatives had become 'progressively enmeshed in parliamentary affairs'.[28] Acceptance of Parnell as a permanent fixture on the political landscape of the United Kingdom is nowhere more apparent than in the correspondence between Edward Jenkinson and Lord Spencer. By 1884, Jenkinson had identified what he regarded as the reformist tendency within the Irish nationalist movement, and was impressed by Parnell's willingness to seek a constitutional settlement of Irish grievances within the British parliamentary system.[29] He had also come to believe that the Government's employment of exceptional legal powers in Ireland, while justified in the short term, had not removed the causes of Irish disaffection and would not eradicate disorder.[30] His conviction that the Liberals were pursuing a fruitless policy in Ireland deepened during the second half of 1884. The Crown's efforts retrospectively to punish crimes committed during the Land War through expanded police powers and alterations to trial procedures, along with irksome controls over the press and public meetings, provoked a stream of criticism. In the two years after August 1882, more than one hundred separate attacks were made upon the administration of justice in Ireland by MPs, including damaging charges that legal officers had displayed sectarian bias in the selection of juries and that innocent men had been sent to the gallows.[31] By the middle of 1884, the reputation of Dublin Castle had fallen to a low point as a result of sexual scandals involving senior government officials, including the former Detective Director of the Royal Irish Constabulary.[32]

Wider changes in the political landscape of the United Kingdom increased Jenkinson's anxiety about Liberal policy in Ireland. Franchise reforms were set to increase greatly the size of the Irish electorate by granting voting rights to small farmers and landless

[28] O'Day, *First Home Rule Episode*, p. 85.

[29] Alan O'Day, *Irish Home Rule 1867–1921* (Manchester, 1998), p. 85.

[30] See **Document 1**. He informed General Sir Garnet Wolseley that the existing administrative machinery made the management of Ireland 'very hopeless work': Elizabeth A. Muenger, *The British Military Dilemma in Ireland: occupation politics, 1866–1914* (Dublin, 1991), p. 70, quoting Jenkinson to Wolseley, 20 January 1884.

[31] 'Return of attacks made by Irish MPs on the administration of justice of Ireland, 1882–1884'; Harcourt to Spencer, 29 October 1884; Spencer to Harcourt, 30 October 1884: AP, Add MSS 77330, 76933.

[32] Spencer to Gladstone, 7 and 11 March 1884; Spencer to Horace Seymour, 9 March 1884: AP, Add MS 76859; Frank Callanan, *T.M. Healy* (Cork, 1996), pp. 89–92.

labourers. It was anticipated that this would secure for Parnell four-fifths of Ireland's parliamentary representation at the next general election. The Liberals had faced a dilemma over this question: under the Franchise Act of 1850, only one in six adult males was allowed to vote in Irish parliamentary elections and, in October 1883, Gladstone questioned whether a larger electorate would be 'favourable or unfavourable to the interests of ultra-nationalism'. Spencer argued that the omission of Ireland from the franchise reform would present Parnell with a 'new & real' grievance. He was supported by Lord Northbrook, who, after consulting Jenkinson (his cousin), was convinced that this would strengthen the hand 'of the more violent of the nationalists, perhaps even those of the dynamite lot'.[33] The Liberals therefore had to face the probability that Ireland would henceforth be entirely divided between Nationalists and Conservatives. In the circumstances, Jenkinson believed that a radical departure in Irish policy was required. On 24 September 1884, he urged Spencer to 'lead England on the Irish question' by acknowledging the Irish aspiration for self-government. He argued that home rule was the 'true solution of the difficulty' and 'the only remedy for Fenianism and Dynamite outrages', and concluded that it would be better if the British presented home rule as 'a gift' rather than have it wrung from them by force.[34]

## George Fottrell, Joseph Chamberlain, and Local Government Reform

By this time, Spencer had become disillusioned with his role in Ireland and believed that the conditions that had made his presence there necessary no longer pertained.[35] As a born administrator, Spencer had an aversion to party politics. He baulked at the prospect of further criticism from the Irish party and believed that his freedom of action was increasingly circumscribed by critics within the Liberal Party. Whereas he had once been certain that English public opinion accepted the 'absolute necessity of repression' in Ireland, he felt that misgivings within the party over its continuation could not be ignored and acknowledged that there was 'no impetus of public opinion' to

---

[33] Gladstone to Spencer, 19 October 1883; Spencer to Gladstone, 20 October 1883; Northbrook to Spencer, 26 November 1883; Spencer to Northbrook, 29 November 1883: AP, Add MSS 76858, 76918.

[34] See **Document 4**.

[35] Horace Seymour to Spencer, 25 July 1884: AP, Add MS 76859. Seymour was private secretary to Gladstone and Spencer's brother-in-law.

help him through his present difficulties.[36] When Jenkinson wrote to
him in September, Spencer found himself 'in the midst of dreadful
abuse' from Irish MPs, with the nationalist press being 'violent and
abusive beyond all precedent'. Nevertheless, he refused to 'run away
from Irish difficulties' and assured Gladstone that he would remain
in Dublin.[37] Much, therefore, depended upon the formulation of
a policy that recognized that resistance to the law in Ireland had
been superseded by organized political opposition to the system of
government. Jenkinson believed that it was important that the Liberals
advertised their good intentions toward Ireland in order to reach
a settlement with moderate home rulers before the Conservatives
regained power. Spencer realized that he had got into 'hopeless
antagonism' with the Irish Parliamentary Party, which made it difficult
for him openly to accept the force of the nationalists' arguments. He
felt unable to acknowledge Parnell as the leader of Irish opinion given
that, as he informed Edward Hamilton, 'he never approaches me
and I cannot approach him'.[38] A means of communicating with the
nationalist leadership was clearly required and so, in early October, Sir
Robert Hamilton recommended the appointment of George Fottrell
as Clerk of the Crown for the County and City of Dublin. This thirty-
five-year-old graduate of the Catholic University was a successful
Dublin solicitor, who had been active in support of Parnell and his
party. He was already known to Liberal ministers, having spent a
brief and controversial spell as solicitor to the Irish Land Commission
in 1881–1882.[39] And, as Jenkinson had suggested, it was to moderate
nationalists like Fottrell that the Government had to turn if it was to
solve the problems of Irish government.

Any accommodation of the Irish party depended upon making
the system of government more acceptable to the majority of the
population. For the first thirty years of the Union, the machinery of
government in Ireland had been recruited almost exclusively from that
section of the Protestant community 'most unpopular with the mass
of the people'; appointees' claims to preferment rested on their loyalty
to the constitutional arrangement that had brought the Castle system
into being. By failing to offer a measure of Catholic participation
in its workings, it has been argued, any chance of building popular
confidence in Irish government and thus securing popular acceptance

[36] Seymour to Spencer, 25 July 1884; Spencer to Seymour, 30 July 1884: AP, Add MS
76859.
   [37] Spencer to Harcourt, 14 September 1884; Spencer to Gladstone, 26 August 1884;
Spencer to Seymour, 30 July 1884: AP, Add MSS 76933, 76860, 76859.
   [38] Spencer to Landsdowne, 16 August 1885, repr. RE, II, pp. 70–74; Spencer to Edward
Hamilton, 23 September 1884: AP, Add MS 76860.
   [39] See Appendix, p. 323.

of the Union was missed.[40] In spite of the introduction of merit as the basis of entry to the civil service in the mid-1850s, patronage continued to play an important part in the recruitment of senior officials, and the distribution of patronage was entangled with party and personal considerations. Lord Spencer, however, believed that 'ability, simple clearness of mind, honesty of purpose and strict impartiality' were the chief qualities required of public servants. In 1871, he declared that the principle upon which he acted was 'never exclude a fit man on account of his religion, but do not on account of his religion give him a place which another is better fitted to hold'.[41]

Fottrell's appointment also owed much to Spencer's desire to display greater probity in his appointment of legal officials. When the clerkship became vacant in the summer of 1884, Hamilton had initially wanted to appoint Samuel Anderson, a crown solicitor who, since 1865, had been intimately involved in the investigation and prosecution of Fenianism. After Anderson's octogenarian father had been forced to stand down as Crown Solicitor for Dublin, the son began to lobby for his position. Because Spencer wanted 'new blood' in the post, Hamilton proposed to compensate Anderson with the clerkship for Dublin.[42] The Chief Secretary, however, objected to the appointment of a man widely regarded as 'the personification of a Castle man' and who appeared to be bargaining for appointments in a highly unethical way.[43] Anderson was notorious in Ireland for 'packing' juries on behalf of the Crown, and Trevelyan complained that parliamentary debate of the issue had brought the Government close to disaster.[44] Fottrell benefited from this dilemma and assumed his new duties on 8 October. His appointment exemplified the growing influence of Catholic professionals within national administration and was, perhaps, the earliest example of the Liberal policy of 'greening' Dublin Castle in anticipation of Irish home rule.[45]

---

[40] Gearoid O'Tuathaigh, *Ireland Before the Famine, 1798–1848* (Dublin, 1990), p. 83.

[41] Spencer to Thomas O'Hagan, 2 November 1871: PRONI, O'Hagan Papers, D 2777/8/159. O'Hagan was the first Catholic to be appointed Irish Lord Chancellor in the modern era.

[42] Spencer to Hamilton, 28 July 1884; Hamilton to Spencer, 28 July 1884: AP, Add MS 77059.

[43] He informed Spencer that Anderson had 'been talking about how much he knows etc.': Trevelyan to Spencer, 28 and 31 July 1884; Hamilton to Spencer, 29 July 1884: AP, Add MSS 76964, 77059.

[44] Hamilton to Spencer, 4 September 1884; Trevelyan to Spencer, 15 August 1884; Spencer to Trevelyan, 21 August 1884; Hamilton to Spencer, 10, 11, and 14 October 1884: AP, Add MSS 77059, 76965, 77060. Anderson retained his crown solicitorship and received a knighthood: *Daily News*, 28 October 1884, p. 3.

[45] *United Ireland*, 28 October 1882; CSO RP 1884/22365; and see Lawrence W. MacBride, *The Greening of Dublin Castle: the transformation of bureaucratic and judicial personnel in Ireland, 1892–1922* (Washington, DC, 1991).

In December 1884, Hamilton told Fottrell that Spencer wanted him to ascertain privately the views of his acquaintances in the Irish Parliamentary Party on questions of government. Fottrell replied that, while he was not prepared to 'pump' his acquaintances for information or betray any confidences, he would attempt to make 'each side acquainted with the views of the other so as to promote harmony between them'.[46] Fottrell's acquaintance with both progressive Liberals, such as John Morley and Charles Russell, and many leading Parnellites made him an ideal intermediary. As his journals demonstrate, he proved to be an important source of intelligence for the Dublin administration during the home rule crisis of 1885–1886.

Fottrell's appointment coincided with the beginning of the end of Gladstone's second administration, as it tried unsuccessfully to resolve internal differences over Ireland. Prior to Fottrell's appointment, Spencer had not been under any pressure to concede to nationalist demands, largely because of improved economic conditions. In February 1884, Spencer reported that boycotting had almost ceased and the 'tone and demeanour of the people' had greatly improved. At the same time, the RIC suggested that 'secret intimidation' was still being exercised by secret societies in the south-western counties, where, Spencer admitted, the Irish authorities had to 'keep a firm hand to repress outrages'.[47] He therefore planned to re-enact several sections of the Crimes Act, which was due to expire in August 1885. Meanwhile, the question of local government reform rose to prominence. In December 1884, Joseph Chamberlain responded to favourable reports on the condition of Ireland by floating a scheme for locally elected councils and a representative central board in Dublin that would control education, the poor law, sanitation, and public works.[48] He argued that this was the only acceptable alternative to home rule, and claimed to have Parnell's approval for the scheme.[49] Fottrell informed Hamilton about this development and supplied him with a copy of Chamberlain's proposals, but the scheme caused considerable unease in Dublin. Spencer had long suspected that Chamberlain was planning to create 'a New Party' when Gladstone retired, and simply

[46] **Journal (13 January 1885).**

[47] Spencer to Lord Granville, 3 February 1884; Spencer to Gladstone, 26 August 1884; Spencer to Granville, 22 October 1884: AP, Add MSS 76884, 76860.

[48] W.H. Duignan to Chamberlain, 24 October 1884; Chamberlain to Duignan, 17 and 19 December 1884: JCP, JC8/3/1/19, 24, 25. See also C.H.D. Howard, 'Joseph Chamberlain, Parnell and the Irish "Central Board" scheme, 1884–5', and 'Documents relating to the Irish "Central Board" scheme, 1884–5', *IHS*, 8, no. 32 (September 1953), pp. 324–361, 240–242.

[49] This claim later caused controversy between Chamberlain and Parnell: see **Journal (3 January 1887)**; Howard, 'Joseph Chamberlain', p. 325; William O'Shea to Chamberlain, 9 August 1888: NLI, MS 5752, fos 338–342, 358–359.

interpreted the central board scheme as an attempt to divide Liberal opinion over the Irish question.[50]

Spencer believed that a new crimes bill should be the Government's first priority and so, on 13 January 1885, he consulted his law officers and police officials, who confirmed that certain core powers could not be safely abandoned.[51] Hamilton urged Spencer to retain some of the most controversial sections of the Crimes Act, including those covering police searches, the prohibition of public meetings, and the suppression of newspapers. Nevertheless, Spencer recognized the limitations of coercion, and acknowledged that over-reliance on emergency powers had obstructed the improvement of relations between the administration and the bulk of the Irish people. The recent extension of the franchise had made it difficult to ignore Irish demands for a more democratic and accountable system of government.[52] Spencer admitted to William Harcourt that government 'by force' was 'odious, and cannot be carried out forever'. If it were ever to become necessary, he added, 'then let us do away with our constitutional forms at once and govern Ireland like India'. This, he conceded, was currently 'impossible' and the only alternative was 'to do all you can to remedy real grievances and, while maintaining law and order, to gradually bring them over to our side'. By supplementing a crimes bill with local government and land purchase reforms, Spencer hoped to diminish the appeal of home rule to 'more moderate nationalists' and overcome the objections of Ulster Liberals to the continuation of coercion.[53] He attached great significance to the spread of Parnellism among public bodies, which had recently manifested itself in a more assertive approach towards Dublin Castle from municipal corporations, which had culminated in Limerick Council's refusal to pay police tax. He therefore favoured measures that might break the perceived connection between the actions of the political ministry and the authority of the Crown.[54]

In February, Hamilton asked Spencer to seek a swift resolution of the Cabinet's difficulties over Ireland in order to forestall further parliamentary criticism of the Irish administration. Spencer

---

[50] Howard, 'Joseph Chamberlain', pp. 332–338; Howard, 'Documents', pp. 242–248; Spencer to William Harcourt, 26 January 1883: HP, Dep 41; **Journal (30 January 1885)**.

[51] Courtney Boyle, 'Minutes of meeting on Crimes Act', 13 January 1885: AP, Add MS 77331. The meeting was attended by Spencer, Henry Campbell-Bannerman, Jenkinson, the Solicitor- and Attorney-Generals, and two divisional magistrates.

[52] Robert Hamilton, 'Renewal of the Crimes Act', 18 January 1885: AP, Add MS 77331; Spencer to Campbell-Bannerman, 25 January 1885: AP, Add MS 76868.

[53] Spencer to Harcourt, 19 January 1885; Spencer to Granville, 25 January 1885: AP, Add MSS 76933, 76884.

[54] See 'Limerick Police Tax', 6 November 1884: AP, Add MS 77318A; Spencer to Gladstone, 26 January 1885: AP, Add MS 76861. He suggested that the viceroy be replaced by a secretary of state and that a royal residency be established in Ireland.

responded by preparing two Cabinet memoranda, the first outlining his legislative proposals and the second evaluating each section of the Crimes Act.[55] Gladstone welcomed a fresh approach to Irish government but decided that Spencer's proposals to abolish the viceroyalty and extend land purchase were not feasible at that time. His plan to extend the jurisdiction of a new crimes bill to the entire United Kingdom also had to be abandoned after the English Law Officers pronounced it unworkable. In order to expedite matters, Gladstone formed a Cabinet committee, composed of Spencer, Campbell-Bannerman, Lord Carlingford, Trevelyan, Harcourt, and Chamberlain, to discuss the framing of Irish legislation.[56] When the committee convened in late April, however, its discussions were hampered by the fact that prior communication between Spencer and Chamberlain had broken down, the significant differences in their respective positions having emerged only the day before.[57] It rapidly became clear that opinion on the Crimes Act was hopelessly polarized. The experience of seeing many poor law guardian boards fall into the hands of nationalists and Land Leaguers during 1880–1882 had made Spencer cautious about wide-ranging local government reform. He argued that it would merely re-ignite political agitation in Ireland, arouse Conservative opposition at Westminster, and antagonize landowners without having the virtue of satisfying the Irish nationalists.[58]

Spencer's reluctance to trust Parnell played a large part in his reluctance to accept administrative reform. He had long endured what he regarded as unjustified personal criticism from Irish nationalist politicians. He deeply distrusted the Parnellites and this proved to be an enduring obstacle to his acceptance of the validity of what, in September 1884, he termed 'the cant phrase "Home Rule"'. He was prepared to consider a 'scheme to create a transitional form

[55] Hamilton to Spencer, 25 February 1885: CSO, RP 1885/14456; Spencer, 'Legislation for Ireland' and 'Prevention of Crime (Ireland) Act, 1882', 23 March 1885: CAB 37/14/19, CAB 37/14/20.

[56] Spencer to Edward Hamilton, 18 March 1885; Gladstone to Spencer, 18 and 30 March 1885; Edward Hamilton to Spencer, 27 April 1885: AP, Add MSS 76861, 76862; Dudley W.R. Bahlman (ed.), *The Diary of Sir Edward Walter Hamilton*, 2 vols (Oxford, 1972), II, p. 862. The committee was to consult Lord Hartington, Hugh Childers, and George Shaw-Lefevre on the question of local government.

[57] See Edward Hamilton to Spencer, 21 March 1885; Gladstone to Spencer, 30 March 1885; Spencer to Edward Hamilton, 25 April 1885; Spencer to Gladstone, 26 April 1885; Spencer, 'Notes of what passed re. Crimes Act in May 1885', 19 May 1885: AP, Add MSS 76861, 76862, 77319. See also Bahlman, *Edward Walter Hamilton*, II, p. 852.

[58] Spencer to Granville, 28 January 1883; Spencer to Harcourt, 15 January 1883: AP, Add MSS 76882, 76930; William L. Feingold, *The Revolt of the Tenantry: the transformation of local government in Ireland 1872–1886* (Boston, MA, 1984).

of government', providing that it could not be interpreted as the product of nationalist pressure, but feared that Chamberlain's scheme raised 'the danger of a Convention'. He warned Gladstone that it would be folly to establish a central authority that might behave as a rival centre of power in Ireland, and one likely to be dominated by men who had, he believed, 'shown themselves so incapable of governing Ireland by their vehemence of language and action, and their persistent efforts to break down law and order'.[59] Spencer was firmly supported by Hamilton, whose own suspicions had been aroused by Parnell's endorsement of Chamberlain's scheme. At this point, both men still regarded the Parnellites as quasi-republicans and predicted that a central board would merely promote 'anarchy and separation', paralyze the Irish executive, and further embitter relations between Britain and Ireland.[60]

At Westminster, opinion on the question remained divided, but Spencer's reputation as an experienced Irish administrator ensured that Chamberlain's proposals were rejected, albeit by a slim majority, on 9 May. Over the following weeks, Spencer and Chamberlain continued to negotiate over Irish legislation, but it was already known that Lord Randolph Churchill had indicated to Parnell that a Conservative administration would not renew the Crimes Act. All the same, three alternative crimes bills, each designed to modify trial procedures and perfect the Irish police system, were considered by the Cabinet on 21 May.[61] Shortly afterwards, Sir Charles Dilke took advantage of a visit to Dublin to seek a compromise on the question of local government. He recorded that Hamilton 'offered as a maximum county boards plus a General Education Board for Ireland to administer all the grants with rating powers and to [be] called a great experiment to be extended if it answered'. Spencer went further and offered four elective provincial boards to discharge many of the duties that Chamberlain had intended to assign to the Central Board, but, lamented Dilke, he 'obstinately refused to take the plunge of making the four Boards into one Board'.[62] On the other hand, when John Morley visited Dublin a few days later, he had found Spencer 'querulous', whereas his discussion with Hamilton, he informed Chamberlain, had pleased him better. Nevertheless, Gladstone correctly suspected that Spencer's intransigence over

[59] **Document 5**; Spencer to Gladstone, 30 April and 10 May 1885: AP, Add MS 76862.
[60] **Document 9**; Spencer, 'Memorandum. Proposed Irish legislation', c.April 1885: AP, Add MS 77319.
[61] Bahlman, *Edward Walter Hamilton*, II, p. 859; Henry Thring, 'Procedure for Trial (Ireland) Bill. Memorandum', 8 June 1885: AP, Add MS 77331.
[62] Sir Charles Dilke's diary, 25 May 1885 (copy): JCP, JC8/2/1.

coercion was in part due to the influence of Dublin Castle. On 6 June, Hamilton, concerned that falling agricultural prices would prevent tenant farmers from drawing further benefit from the Land Act, advised Spencer not to part 'with any power which helps us to deal with [boycotting], or allow the idea in any way to prevail that intimidation in itself is not a crime'.[63] Chamberlain, however, insisted upon Cabinet control over any new Crimes Act, thus making it a potential rather than an operative statute. This move was countered by Spencer who, acting upon Hamilton's advice, declared that present conditions made it likely that most of Ireland would have to be proclaimed upon the bill becoming law. The consequent deadlock was only resolved when a defeat in the Commons over the taxation of beer and spirits gave the ministry an opportunity to resign.[64]

Fottrell had been kept abreast of negotiations over the Crimes Act by John Morley and Thomas Escott, the editor of the *Fortnightly Review* and a confidant of Joseph Chamberlain.[65] Dilke had also consulted him about the central board scheme during his visit to Dublin and was clearly impressed by Fottrell, recording that he and Hamilton 'were the only two men who counted in that city'. Consequently, on the day that the Liberal administration resigned, Chamberlain asked Fottrell to supply him with information on the structure of local government in Ireland.[66] Chamberlain was collaborating with Escott on the final parts of what would be published as *The Radical Programme* and, having already drafted an article on local government in Great Britain, Escott asked Fottrell to supply an equivalent article on Ireland for the *Fortnightly Review*.[67] Fottrell completed his article in just three days and subsequently met twice with Chamberlain to discuss its contents. Fottrell also raised the question of local government with

---

[63] Morley to Chamberlain, 3 June 1885: JCP, JC5/54/615; Bahlman, *Edward Walter Hamilton*, II, p. 876; Hamilton to Spencer, 6 June 1885: AP, Add MS 77060.

[64] Gladstone to Spencer, 5 June 1885; Spencer to Gladstone, 6 June 1885; Hamilton to Spencer, 6 June 1885; Spencer, 'Further notes as what passed re. Crimes Act', 22 June 1885: AP, Add MSS 76862, 77060, 77319. Spencer was advised that the position of Ulster Liberals would improve if the province remained free from the Act: Campbell-Bannerman to Spencer, 5 June 1885: AP, Add MS 76871.

[65] See **Journal (1–31 May 1885)**.

[66] See **Journal (26 May 1885)**; Gwynn and Tuckwell, *Sir Charles W. Dilke*, II, p. 157; **Document 10**. The two became acquainted after Fottrell served on the Irish Land Commission and subsequently corresponded on aspects of the land question: Fottrell to Chamberlain, 30 May 1882: GP, Add MS 44475, fos 210–219; Chamberlain to Fottrell, 6 June 1882: JCP, JC8/4/1/1.

[67] Joseph Chamberlain, *A Political Memoir 1880–92*, edited by C.D.H. Howard (London, 1953), p. 108.

Randolph Churchill at a meeting that Dilke, from whom Churchill then had few political secrets, brought to the attention of Gladstone.[68]

However, Chamberlain's relationship with Fottrell proved to be a liability when he and Dilke proposed to visit Ireland to, as he explained to Michael Davitt, 'see for ourselves something of the present condition of the country & to obtain [. . .] a full expression of the wishes & wants of the people'.[69] While Fottrell was 'well regarded by most of the Irish party', he had some enemies within its ranks. Notable among these was Timothy Healy, who, according to William O'Shea, detested Fottrell. In spite of opposition from Parnell, Healy framed a leader for *United Ireland* assailing his local government scheme.[70] Subsequent attacks on Chamberlain by *United Ireland* were approved by Parnell, who no longer wished to pursue the national councils scheme, and led to the abandonment of Chamberlain's planned visit to Ireland. Chamberlain had been optimistic that his local government scheme would meet Irish demands and was exasperated by the turn of events.[71] He complained to Davitt,

> For a long while past it had been customary for Irishmen to complain, not without reason, that English politicians took no steps to ascertain on the spot the real wishes and opinions of the Irish people; and it certainly seems strange commenting on this complaint that the first two Englishmen who endeavour to relieve themselves from this reproach should be met with insult & offensive imputation.[72]

Although Chamberlain later denied that he developed a personal enmity towards Parnell for abandoning the central board scheme, or that it became the 'stimulating cause' of his opposition towards home rule, Fottrell was to find Chamberlain markedly less sympathetic to his views from this point on.[73]

## Sir Robert Hamilton and Home Rule

The collapse of the Liberal ministry proved to be a turning point in the development of Sir Robert Hamilton's views on Irish government.

---

[68] **Journal (17, 19, 23 June 1885)**; J.L. Garvin, *The Life of Joseph Chamberlain*, 2 vols (London, 1933), I, p. 546; Dilke's diary, 13 July 1885 (copy): JCP, JC/8/2/1; Roy Foster, *Lord Randolph Churchill: a political life* (Oxford, 1981), p. 231.

[69] Chamberlain to Davitt, 1 July 1885: TCD, Davitt Papers, MS 9374/983.

[70] O'Shea to Chamberlain, 13 July 1885: JCP, JC/8/8/1/50; T.M. Healy, *Letters and Leaders of My Day*, 2 vols (London, 1890), I, pp. 249–250; Chamberlain, *Political Memoir*, p. 154; Callanan, *T.M. Healy*, pp. 118–120.

[71] **Journal (5 August 1885)**; Chamberlain to O'Shea, 11 July 1885: JCP, JC/8/8/1/49.

[72] Chamberlain to Davitt, 1 July 1885: TCD, Davitt Papers, MS 9374.

[73] Chamberlain to Davitt, 8 June 1903: TCD, Davitt Papers, MS 9374.

The conversion of Hamilton and, subsequently, of Lord Spencer to home rule mystified supporters of the national council scheme. As Dilke put it, 'I confess that I have never been able to understand why Hamilton and Spencer held out as they did in May against the moderate scheme and have supported the extreme one'.[74] Indeed, for two weeks after Gladstone's departure from office, the Irish Under-Secretary continued to paint an alarming picture of the state of Ireland. He realized that the opportunity to correct 'defects in the existing machinery of the law' had now passed and feared that boycotting and intimidation would soon result. Hamilton also sensed an air of demoralization within the Constabulary and warned that 'another outbreak of crime would throw back the country terribly'.[75] He viewed the future of Ireland 'with the gravest apprehension', and claimed, 'The spirit of the people has not changed. Those who terrorized the country with impunity three years ago are as ready as ever to embark on the same course again.' A fresh outbreak of agrarian crime would, he feared, discredit the executive government and 'indefinitely retard the progress of the country towards quiet and prosperity'. Nevertheless, by the time the Conservative ministry took office, Hamilton had come to accept that the political obstacles to further coercion were insurmountable and was persuaded that Parnell's recent accommodation with the Conservatives would reduce the threat of disorder.[76] Within weeks, Hamilton had not only dropped the idea of further coercing Ireland, but had also embraced home rule as the only practical solution to the country's ills.

While his time with the Irish Civil Service Committee in 1874 would have provided Hamilton with some insight into the machinery of Dublin Castle, he knew relatively little of Ireland's history and political culture. Fottrell's assertion that Hamilton's want of acquaintance with the Manchester Martyrs controversy of 1867 'was a very strong argument in favour of Home Rule for Ireland' struck the Under-Secretary with some force.[77] Hamilton's growing friendship with Fottrell was the catalyst for his conversion to home rule, and he frequently drew upon the young lawyer's expertise in key areas such as legal procedure, education, local government, and land reform. As a result, his views on Irish government changed dramatically during the late summer of 1885.

---

[74] Dilke's diary, postscript to 25 May 1885 (copy): JCP, JC/8/2/1.

[75] Hamilton to Campbell-Bannerman, 15 June 1885: CBP, Add MS 41232, fos 124–125; **Journal (27 June 1885)**.

[76] Hamilton, Memorandum, 18 June 1885: AP, Add MS 77060; Hamilton, Memorandum on agrarian crime, c. June 1885: CP/TNA, PRO 30/6/64 (9).

[77] **Journal (24 May 1885)**.

Hamilton's conversion would have surprised many Liberals given the staunch support that he had given Spencer over coercion and local government in the spring. He had then been confident that Ireland could be pacified by moderate reform supported by a limited number of emergency powers and had therefore encouraged Spencer to resist the claims of militant nationalism. He believed that, by acquiescing to 'legitimate grievances' over land and local government, the Liberals might still divide the nationalist movement between those he described as the 'many honourable men who belong to it' and the fringe of 'born criminals who delight in crime'. The extent of self-government favoured by Hamilton at this time was, however, still quite limited and he regarded the measure, at least in part, as one means of defeating the National League. In conceding a measure of local government, he advised Spencer, 'you will then have cut the heart out of the combination, which is already weakened by the recent land legislation'.[78] Nevertheless, Hamilton had long believed that greater state intervention in Ireland was necessary to stimulate economic development and improve agriculture and transport.[79] In February 1885, having discussed the matter with moderate nationalists such as Edward Dwyer Gray, Hamilton had produced a Cabinet paper that advocated the development of 'free local government' in Ireland and, two months later, he prepared a scheme for converting the National Education Board into a representative body.[80] Yet the sea change in Hamilton's attitude to home rule was largely due to his being made familiar with the opinions of leading Irish nationalists courtesy of Fottrell's social arrangements. Indeed, Hamilton confessed to Fottrell that his home was 'the only place where he was able to meet men in touch with the people'. An important turning point came on 27 July, when Fottrell introduced Hamilton to Sir Charles Gavan Duffy, the veteran Irish nationalist and former prime minister of Victoria. Over the course of two meetings, Gavan Duffy convinced Hamilton of the urgent need to establish a separate Irish parliament in advance of local government reform. The appeal of Gavan Duffy's proposals lay in their legislative safeguards for Irish landowners and the Protestant minority, and an assurance that Parnell's underlying social conservatism would be the dominant influence in an Irish parliament. Hamilton admitted to being 'greatly struck' with what he

[78] Hamilton, 'Renewal of the Crimes Act', 18 January 1885; Hamilton, Memorandum, 18 June 1885: AP, Add MSS 77331, 77060. For Hamilton's proposals, see **Document 9**.

[79] Spencer to Gladstone, 22 May 1883, containing memorandum from Hamilton: *GD*, X, p. 451.

[80] See Hamilton, 'Local government of Ireland', 11 February 1885: CAB 37/14/9.

heard and passed his report to Lord Carnarvon who, unbeknownst to Hamilton, had already arranged to meet with Parnell.[81]

## The Irish Situation, 1884–1885

At this time, the Irish Republican Brotherhood appeared to be serving the wider political interests of Parnellism. On the other hand, Clan-na-Gael, its American counterpart, had retained its freedom to act independently, which made Jenkinson anxious about recent developments in the United States. In August 1884, he learned that the annual convention of the Irish National League of America in Boston had been so completely dominated by Clan-na-Gael delegates that the organization had become a mere 'cloak for Fenianism'.[82] He was particularly concerned by the election of Patrick Egan as its president. Egan had sat on the Supreme Council of the IRB and served as treasurer to the Land League, when he was strongly suspected of having financed the Phoenix Park murders in 1882. Jenkinson advised Spencer that Clan-na-Gael was likely to continue its support for the dynamite campaign in order 'to let Englishmen feel that there is a strong and desperate party of Force behind the constitutional agitators'. He believed that Parnell's public opposition to violence was based 'on grounds of expediency' and warned that if 'constitutional agitation' failed, then more violent action could be expected.[83] Spencer was concerned by the ominous reports that he received concerning Irish republicanism. He was aware that the Fenian movement had never died out in Ireland but, upon resuming the viceroyalty in 1882, he had expressed surprise at just how ubiquitous it appeared to be. He believed that 'treason' lay behind many of the most serious crimes of the Irish Land War and had therefore insisted that the offence of treason felony should come within the provisions of the Prevention of Crime Act. Over the following two years, Spencer had good reason to look out for rural secret societies in the West of Ireland and, in February 1884, warned Lord Granville that it 'must not be supposed that

---

[81] **Journal (28, 30 July, 5 August 1885); Document 11**. Carnarvon was familiar with Gavan Duffy's ideas, having met him on 22 July: CP, Add MS 60825, fo. 38. For the memorandum of his interview with Parnell, see Sir Andrew Hardinge, *The Life of Henry Howard Molyneux Herbert, Fourth Earl of Carnarvon, 1831–1890*, 3 vols (London, 1925), III, pp. 178–181.

[82] Jenkinson to Harcourt, 15 August 1884: HP, Dep 21. The British Government had several agents in America, including Henri Le Caron (Thomas Beach): see his *Twenty-Five Years in the Secret Service: the recollections of a spy* (London, 1892).

[83] See **Document 2**; Jenkinson to Spencer, 17 December 1884; Spencer to Edward Hamilton, 23 September 1884: AP, Add MSS 77035, 76860.

organizations for crime and agitation though considerably weakened are altogether deprived of power'.[84]

Fears over the strength of Fenianism in Ireland were compounded by the failure to eradicate dynamite attacks in Great Britain. Jenkinson's correspondence with Spencer in September 1884 reflected the frustration that he felt while working for the Home Secretary in London. Jenkinson resented the rough treatment that he frequently received from Harcourt, whom he accused of behaving 'like a spoiled child'.[85] Harcourt believed that it was impossible to accommodate Irish nationalism, and confessed to Spencer that he saw 'no ray of light in the future. It is idle to conceal from ourselves', he added, 'that we do and can only hold the country by force. I am afraid that the *via media* of conciliation is impossible – there is no alternative between separation and coercion.'[86] He told Jenkinson that compromise was doomed to fail 'against the inveterate hatred of race', and warned that 'the strong arm' of British power was all that kept the Union together and that the time was 'fast coming when it *must* be used'. Such statements made Jenkinson 'almost despair of the future of Ireland'. To make matters worse, a rift between Clan-na-Gael and the IRB had apparently occurred in February 1885 over the Supreme Council's opposition to the dynamite campaign, thus raising the danger that the minority of IRB members who favoured an 'active' policy might establish a separate 'violent party [. . .] composed of all the extreme men'. At the same time, Jenkinson wanted to take advantage of a fear that violence would harm the interests of the Irish in Britain and was confident that he could manipulate Fenian sentiment in the industrial cities of England.[87] In America, however, the prospects were not so bright. Jenkinson was severely shaken by the murder of one of his agents in New York and had learned that Clan-na-Gael was extending its operations to San Francisco, beyond the surveillance of his agents. 'Things look very ugly all round just now', Jenkinson informed Spencer in March, and a further dynamite explosion at the Admiralty almost ended his career at the Home Office.[88]

[84] Spencer to Granville, 28 January 1883, 3 February 1884; Spencer to Gladstone, 22 April 1883: AP, Add MSS 76882, 76884, 76857. See also **Document 3**.

[85] Jenkinson to Courtney Boyle, 13 August 1884: AP, Add MS 77034.

[86] Harcourt to Spencer, 21 September 1884: AP, Add MS 76933. Harcourt also complained 'in his old strain of the rotten and corrupt state of everything connected with the Irish Administration': Jenkinson to Spencer, 11 November 1884: AP, Add MS 77034.

[87] Jenkinson to Spencer, 2 October 1884, 4 February, 13 March 1885: AP, Add MSS 77034, 77036.

[88] Jenkinson to Spencer, 11 March, 21 May 1885: AP, Add MS 77036; *The Times*, 24 April 1885, p. 8; Jenkinson, 'Confidential memorandum', 22 June 1885: CP, Add MS 60829, fos 57–61.

While Jenkinson battled with the authorities in London, the economic condition of rural Ireland deteriorated and threatened to destabilize the country. This downturn had been accompanied – so the new Viceroy, Lord Carnarvon, told the Prime Minister, Lord Salisbury – by a 'very serious growth in the power of the National League'.[89] There were four main reasons why the influence and popularity of this organization had increased to the point where it had begun to challenge the authority of the state.[90] The first was economic: the agricultural depression that began in 1885 caused a fall in butter and stock prices that not only damaged the livelihood of small producers but also affected large-scale farmers and graziers. This, in turn, began to affect urban traders who were dependent upon the agricultural economy, and the financial position was further damaged when the Munster Bank failed on 14 July 1885.[91]

The second reason for the growth of the National League was its success in gathering clerical support for its programme. Parnell had not been able to consolidate his political hold on Ireland without the support of the Roman Catholic Church. His abandonment of the quasi-revolutionary aims of the Land League in 1882 had started a process of reconciliation with the Catholic hierarchy. Yet, in the early stages of the National League's development, few bishops had actively supported the organization. By the end of 1885, however, the Irish police concluded that a clerical–nationalist alliance was the main reason for the League's rapid expansion. It was asserted that the great majority of active branches owed their success to 'the moral and educational force imparted to their work' by priests who relied upon 'the protection against the law which their clerical status' gave them.[92] During 1882–1884, the Government had found an important ally in the Archbishop of Dublin, Edward McCabe, who disapproved of agrarian agitation and counselled restraint. Spencer regarded McCabe's death, in February 1885, as a serious blow to his administration, particularly as his successor, William Walsh, was a firm supporter of the National League.[93] It is therefore significant that,

[89] Carnarvon to Salisbury, 7 August 1885: CP, Add MS 60825, fo. 58.

[90] See Donald E. Jordan, Jr, 'The Irish National League and the "unwritten law": rural protest and nation-building in Ireland, 1882–1890', *Past and Present*, 158 (February 1998), pp. 146–171.

[91] See **Journal (30 July 1885)**.

[92] 'Summary of Irish National League', Owen Slacke, SRM, 8 March 1883, W.F. Forbes, SRM, 9 March 1883: CSO RPs 1883/6368, 1883/6537 in INLP, carton 6; Slacke, DM, 'Progress of the National League', 10 January 1886: CSO RP 1886/647 in RP 1888/26523; **Documents 41** and **42**.

[93] Spencer to Hartington, 13 December 1883; Spencer to Queen Victoria, 12 February 1885: AP, Add MSS 76899, 76975.

after Fottrell had delivered an address in appreciation of the dead prelate, he ensured that Walsh was one of the first nationalist figures to be introduced to Sir Robert Hamilton.[94]

The National League also benefited from the imminence of a general election. The nationalists had already demonstrated their growing strength by winning four of the six Irish by-elections held in the winter of 1884–1885. By this time, the League had been transformed into a formidable electoral machine, and its membership expanded rapidly in this period.[95] The number of branches, which had stood at 818 in July 1885, grew to 1261 by November, a five-fold increase since 1883. Some of the urban branches existed solely for registration purposes but could be brought into working order whenever they were required.[96] The League also made dramatic progress in Ulster, but remained most popular in the former Land League strongholds of Munster and Connaught, where it presented the danger of another land war. Early in 1885, it was reported that the League's expansion had provided a strong incentive 'for even the hitherto well disposed to join the winning side' and by the end of the year police officials concluded that 'the great mass of the people' had come under its influence.[97]

Finally, the National League's growth had been assisted by government policy. The Prevention of Crime Act was not directly employed against the National League because Spencer believed that its principal aims were constitutional. In February 1884, he had commissioned a report for the Cabinet that clearly distinguished between the objectives of the National League and those of the Land League, which had been suppressed in 1881. The Irish Attorney-General argued that, while the agitation for Irish self-government might be considered disloyal, in the absence of any threat of force, a campaign to abolish the Act of Union could not be regarded as treasonable and he warned that it would be 'a grave and unprecedented step' to prosecute its supporters. A subsequent decision

[94] Thomas J. Morrissey, *William J. Walsh: Archbishop of Dublin, 1841–1921* (Dublin, 2000), p. 47; **Journal (17 February 1885)**.

[95] Brian Walker (ed.), *Parliamentary Election Results in Ireland, 1801–1922* (Dublin, 1978), p. 129; Conor Cruise O'Brien, *Parnell and His Party, 1880–90* (Oxford, 1957), pp. 126–133.

[96] R.B. Beckerson, 'Progress of I.N. League during period from 1st January to 30th June 1885', 15 July 1885; Beckerson, 'Progress report of Irish National League, 30th June to 31st December 1885', 15 April 1886: INLP, carton 6; Francis Cullen, DM, to IG, 6 January 1886: INLP, carton 7.

[97] Slacke, DM, to Jenkinson, 17 January 1885: CSO RP 1885/1279; Thomas Plunkett, DM, 'Progress of the National League: divisional reports for quarter ending 31st December 1885', 4 January 1886: CSO, RP 1886/576 in RP 1888/26523.

to prohibit police surveillance of branch meetings further loosened the Government's control over the League.[98]

Perhaps the most important consequence of the failure to stem the growth of the National League was the resurgence of boycotting. Soon after taking office, Carnarvon concluded that 'silent and highly organized opposition' to the re-occupation of evicted farms was 'rapidly going beyond any legislative enactments which are within Government competences'.[99] Hamilton therefore asked George Fottrell to intervene with the League's secretary, Timothy Harrington, to discourage the intimidation that frequently underpinned boycotting. On 24 September, Carnarvon consulted Fottrell, whom he judged 'a clever, shrewd man', and was advised that the problem stemmed from the critically low level to which agricultural prices had fallen.[100] Carnarvon was assured by Edmund Dwyer Gray that the League's leaders were trying to bring boycotting under control.[101] Nevertheless, recorded cases had increased almost fourfold since the Conservatives had taken office and, during the Cabinet meeting of 6 October, Carnarvon (so Lord Cranbrook recorded) painted a 'picture of Ireland that was in the gloomiest colours'.[102] If, as has been asserted, British politicians in 1885 and 1886 were not concerned with influencing Irish audiences and could therefore afford to ignore 'the rising power and developing branch structure of the National League, the imminence of dark winter nights or of turbulent quarterly rent demands', it was not because they lacked evidence of their existence.[103] In fact, Carnarvon took immediate steps to strengthen the RIC and appointed a new Inspector-General. Meanwhile, Hamilton hoped that his new-found contact with nationalist leaders might prevent a serious crisis and ensured that Fottrell kept him well briefed about Parnellite intentions.

A major concern for Dublin Castle was the reportedly close relationship that had developed between the National League and the IRB. When the League had been established in October 1882, police officials had alleged that militant ex-Land Leaguers were planning

---

[98] Spencer to Hartington, 13 December 1883; John Naish, 'Memorandum: suppression of the Nat. League', 4 February 1884: AP, Add MSS 76898, 77318A. See also **Document 42**.

[99] Carnarvon to Salisbury, 7 August 1885: CP, Add MS 60825, fo. 58.

[100] See **Journal (5 August 1885, 3 February 1886)**; Lord Carnarvon's diary, 24 September 1885: CP, Add MS 60925; O'Day, *Parnell*, p. 97; and see **Document 14**.

[101] For memoranda of Carnarvon's meetings with Gray, see CP/TNA, PRO 30/6/67 (8), (22); Carnarvon to Sir Michael Hicks Beach, 23 September 1885: SAP, D2455, PCC/78.

[102] Nancy E. Johnson, *The Diary of Gathorne Hardy, later Lord Cranbrook, 1866–92: political selections* (Oxford, 1981), p. 576; Carnarvon's diary, 20 October 1885: CP, Add MS 60925.

[103] Cooke and Vincent, *Governing Passion*, p. 17.

to use it to revive the land war and 'set the country ablaze again'. It was reported that the new organization embraced 'the entire scope of the Land League, the Fenian Society and socialist secret societies'.[104] Although no formal alliance existed between the two organizations, during the course of 1884 the police formed the impression that the IRB was using the National League as a vehicle for republicanism. In Cork, the Special Branch reported that republicans were 'willing to assist the National League in every way in their power' in the hope of 'getting men of some position and character' to join their organization.[105] In Ulster, it was claimed that 'the more dangerous politicians of the League' favoured the establishment of IRB branches 'with the view of again playing the game of the old Land League when it becomes necessary to force on public opinion the necessity for a fresh change of the law in favour of the Nationalist or Separatist party'. By the beginning of 1885, shopkeepers and large farmers who a few years beforehand were believed to have 'had their sympathies upon the side of law and order' were now regarded as 'openly disloyal', and it was reported that republican principles were being embraced 'by a more numerous and more intelligent and respectable class than hitherto'. Jenkinson concluded that Fenianism had effectively been 'absorbed by the National League' and reiterated his warning to the Cabinet that, behind their campaign to secure independence by constitutional means, Irish parliamentarians knew that they had 'secret organizations and a party of force at their backs'.[106]

Furthermore, late in 1885, the requirement to select candidates for the general election led the National League to establish branches in areas where agrarian outrages had once been common. In Mayo, it was reported that most of the county's sixty branches existed solely for the purpose of raising funds for arms.[107] On 12 September, Jenkinson furnished Carnarvon with a report from his chief agent in Clan-na-Gael, who, upon visiting republican strongholds in north Kerry, was astonished at the recent change in republican attitudes and claimed

[104]Jenkinson to Spencer, 6 October 1882: AP, Add MS 77031; Henry Blake, SRM to Hamilton, 16 December 1882: CSO RP 1882/46856; J.H. Davies, 26 January 1883: ILL & INL, carton 9.

[105]DICS William Jacques to Butler, DM, 2 February 1884; Andrew Reed, DM to Jenkinson, 4 December 1884; DICS Robert Starkie to Plunkett, 28 November 1884: CSO RP 1885/1279; 'Memorandum explanatory of the aims and objects of the "Irish Republican Brotherhood" or "Fenian Society"', September 1890: TNA, CO 904/16.

[106]DICS Samuel Waters to Jenkinson, 12 December 1884; Slacke, DM to Jenkinson, 17 January 1885; DICS Henry Bouchier to Slacke, DM, 12 December 1884: CSO RP 1885/1279; Jenkinson to Spencer, 11 November 1884: AP, Add MS 77035. See also **Document 8**.

[107]J.H. Davies to Hamilton, 27 March 1886: CSO RP 1886/18485; RIC Special Branch report, c. January 1887: INLP, carton 7.

that 'all but a very few extreme men' had now joined the National League and were ready to support home rule.[108]

Jenkinson was concerned that a 'recrudescence of dangerous Fenianism' might upset the government's tentative accommodation with mainstream nationalists. Dublin was thought to be home to one hundred 'Invincibles', who, Jenkinson claimed, might 'at any moment become active and dangerous' should 'the signal for "active" work' be given. He believed that the forthcoming general election would be a pivotal event, and warned the Home Secretary that, if Parnell failed to obtain some form of home rule by the end of the next parliamentary session, then the Government would face 'a repetition of what happened in 1881 and 1882'.[109] As the fundraising activities of the National League of America gathered pace, Carnarvon received a lengthy report from Howard Vincent, the former CID Commissioner, who had recently toured Ireland. He claimed that Irish parliamentarians dreaded the violent influence of the 'Fenian exiles' in America but could not publicly repudiate them without losing their financial support.[110]

On 17 October, Carnarvon consulted Hamilton, who had learned from Fottrell that Parnell was distributing National League funds to well-known republicans for the purpose of, as the Commissioner of the Dublin Metropolitan Police, David Harrel, put it, 'screwing the sympathies and support of the IRB and Fenian societies in Dublin' for the Parliamentary Party. Harrel suggested that some of this money would find its way to the 'bad lot' in Dublin, who, he believed, were 'being held in reserve for whatever may be needed', and warned Hamilton that 'the movements of the dangerous classes in Dublin at present closely resemble what occurred in 1881–82'.[111] Jenkinson, however, argued that such payments were a regular feature of Irish parliamentary elections, particularly those involving Parnell, and remained confident that the Irish leader would quell any violence prior to the election. Nevertheless, he reminded Hamilton that there was practically 'no difference now between a Nationalist and a Fenian. They both have the same object in view; and both would resort to extreme Revolutionary measures, if they thought it would be to their advantage to do so.'[112] At the same time, Howard Vincent

[108] Jenkinson to Carnarvon, 12 September 1885: CP/TNA, PRO 30/6/62 (27).

[109] Carnarvon's diary, 3 August 1885: CP, Add MS 60925; Jenkinson to Carnarvon, 25 July, 5 August 1885: CP/TNA, PRO 30/6/62 (9), (13); **Document 12**.

[110] Howard Vincent to Carnarvon, 25 September 1885: CP/TNA, PRO 30/6/67 (9); Carnarvon's diary, 17 and 20 October 1885: CP, Add MS 60925.

[111] **Document 18**; Jenkinson to Carnarvon, 10 October 1885: CP/TNA, PRO 30/6/62 (26); Harrel to Hamilton, 15 October 1885: DMP, carton 1.

[112] Jenkinson to Hamilton, 16 October 1885: DMP, carton 1. For a study of this relationship, see M. J. Kelly, *The Fenian Ideal and Irish Nationalism, 1882–1916* (Woodbridge, 2006).

assured Carnarvon that separatism was 'confined only to the most extreme & violent section' of the nationalist movement and there was growing evidence of dissension within its ranks.[113] Members of Davitt's radical agrarian and social democratic wings of the movement already appeared to be pursuing independent objectives. Divisions between those who wished to democratize the leadership of the National League and secure a radical settlement of the land question, and the so-called National Conservatives who supported Parnell emerged at the annual commemoration of the Manchester Martyrs in Dublin, which was the largest and best organized of its kind since 1867 and, as Harrel commented, 'a very significant index' of the current strength of the Fenian organization.[114]

The pro-home-rule sympathies of Hamilton and Jenkinson resonated with Lord Carnarvon. While in many ways an orthodox Tory, Carnarvon's preoccupation with the social and economic condition of Ireland marked him out from most of his Cabinet colleagues. Hamilton had once served on Carnarvon's commission on colonial defences and held a high opinion of his abilities. He soon found that he was permitted to vent his opinions on questions of policy as freely to Carnarvon as he had to Spencer, and, as Lord Ashbourne later observed, Hamilton's views 'had much weight' with the Viceroy. On welcoming Carnarvon to office, Hamilton stated his view that the Irish question remained 'the question of the day', upon the treatment of which depended 'not only the future of this country but grave imperial interests also'.[115]

Carnarvon's outlook on Ireland was also influenced by Gavan Duffy, with whom he had talked and corresponded at some length.[116] He accepted that a return to 'the old methods of Government in Ireland' was impossible and had only accepted the viceroyalty on condition that coercion was to be abandoned. He was reassured by reports of his personal popularity in Ireland and he believed that the ministry might 'risk appealing to good feeling in order to govern under the ordinary law' until agricultural conditions improved and landlord–tenant relations recovered. Carnarvon was also in tune with the views of Edward Jenkinson. Some time before taking office, Carnarvon had requested an interview with him and later fought hard to retain his

---

[113] Vincent to Carnarvon, 25 September 1885: CP/TNA, PRO/30/6/67 (9).

[114] Harrel to Hamilton, 23 November 1885: CSO RP 1885/22351.

[115] Hamilton to Spencer, 13 August 1885: AP, Add MS 77060; Lord Ashbourne's diary, 27 March 1890, repr. A.B. Cooke and A.P.W. Malcolmson (eds), *The Ashbourne Papers, 1869–1913: a calendar of the papers of Edward Gibson, 1st Lord Ashbourne* (Belfast, 1974), p. 26; Hamilton to Carnarvon, 26 June 1885: CP/TNA, PRO 30/6/56, fos 15–16.

[116] O'Day, *Parnell*, pp. 50–51; and see CP, Add MS 60821.

troubled intelligence chief.[117] Although he was aware that Jenkinson was unpopular with the authorities in London, Carnarvon persuaded the Home Secretary, Sir Richard Cross, that Jenkinson's continued presence in the capital was essential for 'the unity & completeness' of police operations against Fenianism. He relied heavily on Jenkinson's ability to counter the security threat and wanted his operation in Great Britain to be maintained at the highest possible state of efficiency. Carnarvon understood that the apparent understanding between the Conservatives and the Irish nationalists could be quickly undermined by a resurgence of republican activity.[118]

During the second half of 1885, Hamilton and Jenkinson supported Carnarvon's efforts to persuade the Cabinet to reach an accommodation with Parnell. Jenkinson was convinced that decisive action should be taken prior to the general election and produced an extensive survey of the current state of Ireland for Carnarvon on 26 September. He suggested that the devolution of power to a representative Irish parliament was the only way of achieving order in Ireland and creating a more durable political union with Great Britain. Over the next two months, he kept the Government informed about developments within republican circles in the United States and across the United Kingdom.[119] The official memoranda prepared by Jenkinson and Hamilton clearly influenced Carnarvon. The Viceroy's reports to the Cabinet in early October reflected their viewpoint as he warned colleagues that Parnell's command over agrarian radicals and American 'extremists' looked increasingly uncertain. With landlords and tenants 'fatally estranged' and a large majority in Ireland set on a national parliament, he warned that present constitutional arrangements could not last indefinitely. And yet, Carnarvon's suggestion that a local parliament was the only viable alternative to crown colony government failed to convince his colleagues that constitutional reform was needed and, in the interests of party unity, he agreed not to press his views.[120] Nevertheless, Hamilton remained convinced that Carnarvon could use his current

---

[117] Harrel to Carnarvon, 19 September 1885: CP/TNA, PRO 30/6/67 (10); 'Lord Carnarvon's notes of his proposals to his colleagues before taking office': CP, Add MS 60823, fos 15–16; Jenkinson to Spencer, 23 April 1885: AP, Add MS 77036.

[118] Carnarvon to Cross, 5, 12, and 25 July 1885; Cross to Carnarvon, 6 July 1885: CP/TNA, PRO 30/6/62 (1), (4), (8), (2); Carnarvon to Cross, 4 and 31 August 1885: BL, Cross Papers, Add MS 51268, fos 147–148, 150–153.

[119] **Documents 15** and **18**; Jenkinson to Carnarvon, 10 October 1885: CP/TNA, PRO 30/6/62 (26).

[120] 'Memo. of important Cabinet on Tuesday 6 October 85': CP, Add MS 60823, fo. 17; Hardinge, *Earl of Carnarvon*, III, p. 193; Carnarvon's diary, 5 and 6 October 1885: CP, Add MS 60925.

popularity within Ireland to at least promote the idea of self-government. After discussing the matter with Fottrell, Hamilton presented his own analysis of the Irish situation and its possible remedies to Carnarvon on 31 October. This important document was later to influence the development of Gladstone's home rule scheme and, along with Jenkinson's paper of the previous month, presented the Conservatives with a forceful case for Irish home rule.[121]

The effort made by Hamilton and Jenkinson to influence political thinking on Ireland cannot be said to have been a concerted one. In fact, over the preceding three years relations between the two men had grown increasingly fraught. From the outset, Jenkinson's dynamic approach to his duties had brought him into frequent conflict with Hamilton, and their working relationship at Dublin Castle came to be seen as 'very anomalous'. Because Jenkinson's responsibilities were never clearly enough defined, Hamilton became frustrated by what he regarded as Jenkinson's inappropriately independent attitude and his refusal to acknowledge him as his superior. The then Chief Secretary was also perplexed by Jenkinson's habit of bypassing Hamilton on matters of policy and found him too independent of his own authority, complaining that he was expected to correspond with Jenkinson 'when it suits his pleasure, as if we were two members of the Government'.[122] Trevelyan did not feel that Jenkinson was shrewd enough to decide when to consult Hamilton, who had begun to suspect that his colleague was creating an *imperium in imperio* in the Chief Secretary's Office.[123] In fact, as Assistant Under-Secretary for Police and Crime, Jenkinson did have complete responsibility for these matters and effectively administered an autonomous department that reported directly to the viceroy. Whenever it did become necessary to consult the Under-Secretary, Jenkinson complained that Hamilton took 'every opportunity to assert in an offensive way his official superiority'.[124]

Spencer recognized that there was 'no real sympathy' between Jenkinson and Hamilton and concluded that both men displayed

---

[121] **Journal (28 October 1885); Documents 13** and **20.**

[122] Trevelyan to Spencer, 14 November 1882, 27 April, 21 December 1883; Hamilton to Spencer, 16 October, 23 November 1882; Hamilton to Trevelyan, 13 November 1882: AP, Add MSS 76950, 76955, 76959, 77058. Jenkinson claimed that Hamilton 'seems to forget that I have held high posts of great trust and responsibility in India, and have had much more experience in administration than he has': Jenkinson to Spencer, 21 October 1883: AP, Add MS 77032.

[123] Trevelyan to Spencer, 21 December 1883: AP, Add MS 76959. Jenkinson's unpopularity in London was put down by his detractors to his 'empire-building proclivities': see Bernard Porter, *The Origins of the Vigilant State: the London Metropolitan Police Special Branch before the First World War* (London, 1987), p. 184.

[124] Jenkinson to Boyle, 26 October, 5 December 1882; Jenkinson to Spencer, 21 October 1883: AP, Add MSS 77031, 77032.

'faults of style and manner'. In spite of his efforts to regularize the relationship between the two men, matters did not improve.[125] In July 1884, Hamilton was incensed by Jenkinson's 'insane' attempt to implicate members of the Irish Parliamentary Party in the dynamite campaign through the use of a female *agent provocateur*. He questioned whether Jenkinson should continue in government service, and complained to Spencer that his colleague's attempts to 'establish a system of espionage such as exists or has existed in continental countries seems to me to be opposed to constitutional government' and was bound to lead to a 'confusion of matters political with matters criminal'.[126] Spencer characteristically took a less serious view of the affair and so Hamilton persisted in his attempts to have Jenkinson removed from the Irish administration. Yet, when he suggested that the decline in crime in Ireland had rendered Jenkinson's position in Dublin redundant, he was opposed by the Home Secretary, who set aside his own differences with Jenkinson to dismiss the idea as a 'spiteful and mischievous' scheme 'to make Robert Hamilton monarch of all he surveys'.[127]

Nevertheless, Jenkinson never ceased to ruffle feathers at the Castle. Trevelyan disapproved of his brusqueness and tendency to place administrative efficiency above political considerations, taking action that often exacerbated Trevelyan's parliamentary difficulties and gave him 'a sense of uneasiness almost amounting to despair'. 'He seems so intent on keeping the peace that he considers nothing else', Trevelyan complained, and suggested that the administration was being driven 'in an arbitrary direction' by a man who appeared to have 'no notion of the higher political and moral aspects of affairs'. He criticized the haste with which Jenkinson often acted 'when it is a question of repression' and bewailed 'the immense unpopularity' he (Trevelyan) had thereby acquired 'from being a willing mouthpiece of what is stern and stiff in the policy of the Government'. Trevelyan found his capacity to defend controversial police actions limited by Jenkinson's reluctance to pass confidential information to the Irish Office, and complained that he was being made into 'a sort of Castlereagh against my own will'.[128]

[125] Spencer to Trevelyan, 16 November 1882, 22 December 1883; Trevelyan to Spencer, 22 December 1883: AP, Add MSS 76950, 76959.

[126] Hamilton to Spencer, 10, 12, and 18 July 1884: AP, Add MS 77059; *FJ*, 12 July 1884, p. 3. For an account of the affair, see Michael Davitt, *The Fall of Feudalism in Ireland* (Dublin, 1904), pp. 438–441.

[127] Spencer to Harcourt, 23 November 1884; Harcourt to Spencer, 23 November 1884; Spencer to Hamilton, 25 November 1884: AP, Add MSS 76933, 77059.

[128] Trevelyan to Spencer, 22 November 1882, 14, 19, and 20 April, 8 May 1883: AP, Add MSS 76951, 76954, 76955.

## Gladstone, the Liberal Party, and the Irish Question

It is probable that Jenkinson's obliviousness to departmental protocol and parliamentary procedure emboldened him to broadcast his opinions in ways that more seasoned officials might never have considered. Frustrated by the Cabinet's indifference to the Irish question, Jenkinson took action that appeared to breach the custom that prevented permanent civil servants from actively engaging in politics. In early November, he secured Carnarvon's permission to have his memorandum of 26 September printed for the information of the Cabinet.[129] Given the sensitive nature of the document, Carnarvon wanted tightly to restrict its circulation. There was, however, an apparent breakdown in communication and Jenkinson, rather than sending a single copy to the Prime Minister as he had been instructed, also prepared copies for Cross, Randolph Churchill, and, remarkably, for Spencer, Northbrook, and Lord Rosebery. Rosebery was the only Liberal politician to receive a copy of the memorandum before Carnarvon had chance to intervene, and yet Jenkinson's decision to send such a sensitive official document to former Liberal ministers at this critical time was significant. He clearly crossed the line that restrained permanent officials from giving privileged information to persons outside government, and Carnarvon quite understandably failed to comprehend how Jenkinson could have so completely misapprehended his intentions, given that the paper had been printed with the Viceroy's consent and would therefore be regarded as carrying official authority.[130] Jenkinson explained that he had not foreseen any objection to his showing an expression of his personal views to interested members of the Opposition.[131] His relationship with Spencer was already well established and, shortly before issuing the memorandum, he had spoken to Northbrook on the question of home rule.

Yet his decision to send a copy of the memorandum to Rosebery requires some explanation. Rosebery could hardly have been described as a specialist on the topic. As he himself had confessed in May 1885, 'My practical knowledge of Ireland is almost nil'.[132] But

---

[129] See **Document 15**.

[130] See **Documents 21–23**; Christy Campbell, *Fenian Fire: the British Government plot to assassinate Queen Victoria* (London, 2002), p. 177.

[131] Jenkinson to Carnarvon, 10 November 1885: CP, PRO 30/6/62 (36); A.B. Cooke and John Vincent, *Lord Carlingford's Journal: reflections of a Cabinet Minister 1881* (Oxford, 1971), p. 139.

[132] Rosebery to Chamberlain, 20 May 1885: JCP, JC5/61/1. His time at the Home Office as parliamentary under-secretary for Scottish affairs had not coincided with Jenkinson's secondment there: Rosebery to Gladstone, 4 June 1883: GP, Add MS 44288, fos 171–172.

it is clear that Jenkinson wanted his paper to reach the highest levels of the Liberal Party, and so it is significant that he wrote to Rosebery at a time when the latter was in frequent conference with Gladstone. Rosebery visited Gladstone at Hawarden on 27 October, just four days before the Liberal leader received Parnell's proposed constitution for Ireland. On 6 November, the day after Rosebery received Jenkinson's paper, Gladstone again asked to discuss the Irish question with him.[133] Although Rosebery had agreed to Carnarvon's request to keep an 'absolute and entire silence on the subject' of Jenkinson's paper, he had been greatly struck by the force of its argument. The following day, Gladstone arrived at Rosebery's country house, where he remained for the next three weeks and, while the evidence suggests that Rosebery kept his word, it is not unlikely that, in the course of his discussions with Gladstone at Dalmeny, he did convey some sense of the apparent urgency of the Irish situation to his party leader.[134]

Gladstone admitted to Rosebery that previous hostility between his ministry and the nationalists had left the Liberals 'in great ignorance of the interior mind of the Irish party' which, he claimed, had 'systematically confined itself to very general declarations'.[135] And yet, Gladstone's stance on the home rule question developed rapidly during his time in Scotland. Shortly before departing, he had told Chamberlain that Ireland was likely to become 'the first & overruling business' of domestic politics,[136] and, immediately after conferring with Rosebery between 10 and 13 November, he was ready to draft his two proposals for Irish self-government. Gladstone appears to have become convinced that the Irish question required a prompt and definitive settlement, and, after discussing Ireland with Rosebery on several more occasions between 16 and 26 November, he returned to Hawarden to await the results of the general election. On 4 December, the Liberal leader confessed to Spencer that he had 'Ireland on the brain' and was more than ever convinced that it would be 'the big subject' in the next parliament.[137]

As had been expected, the general election was a tactical triumph for Parnell, as home rule candidates won 86 of Ireland's 105 parliamentary seats. While Spencer characterized the result as 'dreadful', for Gladstone it represented 'the fixed desire of a nation, clearly and

[133] Rosebery to Gladstone, 6 November 1885: GP, Add MS 44288, fo. 265; Gladstone to Rosebery, 7 November 1885, repr. GD, XI, p. 424. It should be noted that the first letter dealt exclusively with the disestablishment of the Church of Scotland.

[134] See Rosebery to Carnarvon, 10 November 1885: CP, PRO 30/6/62 (35); and p. 41, n. 164 below.

[135] Gladstone to Rosebery, 13 November 1885: GP, Add MS 44288, fos 269–270.

[136] Gladstone to Chamberlain, 6 November 1885, repr. GD, XI, p. 423.

[137] Gladstone to Spencer, 4 December 1885: AP, Add MS 76863.

constitutionally expressed'.[138] In the United Kingdom as a whole, the election again appeared to be a triumph for Parnell. The Liberals had gained 335 seats and the Conservatives 249, the difference between them being made up by the 86 Irish nationalists. The solid Liberal majority that Gladstone had regarded as indispensable for an 'equitable and mature consideration' of the home rule question had not materialized. Yet, while he contended that it was for the Government to deal with Parnell, Gladstone declared himself ready to support a fresh initiative towards Ireland and acknowledged that 'at such a supreme moment' he might have to take on the question himself.[139]

By this time, Edward Jenkinson's belief that home rule should be regarded as a potentially conservative measure was spreading within governing circles. On 9 December, Sir Henry Ponsonby informed the Queen that the idea that nationalist demands must now be either accommodated or strongly resisted had gained ground, but warned that the latter course could be expected to provoke 'a renewal of dynamite attempts at outrage'. He explained,

> Mr. Jenkinson, who sees Irishmen of all descriptions, laments that some form of Irish Local Government was not granted two years ago. The best thing now he believes would be to give local powers to a Central Board on the lines of suggestions to be made by Mr. Parnell, with safeguards against exaggeration, as he thinks Mr. Parnell would then exert himself in the cause of law and order and would be the Conservative leader in the Irish Council.[140]

On 11 December, Jenkinson, perhaps prompted by a suggestion in the *Daily News* that Gladstone now favoured Home Rule, decided to contact the Liberal leader directly.[141] The two men had first met at the House of Commons in November 1882, and, in praising the 'splendid service' that Jenkinson subsequently rendered in Dublin, Gladstone assured Spencer 'I am not at all surprised. He made on me the most decided as well as most favourable impression.'[142] Jenkinson was by now aware that the Conservatives were unlikely to find a satisfactory settlement to the Irish question. When, on 5 November, Jenkinson had discussed the contents of his secret memorandum with Lord Salisbury,

[138]Spencer to Gladstone, 2 December 1885; Gladstone to Rosebery, 13 November 1885: GP, Add MSS 44312, fos 198–201, 44288, fos 269–270.

[139]Gladstone to Rosebery, 13 November 1885: GP, Add MS 44288, fos 269–270; Gladstone to Spencer, 4 December 1885: AP, Add MS 76863.

[140]Sir Henry Ponsonby to Queen Victoria, 9 December 1885, repr. G.E. Buckle (ed.), *The Letters of Queen Victoria, Second Series*, 3 vols (London, 1928), III, pp. 709–710.

[141]*Daily News*, 10 December 1885, p. 5.

[142]*GD*, X, pp. 371, 410; Gladstone to Spencer, 1 December 1882, 27 February 1883: AP, Add MSS 76856, 76857.

the Prime Minister had appeared deeply pessimistic about Ireland and admitted that 'Home Rule could not come from the Conservatives'.[143]

In spite of his past indiscretions, Jenkinson knew that his position as a permanent official prevented him from informing Gladstone of the Prime Minister's views, although Salisbury had made no secret of them when he met Spencer at Sandringham in mid-November.[144] Nevertheless, he did feel at liberty to supply Gladstone with his assessment of the Irish situation based upon what he believed to be happening 'behind the scenes both in Ireland and in America'. This correspondence is of considerable historical importance because it took place shortly before Gladstone brought the question of home rule to the forefront of British politics. Indeed, Jenkinson's letters and the debate they stimulated appear to have directly influenced Gladstone's thoughts and actions during the crucial last weeks of 1885.[145]

Upon leaving office, Gladstone had acknowledged that Parnell's anticipated success at the next general election would 'at once shift the centre of gravity in the relations between the two countries' and pose constitutional questions to which 'an adequate answer' would be required.[146] In early August, Parnell had indicated to him that a wider measure of self-government than that considered in the spring was required, and he subsequently chided colleagues for underestimating the probable consequences of 'a serious dispute with the Irish nation'. Given that Gladstone had scant direct experience of Ireland yet expected the question to 'open [. . .] like a chasm under our feet', first-hand information about conditions there was invaluable to him.[147] In October, Spencer briefed Gladstone in terms that closely resembled those used by Hamilton and Jenkinson in their reports to Carnarvon. He advised him that Parnell had 'united on his side most of the leaders of outrage' but that they would 'hold their hand' until he had 'had a chance to see if he can carry his plans for Home Rule'. He added, 'great anxiety prevails as to whether Parnell can hold the extremists who are very impatient' and warned that unstable relations between landlords and tenants had created 'a very dangerous position', in

[143] **Document 22**.

[144] See **Document 22**.

[145] Jenkinson's correspondence with Gladstone was noted briefly by J.L. Hammond, and has been cited in more recent works by Colin Matthew, Roy Jenkins, Richard Shannon, and Christy Campbell. Nevertheless, the letters are not well known and for many years lay undiscovered in the archives of Macmillan in a collection of documents used by John Morley for his biography of Gladstone: M.R.D. Foot, 'A revealing new light on Gladstone', *The Times*, 6 November 1970, p. 10.

[146] Gladstone to Spencer, 30 June 1885: AP, Add MS 76862.

[147] Katherine O'Shea to Gladstone, 5 August 1885; Gladstone to Rosebery, 10 September 1885: GP, Add MSS 56446, fos 78–83, 44288, fos 242–244; Gladstone to Spencer, 15 September 1885: AP, Add MS 76863.

which it was clear that the Irish Government was 'powerless & in the hands of the Natl. League'. Recent news from Dublin had led Spencer to believe that 'the moderate party' had been overruled and that boycotting would be 'carried on with renewed vigour'.[148]

By December, the situation appeared to have grown even more dangerous. In Ireland, the Constabulary confirmed that the Irish party now dominated political life in most parts of the country. The Inspector-General even paid tribute to the National League's control over its supporters during the general election, its officials having 'formed themselves into a police and watched and prevented the slightest misconduct on the part of their followers'.[149] His subordinates in the south and west of Ireland were, however, more pessimistic about the influence of the League. One divisional magistrate characterized it as an 'open organization for the promotion of crime & agitation', while another reported that the League was now so perfectly organized that the people yielded 'the most implicit obedience to it, even against their own individual interests'. It was characterized as a tyranny enforced by 'a secret organization' that had survived the suppression of the Land League and was now being revived.[150]

Jenkinson was therefore eager to impress upon Gladstone the growing influence of physical-force republicanism within Irish nationalist politics. He identified Clan-na-Gael as 'the main spring of the whole movement' because it controlled the flow of Irish-American money to Ireland and, by means of the Parliamentary Fund, could guide the policies of the Irish Parliamentary Party and the National League in Ireland. He warned Gladstone that the alliance between parliamentarians and Fenians was unlikely to last if Parnell's aspiration for Irish self-government was not met, and that violent agitation, political assassinations, and dynamite attacks might ensue. He therefore urged Gladstone to seize the opportunity offered by Parnell's overwhelming democratic mandate in Ireland to negotiate a settlement before the moderate majority of nationalists lost the capacity to restrain the 'violent' faction. If such an opportunity were to be squandered, he warned, the British Government would find itself 'face to face with open revolution'. Jenkinson assured Gladstone that allowing the Irish to regulate their internal affairs would not encourage separatism. Republicans, he predicted, would remain a

---

[148]Spencer to Gladstone, 5 October 1885: AP, Add MS 76863; and see Hamilton to Carnarvon, 5 and 6 October 1885: CP/TNA, PRO 30/6/57, fos 84–92.

[149]MCR (IG) for November 1885, Reed, 10 December 1885: CP/TNA, PRO 30/6/64 (38).

[150]MCR (SW) for November 1885, Plunkett, DM, 4 December 1885; MCR (W) for November 1885, John Byrne, DM, 4 December 1885, with minute from Carnarvon to Hamilton, 11 December 1885: CSO RPs 1885/23037, 24844.

small and ineffective minority in an Irish parliament dominated by 'a strong Nationalist Conservative Party' that, supported by the Catholic Church, the professional classes, and many large-scale agriculturalists, could be trusted to protect the legitimate interests of the landed and Protestant minorities. Jenkinson suggested that a bipartisan approach to the question might be adopted once the legitimacy of home rule had been conceded. In all, he painted a stark picture of a country 'passing through a great revolution' and, in a passage to which Gladstone appears to have paid particularly close attention, he warned, 'if we do not grant Home Rule now we shall later on either have to agree to "Separation", or have to prevent Separation by force of arms'.[151]

Gladstone found Jenkinson's letter both unexpected and impressive. The arguments that it contained clashed with advice that he was then receiving from party colleagues, who believed that grassroots Liberal opinion was against 'coquetting with Parnell'.[152] The former chief whip, Lord Richard Grosvenor, had warned him that any 'underground communications with the Irish party' might prove disastrous; and Rosebery contended that, when Parnell found himself unable to restrain his more radical supporters in the face of Tory indifference, he would be forced to bargain with the Liberals. He also warned Gladstone of the danger of proposing home rule without first securing the full support of the Liberal Party and British public opinion. A measure that was likely to cause such a 'mighty heave in the body politic', he argued, could only be carried 'by the full use of great leverage'.[153] In spite of this advice, Gladstone informed Jenkinson that he agreed 'very emphatically' with the 'leading propositions' of his letter and was promptly reminded by Jenkinson that failure to settle the question 'on broad and liberal lines' risked 'heavy trouble in the future'.[154] Certainly, the mood around Gladstone already seemed dark. On 12 December, Edward Hamilton recorded, 'The Parliamentary and political situation is bad enough, but it is made still worse by the state in which Ireland is represented to be. According to all accounts that state was never worse.' In spite of there being little violent crime, it was reported that 'a complete reign of terror' existed in Ireland. 'The League is absolutely dominant', he recorded, 'and it seems that we may be within a reasonable distance of a general strike against rent.'[155]

[151] See **Document 27**.

[152] Gladstone to Hartington, 15 December 1885, repr. *GD*, XI, p. 448.

[153] Grosvenor to Gladstone, 14 December 1885; Rosebery to Gladstone, 12 December 1885: GP, Add MSS 56446, fos 182–185, 44288, fos 279–284.

[154] **Documents 28** and **29**; *GD*, XI, p. 445.

[155] Edward Hamilton's diary, 12 December 1885: EHP, Add MS 48642, fo. 48.

Jenkinson's view of Ireland was echoed by another of Gladstone's correspondents. Also on 11 December, James Bryce reported upon a growing feeling that things could not continue there in their present state. The performance of the Conservative Government in the wake of Parnell's electoral success had, he believed, 'given rise to a feeling of contempt for the authority of Parliament' that only a broad measure of self-government could overcome. Bryce, like Jenkinson, believed that most nationalists were not in favour of an Irish republic and he reported that 'the revolutionary party' enjoyed little support outside the larger towns. But he warned Gladstone that Parnell was not a free agent and that, in order to reach a definitive political solution, it was imperative that the Irish leader should state what he and his more extreme backers were prepared to accept.[156] These warnings of incipient revolution clearly surprised Gladstone, who confessed to being 'somewhat stunned' by the abundance and diversity of recent communications on Ireland. Convinced that the dangers of the situation were 'too great, [and] time too precious, for the mere folding of arms', he promptly resumed contact with the nationalist camp through Katherine O'Shea.[157]

First-hand analyses of the Irish situation provided Gladstone with the information he would need if he was to convince British political opinion that home rule was now necessary. Jenkinson's letters to Gladstone had been private expressions of opinion but, with the writer's permission, Gladstone quickly circulated the intelligence to those of his colleagues who stood 'foremost in responsibility as to Ireland'. On 13 December, he hinted to Rosebery (superfluously in this case) that he now had reason to believe that 'very important *permanent* officers believe Home Rule is necessary'.[158] Two days later, Hartington was requested to read and circulate Jenkinson's letters to Granville and Spencer, and did so, after first showing them to Harcourt and Northbrook. While both men were already aware of Jenkinson's opinions on home rule, Harcourt was particularly impressed by the danger of failing to act decisively.[159] Although reluctant to commit himself to home rule at this point, he was, as Henry Labouchere

---

[156] James Bryce, 'Irish opinion on the Irish problem', 11 December 1885: GP, Add MS 44770, fos 5–14.

[157] Gladstone to Granville, 18 December 1885: GP, Add MS 56446, fos 193–195. See also Katherine O'Shea to Gladstone, 10 and 15 December 1885; Gladstone to Katherine O'Shea, 12, 16, 19, and 24 December 1885, all repr. *GD*, XI, pp. 446, 449, 454, 460–461.

[158] Gladstone to Rosebery, 13 December 1885, repr. *GD*, XI, p. 447.

[159] Gladstone to Hartington, 15 December 1885, repr. *GD*, XI, p. 448; Northbrook to Spencer, 17 December 1885, repr. *RE*, II, pp. 85–86; Hartington to Granville, 17 December 1885, repr. Bernard Holland, *The Life of Spencer Compton, Eighth Duke of Devonshire*, 2 vols (London, 1911), II, pp. 98–99; Hammond, *Gladstone and the Irish Nation*, p. 435.

reported to Randolph Churchill, 'preoccupied with the thought that if nothing were done, dynamite would begin again'.[160] But while the sense of urgency imparted by Jenkinson's forebodings galvanized some former ministers into action, those forebodings also stimulated resistance from others. Hartington, who felt starved of information about Gladstone's intentions, commented that, if the terms were as Jenkinson had set them out, it would be 'useless to think of stopping short of separation'. Gladstone's consequent warning that there was currently in Ireland 'a Parnell party and a separation or civil war party, and the question of which is to have the upper hand will have to be decided in a limited time' only served to increase Hartington's resistance to compromise. His assertion that the concession of home rule was tantamount to 'giving way to dynamite' was one that deserved an answer and Rosebery, who now accepted the case for home rule, countered that, while 'no prudent minister disregards dynamite', he should have 'sufficient moral courage not to avoid doing the right thing for fear he should be suspected of fearing dynamite'.[161]

Hartington, however, was not alone in his opposition. Northbrook was surprised that Jenkinson had expressed the case for home rule more strongly to Gladstone than he had in his own conversations with him. After further discussing the question with Jenkinson on 17 December, Northbrook concluded that his cousin's confidence that a conservative majority would 'keep the extremists in check' in a future Irish parliament was misplaced. Northbrook argued that the concession of Irish self-government would immediately dissolve the temporary bond between republicans and home rulers on both sides of the Atlantic. An Irish parliament would, he told Spencer, quickly become 'a platform for further demands and lead either to separation, or to a fight to prevent it, and a fight for which our action would have strengthened our opponents'. This would present the British Government with the 'simply appalling' choice of accepting separation or revoking home rule and thus facing 'the consequences of having to govern Ireland absolutely', alternatives that Northbrook regarded as 'so detestable' that he found it 'very difficult to choose between them'.[162]

On 22 December, Spencer furnished Gladstone with his most recent letters from Jenkinson and Hamilton. Gladstone did not give

[160]Labouchere to Churchill, 23 December 1885: RCHL 1/10. 1199; and see **Journal (3 January 1887)**.

[161] Hartington to Gladstone, 16 December 1885: GP, Add MS 44148, fo. 164; Gladstone to Hartington, 17 December 1885, repr. *GD*, XI, p. 451; Rosebery to Spencer, 31 December 1885, repr. *RE*, II, pp. 96–97.

[162]Northbrook to Spencer, 16 December, 1885, repr. *RE*, II, pp. 85–86 (incorrectly dated 17 December); and see **Document 30**.

Jenkinson's advice on the tactical means of securing home rule as much weight as he had given to his warnings of its necessity, but he was intrigued to learn that Hamilton was also in favour of home rule.[163] Although Gladstone considered the news of Hamilton's conversion to be 'most secret', he immediately used this information to persuade doubters such as Sir Henry James of the virtues of Irish self-government. On 24 December, he informed Rosebery that now both Hamilton and Jenkinson, the latter 'with dark anticipations otherwise', had 'both become Home Rulers'.[164] Notwithstanding the lukewarm reception accorded to Jenkinson's intelligence by some of his colleagues, Gladstone sought to use it to persuade the Conservatives that urgent action was required. An opportunity arose during a chance encounter with Arthur Balfour at the Duke of Westminster's Cheshire home, Eldon Hall, on 15 December. As Richard Shannon has pointed out, on the day previous to this meeting Gladstone had been informed by Frank Hill of the *Daily News* that Salisbury was preparing to make a significant concession to Parnell, provided that he could carry the Cabinet with him, and he received similar information from Canon Malcolm MacColl, who had recently spoken to the Prime Minister.

While this 'flyblown misinformation' may have provided Gladstone with sufficient confidence to confront Balfour directly, it was Jenkinson's disclosures about the current state of Ireland that provided him with his text.[165] What struck Balfour most forcefully during his encounter with Gladstone was the latter's claim to be in possession of

> information of an authentic kind – but not from Mr. Parnell – which caused him to believe that there was a power behind Mr. Parnell which, if not shortly satisfied by some substantial concession to the demands of the Irish Parliamentary party, would take the matter into its own hands and resort to violence and outrage in England for the purpose of enforcing its demands.

When a sceptical Balfour asked whether the government might expect 'to be blown up and stabbed if we do not grant Home Rule by the end of the next session', Gladstone replied that he understood 'that the time is shorter than that'. The puzzle over why Gladstone became convinced that Irish nationalism threatened a 'critical degree of violent action' in mid-December 1885 can therefore be better

---

[163]**Documents 33** and **34**.

[164]Askwith, *Lord James of Hereford*, pp. 158–159; Gladstone to Rosebery, 24 December 1885, repr. *GD*, XI, p. 461. Rosebery replied, 'I have known Jenkinson's opinion for months and it weighed greatly with me. But I had given my word of honour not to mention it': Rosebery to Gladstone, 26 December 1885: GP, Add MS 44288, fos 289–290.

[165]Shannon, *Gladstone*, p. 393; Andrew Roberts, *Salisbury: Victorian titan* (London, 1999), p. 364.

understood in the light of the disclosures recently made to him by Edward Jenkinson.[166]

Some within the Fenian movement had long regarded Gladstonian reformism as the result of their efforts.[167] The threat posed by republicans at this time, however, was not the only concern for Gladstone. He was also mindful of a warning that he had received from Harcourt that, if frustrated in their aims, the Irish party might withdraw *en bloc* from Westminster and establish a national convention in Dublin, thus making an orderly transition to devolved government impossible. This he considered to be the most formidable danger then facing the British Government, and one which brought 'into view very violent alternatives'.[168] In fact, the spectre of Irish secession had haunted Gladstone for some time and had fuelled his drive to establish central boards the previous spring. He also knew that, should Parnell lose his capacity to tame the revolutionary forces within his coalition, the resulting violence might delay the settlement of the Irish question for another generation.[169] Herbert Gladstone, perhaps influenced by Jenkinson's letter to his father, hinted at this possibility in his statements to the press. On 10 December, Gladstone had remarked to his son that the Irish question 'ought for the highest reasons be settled at once'. Yet it is significant that Herbert's first letter on the subject, written on 4 December and published in *The Times* on 12 December, did not allude to any threat of violence in the event of home rule being withheld. Some days later, however, he had come to believe that the British public needed to be aroused to this danger by, as he later put it, 'a cold shower bath, rather than by the customary method of disorder and crime'. His subsequent statement to the National Press Agency, made on 16 December and printed in the *Leeds Mercury* and the *Standard* the following day, hinted that an outbreak of serious disorder in Ireland might undermine the Liberals' capacity to deliver home rule.[170] Privately, Herbert accepted Jenkinson's view that Parnell was prepared to accept 'a reasonable basis' for home rule, but he was also concerned that the Irish leader might 'be forced by the Fenians to go on and make some "show for his money"'. The *Pall*

---

[166]Shannon, *Gladstone*, pp. 393–394; Balfour to Gladstone, 1 July 1886, printed in *The Times*, 5 July 1886, p. 10.

[167]Oliver P. Rafferty, *The Church, the State and the Fenian Threat 1861–75* (New York, 1999), p. 111.

[168]Matthew, *Gladstone*, p. 485; Northbrook to Spencer, 16 December 1885: AP, Add MS 76918; Gladstone to Grosvenor, 7 January 1886, repr. *GD*, XI, p. 475; Shannon, *Gladstone*, pp. 394–395.

[169]Gladstone to Spencer, 6 June 1885: AP, Add MS 76862; and see Loughlin, *Gladstone, Home Rule and the Ulster Question*, pp. 41–45.

[170]Morley, *Gladstone*, III, p. 258; Herbert Gladstone to Lucy Cavendish, 31 December 1885, repr. *GD*, XI, pp. 663–667.

*Mall Gazette* appeared, therefore, to carry an implicit message from Gladstone to Parnell when it stated that 'except in the event of any serious explosion in Ireland that would have the effect of exasperating the popular feeling in England against the Irish the country would in all probability endorse Mr. Gladstone's policy and give him an unmistakable mandate to carry it into law'.[171]

At the same time, Gladstone's political strategy was undermined by the untimely appearance of the 'Hawarden Kite'. Both Northbrook and Rosebery were concerned that, by prematurely announcing his intentions, Gladstone might allow Parnell to manipulate the situation to his own advantage. Gladstone, however, used his contacts within the press to ascertain the private views of leading Parnellites and, with the support and encouragement of Spencer, persevered in his correspondence with Balfour.[172] Emphasizing the fragile nature of the situation in Ireland 'of which every day's post', he claimed, brought him 'new testimony', Gladstone implored Balfour to treat the Irish question as one transcending party politics.[173] Balfour's subsequent reports to Salisbury were, however, guided entirely by party considerations and merely weighed the tactical advantage of forcing Gladstone to bring his potentially divisive proposals before the Liberal Party.[174] Gerald FitzGibbon had already warned Churchill against touching anything so 'red hot' as the national question, predicting that it would be far more advantageous if Gladstone or Parnell were forced to divide their respective followings by doing so.[175] Salisbury, in turn, was contemptuous of Gladstone's appeal for a bipartisan approach to the Irish question, which he interpreted as 'a crude attempt to draw a veil of disinterested patriotism over a contemplated surrender to the Parnellite vote'.[176] Nor did Gladstone's letters to Balfour cut any ice with the Cabinet: Cranbrook dismissed them as 'very Gladstonian and ambiguous & pledging not even himself

---

[171] Edward Hamilton's diary, 15 December 1885: EHP, Add MS 48642, fo. 52; *PMG*, 17 December 1885, p. 8.

[172] **Document 30**. Rosebery to Gladstone, 11 December 1885; Harold Frederic to Gladstone, 17 December 1885: GP, Add MSS 44288, fos 276–278, 56446, fos 186–187; **Document 35**; Gladstone to Spencer, 26 December 1885: GP, Add MS 44312, fos 238–239.

[173] Gladstone to Balfour, 20 December 1885, repr. *GD*, XI, p. 455.

[174] Balfour to Salisbury, 23 December 1885, repr. Robin Harcourt Williams (ed.), *Salisbury–Balfour Correspondence: letters exchanged between the third Marquess of Salisbury and his nephew Arthur James Balfour 1869–1892* (Hertfordshire Record Society, 1988), p. 127; Morley, *Gladstone*, III, p. 259; Matthew, *Gladstone*, p. 483; Roberts, *Salisbury*, p. 366.

[175] See Roy Foster, 'To the Northern Counties station: Lord Randolph Churchill and the prelude to the orange card', in R.A.J. Hawkins and F.S.L. Lyons, *Ireland Under the Union: varieties of tension* (Oxford, 1980), p. 264; FitzGibbon to Churchill, 7 and 22 December 1885: RCHL 1/10. 1149, 1196.

[176] Roberts, *Salisbury*, p. 366. Salisbury claimed that Gladstone's 'hypocrisy makes me sick': Salisbury to Churchill, 24 December 1885: RCHL 1/10. 1199b.

to anything real'.[177] On 9 December, Salisbury informed Churchill that he no longer wished to continue with the pretence of accommodating Parnell. Instead, he proposed to meet parliament with the intention of seducing anti-home-rule Liberals away from Gladstone and declared, 'we can have nothing to do with any advances towards the Home Rulers. The latter case would be quite contrary to our convictions, and our pledges, and would be quite fatal to the cohesion of our party.'[178]

It seemed that intelligent Conservative intuitions about Irish policy would always, in the end, be sacrificed to political opportunism. The encouragement offered by Salisbury to Carnarvon regarding the conciliation of Irish opinion seems to have been little more than a political manoeuvre. Once this tactic had, in the words of Salisbury's latest biographer, 'delivered the electoral goods', it was dispensed with.[179] The Prime Minister's manipulation of the home rule issue was successful because both Parnell and Gladstone underestimated his 'narrow cynicism'. They were mesmerized by the apparent sincerity of Carnarvon's words and actions, and failed to comprehend that the single-minded pursuit of party interest would eventually supervene.[180]

Gladstone's failure to read Salisbury's intentions cost him precious time. His attempt to engage the Conservatives in constructive dialogue over Ireland dragged on into the first weeks of 1886, time that might have been better spent preparing his own party for a new departure.[181] At the same time, by instructing Irish electors in Great Britain to vote against Liberal candidates, Parnell inevitably turned many backbenchers against home rule, and alienated a large section of liberal public opinion, most crucially in Ulster.[182] Parnell was not without his critics within nationalist circles: on 1 January 1886, Michael Davitt predicted that home rule would not come in that year, the Irish having 'Parnell's stupid support of [the] Tories to thank for this'. With some prescience, he confided in his diary,

> Had he [Parnell] stood neutral between both parties in English and Scotch elections Gladstone would have come back to power strong enough to give us a parliament. Popular feeling would not be as incensed against P[arnell] in Gt. Britain and the G.O.M. could have relied upon the rank & file of his party.

[177] Johnson, *Diary of Lord Cranbrook*, p. 588.

[178] Roberts, *Salisbury*, p. 361.

[179] Foster, 'Northern Counties station', pp. 233–261; Roberts, *Salisbury*, p. 360.

[180] Matthew, *Gladstone*, p. 478; Morley, *Gladstone*, III, pp. 260, 284; F.S.L. Lyons, *Charles Stewart Parnell* (London, 1977), p. 309.

[181] See Gladstone to Balfour, 5 January 1886, repr. *GD*, XI, p. 473. The Balfour correspondence was alluded to by the *Daily Telegraph* on 28 June 1886 and Gladstone subsequently consented to its publication: see *The Times*, 1 July 1886, p. 7.

[182] See **Journal (9 December 1885)**.

Davitt feared that the 'bragging of the Parnellites' over the defeat of Liberal candidates would 'destroy all chances' of home rule. When, Parnell subsequently 'boasted' to him of 'having balanced both parties so as to obtain the balance of power himself', Davitt replied that he had merely balanced the English members 'so evenly that he had probably united them against his dictation'. Further discussion of the subject, it was noted wryly, was 'evidently not relished'.[183] It is therefore clear that some of the strongest supporters of Irish independence believed that Parnell's much vaunted electoral success in 1885 was a Pyrrhic victory – a stunning tactical success but a costly strategic blunder.

Meanwhile, in Dublin, Carnarvon's attempt to promote an imaginative approach towards Ireland was floundering. For some time, Randolph Churchill had conducted his own Irish policy from the India Office: his engagement with the Catholic hierarchy on the education question being intended (so he candidly informed FitzGibbon) simply to 'mitigate or to postpone the Home Rule onslaught', in the hope that personal jealousies and 'Fenian intrigues' would meanwhile disrupt Parnell's national alliance.[184] At Dublin Castle, some officials counselled caution. The Attorney-General, Hugh Holmes, and the Assistant Under-Secretary, William Kaye, deemed it unwise to go further than investing elected county bodies with the powers of grand juries, and Holmes warned Carnarvon that even this small concession might be interpreted as the first step towards an Irish parliament. Nevertheless, the Viceroy was increasingly concerned about the state of the country and discussions with Lord Ashbourne and the Chief Secretary, Sir William Hart Dyke, alerted him to the 'extreme danger & difficulty' of the situation. He knew that there was little chance of galvanizing his colleagues into action because Hart Dyke had already warned him of the 'slack mental condition' of the party regarding Ireland. 'They know & understand nothing', he recorded; 'hate the subject – but hate still more a proposal to make any change'.[185]

After consulting Salisbury in late November, Carnarvon concluded that he had little option but to leave office. Nevertheless, he was persuaded to postpone his resignation so as to preserve the illusion of Cabinet unity and so made one last effort to persuade his colleagues to act. At two Cabinet conferences on 14 and 15 December he advocated

[183]Davitt's diary, 1 and 17 January 1886: TCD, Davitt Papers, MS 9545, DN/18. Davitt had publicly criticized Parnell's manifesto at the Manchester Martyrs rally in Dublin: *FJ*, 23 November 1885, p. 7.
[184]Churchill to FitzGibbon, 14 October 1885: RCHL 1/8. 978, repr. Winston Churchill, *Lord Randolph Churchill*, 2 vols (London, 1906), II, p. 4.
[185]Carnarvon, 'Conversation with Attorney Genl.', 16 November 1885; Sir William Kaye to Carnarvon, 20 November 1885: CP/TNA, PRO 30/6/67 (24), (26). Carnarvon's diary, 6, 7, and 21 November, 11 December 1885: CP, Add MS 60825.

constitutional change in Ireland in terms that closely resembled the language employed by Jenkinson and Hamilton. He argued that it was important to recognize the claim of four-fifths of the Irish electorate for self-government and suggested that a committee be formed to draft an 'Irish constitution', just as Jenkinson had recently suggested to Gladstone.[186] But with only Ashbourne to support him, Carnarvon merely secured a vague assurance that the Cabinet would not wholly 'debar themselves' from establishing a parliamentary committee on Irish government, should circumstances allow.[187] He returned to Dublin convinced that the Government would not announce a policy before parliament reconvened, thus leaving the Liberals to make the running on Ireland. The opinion recently offered to him by George Goschen – that Irish policy should consist 'in giving next to nothing & coercing' – was, he believed, one now shared by most of the cabinet.[188] With Irish interests now being equated with short-term party advantage, Carnarvon and Ashbourne had become isolated figures, the latter, Gladstone observed, 'all but cut in Dublin; eyed askance'.[189]

On 1 January 1886, in Carnarvon's absence, the Cabinet unanimously rejected the idea of co-operating with the Liberals over home rule. As Salisbury's most recent biographer concedes, this decision was influenced solely by British imperial interests and sprang from the fear that Irish self-government would encourage separatism in other colonial possessions. With regard to the Irish people themselves, it is argued that 'their aspirations would not have rated on a par with what he [Salisbury] was increasingly coming to see as Britain's greatest contribution to civilisation and mankind, her Empire'.[190]

## Lord Spencer and Home Rule

While the Liberals were aware that Carnarvon had lost all influence over events that were becoming increasingly dangerous, they preferred to leave the Irish question in the hands of the Conservatives. Nevertheless, the appearance of the 'Hawarden Kite' renewed hope

---

[186]Carnarvon's diary, 12 and 13 December 1885: CP, Add MS 60825; **Document 26**. Hamilton's memorandum (**Document 20**) was also printed for the use of the Cabinet.

[187]Roberts, *Salisbury*, p. 362. Carnarvon's desire for conciliation was signalled in an editorial in the *Dublin Daily Express* on 19 December 1885: see *FJ*, 21 December 1885, p. 4.

[188]Carnarvon's diary, 14 and 15 December, 1885: CP, Add MS 60825.

[189]Gladstone to Granville, 22 December 1885, repr. *GD*, XI, p. 457.

[190]Roberts, *Salisbury*, p. 370.

in Dublin that a satisfactory solution might be found and, as the result of the general election became known, Hamilton impressed upon Spencer the urgent need for a significant measure of self-government.[191] The development of Spencer's thinking on this question was a highly important element of the first home rule crisis but is one that has received relatively little attention from historians. Without the support of the former viceroy, whom John Morley considered to have 'a force of moral authority in an Irish crisis that was unique' and whose opinion on Irish questions was 'hardly second in weight to Mr. Gladstone himself', the home rule bill might not have emerged. Though Spencer was not generally regarded as an innovative politician, his reputation for disinterested and practical action and extensive experience of Ireland lent considerable weight to his views. Northbrook informed him that his position on home rule 'was the most important of that of any Englishman almost if not altogether' and, according to Morley, he exerted 'an influence over Liberal opinion without which Mr. Gladstone himself could hardly have gone on'.[192]

Jenkinson's earliest efforts to persuade Spencer to consider home rule had been hampered because, although the viceroy regarded him as 'a liberal broad-minded man', he lacked faith in his political judgment. While Spencer thought Jenkinson possessed ability, energy, and personal integrity, he had frequently remarked upon his lack of 'constitutional instinct or knowledge' and 'inattention to Parliamentary considerations' during his time in office.[193] Yet Jenkinson retained a strong sense of loyalty towards Spencer and continued, while in opposition, to furnish him with his assessments of the political situation in Ireland and America. Hamilton was also eager to keep Spencer informed, but was alert to the sensitivity of communicating with his former chief at what he considered a 'very critical' time for the Government. He confessed to 'a curious feeling that in writing to you I should have to consider whether there is anything I should not say, having so long been accustomed to pour out my mind to you'. Jenkinson, however, was concerned that the intransigent attitude towards Ireland displayed by Chamberlain and Hartington was giving 'strength & encouragement to the extremists'. In September 1885, he exhibited his customary obliviousness to constitutional procedure by offering to meet Spencer in order to pass on 'a great deal of interesting

---

[191] See **Documents 24, 32,** and **37.**

[192] Morley, *Gladstone*, III, p. 261; Morley, *Recollections*, I, pp. 220–221; **Document 30.**

[193] Spencer to Gladstone, 22 April 1883; Spencer to Harcourt, 2 August 1882, 7 March 1884; Spencer to Trevelyan, 26 July, 19 November 1882, 3 November 1883: AP, Add MSS 76857, 76929, 76947, 76951, 76959.

information' and warned him that Britain 'must decide upon one of two courses in Ireland. The present situation cannot last long. Everything is in a most critical & ticklish state.'[194]

Spencer dutifully passed on what he learned from Dublin Castle that autumn to Gladstone, who was to regret not having consulted the former viceroy prior to setting down his home rule proposals in mid-November. Nevertheless, he was subsequently to lean heavily upon the support and advice of Spencer, who cancelled a plan to spend the winter in India in order to be at Gladstone's disposal. But while Spencer confessed that he had no proposals to make at that stage, his views on Ireland were quietly evolving.[195] During his first term as viceroy in 1868–1872, he had become aware of the limitations of Castle government and had once declared, 'I shall soon become a Home Ruler, but for England & Scotland as well as Ireland for if some improvement is not made local questions will be constantly sacrificed.'[196] And yet, during his second term, Spencer could not be convinced that Ireland was sufficiently stable to permit any but the most limited measures of local self-government. After leaving office, however, his views began to change. On 16 August 1885, Spencer furnished Lord Lansdowne with a lengthy analysis of the political state of Ireland. Lansdowne, the owner of a large estate in County Kerry, was deeply hostile to home rule. Free from the shackles of office, however, Spencer at least felt able to consider this prospect. He was convinced that the understanding between Parnell and the Conservatives would soon collapse and he wanted the Liberals to consider some remedy, short of home rule, that might undermine Parnell's appeal to the Irish electorate. He suggested that a wide measure of local government, which stopped short of establishing a central authority, coupled with reforms to Irish administration and university education, might still win back middle-class Catholics to the Liberal cause. If this was to fail, then Spencer reluctantly conceded that an experiment in 'Federal Government with Home Rule' might be unavoidable.[197]

In early December, Spencer learned from Granville that a significant measure of Irish self-government was under consideration, and so travelled to Hawarden where he was shown Gladstone's plans. 'We have had tremendous talks', he told Lady Spencer, but admitted

---

[194] Jenkinson to Spencer, 6 and 12 August, 23 September 1885; Hamilton to Spencer, 13 and 30 August, 15 and 21 October 1885: AP, Add MSS 77036, 77060.

[195] Spencer to Gladstone, 2 December 1885, repr. *RE*, II, pp. 80–81.

[196] Spencer to T.H. Burke, 19 July 1871: NAI, Thomas Henry Burke Papers, box 3.

[197] Spencer to Landsdowne, 16 August 1885, repr. *RE*, II, pp. 70–74.

that he dreaded 'the political prospect more than ever'.[198] Spencer was greatly perturbed when, following Herbert Gladstone's conversations with the press, it was reported in the *Pall Mall Gazette* that he was 'practically convinced' that home rule was now unavoidable. He quickly denied the story but confessed to being 'in a most anxious state' about what line to take on the question. He informed Hartington that he was 'hopeless as to moderate measures', yet could not see his way 'over the difficulties of a bigger one'. Perhaps sensing that Spencer was, as he had privately confessed to being, 'much impressed and oppressed by the gravity of the position', Jenkinson and Hamilton each attempted to stiffen his resolve.[199] Jenkinson had learned from Northbrook that his recent letters to Gladstone had been shown to Spencer and, like Hamilton, he alerted him of the danger of turning the question into a party issue. Each man encouraged the incorporation of all shades of 'constitutionalist' opinion into a public discussion of home rule. Their eagerness for a bipartisan approach to the political crisis in Ireland mirrored that of Gladstone, who simultaneously advised Hartington that 'its becoming a party question would be a great national calamity'.[200]

While Spencer withheld his judgment at this point, he did acknowledge that the events of the previous six months had entirely changed the political landscape and was prepared to declare himself 'dead against simple oppression'. On 17 December, he confided to his private secretary, 'our old methods are hopeless and useless' and the idea that any government might have resort to them made him 'despair of the future'. He confessed, 'I have always been smothering a feeling that some Home Rule would have to be given, but I feel that I have nothing left to smother it with.' It was at this point that Spencer wrote to Hamilton to express this change of heart and subsequently learned of the Under-Secretary's views on the subject. Yet, notwithstanding his private feelings on the question, Spencer was still unwilling to commit himself to home rule and insisted to Gladstone that the question 'must remain a mere matter of speculation'.[201] He first needed to satisfy himself that Irish self-government would not encourage separatism. 'I cannot help thinking', he told Granville, 'that a great deal of the outcry arises from fear of Separation. If that were

[198]Spencer to Gladstone, 5 December 1885: GP, Add MS 44312, fo. 204; Spencer to Lady Spencer, 8 December 1885, repr. *RE*, II, pp. 81–82.

[199]Jenkins, *Gladstone*, p. 527; Spencer to Gladstone, 18 December 1885: GP, Add MS 44312, fos 205–208; *PMG*, 17, 18 December 1885, p. 8. Spencer to Courtney Boyle, 17 December 1885; Spencer to Hartington, 20 December 1885, both repr. *RE*, II, pp. 84, 87.

[200]**Documents 31** and **32**; Gladstone to Hartington, 20 December 1885, repr. *GD*, XI, p. 456.

[201]Spencer to Courtney Boyle, 17 December 1885, repr. *RE*, II, p. 84; **Document 33**.

shown to be impossible, moderate views might prevail.' Jenkinson therefore tried to persuade Spencer that, under home rule, Parnell would still be able to prevent republicans from exerting 'a dominating influence in Ireland'. He argued that British statesmen had to trust that the Irish people would act on 'principles of commonsense' and reject separatism. Spencer believed that the Catholic Church was a very important element in the development of Irish public opinion and he was not convinced that the Catholic bishops would provide a bulwark against separatism. While he accepted that their 'present inclinations' were against separation, he also believed that the parish priests were 'unduly influenced by public opinion' and might therefore be expected to side with whichever political faction proved strongest.[202]

Having carefully discussed the issues of policing, land reform, and taxation with Campbell-Bannerman at Althorp, Spencer spent Christmas Day setting down his views on the implications of Irish home rule for Gladstone. He was inclined to agree with Jenkinson and Gladstone that 'absolute separation' was neither desired by the large majority of home rulers nor would it be 'tolerated' by British public opinion. At the same time, he was concerned that, in disrupting the system of Irish administration, and simultaneously alienating the propertied classes, the British Government would provide 'hostile' nationalists with 'a new & better basis for agitation'. Home rule could only be justified, Spencer believed, if it could be confidently asserted that popular support for a moderate party was strong enough to prevent republicans from ever dominating an Irish legislature. Nevertheless, Spencer's mind was virtually made up, and on 27 December he advised Hartington that he thought the time for fighting home rule had passed, and that 'the sooner one takes the horrible plunge the better before fresh lives are lost and much more disaster is heaped on miserable Ireland'.[203]

Having reluctantly accepted the case for home rule, Spencer soon became frustrated by Gladstone's refusal to discuss the question openly with his colleagues. The Liberal leader, perhaps mindful of Jenkinson's recent correspondence, was concerned by the immediate threat of disorder in Ireland and its implications for home rule: 'what I feel apprehensive about', Gladstone told Spencer on 28 December, 'is the preliminary question shall we have a state of legality in Ireland to start from?' Arguing that this was something only the Government could know, he postponed further action until parliament reconvened and instead continued to press the Conservatives to take 'a strong and early

---

[202]Spencer to Granville, 29 December 1885, repr. *RE*, II, p. 92; **Documents 31** and **33**.
[203]Campbell-Bannerman to Spencer, 27 December 1885; Spencer to Hartington, 27 December 1885, both repr. *RE*, II, pp. 90–91; **Document 36**.

decision of the Irish question'. In the meantime, Gladstone adopted a strategy of proceeding towards home rule by stages in order to draw his colleagues into the process. He was satisfied that, by merely raising the question with his most trusted advisors, he had set in motion a 'slow fermentation of minds' that would convince his party of the necessity of the policy.[204] Spencer therefore cautioned Gladstone that some leading Liberals were not open to persuasion on this matter. Having discussed the Irish question at length with Hartington at Althorp during 30 and 31 December, Spencer informed Gladstone that his guest was very unlikely to fall in with a large measure of home rule and believed, as Hartington himself put it, that the policy 'would utterly smash up the party'.[205] Yet Gladstone remained averse to further consultation while the Conservatives remained in power, a policy that Rosebery claimed was leading to 'open revolt'.[206] He did, however, provide Granville and Spencer with a lengthy analysis of the situation on 26 December, and went into the details of possible lines of action four days later. Perhaps with Jenkinson's recent warnings in mind, Gladstone informed Spencer that, while he thought an instant decision on home rule was unnecessary, he did consider 'the faults & dangers of abstention greater than those of a more decided course'.[207]

Meanwhile, Spencer's own discussions with his colleagues had created the unhelpful impression that, while he saw the offer of home rule as inevitable, he did not believe that the policy would succeed. Both Northbrook and Campbell-Bannerman therefore tried to dissuade Spencer from declaring his hand, fearing that it would only strengthen Parnell's position and thus increase the difficulty of governing Ireland. They thought that if Spencer did not (as Northbrook believed) 'look upon home rule as a good thing in itself, but only as the least of two bad alternatives', and was unable to guarantee that it would not be used as a stepping stone to independence, he ought

[204]**Document 39**; Gladstone to Balfour, 2 and 23 December 1885, repr. *GD*, XI, pp. 455, 459; Matthew, *Gladstone*, p. 489; Gladstone to Granville, 9 December 1885: GP, Add MS 56446, fos 168–169.

[205]Spencer to Gladstone, 31 December 1885: GP, Add MS 44312, fos 245–246; Gladstone to Hartington, 2 January 1886, repr. *GD*, XI, pp. 471–472; Spencer to Granville, 31 December 1885, repr. *RE*, II, p. 96; Hartington to Granville, 17 December 1885, repr. Holland, *Spencer Compton*, pp. 98–99.

[206]Granville to Spencer, 27 December 1885, repr. *RE*, II, pp. 91–92. Gladstone to Granville, 28 December 1885; Spencer to Gladstone, 29 December 1885: GP, Add MSS 56445, fos 138–139, 44312, fos 242–244; Gladstone to Granville, 31 December 1885, repr. *GD*, XI, p. 469; Rosebery to Spencer, 31 December 1885, repr. *RE*, II, pp. 96–97.

[207]Gladstone to Granville, 26 December 1885, repr. *GD*, XI, pp. 462–463. Gladstone to Spencer, 26 December 1885; Granville to Spencer, 28 December 1885, both repr. *RE*, II, pp. 90, 92. Gladstone to Spencer, 30 December 1885, repr. *GD*, XI, p. 467.

to withhold his endorsement.[208] In fact, Spencer questioned whether a general declaration in its favour ought to be made before a detailed scheme had been developed, and reported to Gladstone, 'I confess that I look with dismay at what may occur in Ireland, if Parnell is backed by you in a demand for Home Rule: without a measure being carried at once.' Spencer therefore maintained his public silence and came away from a long meeting with Gladstone, Granville, and Chamberlain in London on 12 January convinced that 'nothing will be said or done in favour of Home Rule'.[209] It was not until the Liberals returned to power in early February that Spencer made what was regarded as the most significant endorsement of Gladstone's policy. As Edward Hamilton recorded,

> The predominance & urgency of the Irish question have made Lord Spencer a most important man. His concurrence in Mr. G's views placing him, as regards Ireland, among the most influential of men. He will do more to soothe apprehensions than any one else; & from the peculiar circumstances he is gaining a great position for himself.[210]

This view was echoed by the new Chief Secretary, John Morley, who later recalled that the 'shock of Spencer's conversion was severe, both social and political', because it gave 'driving point to general arguments for Home Rule. Without his earnest adhesion to revolutionary change in the principles of Irish government, the attempt would have been useless from the start and nobody was more alive to this than Mr. Gladstone himself'.[211]

Before Spencer made his views known, however, Hamilton had assured Fottrell in the strictest confidence that Lord Spencer 'would be sound on the Irish question'. By this time, Fottrell was actively circulating information about the various positions then being taken on the question by leading politicians. While John Morley later denied direct involvement in the home rule question prior to his statement to the Commons on 7 January 1886, he was in regular contact with Fottrell throughout December and later recorded that 'signals and intimations were not wholly wanting from the Irish camp' on the matter at that time.[212] Morley was trying to hold the Liberals

---

[208]Spencer to Granville, 29 and 31 December 1885; Spencer to Rosebery, 30 December 1885; Hartington to Spencer, 3 January 1886; Northbrook to Spencer, 7 January 1886, all repr. *RE*, II, pp. 92–94, 96–100.

[209]Spencer to Gladstone, 8 January 1886; Spencer to Lady Spencer, 12 January 1886, both repr. *RE*, II, pp. 100–102.

[210]Edward Hamilton's diary, 7 February 1886: EHP, Add MS 48643, fo. 3.

[211]Morley, *Recollections*, I, p. 219.

[212]See **Journal (4, 27 January 1886)**; Morley, *Gladstone*, III, pp. 296, 274. Morley did, however, speak in favour of home rule on 21 December 1885.

together over Ireland and promised Chamberlain that he would pass on whatever he learned from Fottrell, while conceding that 'as we all know, all depends on Parnell, and he keeps his own counsel'.[213]

At the end of the year, Morley asked Fottrell to travel to Birmingham to try to persuade Chamberlain to support the idea of an Irish parliament. Fottrell had maintained contact with Chamberlain during the autumn and had been dismayed by the latter's anti-home-rule speech at Warrington on 8 September. He refused, however, to believe that Chamberlain was set against a separate legislature for Ireland until an exchange of letters confirmed that his former collaborator remained committed to the central board scheme.[214] Chamberlain maintained that he wanted Ireland to have 'the widest possible measure of local government consistent with the security and integrity of the Empire', but did not believe, as he told Morley, in the viability of 'anything between my scheme of National Councils & absolute separation'. He blamed the unreasonable and impractical demands of the Nationalists for the abandonment of his own scheme. 'A substantial good', he informed one of them, 'is therefore abandoned for an illusory gain, the shadow is once more preferred to the substance'.[215]

Like Rosebery, Chamberlain did not believe that Parnell could secure home rule from the Conservatives and would therefore have to moderate his demands and approach the Liberals. To negotiate with Parnell at that point, he insisted, ran the risk of providing Salisbury with an opportunity to dissolve parliament and call an election on the question of home rule. Chamberlain set out his position on the question to Sir Edward Russell of the *Liverpool Daily Post*,

> My own policy would be to say to Parnell 'We offered you the utmost that we could conscientiously give, or that we could expect to carry. At the time you approved & promised cooperation: afterwards you changed your mind believing that you could obtain more from the Tories. You threw your whole weight against us in the election, and you prevented us from obtaining the majority which would alone enable us to deal with the matter with any hope of success. You must lie on the bed you have made; you must go to your new friends and see what they will do for you, and we shall wait for the result of your communications'.[216]

Fottrell's efforts to temper Chamberlain's opposition to home rule had been approved by Hamilton and were common knowledge in nationalist circles. The day before their meeting, Timothy Healy

---

[213]Morley to Chamberlain, 24 December 1885: JCP, JC5/54/670.

[214]**Journal (11 September, 5 October 1885)**; **Documents 16** and **17**.

[215]Chamberlain to Morley, 4 December 1885: JCP, JC5/54/669; Chamberlain to George F. Mulqueeny, 6 December 1885: NLI, MS 5752, fos 222–229.

[216]Chamberlain to Sir Edward Russell, 14 December 1885: JCP, JC5/62/24.

commented to Henry Labouchere, 'I don't think F can physic C's disease'.[217] Indeed, such doubts were well founded and Fottrell's talks with Chamberlain had only a temporary effect. Having, in Morley's words, 'kept straight for about a week' after the interview, Chamberlain soon 'relapsed into his sulks'. On 21 January, Chamberlain warned Spencer that recent speeches by Parnell had convinced him that the Irish leader's 'demand is for Legislative Independence as a step to complete Separation'. And on 4 February, Chamberlain informed Morley that, since defining his own plans for Irish self-government the previous summer, he had not altered his opinion 'in the slightest degree'.[218]

## The Conservatives and 'Coercion'

In Dublin, Hamilton longed for a political initiative that might alleviate pressure on the Irish administration. On 14 January, Anthony Mundella informed Spencer of his 'long confidential interviews' with Hamilton, Davitt, and other nationalists. He concluded that the Irish Government now excited 'universal derision' and that the country had 'never been in so deplorable a condition'. Mundella anticipated a return to coercion and had warned Davitt that 'John Bull might be easily roused to put down [the] present state of things in Ireland "by the bayonet!"' Yet Hamilton's response to this – that 'wild and bloody revenge' would ensue – would do little to deter the Conservatives from seeking a showdown with the nationalists.[219]

It should be said that the picture presented to the British Government by the Irish authorities at this time was unclear. The RIC Inspector-General, Andrew Reed, informed Dublin Castle that the anticipated breakdown of law and order in rural areas had not materialized and he reported that National League branches were largely 'on their good behaviour'. With the exception of small parts of country where 'moonlighters' were active, Reed asserted that no 'general conspiracy' against the payment of rent existed and predicted that most tenants would pay if abatements were granted.[220] Hamilton, however, interpreted the latest police reports differently and advised

[217] Healy to Labouchere, 30 December 1885, repr. Algar Thorold, *The Life of Henry Labouchere* (London, 1913), p. 275.

[218] **Journal (27 January 1886)**; Chamberlain to Spencer, 21 January 1886, repr. *RE*, II, p. 103; Chamberlain to Morley, 4 February 1886: JCP, JC5/54/685.

[219] Mundella to Spencer, 14 January 1886, repr. *RE*, II, pp. 102–103. Mundella also assured Davitt that Gladstone was 'resolved to grant H.R. when he can safely do so': Davitt's diary, 10 January 1886: TCD MS 9545/18.

[220] MCRs (IG) for November and December 1885 and January 1886: CP/TNA, PRO 30/6/64 (38), CSO RPs 1886/2395, 1886/6691.

Carnarvon that he hardly took 'so sanguine a view of the state of the country' as Reed. He forwarded a recent report from the Western Division, which stated that lawlessness was increasing as the IRB 'acquired new life' and that the authority of the National League was now being maintained 'by terrorism'. It was anticipated that 'atrocious crimes' would be committed by agrarian secret societies, whose members were now 'beyond the restraining influences of religion'. Reports from other parts of the country were equally worrying. In the midlands, it was reported that the League had fallen under the influence of republicans and that any form of local government was liable to fall 'entirely under Fenian direction'. In the south-east, the National League was reported to have 'assumed a position of authority which has practically superseded the Government of the country' and was so ubiquitous that it would be 'very difficult to put down'.[221] On 12 January, Hamilton reported that the latest reports on the condition of the country presented 'a gloomy picture of the state of affairs' and, flatly contradicting Reed, he claimed that anti-rent combinations were widespread and that 'in the present temper of the people' this would inevitably lead to violence. Two days later, Hamilton summarized the main dangers posed by the National League and offered suggestions for their legal remedy.[222]

Hamilton also tried to alert Liberal leaders to the imminence of agrarian disorder. On 12 January, he informed Edward Hamilton that Ireland was 'in the throes of a revolution' and argued that the Government faced the 'alternative either of letting Ireland govern herself [. . .] or of ruling with a rod of iron'. Given that Hamilton's judgment was usually 'singularly sound and calm', this stern warning carried considerable weight. Gladstone was highly impressed and was reported to be 'loud in his praises of that able and excellent Under Secretary. "What a man", he said, "is Sir Robert Hamilton to hold his ground with such boldness, firmness and sagacity [. . .] and in despite of the ravings, judicial & other, on this side of the water."'[223]

Nevertheless, Hamilton's warnings about the dangerous state of affairs only impelled the Conservatives further towards repression. On 13 December, a Cabinet memorandum claimed that low levels

[221]MCR (W) for December 1885, Byrne, DM, 4 January 1886: CSO, RP 1886/5277; 'Progress of the National League: divisional reports for quarter ending 31 December 1885', Slacke, DM, 10 January 1886, Antoine Butler, DM, 4 January 1886: CSO RPs 1886/647, 1886/210 in RP 1888/26523.

[222]Hamilton to Carnarvon, 12 January 1886: CP, Add MS 60821, fos 16–17; 'Memo. by Mr. Hamilton, dated 14th January 1886 – addressed to Lord Carnarvon' (copy): RCHL 1/11. 1232.

[223]Hamilton to Edward Hamilton, 12 January 1886: EHP, Add MS 48625, fos 1–2; Edward Hamilton to Herbert Gladstone, 14 January 1886: GP, Add MS 56447, fos 6–7; Edward Hamilton's diary, 13 and 15 January 1886: EHP, Add MS 48642, fos 88, 91–92.

of recorded crime in Ireland concealed 'a baneful system of tyranny, carried out and enforced by local branches of the National League', which might soon have to be met with the most stringent measures. It concluded, 'Whenever it becomes evident that the reign of law and of the National League cannot co-exist, the latter must be made to yield at any cost, and it is impossible to say when this necessity may arise.'[224] With conservative opinion in Ireland calling for a permanent measure 'providing for the final extinction of the outward and visible signs' of illegal or seditious organizations, the hawks within the Cabinet concluded that the most recent reports from Ireland demonstrated that Dublin Castle was irresolute and that the National League had to be confronted.[225] On 15 January, Churchill suggested that the League's leaders be arrested for high treason, its offices seized, and parliament requested 'to indemnify [the Government] retrospectively for this breach of habeas corpus'. This draconian and unconstitutional plan divided the Cabinet. When it had been suggested to the Irish Attorney-General he had argued that 'the reputation of everyone engaged in carrying it out would be ruined'. Salisbury therefore concluded that the threat of less drastic action against the League might be sufficient to reassure Irish Unionists, ensure a decisive break between his administration and Parnell, and provide him with an opportunity to relinquish an office from which he was 'feverishly eager' to escape.[226] Contingency planning for a confrontation with the nationalists therefore continued at the War Office, where General Wolseley finalized military plans for the suppression of armed rebellion.[227]

The plan to suppress the National League was met with consternation by those who would have been responsible for its implementation. Hamilton argued that it would prove futile because

[224]Irish Office, 'The condition of Ireland', 13 January 1886: CP, Add MS 60823, fos 100–104. The probable author of the memorandum was the Irish Attorney-General, Hugh Holmes, who briefed the Cabinet on Ireland on 15 January and redrafted the relevant portion of the Queen's speech in similar vein: see A.B. Cooke and J.R. Vincent, 'Ireland and party politics, 1885–7: an unpublished Conservative memoir (I)', *IHS*, 16, no. 62 (September 1968), pp. 168–170.

[225]Fitzgibbon to Churchill, 16 January 1886: RCHL 1/11. 1354; Johnson, *Diary of Gathorne Hardy*, pp. 589–590.

[226]Cooke and Vincent, 'Ireland and party politics', pp. 168–169; Roberts, *Salisbury*, pp. 370–371. Carnarvon was dismayed by Churchill's suggestion to govern Ireland under the Lord Justices and then send Wolseley out as viceroy 'when things grow bad': 'Very remarkable conversation with R. Churchill': CP, Add MS 60825, fo. 132.

[227]NAI, Crime Special Papers, 23614/S; Wolseley to Carnarvon, 14 December 1885: CP/TNA, PRO 30/6/66, fos 198–199. W.H. Smith also ascertained from the Prime Minister of Canada that troubles in Ireland were unlikely to increase the threat posed by American Fenians; Smith to Churchill, 3 January 1886: RCHL 1/11. 1242.

the organization's branch structure was 'far more perfect than that of the old Land League'. It would, he advised Carnarvon, be regarded as 'a declaration of war to the death' by the Irish-Americans who largely funded the League, and he predicted that 'many lives would be lost before the country was again subdued into sullen quiet'. He recalled that, upon showing his Cabinet memorandum to W.H. Smith, the Chief Secretary commented 'You may be right; but not one out of 4 or 5 men in Great Britain is prepared to face "Home Rule"', to which Hamilton replied that an equal number would oppose the suspension of constitutional government in Ireland, which, he believed, was the only logical and plausible alternative.[228] The plan was also considered to be impractical and Reed warned Hamilton and Carnarvon that, in the absence of emergency powers, the Constabulary was not equipped to cope with a general outbreak of crime and disorder. His force would, he declared, be as helpless as they had been during the Land War. This view was echoed by Jenkinson, who believed that the intelligence system that he had developed in Ireland had declined during his absence in London. More than a year earlier, he had warned Spencer 'if ever outrages do break out again [. . .] the present machinery and present system will not be equal to the task. There will be as certainly a break down again as there was a break down in 1881.' He now argued that the RIC required substantial reinforcement before it could cope with the consequences of the League's 'overthrow'. 'It could be like poking the fire', he warned Carnarvon; 'a blaze would follow which could not be extinguished without very exceptional powers and by vigorous action [. . .] The safety valve would be shut down, and instead of one open society, we should have several secret societies in their worst form to deal with.'[229] Such advice was unlikely to have been welcome in Westminster, but Carnarvon had done his best to convince his colleagues to take Jenkinson's advice seriously, telling Sir Michael Hicks Beach that it was 'simple madness' to disregard the danger that Irish republicans would engage 'in outrage of all kinds on the failure of the Irish Parliamentary Party to come to terms with the Government'.[230]

The Cabinet was under pressure from parliament to state its intentions towards Ireland, and it was agreed on 23 January to

---

[228]**Document 44**; Edward Hamilton's diary, 13 February 1886: EHP, Add MS 48643, fo. 13. Hamilton simultaneously briefed Spencer on the situation: see **Document 43**.

[229]Jenkinson to Spencer, 7 November 1884: AP, Add MS 77035; **Documents 42** and **45**.

[230]Carnarvon to Salisbury, 3 and 7 January 1886; Salisbury to Carnarvon, 6 January 1886: CP/TNA, PRO 30/6/62 (48), (53), (52). Carnarvon to Hicks Beach, 3 January 1886: SAP, D2455, PCC/46; Carnarvon to Churchill, 3 January 1886: RCHL 1/11. 1240. Cross to Carnarvon, 4 January 1886; Ashbourne to Cross, 4 and 6 January 1886: BL, Cross Papers, Add MS 51276, fos 2–5.

accommodate Smith, who was alarmed by the sudden growth of an urban 'House League', by announcing firm action against the National League.[231] After signalling an intention to tackle 'concerted resistance to the enforcement of legal obligations' in the Queen's speech, the Government announced the introduction of a bill for the suppression of the League on 26 January.[232] This had the effect, so the Irish Attorney-General later recalled, 'of putting the government out of pain'. Gladstone, however, astutely refrained from challenging the ministry on the issue of Ireland and thus avoided committing himself to home rule at this stage.[233]

## The Home Rule Bill and its Consequences

After the Liberals assumed office on 1 February 1886, Hamilton did all he could to persuade the Irish law officers, including the highly sceptical Lord Chancellor, to serve a home rule administration. He anticipated events by advising Spencer to remain in London to assist in the development of legislation, and to leave Irish administration to John Morley, who enjoyed the trust of the Irish Parliamentary Party. Above all, he wanted to assure the new ministry that Ireland was in a fit state to accommodate constitutional reform. Gladstone and Spencer were aware that the social and political circumstances that had made home rule necessary might also obstruct its implementation.[234] Gladstone had warned Granville that further unrest in Ireland might 'effectually thrust aside' any declaration on home rule and, shortly afterwards, Spencer admitted to Lansdowne that, even if Parnell were to accept the government's proposals, 'the social state of Ireland may be found to be too bad to allow us to proceed'.[235]

Hamilton was eager to assure Spencer that the National League was now doing all it could to curb the excesses of some of its branches, but advised that Ireland remained in a volatile condition. With home

---

[231]Holmes to Kaye, 27 January 1886: CSO RP 1886/1748; and see B.J. Graham and Susan Hood, 'Town tenant protest in late nineteenth- and early twentieth-century Ireland', *Irish Economic and Social History*, 21 (1994), pp. 39–57.

[232]*Her Majesty's Most Gracious Speech to Both Houses of Parliament*, 21 January 1886. A bill was drafted on 27 January: W.F. Cullinan to Ashbourne, 3 February 1886, repr. Cooke and Malcolmson, *Ashbourne Papers*, p. 106.

[233]Cooke and Vincent, 'Ireland and party politics', p. 172. Instead, the Liberals carried an amendment to the address in favour of agricultural labourers against the Government.

[234]**Document 40**; Hamilton to Spencer, 7 February, 28 March 1886; Gladstone to Spencer, 28 December 1885: AP, Add MSS 77061, 76863; Gladstone, 'Secret memorandum', 31 December 1885: GP, Add MS 56446, fos 223–225.

[235]Gladstone to Granville, 18 January 1886: GP, Add MS 56447, fos 10–11; Spencer to Lansdowne, 2 February 1886, repr. *RE*, II, pp. 107–109.

rule close at hand, Hamilton was prepared to accept Reed's opinion that the League's leaders currently thought that it served their cause 'better to preserve peace and order in the country'. Privately, however, he admitted to Edward Hamilton 'that at present Ireland is not governed. We are at the mercy of the National League, who think it good policy to do what they can to keep down actual outrages.'[236] This sense of foreboding was reflected in the reports of some of Reed's senior officers, who painted an even bleaker picture of the country. Reports from the south-west told of strained landlord–tenant relations, impending evictions, widespread boycotting, and whole districts falling into 'a most lawless state'.[237] The prevailing view from the Constabulary was that home rule meant separation, an opinion most fully articulated by the County Inspector of Limerick at the end of February 1886, when he informed Dublin Castle that

All the elements of Fenianism, and the Irish Republican Brotherhood are at present awaiting an opportunity to strike: And keeping quiet merely so long as the milder form of Nationalism acting under Constitutional guise continues to gain ground towards the common good. The National aspiration is independence – pure and simple – and nothing short of actual separation from England will satisfy the people of the Irish race. The more I study their character the more I am convinced of this; and any decided check to the National Movement would, in my opinion, be the signal for an outburst of those elements of Fenianism & Republicanism, which, under different names and guises, lie dormant watching the progress of events.[238]

Setting these warnings aside, Hamilton concentrated on preparing the way for home rule and advised Spencer to put the Lord Lieutenancy into commission, on the ground that 'unless a dummy came here I should dread embarrassment & all our hands at a time like this should be as free as possible'. The appointment of Morley as Chief Secretary and Lord Aberdeen as a subordinate Lord Lieutenant met with the Under-Secretary's approval. Hamilton found that Morley was 'very clear and decided and works without any fuss', and in turn Morley recalled that Hamilton was 'a man of experience and ability, and in firm sympathy with the new policy'.[239] The new arrangement antagonized some Irish Conservatives, who drew attention to the prominent part being taken by Hamilton and Fottrell in policy making.

[236]Hamilton to Spencer, 1 February 1886: AP, Add MS 77061; MCR (IG) for January 1886, Reed, 6 February 1886: CSO RP 1886/6691; Edward Hamilton's diary, 23 March 1886: EHP, Add MS 48643, fo. 52.
[237]CI Q. J. Brownrigg to Plunkett, DM, 3 February 1886: CSO RP 1886/2259.
[238]CI Xaverius Butler to Plunkett, DM, 28 February 1886: CSO RP 1886/4870.
[239]Hamilton to Spencer, 3 and 4 February 1886: AP, Add MS 77061; Morley, *Recollections*, I, p. 221.

On 14 February, Gerald FitzGibbon furnished Churchill with the latest 'local gossip' from Dublin:

> At the Castle, as soon as the swearing was over there was a Cabinet Council of four – i. Aberdeen L.L. ii. John Morley C.S. iii. Sir Robert Hamilton, late of the Orkneys, Privy Council Office, Board of Trade, Navy, and other foreign parts, and iv. George Fottrell, ex solicitor (dismissed) of the Land Commission!!! The Lord Chancellor, Attorney General, and Solicitor General, were in attendance, outside, for three hours, and were never called in at all! So runs the story, and in the evening the Viceroy & Chief Sec. returned to the places whence they came – wiser and more cheerful men – prepared to pacify the Country on Fottrell's lines – which are as follows: A compulsory Land Purchase Bill to be brought in at once, to do whatever is the opposite of 'making the running' for Home Rule – which is to be thought over in the meantime.[240]

The idea that Hamilton drafted Gladstone's first home rule bill persisted for many years. While this is incorrect, it is true that he played an important part in its development.[241] Before Gladstone withdrew to Mentmore to formulate the legislation, Hamilton provided both him and Spencer with copies of his Cabinet memorandum. This evidently made an impression in Whitehall, and Edward Hamilton recorded that the paper practically advocated 'an extensive Home Rule scheme' that exhibited 'full consciousness of the dangers & difficulties surrounding it'.[242] The Irish Under-Secretary subsequently travelled to London to discuss the matter with members of the Cabinet and suggested a number of amendments to Gladstone's proposals on Irish government and finance. Hamilton's views were regarded at Westminster as those 'of a high-minded man who has more knowledge of Irish Executive matters than any one else, who went to Ireland unprejudiced, & whose mind has been bent in this direction solely by conviction'. As such, Edward Hamilton recorded, 'They cannot help weighing with one.'[243]

Three key issues required careful consideration before a home rule bill could be framed – the land question, policing, and the response to home rule in Protestant-dominated areas of Ulster. Within

---

[240]FitzGibbon to Churchill, 14 February 1886: RCHL 1/12. 1380. For Fottrell's account, see **Journal (16 February 1886)**.

[241] *Dictionary of National Biography: second supplement*, p. 382.

[242]**Document 20**; Hamilton to Spencer, 1 and 2 February 1886: AP, Add MS 77061; Edward Hamilton's diary, 11 February 1886: EHP, Add MS 48643, fo. 9; and see John Kendle, *Ireland and the Federal Solution: the debate over the United Kingdom constitution, 1870–1920* (Buffalo, 1989), pp. 42–43.

[243]**Journal (16 February 1886)**; Hamilton to Spencer, 7 February, 24 March 1886: AP, Add MS 77061; 'Sir R. Hamilton's notes. Irish Govt.', 29 March 1886: AP, Add MS 77328; Edward Hamilton's diary, 11 and 13 February, 23 March 1886: EHP, Add MS 48643, fos 10, 12, 52.

each of these policy areas, Jenkinson and Hamilton made significant contributions to the debate. The viability of home rule depended to a large extent upon the future constitutional position of Ulster, yet this question received scant attention from Gladstone because the fate of Ireland's landlords dominated his thinking.[244] The Liberal leader's complacency over this vexed question may have derived, at least in part, from advice he received from Jenkinson, whose views on the probable reaction of Ulster's Protestants to home rule were highly optimistic. Having dismissed the possibilities that Irish Protestants would be persecuted by the Catholic majority or that civil war might ensue, he cited the 'many Protestants in the National Ranks' as evidence of Ulster's acquiescence to home rule.[245]

In fact, Jenkinson's views on Ulster had changed significantly since October 1883. At the height of the National League's 'invasion' of the province, Jenkinson had disobeyed an order from the Chief Secretary to have placards calling for counter-demonstrations removed. Jenkinson had then argued that the Orange Order had a legitimate right to organize in self-defence, which led Trevelyan to charge him with holding 'unstatesmanlike Orange opinions' and being 'absolutely ignorant of the very elements of constitutional government'.[246] The much more sanguine view of Ulster that Jenkinson presented at the end of 1885 was likely to have been music to the ears of Gladstone, who viewed the annihilation of the Liberal Party in Ireland as a political opportunity. He regarded Ulster as a 'fraction of a nation', which was now solely represented 'by Tories or by Parnellites'. 'Perhaps had we large and cordial Ulster support', he admitted to James Bryce, 'it might have abridged our freedom more than it would have enlarged our votes.'[247] Nevertheless, soon after the general election Gladstone's supporters received warnings that the province was far from quiet. In mid-December, Edward Hamilton recorded the views of the Liberal peer Lord Waveney, who reported that 'the Ulstermen are ready to rise to a man if there is any paltering with Parnell'. Bryce also reported that widespread fear that Protestant interests were in jeopardy had provoked fiery language from the Orange lodges.[248] A second report from Bryce in March 1886 challenged Jenkinson's optimistic predictions: he

[244]Matthew, *Gladstone*, p. 487. This matter is most fully considered in Loughlin, *Gladstone, Home Rule and the Ulster Question*.
[245]**Documents 15 and 27**.
[246]Trevelyan to Spencer, 29 October 1883: AP, Add MS 76959.
[247]Gladstone to James Bryce, 2 December 1885, repr. *GD*, XI, p. 439.
[248]It was said that Waveney had returned from Ulster 'an altered man': Edward Hamilton's diary, 17 December 1885: EHP, Add MS 48642, fo. 54; Bryce, 'Irish opinion on the Irish problem', 11 December 1885: GP, Add MS 44770, fos 5–14.

considered that Ulster Liberals were 'practically unanimous in their hostility' to measures that might leave them subject to a nationalist-dominated assembly, and predicted that moderates would join with Tories and Orangemen to oppose home rule. He recommended that the forthcoming bill should restrict the power exercised by a Dublin parliament over Protestant-dominated regions of Ulster, which should in turn be provided with local self-government. Charles Russell tried to assure Gladstone that the violent opinions recorded by Bryce were largely the product of anti-Catholic prejudice, but even he conceded that Liberal opinion in Ulster was largely against home rule.[249]

Jenkinson's optimism about Ulster was not widely shared by those whom he had once served in Dublin. Spencer abhorred sectarianism but accepted that conflict was an inescapable feature of political life in Ulster. The rough treatment that he had received from loyalists during a visit to Belfast in June 1884 hardened his resistance to home rule. 'The North would never agree to it', he had then warned Jenkinson, 'we should at once have civil war between Ulster and the South and West.' This view had been shared by Trevelyan who, in December 1883, had confided to his sister, 'If these people were left to themselves, we should have a mutual massacre; unless they are not quite as brave as they pretend.' While neither man believed that Irish Protestants would suffer persecution under home rule, both understood the alarm felt by Ulster Liberals about the establishment of an Irish parliament. Nevertheless, the true extent of popular loyalist opposition to home rule was not clearly understood by many English Liberals until serious sectarian riots broke out in Belfast in June 1886.[250]

The most pressing administrative issue, one thought by some to be 'the real crux' of the home rule question, concerned the future of the Irish police.[251] Given that the RIC was an imperial armed force that had recently been in conflict with the nationalists, its status under home rule was bound to cause controversy. It was a question that revealed the limit to which British officials were prepared to trust a nationalist government of Ireland as they considered the danger that an independent Irish parliament might use the Constabulary as

---

[249]Bryce to Gladstone, 12 March 1886: GP, Add MS 56447, fos 64–75; Russell to Gladstone, 17 March 1886: GP, Add MS 56447, fos 76–90.

[250]**Document 3**; G.M. Trevelyan, *George Otto Trevelyan: a memoir* (London, 1932), p. 115; Spencer to Gladstone, 31 December 1885: GP, Add MS 44312, fos 245–246. Jenkinson, however, continued to believe that it was 'absurd to believe that Ulster would fight' in the event of home rule: *Liverpool Mercury*, 11 March 1893, p. 5.

[251]The view of Sir Henry Thring: Edward Hamilton's diary, 9 November 1885: EHP Add MS 48642, fo. 5.

an instrument of warfare.[252] It is telling that even Hamilton thought that it might still be necessary to use the Constabulary to protect the Protestant and landed minorities after home rule was granted. In October 1885, he had recommended that the British Government should retain control of the RIC, arguing that the capacity to concentrate this semi-military force at any given point would deter a future Irish government from behaving unconstitutionally. As home rule became more likely in December 1885, concern grew over police morale. Hamilton was aware that the RIC had become demoralized by *ad hoc* reforms to its administration over previous years, and that the prospect of home rule had caused 'great consternation' among its members.[253] On 10 December, Reed warned the Castle that, if his men came to believe that they were to be 'handed over to their enemies the Nationalists and Fenians [. . .] to do with the Constabulary as they think fit', it was not unreasonable to expect that their loyalty would be shaken, 'their interest in the British Government diminish, and their efficiency become seriously impaired (if worse consequences do not follow)'.[254]

Faced by the prospect of mutiny, the Inspector-General sought assurances that the interests of his men would be protected under any new constitutional arrangement. Carnarvon gave Reed his personal assurance that this would be done and, in the light of 'a seditious and very dangerous paper' then being circulated amongst the Constabulary, recommended that the Prime Minister promise to Parliament that the RIC would always remain an imperial force.[255] Spencer, however, doubted whether the imperial parliament would be able to retain control of the RIC after home rule was granted and predicted that local authorities would insist on establishing their own police forces. Consequently, he advised Gladstone that 'this Irish Army' should be disbanded to prevent it being turned against British authority. Gladstone, on the other hand, held 'not the smallest fear' that this would happen. He had always viewed the RIC as an expensive drain upon the Exchequer and believed that it could be harmlessly broken up into about forty county and municipal forces.[256] Nevertheless, threats from leading nationalists to exact 'revenge' upon the police after home rule was secured did little to calm the

---

[252]T. Cooke Trench, 'Seeking for an Irish policy', 12 November 1885; Carnarvon to Trench, 25 December 1885: CP, Add MS 60820, fo. 45.

[253]**Documents 20, 32, 33, 36**, and **37**.

[254]MCR (IG) for November 1885, Reed, 10 December 1885: CP/TNA, PRO 30/6/64 (38).

[255]Carnarvon, 'Mr Reed', 31 December 1885; Carnarvon to Salisbury, 22 January 1886: CP, Add MSS 60823, fo. 97, 60825, fo. 92.

[256]**Documents 36** and **39**; Gladstone to Spencer, 8 September 1882: AP, Add MS 76856.

Constabulary's nerves. Subsequent reports from senior officers, one of whom claimed 'that two thirds of the men would rather resign than serve under a Home Rule Government', forced the new Liberal administration to address the question.[257] Gladstone still refused to accept that policing would present 'an insurmountable difficulty', but others, such as George Trevelyan, were more concerned about the need to curb nationalist ambitions. As Chief Secretary in 1882, he had faced strikes by sections of the Constabulary and Dublin Metropolitian Police and he predicted that the British Government would continue to rely upon the RIC to maintain order in Ireland.[258] His fears were widely shared in Dublin. Hamilton was eager that the force would 'in no circumstances be handed over with their present organization to an Irish Parliament' and, largely due to pressure from the English Lord Chancellor, the Home Rule Bill stipulated that the Constabulary would remain under imperial control.[259]

Some of Gladstone's advisers believed that the safest way to bring the police under Irish control would be to first settle the land question, so that the legal enforcement of contracts would be seen to serve the general public interest. The land question was widely regarded as the biggest obstacle to home rule, largely because its solution threatened the interests of British taxpayers, and it has been cited as the most important reason for the failure of Gladstone's policy. Uncertainty over home rule threatened to destabilize the Irish economy: in December 1885, Carnarvon drew the attention of the Cabinet to 'a sort of panic in certain classes, & a fall of securities' caused by the Hawarden Kite. A month later, Hamilton alerted Spencer to fears that English opinion might turn against home rule because of the alarm caused to British financiers over the security of funds advanced on Irish land.[260] Some proponents of home rule therefore insisted that a prior and definitive settlement of the land question was integral to its success, and it was on this question that Irish officials most actively counselled the politicians.

The success of a land purchase scheme depended upon its capacity to satisfy both Irish landlords and tenants without casting an undue burden on British taxpayers. It was therefore important to persuade rank and file Liberals that a 'scheme of outdoor relief

[257]F.S.L. Lyons, *John Dillon* (London, 1968), pp. 86–87; Brownrigg to Plunkett, DM, 28 February 1886: CSO RP 1886/4870.

[258]Gladstone to Granville, 18 December 1885: GP, Add MS 56466, fos 193–195; Campbell-Bannerman to Spencer, 8 January 1886, repr. J.A. Spender, *The Life of the Rt. Hon. Sir Henry Campbell-Bannerman, GCB*, 2 vols (London, 1923), I, pp. 95–97.

[259]Hamilton to Spencer, 2 February 1886; Lord Herschell to Spencer, 11 April 1886: AP, Add MSS 77061, 77324.

[260]Carnarvon to Cranbrook, 19 December 1885: CP, Add MS 60825, fo. 159; **Document 37**; and see Peter Cain and Tony Hopkins, *British Imperialism, 1688–2000* (London, 2001), p. 130.

for the Irish landlords' was not being contemplated. The scale of the proposed government loan to finance the scheme (Gladstone originally suggested a figure of £113 million) was hotly debated in English constituencies. Progressive Liberals exhibited a strong aversion to the measure, which they regarded as a 'costly attempt to buy the acquiescence of the landlords in a policy of separation', and its adoption precipitated the resignations of Chamberlain and Trevelyan from the Cabinet. The Land Purchase Bill was abandoned soon after its first reading in April 1886 when it was recognized as a political liability, and its close association with the Home Rule Bill was something that Gladstone came to regret. Nevertheless, it has been convincingly argued that the land purchase scheme was far from being a 'dummy' bill and actually formed part of a coherent effort to tackle agrarian unrest and 'lay the foundations of a more secure social order in Ireland'. Fottrell's journal demonstrates that Liberal thinking on the land question was much influenced by the ideas of Sir Robert Giffen, a former Board of Trade economist with whom he held several meetings. Yet Gladstone's decision to adopt land purchase was, at least in part, influenced by views that he received from Ireland.[261]

Land purchase was supported by many Catholic bishops, on the ground that an equitable solution to the land question was necessary if the rural population was to thrive in its native land. Fottrell regarded land purchase as 'a necessary complement to self-government' and Morley relied heavily upon his advice concerning the order in which the land and home rule questions should be tackled.[262] Fottrell recognized that home rule would have a tremendous impact upon the *status quo* in Ireland. He hoped that an equitable land purchase scheme would disarm landowners' opposition to the policy by providing them with the opportunity to dispose of their land at a reasonable price and thus reach an accommodation with Irish nationalism, as had been urged by Isaac Butt in the 1870s. Fottrell's scheme made the Irish state an intermediary between landlord and tenant, providing state aid to landlords who were willing to sell without imposing compulsory purchase on those who were not, and a summary of his paper was circulated to the Cabinet.[263]

As with home rule, Spencer had to be persuaded of the virtues of land purchase. Since 1884, he had been eager to ease stagnation in the Irish land market, which, he believed, had resulted from the

[261] Graham D. Goodlad, 'The Liberal Party and Gladstone's Land Purchase Bill of 1886', *Historical Journal* 32 (1989), pp. 627–641; **Journal (17 January, 16 February, 12 March 1886)**.
[262] Archbishop Walsh to Gladstone, 17 February 1886: GP, Add MS 56447; **Journal (16 February 1886)**.
[263] **Journal (1, 21 March 1886)**.

nationalists raising unrealistic expectations of the Land Act, and he had briefly considered establishing an Irish land bank. He was convinced, however, that the principle of dual ownership established by the Land Act was correct and remained optimistic that the Land Commission would improve landlord–tenant relations. He wanted it to be universally understood that the Act represented a final and definitive settlement of the land question and that there was no profit to be gained from further agitation. Spencer's thoughts on land purchase subsequently changed and, in spite of criticizing aspects of the Ashbourne Act of August 1885, he privately welcomed the measure as a stimulant for the stagnant land market.[264] Jenkinson, however, was not convinced that a workable settlement had yet been achieved and tried to persuade Spencer that comprehensive land purchase was necessary. His administrative experience of India convinced him that problems that had not proved insurmountable in a far larger country than Ireland might also be solved there. Jenkinson's arguments carried weight with Spencer who, in 1882, had considered him for a place on the Land Commission.[265] Having little sympathy for Irish landlords, most of whom he regarded as short-sighted, selfish, and cowardly, Jenkinson had once advised Carnarvon to check 'the excessive zeal' shown towards insolvent tenants by withholding police protection from unreasonable land agents. 'In England', he protested, 'we do not see the military and the Police assisting agents in summarily evicting tenants'. If assistance was to be given, he argued, the Government ought to ensure that it was not being asked to act with undue harshness against tenants. 'Why', he asked, 'in order to put money in the pocket of a landlord should the Government turn a tenant and his family out of his house and ruin him?' At the same time, he did believe that, in spite of their political extinction as a class, Irish landlords ought to have their legitimate interests protected. Like Gladstone, he recognized that, having shaped the country's land code, the imperial parliament was obliged to ensure that the transfer of land to its occupiers was made on terms acceptable to its owners.[266]

Hamilton also believed that a comprehensive land settlement was essential. He, too, had little time for Irish landlords, whom,

---

[264] Spencer to Gladstone, 28 February 1884, repr. *RE*, I, pp. 263–265; Spencer to Granville, 22 October 1884: AP, Add MS 76884; Spencer to Lansdowne, 16 August 1885, repr. *RE*, II, pp. 70–74.

[265] Spencer to Trevelyan, 20 July 1882; Trevelyan to Spencer, 22 July 1882: AP, Add MS 76947. Jenkinson, 'Memorandum on the operation of the Irish Land Commission', 15 July 1882: CAB 37/8/42.

[266] B. Mallet, *Thomas George, Earl of Northbrook* (London, 1908), p. 164; Jenkinson to Carnarvon, 12 September 1885: CP/TNA, PRO 30/6/62 (27); **Document 31**; Goodlad, 'Liberal Party', p. 628.

he considered, had 'too long relied upon English bayonets to protect their rights'. He was, however, alert to the danger that the destruction of Irish landlords as a class would remove an important obstacle to separation, and accepted that the British Government was duty-bound to protect them. On 27 December, Hamilton set out a detailed scheme for facilitating land purchase within a falling market, under which the new Irish state would become the country's largest landowner. He was particularly concerned about the plight of insolvent tenants on large unprofitable landholdings in the west of Ireland and offered advice on rents, land valuation, and the development of safeguards for smallholders.[267] Gladstone resisted Parnell's suggestion that the compulsory purchase of such landholdings would greatly reduce opposition to home rule from landowners. He disliked the idea of state intervention in the land market and was concerned that the Irish tenant's 'long standing antipathy towards the institution of landlordism' would merely be redirected against the Government.[268] But while he saw no virtue in making the state a principal landowner, Gladstone did admit that Hamilton's suggestion for making the Irish parliament responsible for land purchase arrangements was of 'great value' and worthy of further investigation.[269]

As with policing, however, some pro-home-rule Liberals doubted the capacity of an Irish parliament to treat the land question judiciously. The idea that land purchase should precede home rule was partly founded upon doubts about the safety of leaving the matter at the discretion of men whose anti-landlord bias might be the ruin of Irish agriculture. By the end of 1885, Spencer accepted that a comprehensive land purchase scheme was the only means of avoiding a wholesale exodus of the landed interest from Ireland. For him, it also had the advantage of allowing the Land Commission to be dissolved and thus saved from the 'partiality & violence' of the Parnellites.[270] As an Ulsterman, the Irish Attorney-General, Samuel Walker, was also firmly opposed to the Irish state assuming responsibility for the land question on the ground that 'Ulster tenants would not trust an Irish administration to treat them fairly'. He wanted merely to expand the

---

[267]Hamilton to Spencer, 17 January, 3 and 27 February, 2 March 1886; Spencer to Hamilton, 23 February, 1 March 1886: AP, Add MS 77061. Edward Hamilton's diary, 13 February 1886: EHP, Add MS 48643, fo. 13; Hamilton, 'Smallholdings in Ireland', 18 February 1886: GP, Add MS 44632, fos 56–61; and see **Documents 32, 37,** and **43**.

[268]Gladstone to O'Shea, 9 January 1886, repr. *GD*, XI, p. 477; Walsh to Gladstone, 17 February 1886: GP, Add MS 56447, fos 35–40.

[269]Gladstone to Spencer, 14 January 1886, repr. *GD*, XI, p. 479.

[270]**Document 36**; and see 'Confidential. Land purchase. Memorandum of G[eorge] F[ottrell]', 11 March 1886: GP, Add MS 44632, fos 177–184.

Ashbourne Act in order to create a larger land purchase fund. Like Jenkinson, he did not believe that a nationalist-dominated authority would be resilient enough to withstand the demands of Catholic tenant farmers, and recommended that control of land purchase should remain with the imperial parliament.[271] This view was supported by police reports from the south-west that claimed that younger men in disaffected districts were beyond the control of the National League. If nationalist aspirations were checked, it was warned, 'Fenianism would again become rampant' and result in 'the confiscation to their own use of the land and property of the Country'. A consensus therefore developed at Dublin Castle that it would be unwise to trust a settlement of the land question to an Irish legislature. It was an aspect of the Irish question that was to be effectively exploited by Liberal opponents of home rule.[272]

Once the home rule bill had been drafted, Hamilton was opposed to making any amendments that might alienate the Irish Parliamentary Party and so render the legislation unworkable.[273] The progress of the Home Rule and Land Purchase Bills as viewed from the perspective of Dublin political society is vividly recounted by George Fottrell, who, at Morley's request, tried to persuade Chamberlain not to break ranks over Ireland.[274] That Chamberlain was not open to persuasion was regarded as a severe blow. As Balfour intimated to Salisbury, it was Chamberlain and not Hartington who could do most to destroy Gladstone's scheme, and he predicted that they would 'find in him so long as he agrees with us a very different kind of ally from those lukewarm and slippery Whigs whom it is difficult to differ from and impossible to act with'. It was therefore clear that divisions within the Liberal Party would doom the Home Rule Bill and, by early summer, hopes for its success had begun to fade in Dublin.[275]

The manner in which Hamilton and Jenkinson became embroiled in the home rule controversy brought into question their status as permanent civil servants, and had serious consequences for their subsequent careers. After 1854, when the position of Irish under-secretary was made a permanent one, incumbents were expected to abjure involvement in party politics. That the home rule question had

[271] Samuel Walker to Spencer, 10 March 1886: GP, Add MS 56447, fos 56–62.
[272] CI Charles Cameron to Plunkett, 1 April 1886; Plunkett to Hamilton, 2 April 1886: CSO RP 1886/6976; Goodlad, 'Liberal Party', pp. 632, 635.
[273] Edward Hamilton's diary, 23 March 1886: EHP, Add MS 48643, fo. 52; **Document 46**.
[274] See **Journal (12 March 1886)**.
[275] Balfour to Salisbury, 22 March 1886: JCP, JC1/4/4/6; Hamilton to Spencer, 3 June 1886: AP, Add MS 77061; and see W.C. Lubenow, *Parliamentary Politics and the Home Rule Crisis: the British House of Commons in 1886* (Oxford, 1988).

rendered this impossible was attested to when, in 1889, Randolph Churchill advised Arthur Balfour that 'Hamilton & Jenkinson are splendid examples of the danger of not being certain that in yr. permanent officials you have not emissaries from the camp of the enemy.'[276] While both men retained their posts after the Conservatives returned to power in July 1886, it soon became clear that their days in office were numbered. Close study of the Chief Secretary's Office papers of the period indicates that the Chief Secretary, Sir Michael Hicks Beach, and his Attorney-General conducted most of their business through the Assistant Under-Secretary, Sir William Kaye, one of a number of Conservatives within the Irish administration.[277] Hicks Beach had never really trusted Hamilton. In July 1885, he had advised Carnarvon to 'please remember that Sir R. Hamilton is a Whig: and, like a Whig could wish nothing better than that we should follow in the footsteps of the late Govt., with similar failure'.[278] When, in August 1886, Morley assured him that Hamilton was 'in no sense the fountain of the evil' of home rule, Hicks Beach replied that 'he did not see how you could have a vigorous executive when the head of it was a man notoriously hostile to the whole system', and then criticized Carnarvon for 'inviting Hamilton to talk politics'.[279] The Under-Secretary incurred further disfavour for his unenthusiastic response to the appointment of Sir Redvers Buller as Special Commissioner for Cork and Kerry. Buller claimed that the Home Rule Bill had demoralized the entire administrative class and that Irish officials were 'shockingly weak kneed'. He advised Hicks Beach that any attempt to stiffen their resolve would be undermined by the continued presence of Hamilton, whom Buller described as 'a clerk of clerks, whose soul is red tape, and whose idea of initiative is the avoidance of responsibility'. Fottrell documents the subsequent press campaign against the Under-Secretary mounted by *The Times* and *St James Gazette* in the second half of 1886.[280]

Although Hamilton was perturbed by these attacks, he saw 'no immediate prospect of the fulfilment of the kind wishes of the London press' that he should be 'promoted', and was persuaded to avoid becoming embroiled in the controversy. Instead, Spencer publicly

---

[276]Churchill to Balfour, 9 July 1889: BL, Balfour Papers, Add MS 49695, fo. 179.

[277] From 1853, Kaye had registered voters on behalf of the Conservatives and, in 1859, was secretary of the Central Conservative Society of Ireland: Andrew Shields, 'The Conservative Party in Ireland, 1832–67', unpublished PhD thesis (University of Toronto); James Stronge MP to Earl of Mayo, 19 December 1867: NLI, Mayo Papers, MS 43852/7.

[278]Hicks Beach to Carnarvon, 17 July 1885: CP/TNA, PRO 30/6/57, fos 191–193.

[279]Morley to Spencer, 10 August 1886: AP, Add MS 76938.

[280]Buller to Hicks Beach, 16 and 26 October 1886: SAP, D2455, PCC/45; **Journal (5 December 1886)**.

defended Hamilton from accusations of impropriety and privately assured Carnarvon that he had, by and large, arrived at his position on home rule independently of Hamilton's influence.[281] He stated 'with perfect certainty that Mr. Gladstone never saw any paper of Sir R. Hamilton's before he had drawn up the first heads of his policy'. Subsequently, he admitted that he and Hamilton had corresponded in 'general terms' on the question of home rule in mid-December 1885 but Carnarvon, in his concern for Hamilton's reputation, advised Spencer against disclosing this information.[282] In November 1886, Hamilton was persuaded to accept the post of Governor of Tasmania – his removal from Ireland being, he declared, 'entirely the act of the Government' – and he was replaced by Buller.[283] The Liberals' suspicion that the Government had 'really shoved [Hamilton] out of office' meant that the position of Irish under-secretary was subsequently politicized as successive administrations appointed men who were in sympathy with their policies.[284] Sir Joseph West Ridgeway, who succeeded Buller in 1887, did not survive the fall of the Unionist ministry in April 1892, when Morley informed Spencer, 'he will have to go [. . .] He is, I hear in the Castle itself, pure Balfourian and soldier.'[285] A valuable continuity in the exercise of executive authority was therefore sacrificed as the post was successively filled by appointees who, one incumbent commented, 'could not avoid importing the political views of their party in such a way as to influence the whole administration of the executive'.[286]

Edward Jenkinson's position had always been more precarious than that of Hamilton and his support for home rule was to prove even more costly to him. It was some years before Unionists came to suspect that

[281] See his address to National Liberal Federation delegates at Leicester: *The Times*, 26 November 1886, p. 6.

[282] Spencer to Carnarvon, 4 and 5 August 1886; Carnarvon to Spencer, 6 August 1886: CP, Add MS 60830, fos 56–62.

[283] Hamilton to Campbell-Bannerman, 24 November 1886: BL, Campbell-Bannerman Papers, Add MS 41232, fos 313–314; Hamilton to Spencer, 7 and 28 October 1886: AP, Add MS 77061.

[284] Cooke and Vincent, 'Ireland and party politics', p. 333. For a justification of the decision, see *The Times*, 23 April 1895, p. 13; and for Hamilton's defence of his own actions, see **Document 47**.

[285] Morley to Spencer, 12 April 1892: AP, Add MS 76940; MacBride, *Greening of Dublin Castle*, pp. 49–51.

[286] David Harrel, *Recollections and Reflections* (unpublished, 1926), p. 91: TCD, MS 3918a. The notion that Harrel was himself above politics is belied by his remark to Carnarvon in 1885 that he 'dreaded for Ireland the return of a Liberal Govt.', and his later tribute to Arthur Balfour as 'a real benefactor to Ireland': Flanagan, 'Chief Secretary's Office', p. 209; Carnarvon, 'Conversation with Harrel', 28 November 1885: CP/TNA, PRO 30/6/67, fo. 29; Harrel, *Recollections*, p. 102.

he had warned Gladstone of the imminent dangers of withholding home rule. And yet, while the reasons for his removal from office were chiefly administrative, his position was also undermined by more immediate political contingencies. As Chief Secretary, John Morley wished to placate Parnellite demands for the retrenchment of Irish expenditure and therefore abolished the post of Assistant Under-Secretary for Police and Crime.[287] Jenkinson's Indian background had always made him an object of intense suspicion to Irish Nationalists and, with his home rule sympathies apparently unknown to them, they associated him with acts that, as Morley explained, 'the most active members of Mr. Parnell's party have always felt themselves bound publicly to denounce, and about which they still profess to feel bitterly'.[288]

Jenkinson continued his secret service work in London during 1886, but the Liberal Home Secretary, Hugh Childers, was no more willing to provide him with a permanent position than his predecessor had been. Although Jenkinson's freedom of action was increasingly circumscribed, he persevered in trying to persuade the subsequent Conservative ministry that a definitive settlement of the Irish question was still within reach.[289] Meanwhile, it was increasingly clear that the functions assigned to him were incompatible with the independence of the Metropolitan Police and his position as 'Secret Service Commissioner' eventually became untenable.[290] By September 1886, the Prime Minister considered the circumstances of Jenkinson's employment to be 'very unsatisfactory.' He had, so Harcourt informed Spencer, 'made himself impossible' and, on 10 December 1886, the Home Secretary informed Jenkinson ('without a word of thanks') that his engagement was to be terminated.[291] Nevertheless, Lord Salisbury thought that he had served the British government well 'and ought

---

[287] O'Shea to Parnell, 28 December 1888: JCP, JC8/8/1/117. Hamilton to Spencer, 7 February 1886; Spencer to Hamilton, 8 February 1886: AP, Add MS 77061.

[288] Porter, *Origins of the Vigilant State*, p. 44. Morley to Childers, 16 February 1886; Godfrey Lushington to Childers, 23 February 1886: TNA, HO 144/721/110757. Timothy Healy had once characterized Jenkinson as 'a species of Mokanna': *FJ*, 14 November 1884, p. 3.

[289] Jenkinson to Churchill, 9 August 1886, containing confidential and very secret memoranda dated 25 July and 5 August 1886: RCHL 1/14. 1646, 1647; Jenkinson to Buller, 27 November, 2 December 1886: TNA, Buller Papers, WO 132/4A.

[290] Lushington, Memorandum, *c*.31 May 1886; Lushington to Henry Matthews, 31 October 1886: TNA, HO 144/721/110757; Childers to Harcourt, 3 June 1886: HP, Dep. Adds 18.

[291] Salisbury to Ashbourne, 13 September 1886, repr. Cooke and Malcolmson, *Ashbourne Papers*, p. 165; Harcourt to Spencer, 16 December 1886: AP, MS 76934. Matthews to Jenkinson, 10 December 1886; Jenkinson to Matthews, 12 December 1886; Home Office minute to Treasury, 14 January 1887: TNA, HO 144/721/110757. Northbrook to Spencer, 12 December 1886: AP, Add MS 76918.

not to be cast adrift'. He regarded Jenkinson as 'a shrewd spy, with a good nose' and, in February 1888, suggested that the Foreign and India Offices place him in Paris 'to try and get Russian information for us'. Nothing came of the plan, however, and Jenkinson's career in public service was over.[292]

Although Fottrell's career suffered less than those of Hamilton and Jenkinson, he was viewed with deep suspicion by Conservatives in Dublin, where he was regarded simply as 'the Land League lawyer'.[293] His claim to have refused a place on the Royal Commission on Land in 1886 because of his brother's illness should be considered against the fact that his inclusion had not been popular in Conservative circles. *The Times* implied that his appointment would conflict with his professional work on behalf of tenant farmers and Churchill referred to him simply as 'a snake' who had 'been warned off'.[294]

In spite of the removal of Hamilton and Jenkinson from Dublin, their ideas continued to influence policy makers. After the failure of home rule, both men maintained that the situation would have been much worse if the principle had not been adopted by at least one of the British political parties. As F.S.L. Lyons commented, the Bill

> symbolized a mighty change in Ireland's affairs. At last a great statesman and a great party had been brought to embody Irish aspirations in legislative form. Compared with this, from which it was assumed there could be no going back, the immediate fate of the bill was of secondary importance.[295]

Gladstone had brought Parnell's aspirations for Ireland within the realm of practical politics. With hindsight, it seemed that the capacity of republicans and radical agrarians to disrupt the government of Ireland had been overestimated in the winter of 1885. But if an attempt had been made to suppress Parnell's movement early in 1886, then radical forces might have come to the fore in a conflict with the British authorities far more violent than that which subsequently occurred during the Plan of Campaign. Above all, Hamilton thought it was important that Gladstone's election defeat in July 1886 should not be popularly regarded as 'an emphatic "no" to a Home Rule policy for Ireland'. If the Irish were to believe that, then, he feared, resort would be had 'to other than constitutional means'. Testimony that this had been averted was offered to Gladstone when the militantly

---

[292]Salisbury to Cross, 12 January 1887, 21 February 1888: BL, Cross Papers, Add MSS 51263, fos 137–138, 51264, fos 6–8.
[293]Buller to Ridgeway, 15 November 1887: HMC, Sir Joseph West Ridgeway Papers, NRA 6957; *The Times*, 13 July 1897, p. 10.
[294]*The Times*, 1 October 1886, p. 7; Churchill to Ashbourne, 30 September 1886, repr. Cooke and Malcolmson, *Ashbourne Papers*, p. 103.
[295]Lyons, *Parnell*, p. 345.

nationalist councillors of Limerick assured him that he had placed 'the cause of Irish liberty in a position from which it cannot be driven'.[296] Parnell's success in securing a place for home rule within the mainstream of British politics also convinced influential Irish-American republicans that persisting with constitutional politics would be the most productive path towards independence. Contrary to Jenkinson's expectations, Patrick Ford, who had pledged his support for Parnell in 1884, did not alter his allegiance after the defeat of the Home Rule Bill. While the IRB remained active in Ireland, the forces of revolutionary nationalism, it seemed, were not powerful enough to divert Parnell's followers from the parliamentary course once the principle of home rule had been conceded.[297]

Between 1887 and 1891, Arthur Balfour dealt with the Irish nationalist movement with renewed coercion, piecemeal reforms, and an orchestrated public campaign designed to discredit Parnell and his party. While the Special Commission on 'Parnellism and Crime' failed to prove charges against Parnell himself, it inflicted mortal wounds to the home rule cause in the eyes of British public opinion, thus making the Irish party's subsequent schism over the O'Shea divorce case more damaging than it need have been.[298] In Ireland, the partial suppression of the National League and the consequent reappearance of what Balfour characterized as 'retail assassination' appeared to suit Unionist purposes. Balfour informed the Cabinet that he regarded 'with unmixed satisfaction this reversion to former types of Irish discontent, which, if it be completely carried out, will entirely destroy all that was original and effective in the policy initiated by Parnell in 1879'. His staff took great pains to collect evidence to demonstrate that the ultimate objective of the home rule movement was 'not union with England, but separation, and the formulation of a distinct and individual nationality'. It is ironic that some of the ammunition that Balfour gathered against the Parnellites came from the pen of Jenkinson, whose memoranda of 1885 were reprinted for the Cabinet in March 1889 and used to justify policies quite different from those advocated by their author.[299]

[296]Hamilton to Spencer, 19 July 1886: AP, Add MS 77061; 'Address from the mayor, aldermen, & burgesses of the borough of Limerick to the Right Honourable William Ewart Gladstone MP, 23 September 1886': GP, Add MS 56447, fos 141–143.

[297]MCR (W) for October 1886, Byrne, DM, 31 October 1886: CSO RP 1886/21972.

[298]See Margaret O'Callaghan, *British High Politics and a Nationalist Ireland: criminality, land and the law under Forster and Balfour* (Cork, 1994).

[299]Balfour, 'Confidential. Political condition of Ireland', January 1889; 'Secret Societies in Ireland and the United States', 26 March 1889: CAB 37/23/13, CAB 37/23/5 (**Documents 8** and **15**). See also Campbell, *Fenian Fire*, pp. 177–178.

The political journal of George Fottrell and the correspondence generated by Edward Jenkinson and Sir Robert Hamilton demonstrate that, by 1885, important figures in Irish government believed that the time had come for the Irish people to be given, as Jenkinson put it to Gladstone, 'the right to regulate their own internal affairs, the right to preserve their revenues for their own advantage, and to make their own laws'. For Hamilton, the underlying principle was that 'without sacrificing Imperial interests the country should be governed in accordance with the views of the people and not against them'.[300] Like Fottrell, both officials questioned the continued viability of British government in Ireland and shared the view that alternative methods had neither secured lasting peace nor politically integrated the country into the United Kingdom; as Matthew has stated, 'despite all efforts the integration was the other way, towards an Ireland largely integrated by a demand for Home Rule'. As the dangers of persisting with former methods of government became clearer, Hamilton and Jenkinson concluded that only two alternatives remained – granting self-government or repression and disenfranchisement.[301]

If nothing else, Hamilton and Jenkinson did much to persuade Lord Spencer to accept home rule. As John Kendle has explained, 'Gladstone would not have moved, could not have moved, without Spencer'. The task had not been easy because Spencer had been a victim of his own success. By suppressing crime and securing British institutions in Ireland during 1882–1885, he had convinced many British politicians that they could continue to govern the country largely on their own terms. Support for home rule was made more difficult to secure because some leading Liberals believed that the difficulty of governing Ireland had been exaggerated.[302] Furthermore, Spencer had endured years of personal abuse from Irish nationalists, and had left the country, as Gladstone knew, 'the butt of all the sharpest arrows of Nationalism and disaffection'. Understandably, Spencer harboured strong doubts about Parnell's fitness for government and, late in 1885, told Hartington, 'I get at times sick at the idea of giving up to such men!! With such a history belonging to them!!' Even after he had accepted the case for home rule, he confessed that he still found it 'odious to deal with men who have tolerated methods of agitation such as those of the Land League, and who have not when they could exerted themselves to put down outrages'. At the same time, Spencer

---

[300] See **Documents 27** and **46**.
[301] Matthew, *Gladstone*, p. 472; **Documents 27**, **32**, and **40**.
[302] Kendle, *Ireland and the Federal Solution*, p. 43; Matthew, *Gladstone*, p. 451; Jonathan Parry, *The Rise and Fall of Liberal Government in Victorian Britain* (New Haven, CT, 1993), p. 292; Mallet, *Northbrook*, p. 233.

knew that there was no evidence to suggest that Parnell bore direct responsibility for crimes committed during the Land War.[303] He told an audience in Newcastle that, while nationalist leaders had too often remained silent 'when words would have been golden', he could say 'without doubt or hesitation' that he had 'neither heard nor seen any evidence of complicity in any of these crimes by the leaders of the Irish party'. Indeed, as Spencer drew satisfaction from the fact that it might soon be Parnell's turn to 'deal with the extremists', he admitted that this task would not be 'as tough as ours could be with the Parnellites against us'.[304]

The viewpoint offered from Dublin Castle in 1885 was persuasive because it represented Irish self-government as an essentially conservative measure that would marginalize extremism. It was confidently asserted that Parnell's popular conservatism would provide an effective bulwark against republicanism and dominate all other strands of Irish nationalism indefinitely. Liberal politicians were encouraged to believe that home rule was not a danger but a source of strength and that the risk of separation lay in its postponement. It was, it has been argued, 'the boldest of all possible attempts to save Ireland for constitutionalism and from Fenianism' and Gladstone calculated that, for fiscal reasons alone, Parnell would adopt a 'common sense' approach to self-government and entirely reject separation from Great Britain.[305]

There were, however, more negative reasons for the promotion of home rule. It derived, in part, from a sense of failure and a desire to be rid of the irksome and exhausting duties of Irish government and its attendant cycle of protest, disorder, repression, and crime. During the election campaign of 1885, John Morley had painted a picture of a demoralized Irish executive and it is true that Hamilton and Jenkinson were clearly dispirited by the experience of governing Ireland against its will. They were particularly disappointed to see the temporary successes achieved between 1882 and 1885 appear to evaporate. Spencer was forced to accept that the Conservatives' 'surrender' to the Irish nationalists over coercion in June 1885 had made the Liberals 'see-saw policy' of repression and reform redundant. Hamilton confessed to Edward Hamilton that he had started to come round to home rule 'immediately after Lord Spencer's

---

[303]Gladstone to Spencer, 30 June 1885: AP, Add MS 76862; Spencer to Hartington, 27 December 1885, repr. *RE*, II, p. 91. 'Draft taken from a letter to Lord Lansdowne when Mr. Gladstone's Government was formed in 1886'; Spencer to Edward Hamilton, 23 September 1884: AP, Add MSS 77329, 76860.

[304]I.S. Leadham, *Parnellism and Conservatism, or the Accusers in the Dock* (London, 1887), p. 27; 'Draft taken ... in 1886': AP, Add MS 77329.

[305]Matthew, *Gladstone*, p. 506.

policy had been reversed, or (rather) allowed to fall through'. It had, he admitted 'been a fragile enough edifice to build up', one 'reared with the greatest difficulty; and it was impossible to set it up again, when once it had been pulled down'.[306] Personal stresses added to the sense of frustration. Jenkinson had been under particular strain for a number of years, having lived separately from his family and foregone all recreation. His experience told him that the odds were '8 to 1 in favour of the Dynamiter' and that his rare victories over the bombers did not 'go to the root of the matter'. After the explosions at the House of Commons in January 1885, he had confessed to feeling as though he had 'passed through some tremendous storm, and had come out of it a complete wreck'.[307] A year later, Carnarvon provided Salisbury with a vivid insight into an assignment that was 'not only laborious & difficult, but personally very dangerous'. Jenkinson was reportedly 'obliged to take his life in his hands' by meeting informants in the East End of London, work that he admitted to finding 'most uncongenial [. . .] and repulsive'.[308] Clearly, his cloak-and-dagger lifestyle took its toll and a desire to be free of it is likely to have encouraged him to reassess the future of Irish government.

The accusation that Gladstone deliberately exaggerated the gravity of the Irish situation in December 1885 in order to justify his remaining at the centre of the political arena seems unduly harsh when one considers the grave reports that he was then receiving from Ireland. Nevertheless, one unintended consequence of the emphasis that Jenkinson placed upon the danger posed by Irish republicanism was that it encouraged Gladstone to develop his home rule policy with damaging haste, in the belief that Ireland was on the verge of anarchy. Gladstone later defended his actions by arguing that 'once the subject was ripe, the time for action had come. We were not to wait until it was over-ripe.'[309] But Hamilton and Jenkinson clearly thought that bipartisanship and a process of consultation were indispensable for the success of home rule, and warned that the Liberals risked political disaster if they attempted to carry the issue on their own. It was typical of a man schooled in the ways of colonial administration that Jenkinson argued that only a gradual devolution of power would enable the Irish

---

[306]Lord Eversley, *Gladstone and Ireland* (London, 1912), p. 285; Spencer to Lansdowne, 2 February 1886, repr. *RE*, II, pp. 107–109; Edward Hamilton's diary, 13 February 1886: EHP, Add MS 48643, fos 13–14.

[307]See **Document 2**; Jenkinson to Spencer, 17 December 1884, 4 February 1885: AP, Add MSS 77035, 77036.

[308]Jenkinson to Cross, 11 August 1885: TNA, HO 144/721/110757; Carnarvon to Salisbury, 7 January 1886: CP/TNA, PRO 30/6/62 (53).

[309]Parry, *Liberal Government*, p. 296; Gladstone, 'The Irish Question, 1886', 18 August 1886: GP, Add MS 44699, fos 209–231.

to acquire the 'gradual political education' they needed to 'fit them for self-government'.[310] Nevertheless, this was an approach that was apparently shared by both John Dillon and Parnell himself: Carnarvon claimed that, during their clandestine meeting on 1 August 1885, Parnell accepted 'the need for a "gradual growth" of self-government in order to "accustom the people" to the exercise of responsibility'.[311]

The documents reproduced in this volume challenge the idea that late Victorian high politics was played out without serious reference to Irish events. They reveal that the condition of Ireland was a significant factor in Gladstone's decision to formulate a home rule policy during 1885–1886 and demonstrate that Dublin Castle's concern over the growing strength of Irish republicanism significantly accelerated the development of legislation. For a number of Liberal administrators and politicians, the devolution of power in Ireland was the only effective means of securing public order, political union, and strategic safety, by 'creating an empire whose cohesion came from decentralized power'.[312] Nevertheless, as George Fottrell was to find out, opponents of home rule viewed the policy as an aspect of Fenianism rather than the means of its defeat, and many Liberals were prepared to follow Chamberlain and fight to prevent what they regarded as the dismantling of the Empire. Political opposition to home rule was grounded on English and imperial rather than Irish grounds and Hamilton was criticized for failing to take these aspects of the question seriously enough. The former chief secretary, Henry Campbell-Bannerman, reminded Spencer, 'I think, indeed, that those of us who have had to do with Ireland and know the hideous difficulties of its government are naturally disposed to take too light a view of the dangers to the Empire of the alternative to which we deem ourselves driven.' But many of the Liberals who disliked Parnell's demands still recognized that they were compatible with their own desire to balance the integration of smaller 'regional' territories into a larger nation state. The documentary evidence reproduced here suggests that the experience of governing Ireland during the turbulent years of 1882–1885 convinced those most intimately involved that home rule was a natural development of the principle of popular, responsible self-government, and was the only means of persuading Irish nationalists to confine their struggle for independence within the bounds of the British constitution.[313]

---

[310]**Document 2**.

[311]**Journal (28 July 1885)**; O'Day, *Irish Home Rule*, p. 99.

[312]Matthew, *Gladstone*, pp. 468–469.

[313]Campbell-Bannerman to Spencer, 8 January 1886, repr. Spender, *Campbell-Bannerman*, I, pp. 95–97; Matthew, *Gladstone*, pp. 437, 467.

# EDITORIAL NOTE

Sir George Fottrell placed a number of newspaper cuttings in his journal, most of which have not been reproduced. Some passages of text, chiefly those listing the contents of memoranda or parliamentary bills, have also been excised and referenced. Wherever possible, the journal has been cross-referenced with the documentary evidence to which it relates. Fottrell's statements have been explored by means of editorial notes based on manuscript, newspaper, and secondary sources. Their veracity has been tested wherever possible, with attention being drawn to any statement of fact that is proven to have been inaccurate. Biographical notes are largely confined to the period covered by the journal and minor spelling mistakes and other errors in the text have been silently corrected. Occasional stylistic infelicities have been left unaltered, though in some places punctuation and capitalization have been added for reasons of clarity and consistency. Latin phrases, foreign words, and the titles of publications have been printed in italics and missing words have been written in full within square brackets.

In the case of the documents reproduced in this volume, only minor corrections have been necessary and the small amount of material excised from the text has been summarized. The names and addresses of the recipients of the letters, greetings, and signatures, etc. have been omitted and the relevant information included in the title of the document.

A list of abbreviations is provided on p. xi of this volume.

# THE POLITICAL JOURNAL OF SIR GEORGE FOTTRELL

13 Jany. 1885

I think it may perhaps at some future stage of Irish politics prove useful to have from an eye witness some notes of the events now passing in Ireland or rather some notes of the inner working of the Government and of the Irish party. I have rather exceptional opportunities of noting their working. I have since I attained manhood been a consistent Nationalist and I believe that the leading men on the national side have confidence in my honour and consistency. On the other hand I am a Crown official & I am an intimate personal friend of Sir Robert Hamilton,[1] the Under Secretary for Ireland. My first introduction to him took place about 18 months ago. I was introduced to him by Robert Holmes,[2] the Treasury Remembrancer. At that time Sir Robert was Mr. Hamilton & his private secretary was Mr. Clarke Hall who had come over temporarily from the Admiralty. Mr. Hamilton was himself at that time only a temporary official. Shortly afterwards he was induced to accept the permanent appointment as Under Secretary. From the date of my first introduction to him up to the present our acquaintance has steadily developed into a warm friendship and I think that Sir Robert Hamilton now probably speaks to me on Irish matters more freely than to anyone else.

I have always spoken to him with similar freedom and whether my views were shared by him or were at total variance with his I have never concealed my opinion from him.

I was in last October appointed Clerk of the Crown for Dublin City & County & I believe my appointment was the result of Sir R. Hamilton's intervention. I had not asked for the post. My first interview with Lord Spencer[3] was that at which he offered me the post. A note of the conversation on that occasion is in my locked note book which I had when in the service of the Land Commission.

In December 1884 Sir R. Hamilton sent for me to ask me my opinion as to the best tribunal to deal for Ireland with the question

[1] See appendix.
[2] Robert William Arbuthnot Holmes (1843–1910), Treasury Remembrancer and Deputy Paymaster for Ireland (1882–1908).
[3] See appendix.

of Boundaries under the Redistribution of Seats Bill.[4] He told me his notion was to make the Irish Boundaries Commission out of exactly similar elements to those out of which the Scotch Boundaries Commission[5] had just been formed, viz. Sir J. Lambert,[6] the Head of the Ordinance Survey Dept., Sir F. Sandford,[7] the Chief English Boundaries Commissioner & 1 barrister.

I agreed in the wisdom of this. He then asked who would be the best barrister & he said Naish[8] had recommended Piers White QC.[9] I cordially agreed.

He subsequently told me he had been asked by Lord Spencer to get me to ascertain my views of Gray MP[10] & Sexton MP[11] on the subject & he asked me had I any objection privately to make the inquiry. I replied that my position of mind was that I would not on any account 'pump' the Irish members & then detail to the Government anything which I thought the members might wish to conceal nor would I pump him or any other member of the Government & then detail to the Irish members anything which he might wish to conceal but that I would willingly undertake any trouble with a view of making each side acquainted with the views of the other so as to promote harmony between them.

Gray was in London & so was Sexton. I saw Tim Healy MP.[12] He preferred Carton[13] to Piers White but he admitted that White would command confidence on all sides for his integrity and high character. I arranged to lunch with Sir R. Hamilton on the following Sunday. When I had lunched he said that Lord Spencer wished to see me. I walked over to the Vice Regal Lodge & had a long talk about the

---

[4] Bill for the Redistribution of Seats at Parliamentary Elections: *PP* 1884–5, IV, 85.

[5] Report of the Boundary Commissioners for Scotland: *PP* 1884–5, XIX, 499.

[6] Sir John Lambert (1815–1892), Permanent Secretary to the Local Government Board (1871–1882).

[7] Sir Francis Sandford (1824–1893), first Baron Sandford (1891), Secretary for the Education Office (1870–1884).

[8] John Naish (1841–1890), Attorney-General (1884–1885) and Lord Chancellor of Ireland (1885, 1886).

[9] A Roman Catholic barrister and liberal, later Chairman of the Liberal Union of Ireland: see Hamilton to Spencer, 5 December 1884: AP, Add MS 77060; *The Times*, 15 March 1888, p. 9.

[10] Edmund Dwyer Gray (1845–1888), Nat. MP for Co. Carlow (1880–1885) and for St Stephen's Green Division, Dublin (1885–1888), owner of the *Freeman's Journal*.

[11] Thomas Sexton (1848–1932), Nat. MP for Co. Sligo (1880–1885) and for Sligo South (1885–1892), Lord Mayor of Dublin (1887–1889).

[12] Timothy Michael Healy (1855–1931), Nat. MP for Co. Monaghan (1883–1885), for Londonderry South (1885–1886), and for Longford North (1887–1892), Governor-General of the Irish Free State (1922–1928).

[13] Richard Paul Carton (1836–1907), Commissioner of National Education, Chairman of the Queen's Colleges Commission (1884–1885).

Boundaries Commission. I strongly urged the importance of making the Scotch & Irish Commissions identical. I told Healy's opinion but I said that personally I had a much higher opinion of Piers White's ability than of Carton's.[14]

On that evening Lord Spencer sent Mr. Courtney Boyle,[15] his private secretary, specially to London to arrange if possible for the appointment of the Commission on the suggested lines & the Commission was next day appointed consisting of the following –

Sir J. Lambert – Sir F. Sandford

Piers White QC – Major McPherson[16]

& Richard Burke [sic],[17] Local Govt. Board Inspector.

All the Irish papers Whig, Tory & Nationalist approved of the Commission.[18]

One day in December last Sir R. Hamilton went with me to Bray for a long walk. On our way out in the train we discussed the question of the renewal of the Crimes Act. I opposed its renewal except under the direst necessity. He admitted that his own view was that most of the provisions of the Act might be allowed to lapse but that it would be requisite to re-enact the change of venue clause & the special jury clause.[19]

I urged the pressing importance of bringing in a County Government Bill for Ireland. He admitted this – we discussed the details as to the multiple vote & as to giving some supervising power to the Local Government Board.[20]

[14] Spencer informed Sir Charles Dilke, 'From sources independent of Sir R. Hamilton I hear that a row is getting up about the question': Spencer to Dilke, 10 December 1884: AP, Add MS 76924.

[15] Courtenay Edmund Boyle (1845–1901), private secretary to Lord Spencer (1868–1874, 1882–1885), Assistant-Secretary to the Local Government Board (1885) and the Board of Trade (1886).

[16] John Cosmo Macpherson (Farquharson) (1839–1905), officer of Royal Engineers (1859–1896), Executive Officer of the Ordnance Survey of the United Kingdom (1887–1894).

[17] As inspector for Dublin, Bourke had represented the Treasury in the settlement of arrears. Spencer claimed that he and White were the 'most influential' men available and that their impartiality was guaranteed: Spencer to Edward Gibson, 16, 19, and 26 December 1884, repr. A.B. Cooke and A.P.W. Malcolmson (eds), *The Ashbourne Papers, 1869–1913: a calendar of the papers of Edward Gibson, 1st Lord Ashbourne* (Belfast, 1974), pp. 179–180.

[18] See *The Times*, 3 December 1884, p. 12. For findings, see Report of the Boundary Commissioners for Ireland: *PP* 1884–5, XIX, 499.

[19] In the belief that 'anything that makes punishment more certain aids the prevention of crime', Hamilton recommended that these clauses become permanent laws: 'Memo. on the renewal of the Prevention of Crimes Act', 18 January 1885: AP, Add MS 77331.

[20] The Local Government Board, established in 1872, assumed responsibilities for medical treatment and public hygiene formerly vested in the Poor Law Commissioners.

Some days afterward he read for me at the Castle two memoranda which he had written for Lord Spencer – one on the subject of state advances & the other on the subject of County Government.[21]

Gray returned from London some time in Dec. I spoke to him on the subject of the Crimes Act renewal[22] & the introduction of a County Government Bill. He quite agreed with my view that if the latter bill was introduced & pushed on by the Government it would do more than anything else to quiet the country. I afterwards explained fully to Sir R. Hamilton Gray's view & mine.

Some day early in the present month Sir R. Hamilton read for me a memorandum which he had written for Lord Spencer suggesting the best course to be followed by the Government in relation to Irish business in Parliament.[23] This memorandum was very able & manly. It strongly urged the introduction of a County Government Bill at once.

I told Sir R. H. that I intended to write a memorandum on the same subject & that Charles Russell[24] would give it to Mr. Gladstone.[25] Sir R. H. approved of this course. I invited him to dine on Wednesday 7 Jany. to meet C. Russell & Gray.

On 7 Jany Russell, Gray, Hamilton, R. Holmes & Jonathan Hogg[26] dined with me. A few days previously I wrote the promised memorandum[27] & gave it to Hamilton to look over it. When he came to dinner he told me that he was delighted with the memorandum & that he was so struck with it that he had read it to Lord Spencer who also was really struck with it. Hamilton said, "It was just the complement of my memorandum as it dealt with the party aspect of the question which mine did not." I am in great hopes that the Government will introduce a County Government Bill for Ireland in the coming session.

[21] See 'State interference with industrial enterprise', 1 December 1884 and 'Statement as to Local Government of Ireland', 11 February 1885: CP/TNA, PRO 30/6/127 (8), (11).

[22] The Prevention of Crime (Ireland) Act, 1882 (45 & 46 Vict., c. 25) was due to expire and the Liberal ministry was considering its renewal.

[23] Hamilton argued that the concession of a measure of local government would remove a popular grievance and thus assist the operation of the Land Act: 'Memo. on the renewal of the Prevention of Crimes Act', 18 January 1885: AP, Add MS 77331.

[24] Charles Russell (1832–1900), first Baron Russell of Killowen (1894), Lib. MP for Dundalk (1880–1885) and for South Hackney (1885–1894), KCB (1886), Attorney-General (1886, 1892–1894), Lord Chief Justice (1894).

[25] William Ewart Gladstone (1809–1898), Lib. MP for Midlothian (1880–1895), Prime Minister (1868–1874, 1880–1885, 1886, 1892–1894).

[26] Jonathan Hogg (1847–1930), Chairman of William Hogg & Company, treasurer of the Liberal Unionist Party and committee member of the Irish Loyal and Patriotic Union (1886), Governor of the Bank of Ireland (1901–1902).

[27] See **Document 7**.

Afterwards Gray & Hamilton had a long & earnest conversation on politics for fully two hours.

Hamilton takes a deep interest in the cutting down of the Irish Bench to reasonable limits & putting an end to the awful extravagance of the Irish legal establishment generally. He has told me several times that he reads over every now & then my article on the Irish judicial establishment in the *Fortnightly Review* published in 1875[28] & that he thoroughly agrees with it.

I got Sexton last year to move for a return shewing the amount of civil business transacted before the Judges in Dublin & on circuit. It discloses a state of things conclusively proving that the Irish Judges have scarcely any legal business to occupy them.[29]

The Bench is sure to be considerably reduced. On yesterday a meeting of the 'Benchers' was held. A letter from Lord Spencer was read asking for their opinion as to reducing the Irish circuits to 4. This was strongly condemned. Baron Dowse[30] moved that the Home Circuit might be abolished. This motion shewed an equal number of Benchers for & against & therefore the resolution was carried. This is satisfactory as it puts the Judges completely in the wrong. The *Freeman* attacks them strongly today.[31] I find that Benjamin Whitney[32] & George Tyrell[33] two staunch Tory Solicitors are just as favourable as I am to cutting down the bench & bar places & emoluments to reasonable limits.

14 Jany. 1885

I went to the Under Secretary's Lodge today to see Sir R. Hamilton who was laid up with a cold. We had a talk about the Judges & he told me that those Judges who had opposed the abolition of the Home Circuit, finding that there was a division of opinion among the Judges, had now come round to the theory that there ought to be only 4 circuits. We conversed about the reduction of legal charges in Ireland. He told me that he had reduced them from

[28] 'The Irish Judges', *Fortnightly Review*, 23 (March 1875), pp. 408–421, and see his *The Irish Judges and Irish Chairmen* (Dublin, 1876).

[29] See Return of Civil Cases in Ireland tried in Dublin and on Circuit, 1873–82: *PP* 1884, LXIII, 327.

[30] Richard Dowse (1824–1890), Lib. MP for Londonderry city (1868–1872), Baron of the Exchequer (1872–1890).

[31] See *FJ*, 13 January 1885, p. 3.

[32] Sir Benjamin Whitney (1833–1916), Clerk of the Crown and Peace for Mayo, founder of Whitney & Moore, solicitors (1882).

[33] George Gerald Tyrell, Clerk of the Crown and Peace for Armagh.

over £100,000 to £79,000.[34] He also said he had very considerably reduced the constabulary estimate by stopping recruiting altogether for the present. The usual number of recruits per annum being 800 (eight hundred), he had reduced it to 30 for the past year – the annual wasting of the constabulary is about 800.[35]

We spoke about the payment of Crown witnesses & I recalled his attention to the witnesses' expenses in the trial of Fitzgerald,[36] the supposed Fenian outrage monger in Dec. last, where I found that Mr. Peyton[37] had recommended payment at a lower rate to Mr. O'Reilly,[38] the Hotel Keeper, than to other witnesses in a similar rank of life. O'Reilly being the only Crown witness who gave evidence with hesitation for the Crown, that is, he was most guarded in saying that he could not conclusively identify the prisoner. Sir R. Hamilton said he feared my suspicions were too true & that it apparently had been a habit with Crown Solicitors to pay witnesses "by results". He is most strongly opposed to any such detestable system & he said he had issued instructions which would make it clear to Crown Solicitors that such a practice would not be tolerated by the Government. He has also put an end to the system of supporting Crown witnesses in a lavish fashion pending the trials at which they are to give evidence.[39]

I mentioned to him that in relation to the change of venue clauses of the Crimes Act I believed that the Queen's Bench had, without any Crimes Act, full power to change venues in Criminal Cases. He said that if this was so it was most important & I promised to look up the law & let him know how it stood on the subject.

---

[34] Hamilton proposed to cut estimated expenditure on law charges and criminal prosecutions for 1885–1886 from £99,031 to £79,206: Hamilton to Spencer, 5 and 23 December 1884: AP, Add MS 77060; Hamilton to Sir Henry Campbell-Bannerman, 29 January 1885 and Hamilton to Sir Ralph Lingen, 30 January 1885: CSO RP 1885/1692 in RP 1885/2366.

[35] Between 1883 and 1885, the authorized force strength fell from 14,277 to 12,500: Treasury Blue Notes, 1894–1895: TNA, T165. For RIC expenditure, see CSO RPs 1884/15076, 1884/11841, 1885/4011.

[36] Patrick Neville Fitzgerald (1851–1907), commercial traveller, representative for Munster on the Supreme Council of the IRB (1878), tried and acquitted of treason felony in November 1884: see Owen Magee, *The IRB: the Irish Republican Brotherhood from the Land League to Sinn Fein* (Dublin, 2005), pp. 127–129.

[37] Randle Peyton (b. 1820), crown solicitor for Leitrim, Sligo, and Roscommon (1874–1885).

[38] Edward Albert O'Reilly, hotel proprietor in Wormwood-gate, Dublin. For his deposition, see *Queen against Jeremiah Lowry and Others: brief on behalf of the Crown*: NLI, MS 5508.

[39] Hamilton proposed that all crown witnesses should be paid at the minimum rate unless satisfactory reason was given for paying more: Hamilton to Spencer, 23 December 1884; circular to crown solicitors, 12 January 1885: CSO RP 1885/2366.

I lent him A.M. Sullivan's[40] memorandum for the Pope respecting the Parnell fund to read.[41] J.E. Kenny[42] had lent this to me.

## 15 Jany. 1885

I sent to Hamilton a carefully prepared memorandum shewing the law & practice in Ireland in relation to the power of the Queen's Bench Division to change the venue in Criminal Cases.[43]

## 16 Jany. 1885

I rode out to see Hamilton at the Under Secretary's Lodge. We discussed the above mentioned memoranda [sic] which he told me he had sent to his private secretary, without telling him from whom it came, in order that he might ask the Atty-Genl. why it was that the Government had set such store by the clause in the Crimes Act in relation to change of venue.

We discussed Dilke's[44] & Chamberlain's[45] recent speeches.[46] Hamilton's view is that these two statesmen have agreed between them that at the General election they will bid for the radical vote in England with a view of forming a radical Government of which Chamberlain would be Prime Minister. He believes that Gladstone will not continue in office as First Lord after the end of the coming session.

## 17 Jany. 1885

I met Thomas A. Dickson MP[47] today. I asked him how the Liberal Party now stood in the north of Ireland. He replied that if there was to

---

[40] Alexander Martin Sullivan (1829–1884), Home Rule MP for Co. Louth (1874–1880) and for Co. Meath (1880–1882), editor and proprietor of *The Nation* (1858–1877), author of influential accounts of Irish history.

[41] Sullivan penned several articles on the matter for *The Nation* in May 1883 and, in January 1884, published his *Observations* on the religious and political situation in Ireland for the information of church leaders: T.D. Sullivan, *A.M. Sullivan: a memoir* (Dublin, 1885), pp. 153–157.

[42] Joseph Edward Kenny (1845–1900), Nat. MP for Co. Cork South (1885–1892), surgeon to the North Dublin Union Hospital.

[43] And see his 'Memorandum showing the usual course of criminal proceedings in Ireland', 22 December 1884: CSO RP 1885/2366.

[44] Sir Charles Wentworth Dilke (1843–1911), Lib. MP for Chelsea (1868–1886), President of the Local Government Board (1882–1885).

[45] Joseph Chamberlain (1836–1914), Lib. MP for Birmingham (1876–1885), Lib. U. MP for Birmingham West (1885–1914), President of the Board of Trade (1880–1885), President of the Local Government Board (1886).

[46] Dilke spoke at Kensington on 13 January: *The Times*, 14 January 1885, p. 6; Chamberlain appeared at Ipswich the following day: *The Times*, 15 January 1885, p. 7.

[47] Thomas Alexander Dickson (1833–1909), Lib. MP for Co. Tyrone (1881–1885), Lib. U. MP for St Stephens Green Division, Dublin (1888–1892).

be any attempt to renew the Crimes Act the Liberal party in Ireland would be annihilated & that, for his part, if any such attempt were made he would denounce it.

### 23 Jany. 1885

I wrote to Dickson a few days ago suggesting that he would write to Lord Spencer or Sir R. Hamilton expressing the opinions which he had expressed to me in the above conversation. He replied that he had done so already.

I received from Charles Russell two letters of which I kept copies & then returned them. One was from Sir Charles Dilke to whom Russell had sent a copy of my memorandum on County Government. Dilke's letter was simply, "But I should regard it as a great calamity that a County Govt. Bill for Ireland should be introduced before County Govt. for England". The other letter was from Herbert Gladstone who says that he had given the memorandum to his father who had read it in the train on his way from Hawarden to London & that he was greatly struck with its clearness & force & that he had sent it to Lord Spencer for his opinion.[48]

I showed these letters on yesterday to Sir R. Hamilton.

### 30 Jany. 1885

Russell has sent me Chamberlain's letter to him on the same subject. Chamberlain's letter encloses a copy of a letter which he wrote to Mr. Dingnan[49] [sic] of Walsall on 17 Dec. 84 in which Chamberlain pronounces in favour of an extension of local government to Ireland which would include among the matters to be exclusively dealt with by an Irish Assembly all questions of education & land law.[50]

I not only shewed this letter to Sir R. Hamilton but I gave him a copy of it.

### Feby. 1885

I met T.A. Dickson MP at the levee.[51] He promised to call on me to discuss fully as to the danger &c. of renewing the Crimes Act. He

---

[48] See **Document 7**. Gladstone returned to London early on 20 January 1885: *GD*, XI, p. 279.

[49] William Henry Duignan (1824–1914), Director of the Walsall Wood Colliery Company, Mayor of Walsall (1868–1869). An antiquarian and etymologist, he travelled widely within the United Kingdom: C.D.H. Howard, "'The man on a tricycle": W.H. Duignan and Ireland, 1881–5', *IHS*, 14, no. 55 (March 1965), pp. 246–260.

[50] Chamberlain to Duignan, 17 December 1884: JCP, JC8/3/1/24.

[51] The first levee of the season was held on 3 February 1885: *The Times*, 3 February 1885, p. 6.

called & showed me a proof copy of a lecture proposed to be delivered by him in Liverpool in a few days but he said that owing to the dynamite explosion in the Houses of Parliament it would be impossible to address any English meeting on Irish affairs.[52] The proposed lecture is admirable in tone. It goes dead against any renewal of the Crimes Act & urges the immediate granting of County Boards. I was so struck by the manly tone of the lecture that I told him all I had done & read for him the memoranda & letters. He was very much pleased & said that now that he found I had paved the way, by expressing so strongly to the Executive the importance of relying on an extension of freedom instead of resorting to coercion, he would work still harder to inculcate the same advice. I advised Dickson to publish his lecture as a pamphlet.[53]

13 Feby.

I received a letter from Dickson stating that he had strongly urged his views again but he feared without avail as "Redmond's speeches were quoted as an evidence of the necessity for renewing the Crimes Act".[54]

17 Feby.

I met T. Harrington MP,[55] he said he wished to warn me that I was much blamed because I had undertaken the task of bringing about an understanding between Sir R. Hamilton & Dr. Walsh[56] of Maynooth, who has just been appointed Vicar Capitular on the death of Cardinal McCabe which took place a few days ago.[57] I replied that if the accusation against me was that Hamilton & Dr. Walsh dined at my table together some months ago I plead guilty but I must reserve to myself the right of inviting to my private table any guest I please.

---

[52] The explosion occurred on 24 January 1885: K.R.M. Short, *The Dynamite War: Irish-American bombers in Victorian Britain* (Dublin, 1979), pp. 205–208.

[53] See Thomas A. Dickson, *Committee on Irish Affairs, Paper No. 4: an Irish policy for a Liberal Government* (London, 1885).

[54] William Hoey Kearney Redmond (1861–1917), Nat. MP for Wexford (1883–1885), for Fermanagh North (1885–1892), and for Clare East (1892–1917). During demonstrations at Carndonagh, Co. Donegal and Newtonbarry, Co. Wexford, Redmond had advocated the boycotting of tenants occupying evicted farms: *The Times*, 2 February 1885, p. 6; 3 February 1885, pp. 6, 9.

[55] Timothy Charles Harrington (1851–1910), Nat. MP for Co. Westmeath (1883–1885) and for Harbour Division, Dublin (1885–1910), Secretary of the Irish National League (1882–1891), proprietor of the *Kerry Sentinel*.

[56] William Joseph Walsh (1841–1921), professor of moral theology and President (1880–1885) of St Patrick's College, Maynooth, Archbishop of Dublin (1885–1921).

[57] Edward MacCabe (1816–1885), Archbishop of Dublin (1879–1885). He died suddenly on 11 February.

24 Feby.

It is announced in today's papers that the Prince and Princess of Wales will visit Ireland early in April & will hold a levee & drawing-room & that in anticipation of their so doing the Lord Lieutenant's levee advertised for early in March is abandoned.[58]

There is much speculation as to the meaning of this move. In Parliament last night Gladstone in reply to Lewis[59] of Londonderry point blank refused to say whether the Crimes Act would be renewed.[60] My impression is that it will not.

28 Feby.

The division took place last night on the motion for a vote of censure on the ministry in relation to their Egyptian policy & conduct. The division showed a majority of only 14 for the ministers. The Irish party numbered 42 & voted solid against the ministers.[61]

I saw Sir Robt. Hamilton this morning & I urged him very strongly to do everything he could to induce the ministry at once to announce the proposed introduction of a County Government Bill for Ireland. He thoroughly agreed with me that it would be wise to introduce a bill for this purpose without delay & agreed also that the very fact of the Irish party having voted against the ministry would enable the ministry to escape odium in England in the event of introducing such a bill, by showing that its introduction was not the result of any bargain or 'treaty'.

2nd March

Robert W. Holmes, Brougham Leech,[62] Mr. Williams, Solicitor of Wakefield[63] & myself today held our first meeting as Commissioners to enquire into the working of the Registry of Deeds Office.[64]

---

[58] See *The Times*, 24 February 1885, p. 10.

[59] Sir Charles Edward Lewis (1825–1893), Con. MP for Londonderry city (1872–1886) and for Antrim North (1887–1892).

[60] Gladstone declined to discuss the legislation until after the Redistribution Bill was passed: *Hansard*, CCXIV, cols 1047–1048.

[61] See *The Times*, 2 March 1885, p. 8. On 23 February, John Morley had tabled a motion opposing the ministry's plan to send troops to Khartoum: *Hansard*, CCXIV, col. 1071.

[62] Henry Brougham Leech (1843–1921), professor of international law and jurisprudence at Dublin University (1878–1888). A pronounced unionist, he wrote 'Is Ireland overtaxed?' in reply to Robert Giffen's home rule proposals ( **Journal, 17 January 1886**): *The Times*, 11 May 1886, p. 16; 26 March 1921, p. 11.

[63] William L. Williams, solicitor to the justices of the West Riding, Yorkshire, registrar to the West Riding Registry, Wakefield.

[64] The commission was established by the Treasury in December 1884 to recommend improvements: see Registry of Deeds Office (Dublin): *PP* 1887, LXVII, 431.

10 March

On today the voting of the Parish Priests & Chapter of Dublin for the selection of an archbishop took place.[65] The result was as follows,

| | | |
|---|---|---|
| Dr. Walsh – | 46 | |
| Dr. Donnelly[66] – | 12 | Only one absentee Dr. Verdon[67] |
| Dr. Tynan[68] – | 3 | who is in Rome. |
| Dr. Woodlock[69] – | 2 | |
| | 63 | |

I received a letter from C. Russell asking could I suggest any medium course as to the renewal of the Crimes Act. I wrote in reply strongly urging him to use his influence with the ministry to dissuade them from asking for its renewal at all.

31 March

Sir R. Hamilton returned this morning from Gibraltar after an absence of nearly a month on a trip for his health. I saw him for a few minutes & remarked to him that the absence of crime in the country was almost complete & that I hoped we had therefore heard the last of attempts to renew the Crimes Act. He said that when he saw the newspapers at Portsmouth he was struck by observing news of disturbances and upheavals in almost every part of the British Dominions except Ireland. He says he has not read a line or heard a word spoken about Ireland for a month.

1st May

In London staying at the National Liberal Club. I came over at the instance of the Council of the Irish Law Society to smooth the passage through the House of Commons of the bill introduced by Lord Fitzgerald[70] in the House of Lords to amend the law relating to the status &c. of solicitors in Ireland.[71]

---

[65] See *The Times*, 11 March 1885, p. 10.

[66] James Donnelly (1823–1893), Bishop of Clogher (1864–1893).

[67] Michael Verdon (1838–1918), Vice-rector of the Irish College in Rome, Bishop of Dunedin (1896).

[68] Patrick J. Tynan, private secretary to Cardinals Paul Cullen and Edward McCabe.

[69] Bartholomew Woodlock (1819–1902), President of All Hallows College, Rector of the Catholic University, Dublin, Bishop of Ardagh and Clonmacnois (1879–1895).

[70] John David Fitzgerald (1815–1889), first Baron Fitzgerald (1882), Lib. MP for Ennis (1852–1860), justice of Queen's Bench, Ireland (1860–1882), Lord of Appeal (1882–1889).

[71] Bill to amend Laws for Regulation of Profession of Solicitors in Ireland: *PP* 1884–5, V, 473.

I saw John Morley,[72] MP for Newcastle, at the House & had a long talk with him. He asked me as to the condition of Ireland regarding crime & I told him that the country was practically free of crime & that unless there should happen to be a very bad harvest this year immunity from crime would probably continue. He told me that the question of renewal of the Crimes Act was at present under the consideration of the Cabinet & that the only member of the Cabinet really urgent in favour of renewal was Lord Spencer, but that as he insists upon the renewal he is backed up by Lord Hartington[73] & others. He believes that if non-renewal be decided upon Lord Spencer would resign & that Trevelyan[74] considers himself bound in honour to unite his fortunes with Lord Spencer's on this question, so that Spencer's resignation would also mean Trevelyan's secession & the united effect would probably be to burst up the Cabinet. Morley will steadily and determinedly oppose the renewal. He asked me what provision in the Crimes Act did I regard as most important. I told him that Sir R. Hamilton considered the most necessary to be – change of venue – special juries & tribunal of 2 resident magistrates for summary trial of boycotting & such like offences. Morley says that Jenkinson[75] told him the most important provision was – secret inquiries – & charging compensation for injuries on the incriminated localities.[76] He says also that Dilke & Chamberlain will not consent to renewal of the Crimes Act unless a compensation be made by introducing some important reform of Ireland at the same time. I suggested that if this was so the radicals ought to press for the introduction of a bill for County Boards in Ireland this session. Morley suggests the immediate establishment in Ireland of a representative board of say 50 members for all Ireland with Parnell[77] at their head, leaving to this board the settlement of land questions & the distribution of all money constituted by Ireland towards education. He promises to come to Ireland at Whitsuntide.

---

[72] John Morley (1838–1923), first Viscount Morley of Blackburn (1908), Lib. MP for Newcastle upon Tyne (1883–1895), Chief Secretary for Ireland (1886, 1892–1895).

[73] Spencer Compton Cavendish (1833–1908), Marquess of Hartington (1858) and eighth Duke of Devonshire (1891), Lib. MP for North-East Lancashire (1880–1885) and for Rossendale (1885–1891), Chief Secretary for Ireland (1870–1874), Secretary of State for War (1882–1885).

[74] George Otto Trevelyan (1838–1928), second Baronet (1886), Lib. MP for Hawick Burghs (1868–1886) and for Glasgow Bridgeton (1887–1897), Chief Secretary for Ireland (1882–1884), Chancellor of the Duchy of Lancaster (1884–1885), Secretary of State for Scotland (1886, 1892–1894).

[75] See appendix.

[76] For the clauses of the Prevention of Crime (Ireland) Act, 1882, see Virginia Crossman, *Politics, Law and Order in Nineteenth-Century Ireland* (Dublin, 1996), pp. 224–226.

[77] Charles Stewart Parnell (1846–1891), Nat. MP for Co. Meath (1875–1880) and for Cork city (1880–1890), President of the Irish National Land League (1879–1881) and of the Irish National League (1882–1890), Chairman of the Home Rule Party (1880–1890).

2$^{nd}$ May

I called at the Thatched House Club[78] to see if Escott,[79] the Editor of the *Fortnightly Review* was there. He was & he asked me to call on him tomorrow as he was very anxious to talk over some matters with me.

3$^{rd}$ May

I called on Escott. He wanted to get all the information he could about the Crimes Act. I explained its main provisions to him & told him the clauses which Sir R. Hamilton attached most importance to. He then told me that the Cabinet was at open war about the question of renewal or non-renewal & that a minister had as much as told him that it was about an even chance that the Cabinet would break up on the question. Escott's view is that Lord Spencer is the only member urgently anxious for renewal but that he is dogged on the point & that if he brings Lord Hartington & the Whig section of the Cabinet with him the result will be that Lord Spencer will wreck the Government & that Gladstone, Chamberlain & Dilke will retire from the Cabinet. If Gladstone retires Escott thinks he, Gladstone, will never again join in public life but if, on the other hand, Gladstone can retain power he believes that he will not abandon public life while he lives. He says that Dr. Andrew Clark[80] has practically told Gladstone's family that if the Prime Minister retires from public life he will probably die in a few months.

I find that Escott hates Wilson[81] of the *Times*. He says he is an ill-conditioned dyspeptic canting fellow.

4 May

I saw Sir Robert Hamilton today & told him what Morley & Escott had mentioned to me. He said that he was not altogether surprised at what I mentioned although he had not heard any details. He repeated that the only provisions in the Crimes Act he laid much stress by are those for change of venue – special juries & making intimidation a crime. These he considers absolutely necessary. The change of venue

---

[78] The Royal Navy Club of 1785, which met at the Thatched House Tavern in St James Street, before relocating to Willis's Rooms in 1862.

[79] Thomas Hay Sweet Escott (1844–1924), journalist and editor of the *Fortnightly Review* (1882–1886).

[80] Sir Andrew Clark (1826–1893), Physician to the London Hospital (1853–1886), President of the Royal College of Physicians (1888–1893), personal physician to W.E. Gladstone (1866–1893).

[81] Edward Daniel Joseph Wilson (1844–1913), contributor to and leader writer for *The Times* (1870–1903). His opposition to the Land League and home rule was described as 'the great work of his life': *The Times*, 30 June 1913, p. 11.

provision he would extend to England, & he says that the intimidation provisions are virtually in force already in Scotland.

He added that what he would wish to see done this year is the enactment of

(a) a measure renewing the provisions above stated.
(b) a measure establishing County Government.
(c) a measure abolishing the Viceroyalty.

He is in hopes that the very acuteness of the crisis in the Cabinet respecting (a) may enable (b) & (c) to be brought forward & carried this session.[82]

He was very anxious to obtain from me an explanation of the absence of all the Irish Bishops from the Prince of Wales's levee.[83] My explanation is that the Bishops are no longer leaders but followers & that in absenting themselves they simply yielded to the popular wish to show disapprobation of Lord Spencer's regime.

## 14 May

I saw Sir R. H. at the Castle today & spoke about the Crimes Act & County Government. He did not state what course the ministry would pursue, in fact he said that he did not yet know what decision had been arrived at, but he plainly expected that a County Government Bill would be introduced & pressed this session.

We spoke about the prospects of Dr. Walsh being appointed Archbishop of Dublin & he agreed with me that it would be a misfortune if he were not appointed. "What we want" said he "in public positions in Ireland is men who approach their duties with sympathy for the people – Such men command influence with the people & the sense of responsibility developed by their position sobers them even if at first they may be extreme in their views".

## 16 May

The papers of this morning contain Gladstone's statement made last night as to the intentions of the Government. The statement is very disappointing – no County Government Bill, no Purchase Bill, nothing but some "valuable & equitable" provisions of the Crimes Act, to use Mr. Gladstone's words.[84]

The Ministers are certainly though I suppose unwittingly playing into Parnell's hands. He will now be able to lash the constituencies in Ireland into a rage on the very eve of the General election.

---

[82] See **Document 9**.
[83] The levee took place on 9 April 1885: *The Times*, 10 April 1885, p. 10.
[84] See *Hansard*, CCXCVIII, cols 626–631.

18 May

The newspapers this morning announce the new Irish Law Appointments:[85] John Naish Chancellor, Samuel Walker[86] Attorney General & The MacDermot[87] Solicitor General.

I saw Sir R. H. today. He said that he never suffered more blank disappointment than in reading Gladstone's speech announcing Crimes Act renewal & no reforms for this session. He also said that when history comes to be written men will see how different a part Lord Spencer has played from that which is popularly attributed to him.

21 May

Mr. Gladstone on yesterday mended his hand by stating that the ministry had on consideration resolved to introduce a Land Purchase Bill and a Labourers Act Amendment Bill for Ireland.[88]

24 May

This is Whitsunday. Sir R. Hamilton, R. Adams[89] & L. Waldron[90] came out to me to Ballybrack to have a ramble about the hills. Sir R. spoke to me about the renewal of the Crimes Act & I again strongly opposed the clauses giving to the Attorney General power to change venues & require special juries. After we had walked to the top of the scalp we all sat down for a rest and the conversation happened to turn upon Parnell. Some one asked what was the motive power in Parnell. Adams replied that he believed Parnell's strongest passion was hatred of England. Sir R. H. asked why should Parnell hate England, was he not educated in Cambridge? Adams replied that he believed Parnell had stated that while at Cambridge & up to the date of the execution of the 'Manchester Martyrs'[91] he had not devoted a

---

[85] The appointments became necessary upon the sudden death of Sir Edward Sullivan, the Lord Chancellor of Ireland: *The Times*, 18 May 1885, p. 10.

[86] Samuel Walker (1832–1911), Lib. MP for Londonderry (1884–1885), Solicitor- and Attorney-General for Ireland (1883–1885, 1885, 1886), Lord Chancellor for Ireland (1892–1895, 1905–1911).

[87] Hugh Hyacinth MacDermot (1834–1904), Solicitor- and Attorney-General for Ireland (1885, 1886, 1892–1895).

[88] See *Hansard*, CCXCVIII, cols 971–972.

[89] Richard Adams (1846–1908), journalist for the *Cork Examiner* and the *Freeman's Journal* (1868–1873), barrister on the Munster circuit (1873–1894), county court judge for Limerick (1894).

[90] Laurence Ambrose Waldron (1858–1923), Chairman of the Dublin and Kingston Railway and Dublin United Tramways (1896), commissioner of National Education, son of Laurence Waldron MP (1811–1875).

[91] William Allen, Michael O'Brien, and Michael Larkin were executed on 23 November 1867 for the murder of a police sergeant during an attempt to rescue the Fenian leader Thomas Kelly from custody in Manchester.

thought to Irish politics, but that he was driven wild with rage at that event & began then to study Irish political questions with eagerness and as a result he has acquired a downright hatred of England. Sir Robert then amazed us by asking who were the Manchester Martyrs & why did their execution excite anger in Ireland. Adams explained the particulars of the offence & of the trial of Allen, Larkin & O'Brien & the facts seemed quite new to Sir Robert. I could not resist the temptation of pointing out to him that his want of acquaintance with the details or even with the outlines of an event which had thrilled the Irish Race all over the world was a very strong argument in favour of Home Rule for Ireland, for if he, an able and keen man always alive to public events passing around him, knew so little about an event which every Irishman was fully acquainted with & which had caused fierce controversy for years in Ireland it was reasonable to assume that the majority of Englishmen were still less acquainted with Irish affairs. This observation evidently went home. Sir Robert was silent for many minutes & he plainly felt the force of what I had said.

In the evening, Sir R. H., Adams, Waldron, Richd. O'Shaughnessy,[92] late MP for Limerick, & G.V. Hart,[93] Revising Barrister for Dublin, dined with me.

## 26 May

I dined this evening with E. Dwyer Gray MP, the company included Dr. Walsh, Vicar Capitular, Sir Charles Dilke MP, Lyulph Stanley MP,[94] Lord Brownlow,[95] the Bishop of Bedford,[96] Chief Justice Morris,[97]

---

[92] Richard O'Shaughnessy (b. 1842), Home Rule MP for Limerick city (1874–1883), twice considered for the post of Under-Secretary for Ireland: Trevelyan to Spencer, 17 May 1882; Spencer to Trevelyan, 4 March 1883: AP, Add MSS 76944, 76952.

[93] George Vaughan Hart (1841–1913), Revising Assessor for Dublin (1881–1891), Regius Professor of Feudal and English Law, Trinity College (1890–1909).

[94] Edward Lyulph Stanley (1839–1929), fourth Baron Sheffield (1909), Lib. MP for Oldham (1880–1885).

[95] Adelbert Wellington Brownlow Cust (1844–1921), third Earl Brownlow (1867), Con. MP for Shropshire North (1866–1867), Parliamentary Secretary to the Local Government Board (1885–1886), Paymaster-General (1887–1889).

[96] The Revd William Walsham How (1823–1897), Bishop-suffragan of Bedford (1879–1888), Bishop of Wakefield (1888–1897). Brownlow and How were members of the Royal Commission on the Housing of the Working Classes, which was then sitting in Dublin: *The Times*, 27 May 1885, p. 6.

[97] Michael Morris (1827–1904), first Baron Killanin (1900), Lib. MP for Galway (1865–1867), justice of Common Pleas (1867–1887), Lord Chief Justice of Ireland (1887–1889), an opponent of home rule but a critic of the shortcomings of Irish government.

Jesse Collings MP,[98] Thos Dickson MP, Alderman Meagher MP,[99] the Lord Chancellor & others.[100]

I sat beside Jesse Collings. He told me that he & Chamberlain live together in London. He believes that Chamberlain is more likely than Dilke to become Prime Minister & he thinks that Dilke shares this view. He says that Dilke & Chamberlain are thoroughly loyal to each other. But for the fact that the complication about Russia was not quite at an end he believes that both Dilke & Chamberlain would have left the Cabinet before the 15th May. They are determinedly hostile to any renewal of the Coercive Act & nothing but the fear of being thought cowardly for deserting the Cabinet in the midst of their foreign troubles would have induced them to remain members of a Cabinet pledged to renew any portion of the Crimes Act. He says that both Chamberlain & Dilke are in favour of a scheme which would virtually be Home Rule & are in favour of granting it at once. They would have not only County Boards but also a Central Assembly or Council in Dublin, elected not appointed & endowed with legislative powers in relation to all matters affecting Ireland alone. He is MP for Ipswich, a constituency in which there is not a single Irishman, & yet he says that owing to his persistently supporting the Irish party & boldly expressing in Parliament & to his constituents his belief in liberty as the only panacea for Ireland his constituents are practically united in condemning coercion & advocating extension of free institutions to Ireland.

After dinner, when we had gone up to the dining room, I took Dickson to one side to learn from him the explanation of the election in Antrim last week at which Sinclair[101] the Liberal Candidate succeeded in beating Lord O'Neill,[102] the Tory Candidate, by 139 votes.[103] Dickson explains the election as a protest against coercion.

He says that he, Dickson, put prominently before the Presbyterian voters the iniquity & folly of renewing any portion of the Crimes Act & that his sentiments on this point were enthusiastically cheered. Sinclair pledged himself to oppose coercion in every form. While we were speaking Sir Charles Dilke came over, sat down beside me & entered into an animated discussion in reference to the Crimes

---

[98] Jesse Collings (1831–1920), Lib. MP for Ipswich (1880–1886), Parliamentary Secretary to the Local Government Board (1886).

[99] William Meagher, Lord Mayor of Dublin (1884), Nat. MP for Co. Meath (1884–1885).

[100] For Dilke's account of the evening, see his diary, 26 May 1885 (copy): JCP, JC8/2/1.

[101] William Pirrie Sinclair (1837–1900), Lib. MP for Co. Antrim (1885) and for Falkirk district (1886–1892), favoured reform of Irish government but opposed home rule.

[102] Edward O'Neill (1839–1928), second Baron O'Neill (1883), Con. MP for Co. Antrim (1863–1880), owner of 66,000 acres at Shanes Castle, Co. Antrim.

[103] The election took place on 21 May 1885; Sinclair polled 3971 votes and O'Neill 3832.

Act. I openly told him that in my opinion Lord Spencer was wrong in asking to have those provisions of the Act renewed which would give the Attorney General of the day the power of changing venues & obtaining special juries merely by his own fiat. He asked why I held this opinion & I replied because under the Common Law the Judges have the power of changing the venue when it is proven to them that a fair trial cannot be had in the venue where the crime was committed. This seemed new to Sir Charles & [he] was much struck with it & wrote it down. I told him that I had prepared some time ago a memorandum giving full particulars as to the state of the law in relation to change of venues[104] & he asked me to let him have a copy of it & also if I could to let him have a memorandum expressing generally my views on the Crimes Act. I promised to send these to him.

We had an interesting chat about the authorship of the letters of Junius.[105] Sir C. Dilke's grandfather[106] was perhaps the best informed man in England on this question. He was quite satisfied that the letters were not written by Sir Philip Francis[107] or by Lord George Sackville.[108] He never formally accepted the claims of any one man to be the author but he considered that in all probability the author was either Dr. Mason,[109] Chaplain to the King, or John Wilkes.[110] Sir Charles Dilke said that his grandfather regarded Macaulay[111] as a slap dash writer who did not use sufficient diligence in investigation before writing.

[104]See **Journal (15 January 1885)**.

[105]Junius was the pseudonym of the writer who contributed a series of brilliant polemical letters to the *Public Advertiser* between 1769 and 1772, fiercely criticizing the ministries of the Duke of Grafton and Lord North: Francesco Cordasco, *Junius and His Works: a history of the letters of Junius and the authorship controversy* (Hillsdale, NJ, 1986).

[106]Charles Wentworth Dilke (1789–1864), editor of the *London Magazine* (1824) and the *Athenaeum* (1830), author of several influential articles on the subject of Junius.

[107]Sir Philip Francis (1740–1818), amanuensis to William Pitt (1761–1762), councillor of the Governor-General of Bengal (1774–1780), MP for the Isle of Wight (1784–1790), for Bletchingly (1790–1798), and for Appleby (1802–1807), first identified as Junius by John Taylor in 1816, a view supported by modern statistico-linguistic analysis: Alvar Ellegard, *Who was Junius?* (Stockholm, 1962).

[108]George Sackville Germain (1716–1785), first Viscount Sackville (1782), British general but dismissed from the service for neglect of duty at the battle of Minden (1759), MP for Dover (1741–1746), for Hythe (1761–1768), and for East Grinstead (1768–1782), Chief Secretary for Ireland (1751–1756), Colonial Secretary (1775–1782), adopted the name Germain in 1770.

[109]William Mason (1725–1797), King's chaplain (1757), canon of York (1762), prominent in agitation for parliamentary reform (1780), literary executor for Thomas Gray; see his *The Poems of Mr. Gray, to which are prefixed memoirs of his life and writings* (York, 1775).

[110]John Wilkes (1727–1797), MP for Aylesbury (1757, 1761) and for Middlesex (1768–1769, 1774–1790), co-founded the *North Briton*, arrested for libelling George III (1763) and expelled from the House of Commons in 1769, when his case was taken up by Junius.

[111]Thomas Babington Macaulay (1800–1859), first Baron Macaulay (1857), Lib. MP for Calne (1830–1832), for Leeds (1832–1834), and for Edinburgh (1840–1847, 1852–1856),

27 May

John Morley MP for Newcastle called on me today. I told him of the conversation which I had last evening with Dilke & he was much pleased at Dilke asking for the memorandum from me. He mentioned that after he (Morley) had seen me in London he met Dilke & told him my views, adding that "Fottrell is a man whose scent of Irish difficulties I have now for some years found to be rarely at fault".

Morley told me what he knew about the late Cabinet struggles on the subject of the Crimes Act & from what he told me, joined to what I had already heard from Jesse Collings, I think that events occurred somewhat in this way –

Lord Spencer demanded a renewal of such portions of the Crimes Act as would give –

1. Change of venue
2. Special jury } on the fiat of the Attorney General
3. Summary jurisdiction in cases of boycotting and intimidation
4. Secret enquiry.

Chamberlain, Dilke & Gladstone strongly opposed any renewal but after a big fight they gave in, whereupon Lord Spencer said "I am not going back to Ireland with a rod in pickle & nothing else". When asked what else he wanted, he said a County Government Bill for Ireland. Chamberlain & Dilke promptly agreed but they said in effect "understand that what we mean is a bill which will not alone establish Boards in each County for the business of such County exclusively but which will also establish a central elective assembly in Dublin with legislative powers for exclusively Irish affairs." This proposition struck Lord Spencer as too rapid & sweeping & thereupon it was resolved that no bill dealing with Local Government should be introduced this session. It was also agreed that no Land Purchase Bill should be introduced.

So matters remained until the 20 May when Gladstone, dreading the effect of Dickson's crusade against the Government on account of the policy of coercion & no remedial legislation, suddenly announced in Parliament without consulting Dilke or Chamberlain that the Government would introduce a Land Purchase Bill. This was regarded by Chamberlain & Dilke as a cancellation of the entire Cabinet agreement & accordingly they are now pressing again to have coercion abandoned *in toto*.

Paymaster-General of the Forces (1846–1848), professor of ancient history in the Royal Academy (1850).

28 May

I read for Morley portions of the memorandum which I am preparing for Dilke & he highly approved of them. He told me that but for the Russian complication[112] & the certainty that Lord Salisbury's[113] advent to power would mean a Russian War, not only Chamberlain and Dilke but even Gladstone himself would have resigned sooner than sanction a renewal of any part of the Crimes Act.

He tells me that since Trevelyan has left Ireland his views have been much modified, so much so that when at the Cabinet Council he urged objection on principle to a renewal of any part of the Crimes Act, Lord Spencer blurted out, "It is strange that when you were my Chief Secretary you never expressed these lofty sentiments."

I took Morley up to the Castle to lunch with Sir R. Hamilton. No one was present save the three of us. After lunch we discussed with our cigars the question of renewal of the Crimes Act. Sir Robert advocated the renewal of the provisions for change of venue, special jury & summary jurisdiction for boycotting. Morley & I took the opposite side. In the course of the discussion Sir Robert astounded me by saying that the Conspiracy Act of 1875[114] did not apply to Ireland. I replied that within the last few days I had occasion to look into the Act & that I was quite clear it did apply to Ireland. Sir Robert said that the burden of the advice given to him & Lord Spencer by the legal adviser of the Castle[115] was to the effect that the Act did not apply.

Morley expressed his profound astonishment at this statement and mentioned that he had met at Edward Gibson's MP[116] last evening

---

[112] A skirmish at the Afghan–Russian border on 30 March had threatened to bring Britain and Russia into armed conflict: see R. A. Johnson, 'The Penjdeh incident, 1885', *Archives: The Journal of the British Records Association*, 24, no. 100 (April 1999), pp. 28–48.

[113] Robert Arthur Talbot Gascoyne Cecil (1830–1903), third Marquess of Salisbury (1868), Con. MP for Stamford (1853–1868), Foreign Secretary (1878–1880, 1885–1886, 1886–1892, 1895–1900), Prime Minister (1885–1886, 1886–1892, 1895–1902).

[114] The Conspiracy and Protection of Property Act, 1875 (38 & 39 Vict., c. 86) was designed to regulate picketing during trade disputes. Section seven made it an offence, punishable by up to three months' imprisonment, to compel another person to abstain from doing any act that they had a legal right to do by violence or intimidation: A.E. Musson, *British Trade Unions 1800–1875* (London, 1972), pp. 62–63; RIC Inspector-General's circular, 31 January 1881: TNA, HO 184/116.

[115] The Law Adviser counselled the Irish executive and magistracy on points of law. The post was abolished in 1883.

[116] Edward Gibson (1837–1913), first Baron Ashbourne (1885), Con. MP for Dublin University (1875–1885), Attorney-General (1877–1880) and Lord Chancellor of Ireland (1885–1886, 1886–1892, 1895–1905).

at dinner the Master of the Rolls,[117] and that he (the Master) has told him not only that the Act did apply to Ireland but that in his opinion it would enable the Executive to deal with all questions such as intimidation or boycotting which might arise in Ireland.

Sir Robert's objection as to the change of venue has something in it. He says he was advised that under the ordinary law a change of venue could not be moved for until after a bill had been found against the accused by the Grand Jury of the venue in which the crime was committed & that therefore a change of venue would always involve a delay of the trial. There is something in this but not much. The delay would be more prejudicial to the prisoner than to the Crown. Morley rather 'stumped' Sir Robert by quoting the evidence of Lord (then Mr. Justice) Fitzgerald before the Lords Committee on Irish Jury Law[118] (in 1881 I think) in which that Judge strongly expressed his dissent from the proposal to give to the Attorney General the power by his simple fiat of changing venues. Hamilton thinks that at the General election the Liberals will have an overwhelming majority in England & Scotland.

## 29 May

Having completed my memorandum as to the Crimes Act[119] I forwarded it today to Sir Charles Dilke in the Reform Club whither he always, as I learn from Morley, gets his private letters addressed so that they may not be opened by his secretary.

## 30 May

I saw Morley today at the Shelbourne Hotel[120] and told him I had forwarded the memorandum to Dilke but that I had been turning over in my mind whether it would not be improper for me, an Irish Crown official, to give a copy to him who had a motion down in his name in opposition to the ministry.[121] He pondered for a moment & then said "you are quite right & I shall not take a copy. We Liberals in England shall have occasion during the next 10 or 15 years to make

[117] Andrew Marshall Porter (1837–1919), Lib. MP for Co. Londonderry (1881–1883), Solicitor- and Attorney-General for Ireland (1881–1883, 1883), Master of the Rolls (1883–1906).

[118] The committee was appointed in May 1881: Select Committee of the House of Lords on the Operation of Irish Jury Laws as regards Trials by Jury in Criminal Cases: *PP* 1881, XI, 1. For Fitzgerald's evidence on venue changes, see pp. 454–457.

[119] Not traced.

[120] 27 St Stephens Green, Dublin.

[121] On 21 May, Morley gave notice of an amendment to a proposal to renew the Crimes Act on the ground that the cessation of exceptional crime made it unnecessary: *The Times*, 22 May 1885, p. 6, and see his letter to the editor (1 June 1885), *The Times*, 3 June 1885, p. 8.

great use of you so don't play yourself out but act with circumspection. I am glad you suggested to me the distinction between giving such a memorandum to a Cabinet minister & giving it to an outsider, especially to a member who has given notice of a hostile motion on the subject dealt with by the memorandum".

31 May

I today wrote to Sir Robert Hamilton, who is on a fishing excursion at Lough Sheelin,[122] telling him I had prepared the memorandum & forwarded it to Sir Charles Dilke & telling him that if he wished to see a copy of it I should take one to him on his return to Dublin. I thought it more honourable and manly to write this to Sir Robert, lest he or Lord Spencer might fancy that I was plotting behind their backs.

I had a long talk on yesterday with William O'Brien MP[123] & also with T. Harrington MP. They believe that the ministry will not press any portion of the Crimes Act even though they may introduce a bill containing some of its provisions. Harrington says his mind inclines to the belief that at the General election the Irish party will aid Dickson MP and candidates of his stamp against the Tories in Ulster, but that nothing is yet decided. He does not think that the Liberals will have an overwhelming majority in England & Scotland because he thinks that, as all constituencies will under the Franchise Act be 'one man' constituencies,[124] local influences will be stronger than ever & that in the Counties local influences will tell for the Tories. O'Brien's view seems to agree as to this.

I urged O'Brien to direct his attention to working up in *United Ireland*[125] solid practical questions such as, the working of the new Constitution in Canada since the legislative functions were divided between one Central Dominion Parliament & two Provincial Assemblies; the working of the new Constitution of Hungary since it obtained Autonomy;[126] the development of manufactures in Belgium; the local administration of Switzerland. He promised to do what he could in this direction but he said that it is very difficult to obtain writers competent to work up such subjects in an interesting manner. We discussed County Government & a Central Assembly in Dublin.

---

[122] A trout fishery situated on the border between counties Cavan, Meath, and Westmeath.

[123] William O'Brien (1852–1928), Nat. MP for Mallow (1883–1887) and for Cork North-East (1887–1892), editor of *United Ireland* (1881–1890), founder of the United Irish League (1900).

[124] In December 1884, the Representation of the People Act abolished all two-member constituencies.

[125] A weekly newspaper established by the Land League in 1881.

[126] In 1867, the Canadian Confederation was created by the British North America Act, and the Dual Monarchy of Austria-Hungary was established by the Ausgleich.

He says that Parnell would not accept any settlement which would not leave to Irish control the Police Force of the whole of Ireland, nor would he consent to the Central Assembly being elected indirectly by the County Boards instead of directly by the constituencies.

He expressed a high opinion of Lord Hartington.

1 June

I went to the Four Courts[127] today to see John Naish take his seat as Irish Lord Chancellor. I am 36 years of age & I remember already to have seen eight different Irish Chancellors & of them only two, viz. John Naish & John Thomas Ball,[128] are now alive. *Eheu fugaces, Postume, Postume, labuntur anni!*[129]

5 June

I dined last night with Dr. Nedley.[130] Among the guests was Sir Rowland Blennerhassett,[131] MP for Kerry, who told some anecdotes of much interest. Among them was the following. In the year 1874 Sir Rowland was staying with Lord Acton[132] & Mr. Gladstone was also there. Sir Rowland & Gladstone had one evening a warm discussion as to the abilities as a statesman possessed by the Duke of Wellington.[133] Gladstone depreciated & Sir Rowland praised him. Next morning Sir Rowland was walking in the demesne when Gladstone joined him & renewed the discussion, & as an instance of the folly and weakness of judgement shewn by the Duke in politics he told that on one occasion the Duke & Sir Robert Peel,[134] being members of the same Cabinet, the council was breaking up when the Duke who was standing with his back to the fire called Peel and said to him "Peel I wish you would turn

---

[127] Designed by James Gandon and built on Merchants Quay, Dublin (1786–1802), the seat of the Irish high court was named after its four oldest divisions: Chancery, King's Bench, Exchequer, and Common Pleas.

[128] John Thomas Ball (1815–1898), Con. MP for Dublin University (1868–1875), Lord Chancellor of Ireland (1875–1880).

[129] 'Alas, Postume, Postume, the fleeting years are slipping by', the opening lines of Horace, Ode 2.14.

[130] Thomas Nedley (1820–1899), surgeon to the vice-regal household and Dublin Metropolitan Police, member of Lord Randolph Churchill's Dublin circle: Roy Foster, *Lord Randolph Churchill: a political life* (Oxford, 1981), pp. 40–42.

[131] Sir Rowland Blennerhassett (1839–1909), Lib. MP for Kerry (1880–1885).

[132] John Emerich Edward Dalberg Acton (1834–1902), first Baron Acton of Aldenham (1869), Lib. MP for Carlow (1859–1865), co-founder of *The English Historical Review* (1886).

[133] Arthur Wellesley (1769–1852), first Duke of Wellington (1814), Chief Secretary for Ireland (1806–1808), Master-General of Ordnance (1818–1822), Foreign Secretary (1822–1827), Prime Minister (1828–1830).

[134] Sir Robert Peel (1788–1850), Chief Secretary for Ireland (1812–1818), Home Secretary (1822–1827, 1828–1830), Prime Minister (1834–1835, 1841–1846).

over in your mind how land transfer could be simplified in Ireland, I don't understand how it is to be done but I am quite satisfied that it must be done for unless the land system there be changed as to enlarge the number of owners of land, there will be a strike against rent before this century is over & if that occurs then the resources of Constitutional Government will have been almost exhausted". This dictum Mr. Gladstone regarded as conclusive evidence of the Duke's want of judgement.

In Mr. Gladstone's Guildhall speech in 1881 made as a prelude to the arrest of Parnell, Gladstone amid cheers said "Mr. Parnell will find that the resources of civilization are not yet exhausted".[135] Sir Rowland says that this was clearly an allusion to the Duke's dictum & was so understood by those who remembered the incident related by Gladstone to Sir Rowland.

Sir Rowland told a thing which was new to me, viz. that Lord Palmerston[136] when Prime Minister urged J.D. Fitzgerald (now Lord Fitzgerald) to give up the bar & accept the post of Chief Secretary for Ireland but that Fitzgerald said he could not afford to do it.

Sir Rowland says that Lord Spencer recommended Naish for the Irish Chancellorship but Gladstone was opposed to him & in consequence the post was offered to Lord Fitzgerald but on the condition that if the bill now before Parliament for reducing the number of Irish judges & reducing the salary of the Chancellor from £8000 to £6000 should pass, Lord Fitzgerald should take the reduced salary.[137] He refused the offer. Sir Rowland thinks that even then Naish would not have got the post only for Sir Henry Thring,[138] the parliamentary draughtsman, who has a very high opinion of Naish & spoke very strongly in his favour to Mr. Gladstone.[139]

The conversation turned upon Mr. Trevelyan MP and Sir Rowland said that Mr. Trevelyan was anything but a well read man, even in the literature of the period about which he wrote. I said that his early years of Charles James Fox was a book not only very charming in style, but written apparently from an abundance of knowledge, & that in

[135] The speech was delivered at Leeds Cloth Hall on 7 October 1881 and Parnell was arrested six days later.

[136] Henry John Temple (1784–1865), third Viscount Palmerston (1802), Secretary of State for War (1809–1828) and for Foreign Affairs (1830–1834, 1835–1841, 1846–1852), Prime Minister (1855–1858, 1859–1865).

[137] Bill to amend Supreme Court of Judicature Act (Ireland), 1877: *PP* 1884–5, V, 531.

[138] Sir Henry Thring (1818–1907), first Baron Thring (1886), Parliamentary Draughtsman (1850) and Counsel to the Treasury (1869). He prepared the Home Rule Bill of 1886.

[139] Gladstone finally conceded to Spencer's request when Fitzgerald endorsed Naish as the best administrator among the candidates: Spencer to Gladstone, 18, 24, 26, and 29 April, 6 May 1885; Gladstone to Spencer, 25 April, 8 May 1885; Edward Hamilton to Spencer, 6 and 11 May 1885: AP, Add MS 76862.

reading it one was led to feel that the author was using up only a very few of a large quantity of material in his mental store.[140] Sir Rowland as an example of the narrow range of Mr. Trevelyan's reading said that on one occasion he (Sir Rowland) asked him what he thought of some statement in De Tocqueville's *Ancien Regime et la Revolution*[141] & to his astonishment he found that Trevelyan had never read the book or even heard of it.

I knew Mr. Trevelyan pretty well when he was here as Chief Secy & it certainly did surprise me to find how few books he had in any of his rooms. Indeed it would be little exaggeration to say that he had not any books at all & his pictures as he told me himself one day were not his, but belonged to Jephson,[142] his private secretary, who removed them when he married the rich London girl who has set him up in life.

7 June

Sir Rowland Blennerhassett came out to me today to Ballybrack to lunch after which we had a chat of several hours duration while we smoked our cigars. He had previously sent me the *Contemporary Review* for June 1885 containing an article by him on Peasant Proprietorship in Ireland in which, after giving much information of interest on the subject of the creation of an occupying proprietary in foreign countries, he recommended the establishment in Ireland of a Land Commission to purchase from such landlords as would be willing to sell their lands at 22 years['] purchase of the judicial rent.[143] We discussed this article & I dissented from many of its recommendations & I told Sir Rowland that in my opinion Irish landlords as a rule were not likely to get more than 15 or 16 years['] purchase of their rents. He said that the article was written by him last year to influence Mr. Gladstone & to induce him to bring in a land purchase bill & that it had been privately printed & circulated among the members of the Cabinet.[144] He believed it did not convert Gladstone who has previously been opposed to any purchase scheme. I knew that Gladstone had been opposed to the policy of aiding purchase by tenants on anything like a large scale & I told Sir Rowland the following anecdote in

---

[140] *The Early History of Charles James Fox* (London, 1880).

[141] Charles De Tocqueville, *L'Ancien Regime et la Revolution* (Paris, 1856).

[142] Henry Jephson (1844–1914), private secretary to the Under-Secretary and Chief Secretary of Ireland (1872–1884), he married Julie Reiss in 1884. His works include *The Platform: its rise and progress* (London, 1892).

[143] 'Peasant proprietors in Ireland', *Contemporary Review*, 47 (June 1885), pp. 866–881.

[144] See W.F. C[ullinan], 'Purchase of land (Ireland). Notes on the various schemes proposed from time to time', 30 June 1885: CAB 37/15/35.

connection with land purchase. When Gladstone's Land Bill of 1881[145] was passing through Committee I urged Charles Russell to move that the entire purchase money should be addressed. I could not persuade him to do this but I did induce him to propose an amendment in favour of advancing four-fifths of the purchase money. He moved this amendment whereupon Gladstone left his seat on the Treasury Bench, came to Russell sat down beside him & said "Don't press this amendment, it is a small thing in itself as the difference between $3/4$ & $4/5$ is trifling but moreover it is unnecessary for believe me I have made the tenure clauses of the bill so attractive that I shall by them wean the Irish peasant from the idea of purchasing his holding".[146]

Sir Rowland capped this by telling me that when some years ago he in conversation said to Gladstone that it was absolutely necessary for permanent peace in Ireland to bring about a sale of a large part of the land here to the tenants, Gladstone roundly accused him of trying to undermine the Irish landlords & to render society here wholly democratic.

We alluded to the effect produced upon Irish politics by the execution of the Manchester Martyrs a propos of which Sir Rowland mentioned at the time of their conviction D'Israeli [sic][147] was in power & he was anxious that Allen, O'Brien & Larkin should not be hanged, but Gladstone let it be conveyed to him that any reprieve should be denounced by him, Gladstone. Sir Rowland knew that this was so by reason of a communication which he had at the time with Lord O'Hagan, then Judge O'Hagan.[148] O'Hagan had been a pet of Gladstone's & Sir Rowland knowing this urged O'Hagan to write strongly to Gladstone to get him to use his influence in favour of commuting the capital sentence. Gladstone replied in a letter couched in what Sir Rowland calls 'The English Grocer politician's style' denouncing the idea of asking for a reprieve & telling O'Hagan that he, Gladstone, felt it was intolerable that in the first centre of England's manufacturing industry a policeman should be shot down, & that he, Gladstone, would denounce any attempt to obtain mercy for, or a remission of the capital sentence passed upon Allen, O'Brien & Larkin. Disraeli had in this as in many other instances a true instinct; Gladstone had no instinct at least for Irish affairs. He has reasoning

---

[145] Bill to Further Amend Law Relating to Occupation and Ownership of Land in Ireland: *PP* 1881, III, 7.

[146] For Russell's proposed amendments, see *Hansard*, CCLXI–CCLXIII.

[147] Benjamin Disraeli (1804–1881), first Earl of Beaconsfield (1876), Chancellor of the Exchequer (1852, 1858–1859, 1866–1868), Prime Minister (1868, 1874–1880).

[148] Thomas O'Hagan (1812–1885), first Baron O'Hagan (1870), Lib. MP for Tralee (1863–1865), justice of Common Pleas (1865–1868) and Lord Chancellor of Ireland (1868–1874, 1880–1881).

power & he has a desire to do right, but he never understands an Irish situation intuitively. For example, it is amusing to hear that when Gladstone came over to Ireland shortly after having written his pamphlet on 'Vaticanism',[149] he mentioned that the cordial reception afforded to him by priests & people shewed that the Irish clergy were of his mind as regards 'Vaticanism' & were opposed to Pope Pius the 9th.[150] Disraeli would never have made such a blunder. Again, Disraeli as far back as 1870 saw that for the stability of society in Ireland it was necessary to increase the number of owners of land here, & he was anxious that the entire fund arising from the disestablishment of the Irish Church should be used as a guarantee fund to save harmless the state against loss in a big scheme for sale to tenants in Ireland, but Lord Cairns[151] opposed him & he therefore kept his counsel to himself.[152] (This anecdote was told to me about 18 months ago by the Marquis of Waterford.[153]) In this instance his instinct was right, while Gladstone shews that he lacks instinct.

Disraeli was an awful sinner against Ireland. He saw the light, but he deliberately avoided it because it did not suit him to follow it. Gladstone has sinned through what theologians call 'invincible ignorance'.

When Sir Rowland was at the University of Berlin he became acquainted with Prince Bismarck[154] & he has kept up the acquaintance ever since. He has a very high opinion of his massive sense. Bismarck is in public awfully rude, in private life Sir Rowland says that he is only rude if he happens to dislike you, but if he regards one with favour or thinks that there is anything in one, he is very pleasant & courteous. His mainspring politically is 'Socialism'. He regards the struggle between Capital & Labour as the great problem of the near future & all his influence is exerted to increase the share of profit now conceded to Labour by Capital. He is detested by the big merchants of Germany & it is owing to the preponderance of merchants & manufacturers or,

---

[149] *The Vatican Decrees and Vaticanism* (London, 1874) and *Vaticanism: an answer to replies and reproofs* (London, 1875).

[150] Giovanni Maria Mastai-Ferretti (1792–1878). As Pope Pius IX (1846–1878), he promulgated the dogma of papal infallibility.

[151] Hugh McCalmont Cairns (1819–1885), first Earl Cairns of Garmoyle (1867), Con. MP for Belfast (1852–1866), Lord Justice of Appeal (1866–1868), Lord Chancellor (1868, 1874–1880).

[152] See E.D. Steele, *Irish Land and British Politics: tenant-right and nationality 1865–70* (Cambridge, 1974).

[153] John Henry de la Poer Beresford (1844–1895), fifth Marquess of Waterford (1866), Lib. MP for Co. Waterford (1865–1866).

[154] Otto Eduard Leopold, Prince von Bismarck (1815–1898), Prime Minister of Prussia (1862–1873, 1873–1890), Chancellor of Germany (1871–1890).

in other words, of representation of capital in the German Parliament that Bismarck is so often defeated in the Chamber.[155]

Bismarck demands a strong Central Government for dealing with foreign affairs but for domestic purposes he is quite opposed to centralisation. For example he had always opposed the substitution of an Imperial sign on the coinage, in place of the sign of the country, duchy or whatever it may be which issues the coin. Prussia has on its coins the head of King William,[156] Bavaria has on its coin the head of its own chief & Bismarck says that it should so continue.

Sir Rowland says that Sir Henry Thring is opposed to the renewal of any part of the Crimes Act, he (Sir Henry Thring) says "Those d—d fellows at Dublin Castle are always asking for more powers even when they have them already".[157]

Sir Rowland expressed a high opinion of the straightforwardness & ability of the Marquis of Hartington. I told him that Wm O'Brien had said much the same thing & he told me that the Marquis of Hartington had told him that he held a high opinion of Wm O'Brien because he was so transparently honest.

We spoke about the prospect of the Crimes Act smashing up the ministry, Sir Rowland believes that the Crimes Act renewal bill will not alone not be pressed but that it will not be even introduced & that still Lord Spencer will not resign.

## 9 June

While I was writing this last night the note of my conversation with Sir Rowland Blennerhassett, Mr. Gladstone was fighting in the House of Commons the death struggle of his ministry. Mr. Childers,[158] the Chancellor of the Exchequer, had to provide 11 millions sterling for war expenses in the Sudan & Afghanistan. He proposed to raise this sum partly by an increase in the Income Tax and partly by an increase of 2/- per gallon on whiskey and a slight increase on beer. Against the increase of the whiskey & beer duties the Irish party & the Conservatives united with the result that at half past one of the morning the ministry was defeated by 12 votes.[159] The Irish party was

---

[155] See Rowland Blennerhassett, 'Prince Bismarck', *Nineteenth Century*, 26 (June 1890), pp. 688–707.

[156] Wilhelm of Hohenzollern (1797–1888), King of Prussia (1861–1888), Emperor of Germany (1871–1888).

[157] For Thring's formal position, see his 'Procedure for Trial (Ireland) Bill: memorandum', 6 June 1885: AP, Add MS 77331.

[158] Hugh Culling Eardley Childers (1827–1896), Lib. MP for Pontefract (1860–1885) and for Edinburgh South (1886–1892), Chancellor of the Exchequer (1882–1885), Home Secretary (1886).

[159] The motion was rejected by 264 : 252. See *Hansard*, CCXCVIII, col. 1511.

organised for the fray very quietly, no preliminary public whip was made but the members were quietly got over from Dublin & elsewhere & a solid muster of 38 of the party surrounded Parnell. They marched in a body into the opposition lobby and when a few minutes later the division list was handed to the opposition teller and it was known that the Government was defeated a scene ensued which beggars description. Lord Randolph Churchill[160] stood up on the seat and whirled his hat round his head yelling like a red indian, the contagion spread like wildfire, Healy, O'Brien & almost the entire body of Irish members with one accord burst into a roar of "coercion", "Spencer", "Buckshot".[161] The uncontrolled excitement lasted for several minutes, Parnell being apparently the only cool man present. His only sign of emotion was a slightly increased pallor of the cheek.

Trevelyan said to Sir Wm. Harcourt[162] (I suppose not intending his observation to be overheard but it was overheard by Dawson[163]) "I knew that Lord Spencer would do it".

Mr. Gladstone moved the adjournment of the House till today.

On reaching my office this morning I found awaiting me a letter from Mr. Joseph Chamberlain MP, the President of the Board of Trade, reminding me that he had been introduced to me some time ago in London and asking me to get him information on the following points

1. The details of the system – list and functions of the several local authorities in Ireland, their composition and mode of election or nomination & details as to the system of Castle Administration.

2. Illustrations of the delay, irritation, inefficiency or extravagance produced by this highly centralised & non-representative administration.[164]

---

[160] Lord Randolph Churchill (1849–1895), Con. MP for Woodstock (1874–1885) and for Paddington South (1886–1890, 1892–1895), Secretary of State for India (1885–1886), Chancellor of the Exchequer (1886).

[161] A reference to a former Irish chief secretary, William Forster, who had authorized the use of buckshot as a 'non-lethal' alternative to round shot when policing Land League demonstrations: Stephen Ball, 'Crowd activity during the Irish Land War, 1879–90', in Peter Jupp and Eoin Magennis (eds), *Crowds in Ireland, c. 1720–1920* (Basingstoke, 2000), pp. 212–248.

[162] Sir William George Granville Venables Vernon Harcourt (1827–1904), Lib. MP for Derby (1880–1895), Home Secretary (1880–1885), Chancellor of the Exchequer (1886, 1892–1895), professor of international law, Cambridge University (1869–1887).

[163] Charles Dawson, Nat. MP for Co. Carlow (1880–1885), Lord Mayor of Dublin (1882–1883).

[164] See **Document 10**.

I also found a long letter from Escott, the Editor of the *Fortnightly Review*, enclosing a rough draft of an article on local government in England, Ireland & Scotland written by or at the direction of Chamberlain and asking me as a personal favour to lick the Irish portion into shape. His letter is very urgent and he says in it that I can have as much space as I wish in the *Fortnightly Review* for the Irish portion of the article. I replied stating that I would be in London on the morning of the 12th inst & that I would call on him with all the materials which I can collect.

I called to the Castle to see Sir Robert Hamilton who wrote to me on yesterday asking me to let him see my memorandum on the Crimes Act. He was in very low spirits. He acknowledged that any renewal of the Act was now hopeless and he is in dread that intimidation will raise its head afresh and in a formidable shape & that he will not be able to cope with it by the ordinary law.[165] He was really affected as he spoke to me & almost with tears in his eyes he said that he was grieved to the heart to see men whose good intentions he recognised working against him to prevent the Executive getting powers which he believed essential to peace & quiet in Ireland. I said "Sir Robert I have worked against you in this matter & I have used every means to persuade you & others that there is no part of the Crimes Act essential, but I plainly tell you I should be doing an unkind as well as a mean action if I told you anything which I did not honestly believe. My judgement may be wholly wrong but anyway if I am to be of any use to you or to Ireland it is by honestly proclaiming not what is palatable but what I believe to be true". He shook my hand warmly & I don't think my sturdy stand against his opinion & wishes will lessen, but rather I think it will tend to cement, our friendship.

Later in the day I saw Sir Robert for a moment & he told me that Mr. Gladstone has resigned & that he would go tonight to Balmoral to place his resignation in the hands of Her Majesty.

12 June

I arrived in London this morning and am staying with Charles Russell QC for a few days. I called on Mr. Chamberlain and had a discussion of about an hour's duration with him on the subject of the article for the *Fortnightly Review* on Local Government in Ireland. His scheme is

(a) County Councils elected one third by landlords & two thirds by tenants

---

[165]Hamilton had stated, 'I cannot conceive of anything which would be more disastrous to the preservation of order than that the idea should get abroad that intimidation is no longer a crime': Hamilton to Spencer, 6 June 1885: GP, Add MS 44312, fos 145–146.

(b) Central Assembly in Dublin elected by the County Councils but in the election the representatives of the landlords & tenants respectively on the County Councils would vote separately eg if the number of members to be sent by each County Council to the Central Assembly should be 3, the landlord representatives should elect one member & the tenant representatives should elect 2 members. He justifies this proposition by saying that the local taxes are contributed in the proportion of $^1/_3$ by landlords & $^2/_3$ by tenants. What he told me satisfies me that he & Parnell have discussed the matter & that the scheme proposed is the result of an understanding between them. I have promised Escott & Chamberlain that I will write the entire article.

Chamberlain told me that while the fight in the Cabinet about the Crimes Act was going on, he & Dilke wanted to get the above scheme introduced into Parliament this session. It would have been a tough job to carry it but they were prepared to go to work at once on it & make a great effort to get it through this session. This information tallies with what I heard from John Morley on the 27th May.

I learned a strange thing today. The Prince of Wales recently met Charles Russell & he spoke very earnestly to him about the Crimes Act & in favour of its renewal. Russell took a determined stand against its renewal & the Prince urged him strongly to modify his attitude & withdraw from opposing the renewal. Russell would not budge an inch & he believes that the action of the Prince is the result of his recent visit to Lord Spencer.[166]

The Queen has accepted Mr. Gladstone's resignation.

15 June

I completed the article on local government last evening & took it this morning to Escott. He was surprised at the rapidity with which I had done it.

I attended at the opening of the House of Commons today & witnessed a curious scene. The first order of the day was the consideration of the Lords amendment in the Redistribution of Seats Bill. Sir Drummond Wolfe [sic][167] moved the adjournment of the question on the ground that the Lords had introduced into [the] bill clauses for accelerating the completion of the revision so as to allow the new election to take place in November. Sir Charles Dilke

[166]The Prince of Wales paid a state visit to Ireland in April 1885 (see **Journal 24 February, 4 May 1885**).

[167]Sir Henry Drummond Wolff (1830–1908), Con. MP for Portsmouth (1880–1885), member of Churchill's 'fourth party'.

explained that these clauses had been introduced at the insistence of Lord Salisbury to save both houses the trouble of considering a separate bill for the purpose. Sir Stafford Northcote[168] confirmed Dilke's statement & therefore everyone expected to see Sir D. Wolfe's [*sic*] opposition collapse, but instead of any collapse what occurred was that Lord Randolph Churchill stood up &, throwing over both Lord Salisbury & Sir Stafford, vigorously supported Sir Drummond Wolfe's [*sic*] motion & to the still greater surprise of everyone present, up stood Sir Michael Hicks Beach[169] & took the same line. A division was challenged with the result that into the Government lobby walked Sir Stafford Northcote & Sir Richd. Cross,[170] & into the opposition lobby walked Lord Randolph Churchill, Sir Michael Hicks Beach, Chaplin[171] & several other prominent Tories. The division showed 331 for the ministry & 35 for the Churchill opposition.[172]

The division is a subject of amusement to the Radicals who consider the new ministry as broken up before it could be formed.

16 June

Lord Randolph Churchill has triumphed. Sir Stafford Northcote has been thrown over by Lord Salisbury. He is not to lead the House of Commons but is to be 'kicked up stairs'. He takes a peerage & some office of dignity & unimportance, Lord Privy Seal or some such post.[173] Sir Michael Hicks Beach is to be Chancellor of the Exchequer & leader of the House of Commons & Lord Randolph is to be Secretary of State for India with a seat in the Cabinet.

17 June

I got the proof of the article on local government this morning & having revised it I took it to Escott. He asked me to see Chamberlain about it. I did so & I found him writing out a speech which he is to

---

[168] Sir Stafford Henry Northcote (1818–1887), first Earl of Iddesleigh (1885), Con. MP for Devon North (1866–1885), Chancellor of the Exchequer (1874–1880), First Lord of the Treasury (1885–1886), Foreign Secretary (1886–1887).

[169] Sir Michael Edward Hicks Beach (1837–1916), first Earl St Aldwyn (1915), Con. MP for East Gloucestershire (1864–1885) and for Bristol West (1885–1906), Chief Secretary for Ireland (1874–1878, 1886–1887), Chancellor of the Exchequer (1885–1886, 1895–1902).

[170] Sir Richard Assheton Cross (1823–1914), first Viscount Cross of Broughton-in-Furness (1886), Con. MP for Lancashire South-West (1868–1886), Home Secretary (1874–1880, 1885–1886), Secretary of State for India (1886–1892).

[171] Henry Chaplin (1840–1923), first Viscount Chaplin (1916), Con. MP for Mid-Lincolnshire (1868–1906), Chancellor of the Duchy of Lancaster (1885–1886).

[172] The result was 333 : 35. See *Hansard*, CCXCVIII, cols 1540–1555.

[173] He was appointed First Lord of the Treasury.

deliver tonight at Holloway,[174] so I arranged to call on him on Friday next to discuss the article.

I saw Lord Randolph Churchill at the Carlton Club & had a long talk with him about Ireland.[175] He asked me did I believe the ordinary law was sufficient to keep the peace in Ireland. I said yes & he then told me he had all along opposed coercion & that he believed it was to his action that the Irish party might attribute the abandonment of coercion because his action had stimulated the Radicals to take up a strong attitude in opposition to coercive legislation for Ireland. He is in favour of County Boards in Ireland but he saw great difficulties in giving a National Council, but he thinks that if the Tories come in at the General election they will offer to the Irish party a scheme of local government for Ireland so wide that the Irish party will be sorry to lose it. He does not believe it is probable that the Tories will have an absolute majority at the election because they have against them Ireland, Scotland & Wales, but he said "If our party show sense & courage we may at the election win 280 seats & this number would enable us to carry on the Government by an understanding with the Irish party."

He has a great admiration for Parnell whom he considers a greater man than O'Connell.[176] He says that Parnell's instincts are Parliamentary & Constitutional & he looks to him as a Conservative force among the Irish party after the election, when there will be probably many new & young men in this party whom he will have to control.

We spoke about Lord Spencer & I said that while I had a high opinion of Lord Spencer's character I regarded him as a man who from his condition of mind could never understand Ireland. Lord Randolph said "I have a very poor opinion of Lord Spencer, I have always told his colleagues that it was a gross blunder to make him Lord Lieutenant of Ireland for he is a small minded, vain, obstinate, dull man".

I find that on the subject of land purchase in Ireland Lord Randolph is in favour of allowing any scheme for the purpose to be carried out by the County Boards to whom, & not to the tenant farmers, the state should advance money.[177]

---

[174] See *The Times*, 18 June 1885, p. 7.

[175] See Dilke's diary, 13 July 1885 (copy): JCP, JC8/2/1; and Foster, *Lord Randolph Churchill*, p. 231.

[176] Daniel O'Connell (1775–1847), co-founder of the Catholic Association (1823), MP for Clare (1828–1847), founder of the Loyal National Repeal Association (1840), Lord Mayor of Dublin (1841–1842).

[177] For Fottrell's position on this question, see Fottrell to Churchill, 13 July 1885: RCHL 1/6. 690.

The impression left upon my mind by my conversations with Chamberlain and Lord Randolph is that there is remarkably little difference between the political opinions held by one & those held by the other.

18 June

I called on W.H. Smith MP[178] this morning at his house no. 3 Grosvenor Place & had a long and interesting conversation with him about Ireland. He asked me did I think that the ordinary law of the land would suffice to keep peace there & I said certainly for this up to the meeting of the new Parliament, but that if there was then no attempt made to remedy the centralised system of government in Ireland so as to give power to the localities & to Irishmen at home to manage local and domestic matters in Ireland there would be such a revulsion of feeling that a very serious agitation would at once begin & that it might lead to crime. I also told him that the fact of last harvest having produced abundant food & turf rendered any immediate outbreak of crime highly improbable. He said he quite understood my view but that the influence of a dry season in Ireland in producing comparative content by reason of an abundance of fuel was one which Englishmen could not understand.

He is evidently in favour of abandoning coercion of every kind. We discussed the question of land purchase in Ireland. He is quite opposed to Government fixing any definite number of years' purchase of the landlords' interest & I think he would be anxious to let the Irish Counties borrow the purchase money on the security of the rates & then lend it to the tenant purchasers. However, he thinks that possibly a measure might be carried this session to enable the entire purchase money to be lent direct by the state on the condition that the vendors should allow proportion of the purchase money to be retained for a certain number of years as a guarantee. He asked me what would I think of a plan which would hold out to the tenant purchaser an inducement to pay up his instalments more rapidly than contract would bind him to do, & when I replied that if such a plan could be devised it would be most useful & likely to be availed of he told me he had got calculations made very carefully which shewed him that an instalment of say £12 payable 35 years hence could without loss to the state be redeemed now by a payment of say £5, so that it would be possible to hold out a strong inducement to the tenant purchasers

---

[178] William Henry Smith (1825–1891), Con. MP for Westminster (1868–1891), Secretary of State for War (1885, 1886), Chief Secretary for Ireland (1885–1886), First Lord of the Treasury and Leader of the House of Commons (1887–1891).

in a good year to pay up more than the year's instalment. This seems very simple & I told him I thought it would be effective.

19 June

I saw Chamberlain today at his house. We discussed the article which I had written for the *Fortnightly Review* & he expressed himself much pleased with it & said "it will kick up the devil of a row". He mentioned that before he had written the memorandum which had been sent to me as the basis of the article, he had obtained from Parnell a written memorandum of his views on the subject & in Parnell's memorandum there was no mention made of handing over the control of the police to County Boards or to the National Council.[179] He therefore struck out the sentence in the article which stated that the control of the police should be vested in the County Boards, but at the same time he said that he did so not because of his own unwillingness to entrust the police to the Board but because he feared the proposal might arouse bitter & dangerous opposition.[180]

The newspapers this morning referred to a hitch which had arisen in Lord Salisbury's arrangements for forming a Cabinet, but they did not state how the hitch had arisen.[181] Chamberlain told me that Lord Salisbury had asked for a pledge from Mr. Gladstone's ministry on two points –

1st That the Liberals would not oppose any financial proposals which the new Government might make for raising taxes to pay the expenditure for the year or else that the new Chancellor of the Exchequer should be at liberty to pay the bills simply by issuing Exchequer bills & thus tide over the difficulty till next year.

2nd That the entire time of the House of Commons should be given to the new Government till the end of the session. Chamberlain said that he had opposed the proposition to give such pledge which he considered manifestly unreasonable. The result of the deadlock might be that the Liberals would have to come back to power again. I said I hoped not, for I thought it would be much better for them to be free for the few months preceding the General election, to which Chamberlain replied that he agreed with me but that it was to be remembered that if the Liberals came back now, they would go into office on very different terms from those which existed before they had resigned,

[179] See William O'Shea's memorandum, 14 January 1885: JCP, JC8/8/1/36, repr. *The Times*, 13 August 1888, p. 8; and see 'A scheme for the improvement of local govt. in Ireland': AP, Add MS 77329.

[180] See Richard Barry O'Brien, *The Life of Charles Stewart Parnell, 1846–1891*, 2 vols (London, 1899), II, p. 138.

[181] See 'The political crisis', *The Times*, 19 June 1885, p. 6.

because coercion was now dead & that was the only question about which the Cabinet was in danger, as under no circumstances would he & Dilke have continued members of a Cabinet pledged to coercion. I said that if the Liberals returned to power he ought to come over to Ireland as Chief Secretary, but he answered that he would not do so, that they would put the Vice-Royalty in Commission, appoint a Chief Secretary who would not object to Dilke & Chamberlain coming over to Ireland & making speeches, & that he & Dilke were quite prepared to go over to Ireland in this fashion, but that it would be worse than useless for him to go over at present as Chief Secretary because he would not do better as Chief Secretary than any one else in as much as he, under the present system of Government, would have no bodies of authority & persons of popular confidence to whom he could refer for information & that he would therefore have to rely on the police.

## 21 June

This being Sunday I arranged with Charles Russell to go down to Epsom to see the Country House, Tadworth Court, which he has bought & for which he is paying £22,000. It is a very handsome old place with 150 acres of a park. The house is between 2 & 3 centuries old & is very fine.[182]

The political crisis still continues.

## 19 [22] June

I today saw Oxford for the first time. Laurence Waldron & young Charles Russell[183] came with me. I was deeply impressed with the venerable & artistic air of most of the Colleges, especially of Oriel, Trinity, Magdalen & Christchurch.

## 23 June

The crisis is over. Lord Salisbury has not received the assurances which he asked for, but he received some general expression of good will from Gladstone.

I attended the House of Commons today & heard Gladstone announce that Lord Salisbury had definitely accepted office. Mr. Gladstone immediately moved the adjournment of the House and then the members of Gladstone's ministry left the front bench on the

---

[182]The house was built by Leonard Wessel at Banstead in 1694.
[183]Charles Russell (1863–1928), son of Sir Charles Russell, solicitor to the Canadian government (1896).

Government side of the House and on tomorrow they will take their places on the opposite bench.[184]

I dined with Mr. Chamberlain at his house, 40 Prince's Gardens. The party consisted of Sir Charles Dilke, John Morley, Jesse Collings, Chamberlain, his daughter and myself. The conversation during dinner was all political & Miss Chamberlain[185] joined in it & seemed to understand the drift of it very well. Chamberlain asked me to get him definite information as to the personnel of the Irish Board of National Education, & as to the powers of the board and also as to the amount of interference exercised by the Local Government Board on Municipal Councils & Boards of Guardians in Ireland.

Chamberlain is personally in favour of handing over the control of the police to elective County Boards in Ireland. My opinion was asked & I said that while theoretically it would be right to vest control of the police in the Boards, I could not conceal from myself as a practical politician that the transfer of police jurisdiction to popular boards would at present be a dangerous experiment because I felt satisfied that in agrarian disputes for rent &c. the popular boards would not aid the Sheriff in carrying out unpopular proceedings. Morley took my view & quoted a statement made to him a couple of years ago by John Dillon MP[186] who said "If you give us the police, the English control of Ireland is at an end". Collings took part against me, Dilke held his tongue.

I have now had a few opportunities of judging of Chamberlain & of Dilke & my impression is entirely in favour of Chamberlain as the abler & bigger man. Dilke is clever, knows a good deal & has his knowledge carefully docketted. He has not a spark of genius nor a trace of humour. He is noisy & self-assertive – tells stories without much point & laughs loudly at them. He says things of his supposed friends which shew a womanly spite. I should say he has no political instinct but he reads his brief carefully & is painfully accurate & respectable. I think he knows that Chamberlain is his superior. They are very friendly & seem to rely thoroughly on each other. I fancy that Dilke is a man without any bowels of compassion & that he would ride roughshod over any one who stood in his way. Chamberlain has a much better manner than Dilke. He is more open & less self conscious. He speaks frankly or, if not really frank, he is able enough to impress his hearers with his

[184] *Hansard*, CCXCVIII, cols 1618–1622.

[185] Beatrice Chamberlain (1862–1918), eldest daughter and (prior to Chamberlain's second marriage in 1888) chatelaine of his household: Peter Marsh, *Joseph Chamberlain: entrepreneur in politics* (New Haven, CT and London, 1990), p. 301.

[186] John Dillon (1851–1927), Nat. MP for Co. Tipperary (1880–1883) and for Mayo East (1885–1918), co-leader (with William O'Brien) of the Plan of Campaign (1886–1892), Deputy Leader of the Irish Parliamentary Party (1900–1918).

frankness. He has political instinct & his politics seem to have their root in a desire to improve the condition of the masses. I do not mean to say that he is not ambitious, but I do think that Chamberlain is capable of making personal sacrifices for the good of others & I doubt if the same could be said for Dilke.

The new Lord Lieutenant for Ireland is to be Lord Carnarvon[187] & the Chief Secretary is to be Sir William Hart Dyke.[188] We discussed the character of these politicians & I found that all present had a very poor opinion of Lord Carnarvon. They say he is small & antipetty. He means however not to be a cypher. He sent today for Courtney Boyle, Lord Spencer's late private secretary, & for Mr. Campbell Bannerman,[189] the Chief Secretary, to coach him on Irish affairs. Of Sir W. Hart Dyke the company agreed that he is a kindly good natured fellow with very little capacity. Edward Gibson, the Irish Lord Chancellor, is to have a seat in the Cabinet & a peerage.

## 24 June

I met Sir Rowland Blennerhassett at the Athenaeum Club. He introduced me to Lord Houghton[190] whom I was anxious to see as I remembered to have read somewhere that he said he had himself performed the miracle of the liquefaction of the blood of St Januarius.[191] I asked him about this statement & he told me that on one occasion he was travelling with the late Archbishop McHale[192] in Italy and that they put up at the Convent in which the blood of St Januarius is deposited. It is kept in a cellar or underground cave. Dr. MacHale told the superior that Lord Houghton believed in the miracle whereupon the Superior said that Lord Houghton could next day hold the vessel containing the blood & that he would see it liquefy. On the next day accordingly the vessel was brought up from the cave & handed to Lord Houghton, who was told to hold it up before the people in the Church. He did so and the blood or whatever other

---

[187]Herbert Henry Howard Molyneaux (1831–1890), fourth Earl of Carnarvon (1849), Colonial Secretary (1866–1867, 1874–1878), Lord Lieutenant of Ireland (1885–1886).

[188]Sir William Hart Dyke (1837–1931), Con. MP for Mid-Kent (1868–1885) and for Dartford (1885–1906), Chief Secretary for Ireland (1885–1886).

[189]Henry Campbell-Bannerman (1836–1908), Lib. MP for Stirling Burghs (1868–1908), Chief Secretary for Ireland (1884–1885), Secretary of State for War (1886, 1892–1895), Prime Minister (1905–1908).

[190]Richard Monckton Milnes (1809–1885), first Baron Houghton (1863), Con. and Peelite MP for Pontefract (1837–1862), President of the London Library (1882–1885), scholar and advocate of religious equality.

[191]Patron saint of Naples. As bishop of Beneveto, he was beheaded in 304 during Diocletian's persecution of the Christians. The miracle is said to happen twice a year at the Duomo in Naples and at the Church of San Gennaro at Solfatara in Pozzuoli.

[192]John McHale (1791–1881), Archbishop of Tuam (1834–1881).

substance was in the vessel did gradually change from a viscous substance to a fluid. Lord Houghton attributes the liquefication to the change in the temperature. The vessel is shaped somewhat like a carriage lamp & the hand has of course considerable power of altering the cool temperature in which the vessel while in the cellar was placed.

Lord Houghton knew Daniel O'Connell. He remembers a conversation which they had about repeal of the Union, this took place about the year 1847. Lord Houghton asked O'Connell did he consider Repeal feasible & O'Connell replied, that he could not tell how long the change might take to come about, but he felt sure that in the long run Ireland would be politically connected with the only country in Europe of the same religion as herself, & near enough to protect her, he meant France.

Sir Rowland Blennerhassett is doing his best to induce the Tory Cabinet to bring in a purchase bill for Ireland this session. I told him he might put out of his head all thought of inducing the Tories to propose a bill fixing the price at which the land is to be purchased.

A telegram has been this morning received from Rome announcing that the Pope has appointed Dr. Walsh Archbishop of Dublin.

27 June

Lord Spencer today held a farewell reception & then left Ireland for good. I was detained in court all day & therefore I was not able either to attend the reception or watch Lord Spencer's progress through Dublin on his way to Westland Row.[193] I told him in confidence my share in the production of the article in the coming number of the *Fortnightly* on local government.[194] Sir Robert asked me for the outlines of Chamberlain's scheme, & when I had told them to him he asked me how Chamberlain proposed to deal with the question of ascertaining the amount to be contributed each year by the Imperial Exchequer to Irish domestic purposes. I said that Chamberlain proposed to leave this question to be dealt with each year by the Imperial Parliament. "Then", said Hamilton, "a serious danger will arise for on this side of the Channel you will have in the Central Council of Ireland a body possessed of national authority who will keep constantly demanding an increased contribution from the Imperial Exchequer, and if this

---

[193] See Fottrell to Spencer, 2 July 1885: AP, Add MS 77152. Spencer made farewell visits on 19 June and departed from Kingstown on 22 June: *The Times*, 20 June 1885, p. 12; 23 June 1885, p. 6.
[194] 'The Radical Programme (No. VII): local government in Ireland', *Fortnightly Review*, 44 (July 1885), pp. 1–16. For Gladstone's view of this article, see *GD*, XI, pp. 652–653.

demand be refused there will be a risk of great friction between the National Council & the Imperial Parliament. The National Council would then be opposed to the Imperial Parliament & to whatever Executive would remain in Ireland to represent the Home Office, in whom the control of the police would be vested, & no Executive could stand against the declared hostility of so strong a body as the National Council!".

Sir Robert then said "you have been very frank with me & I shall now be frank with you. I recommended Lord Spencer to suggest to the Cabinet (a) the immediate establishment of County Boards with owners & occupiers representatives on them (b) a Central Board elected partly by the ratepayers & partly by the managers of the national schools throughout Ireland (c) that to this Central Board should be given the entire control of primary education in Ireland & the distribution of the Imperial grant as well as of local contributors for education, the imperial grant to be definitely fixed at the figure which would represent the average of the last five years, such figure to remain fixed irrevocably for 5 years, leaving it to the Central Board to supply by local taxation any further money which might be needed".

This, said Sir Robert, "would have been a start in the direction of free local government. It would have trained Irishmen to undertake the work of administration while at the same time, as the Central Board would be one created to deal only with education, it would not have had such a strong position as would enable it to be a menace to the Executive in Ireland or to the Imperial Parliament."[195]

Before we could finish the discussion Sir Thomas Steele,[196] Commander of the Forces, came in to consult Sir Robert Hamilton as to the necessity of providing a military escort for Lord Carnarvon, who is to arrive on Monday morning as Lord Lieutenant of Ireland & therefore I left & adjourned our discussion till some other occasion.

28 July

Since I wrote the preceding note, events have moved quickly. Lord Carnarvon has assumed his duties as Lord Lieutenant & has made himself quite a popular character. He drives about Dublin without an escort and he has made several speeches in answer to addresses and in many of these utterances he has shown a breadth of sympathy which is in strong contrast with the rigid replies of Lord Spencer, whose honesty of nature was appreciated by those

---

[195] See **Document 9**.
[196] Sir Thomas Montague Steele (1820–1890), commander of Dublin military district (1872–1874), Commander-in-Chief in Ireland (1880–1885).

few who know him well, but whose haughty, unintentionally haughty, & cold demeanour rendered it impossible for him to impress Irishmen favourably.

Parnell has brought forward a motion for an enquiry into the Maamtrasna, Barbavilla, & Crossmaglen convictions & he rested his case mainly upon the first named of these cases.[197]

The Tory Government yielded in the main to his motion. They refused a public enquiry, but they promised that the Lord Lieutenant would himself carefully enquire into the cases. As a result of this concession there has been a furious howl from the Liberal press in England & the Tories are denounced as traitors and immoral politicians because they have "surrendered to Parnell". It will be interesting to watch whether this alleged agreement with Parnell will seriously injure the Tory party in England at the General election.

Edward Gibson, the Irish Lord Chancellor, has been created a peer under the title of Lord Ashbourne. He has introduced a Land Purchase Bill which if it passes ought to do a deal of good to this country by promoting the purchase by tenants of their holdings.[198] I had some slight influence on the policy of the Bill. I was asked by Robert Holmes to call on Lord Ashbourne in reference to the Bill which it was known he was preparing. I did so & I soon saw that his notion was to leave the working of the bill to one of the existing Land Commissioners & to one additional Commissioner. I pointed out to him that if he followed this line his bill would inevitably fail because there was not a possibility that the existing commissioners could perform successfully their present work of dealing with appeals from the sub Commissioners, much less perform that work plus the work of land purchase. He then asked what would I suggest. I said that the best thing would be to appoint a separate Commission & give them power to utilise such portions of the Land Commission staff as might be suitable for the purposes of this work. I pointed out that 2 Commissioners would probably suffice for the work at the beginning & that a salary of £2000 a year would command good men. Lord Ashbourne said the session was so far advanced that it would be impossible in the time at the disposal of the Government to elaborate a scheme for appointing an entirely fresh Commission & that the new man or men selected should be grafted on the existing Commission. I replied that if they were to be grafted they should be

[197] On 17 July, Parnell requested that the government 'institute strict inquiry into evidence' surrounding these and two other 'agrarian' cases: *Hansard*, CCXCIX, cols 1064–1150.

[198] Bill to Provide Greater Facilities for Sale of Land to Occupying Tenants in Ireland: *PP* 1884–5, II, 305; *Hansard*, CCXCIX, cols 1040–1049.

grafted in such a way as would leave them entirely independent of the existing Commissioners, for if not failure was inevitable. He asked me whom would I suggest as Commissioners. I said Mr. Edmund Murphy[199] of Dunfanaghy, the Board of Works Arbitrator, was in my opinion the man best suited of all the men I knew for the post of Commissioner & that he certainly ought to be selected as one of the new men, & as for the other I said that the Government ought to try to get a man like myself. I said that I mentioned myself with perfect freedom in as much as the post would be no gain to me at all, because my present post of Clerk of the Crown & my private practice placed me financially in fully as good a position as a Commissionership could do.

Lord Ashbourne adopted my suggestions in the main points.

John Dillon has come back from America.[200] He seems to be in excellent health. He spent last Sunday fortnight with me & we had a long talk about Irish affairs. I explained to him what I had done in connection with the article in the *Fortnightly* attributed to Chamberlain. He agreed with me that it was a gain to get Chamberlain committed even so far. He, John Dillon, is anxious that the process of obtaining freedom of Government in Ireland should be gradual, for he believes that the more gradual it is the more usefully it will be availed of by the Irish nation. I told him that Chamberlain's own view is that the control of the police should be vested in the County Boards. John Dillon said that if County Boards were established & if large powers of taxation & of local control were vested in them, it was inevitable that the control of the police should be soon given to these Boards, because once it became apparent that the police force was being maintained merely to assist landlords in getting their rents, the English people would kick against paying an enormous yearly sum merely for the benefit of Irish landlords, & the Irish people would never consent that the charge of this huge force should be thrown on Irish rates unless control of the force was vested in Irish boards.

We spoke about the Land Purchase Bill. John Dillon's opinion is that it will be availed of largely if the landlords shew a willingness to accept reasonable prices for the land, & if they do not he thinks there will be something like a strike against rent so as to bring the landlords to their senses. His view is that the purchase price of Irish land will be almost 16 years['] purchase of the judicial rent. Sir Robert Hamilton

---

[199]He later served briefly on the Evicted Tenants Commission: *FJ*, 15 October 1892, p. 5.

[200]In 1883, Dillon temporarily withdrew from politics and spent two years on his brother William's ranch at Castlerock, Colorado: F.S.L. Lyons, *John Dillon* (London, 1968), pp. 70–71.

says about 15 years['] purchase is the figure he would prophesy as the average.

On last evening I had a very interesting dinner party here at Dunmera.[201] The company was Sir Charles Gavan Duffy,[202] Sir Robert Hamilton, Lord Justice Barry,[203] Professor Galbraith,[204] Richard Owen Armstrong,[205] Laurence Waldron, Major Miley,[206] my father[207] & myself. After dinner we had a long discussion on the subject of Home Rule. Duffy propounded the proposition that it would be safer to grant a separate Parliament at once to Ireland than to begin by establishing County Boards and a Central Council such as Chamberlain suggested. Hamilton took the opposite side. I suggested that the main difficulty was the question of landlord & tenant, because if complete freedom of legislation were conferred on the Irish Parliament there would be a risk of the landlord's interest being practically confiscated. Duffy said that this difficulty could be met. I asked how. He replied by enacting in the Act giving the separate Parliament a provision that there should not be any compulsory expropriation of landlords, & that in the Act a maximum price of say 20 years['] purchase should be fixed as the limit for state advances for purchase, but that subject to this maximum limit both landlord & tenant should be left free to bargain for the price of all land to be sold. Duffy suggested that provisions could also be inserted for securing full freedom to Protestants against Catholic oppression. I said that I believed such provisions would be wholly unnecessary as there was really no danger of Catholics in Ireland striving to oppress Protestants.

I suggested as the next greatest danger the question of a protective tariff. Duffy met this by saying that a provision could be introduced prohibiting the imposition of a protective tariff, but leaving liberty to the Irish Parliament to grant bounties if they thought it wise to do so. He believes that such bounties would be & ought to be given.

[201] His home at Ballybrack, Co. Dublin. A keen cyclist, Fottrell regularly made the round trip to his office in Dublin: *Irish Times*, 2 February 1925, p. 8.

[202] Sir Charles Gavan Duffy (1816–1903), founder of *The Nation* (1842), of the Irish Confederation (1847), of the Tenant League (1850), and of the Independent Irish Party (1852), Prime Minister of Victoria (1871–1872).

[203] Charles Robert Barry (1823–1897), Lib. MP for Dungarvan (1865–1872), justice of Queen's Bench, Ireland and Lord of Appeal (1872–1883).

[204] Joseph Allen Galbraith (1818–1890), professor of mathematics, Trinity College, Dublin, advocate of Irish home rule.

[205] Richard Owen Armstrong, Director of the Artisans' Dwellings Company of Dublin.

[206] James Miley (1846–1919), military officer on departmental staff (1875–1898), Secretary of Finance for the Military Department, Government of India (1898–1902).

[207] George Drevar Fottrell Snr (1813–1887), solicitor. Fottrell's mother, Ellen, had died in 1867, aged forty-six.

Hamilton asked would Duffy propose to have both an Irish Parliament & Irish representatives in the Imperial Parliament. Duffy's reply was to the effect that he personally would care very little whether the Irish had representatives in the Imperial Parliament or not, provided that the Irish people were not called on to contribute to foreign wars but that his belief was that the best course for both countries would be:

(a) to fix now once & for all the ratio of contribution by Ireland for ordinary Imperial purposes.

(b) to enact that Ireland should send representatives to Westminster.

(c) to enact that Ireland should contribute to the expense of foreign wars in the proportion of her ordinary contribution to Imperial expenses.

Hamilton said would not this give to Ireland more than Canada or any other British Colony possessed. I said no. Canada it is true has no representatives in the Imperial Parliament, but on the other hand she is not called on to contribute to Imperial expenses; the moment you decide that Ireland must contribute to the expense of foreign wars you must necessarily give her a voice in deciding whether or not such wars are to be undertaken.

I called today to the Castle to see Sir Robert Hamilton. I found him quite enthusiastic in his delight at our discussion of last evening. He was greatly struck with Duffy who he says is one of the most interesting men he has ever met. He told me that this morning he was with Lord Carnarvon to whom he mentioned where he had been dining last evening & the company whom he had met, & that he mentioned to Lord Carnarvon that my house was the only place where he was able to meet men in touch with the people. He detailed to Lord Carnarvon the whole discussion which we had & which evidently has made a great impression on him (Hamilton). He said that there was one point suggested last evening about which he had grave doubts, viz. that if an Irish Parliament were granted at once there were many moderate men now without any influence on public affairs in Ireland who would seek to be elected to the Irish Parliament & would form a moderate party there. He asked what was my opinion in the matter. I said that I felt satisfied there would be many moderate men who would obtain influence in an Irish Parliament but who were at present absolutely kept out of public life because they had nothing round which they could rally, they could not honestly support the existing order of things because they regarded it as a rotten condition of things, but they would rally round a man who in an Irish Parliament would seek to prevent headlong legislation. Hamilton said that if he were satisfied on this point he would be glad to see an Irish Parliament established at once.

We laughed at the way in which Chamberlain's suggestions in the *Fortnightly Review* of this month were derided last evening by all the company as being entirely inadequate. It is certainly a very good criterion of the rapidity with which we are moving to find that on the 27[th] day of the month a scheme is, by a mixed company of Irishmen, decried as wholly inadequate which on the 1[st] of that month was denounced as revolutionary.

## 30 July

This mornings papers announce that Farquharson, the manager of the Dublin Branch of the Munster Bank, absconded on the day before yesterday & that his accounts shew defalcations amounting to £70,000.[208]

I breakfasted this morning with Sir Charles Gavan Duffy at the Shelbourne Hotel. Our party consisted of Sir Charles and his wife,[209] Sir Robert Hamilton & myself. I had suggested to Duffy on the evening when he dined with me that it would be useful if he & I and Hamilton could meet somewhere to have a quiet chat about Irish affairs & acting on this hint he asked us to breakfast. When we had finished our meal Lady Duffy retired & we lighted our cigarettes & straightaway plunged into an animated discussion. Our subject was the establishment of an Irish Parliament. Hamilton remarked that he had been carefully considering the arguments put forward by Duffy at my house on the 27[th] July in favour of the immediate establishment of an Irish Parliament, but that there was one matter about which he was in grave doubt, viz. how in such an assembly it could be secured that property would be adequately represented. Duffy replied that the difficulty had occurred to him and that he was satisfied it could be met in more ways than one, but that one way of effectually securing an adequate representation of property seemed to him quite feasible. His proposal was that Ireland should be divided into say 33 or 34 electoral districts corresponding in general to the Irish Counties & that each district should return to the Parliament 3 members, but that each elector should be permitted to give not 3 but only 2 votes & (as I understand his proposal) that our elector should be at liberty to give both his votes to one candidate. The result would be that the landlord

[208]Farquharson fled to Spain and subsequently evaded arrest: *The Times*, 30 July 1885, p. 10; 31 July 1885, p. 10; 1 August 1885, p. 5; 3 August 1885, p. 4.

[209]Louise (née Hall), a niece of Duffy's second wife, Susan (d. 1878), became his third wife in 1881. They had four children before Louise died in childbirth in February 1889.

minority would file all their votes in favour of a single candidate in each constituency & that they would thereby secure at the onset one third of the representation. With such a proportion secured to the landlords at the start they would, amid the ever varying contingencies of a Parliament, be able to make their influence felt because on many questions they would be able in practice to attract the support of a section of the non landlord representatives, & a compact body of 33 members out of 100 would always be so powerful a factor in divisions as to be certain of wielding substantial influence. Hamilton urged that such a system of minority representation would be a novelty in the history of the World, but Duffy promptly met the objection by pointing out that a system of representation such as he advocated had been for some years in operation in the Cape of Good Hope, where it had been found to work well.[210] I pointed out to Duffy that the fact of both Hamilton & myself being ignorant of the fact that such a system existed in the Cape of Good Hope was a strong argument in favour of the suggestion which I had made to him (Duffy) at a former interview, that he should write, for say the *Freeman*, a series of short articles describing the constitution of several colonies of Great Britain. He acquiesced in the wisdom of this suggestion & promised to act on it.

I asked him would he propose to have in Ireland two chambers or only one. He replied "certainly two. I should have both a lower chamber or House of Commons & an upper chamber or Senate. The Senate should consist of say 60 members, whose qualification should be laid down in the Act establishing the Parliament. They should consist for example of certain ex officio members, e.g. the Catholic Primate & the Protestant Primate & of members elected by a constituency more limited than that which would elect the members of the lower chamber, say for example that for the lower chamber the constituency should be founded on household suffrage and for the Senate that it should be founded on a £20 annual valuation. The first members of the Senate should be named in the Act of Parliament establishing the constitution and they should be selected so as to give a fair representation to the several schools of political opinion in Ireland".

Duffy considers that a constitution established on such a basis as he described would be absolutely a protection against any violent inroad upon the rights of property.

Hamilton was greatly struck with Duffy's views & thanked him cordially for the information which he had given. After Hamilton & I had taken our departure we walked together as far as Trinity College

---

[210] See Alpheus Todd, *Parliamentary Government in the British Colonies* (London, 1880), pp. 64–74.

& Hamilton spoke as if he considered that Duffy's views might be put into action in the course of the next few months.

I should mention that when Duffy had developed his views I said "but as a matter of practical politics what would you suggest as a means of giving prompt effect to your opinions". His reply was that the ministry should privately take counsel with Parnell as the recognized leader of the Irish people and that they should promise him privately that if they came back into power at the General election they would bring forward a scheme for establishing an Irish Constitution, & that the details of the scheme should meanwhile be settled by a small private commission of say 5 or 6 men of whom Parnell should be one.

1ˢᵗ August

Hamilton has a very high opinion of Lord Carnarvon's abilities as well as his character.

2ⁿᵈ August

Dr. Walsh was today consecrated Archbishop of Dublin.

5ᵗʰ August

I saw Sir Robert Hamilton today at the Castle. He read for me a very full report which he had made immediately on his return from breakfasting with Sir Charles Gavan Duffy on the 1ˢᵗ inst.[211] This report which is an almost word for word reproduction of the discussion between Sir Robert Hamilton, Sir Charles Gavan Duffy and myself was prepared in order that it might be laid before Lord Carnarvon, & it was sent by Sir Robert to Lord Carnarvon the evening of the 1st inst. Lord Carnarvon was at that time in London.[212] The fact of our conversation having been reduced promptly to writing and forwarded to the Lord Lieutenant who is also a Cabinet Minister is significant.

Parnell on last evening made a very broad & statesmanlike speech in Parliament on the second reading of the Irish Land Purchase Bill.[213] It was extremely moderate and was plainly intended to help on the working of the Purchase Scheme. Davitt[214] has for the last couple

---

[211] See **Document 11**.

[212] Where he was secretly meeting with Parnell at 15 Hill Street, Mayfair: L.P. Curtis, *Coercion and Conciliation in Ireland, 1880–92: a study in Conservative Unionism* (Princeton, NJ, 1963), pp. 49–54.

[213] See *Hansard*, CCC, cols 1103–1108.

[214] Michael Davitt (1846–1906), chief arms purchaser for the IRB, imprisoned on a charge of incitement to murder (1870–1877), instrumental in the foundation of the Land League of

of weeks been unsparing in his denunciation of the bill as a mere measure of relief for Irish landlords. Parnell's speech therefore means war between himself & Davitt & in such a contest I shall back Parnell to win all along the line.

I saw Harrington MP today at the rooms of the National League & had a long talk with him about the political situation. I told him that the Solicitor General for Ireland (John Monroe)[215] had mentioned to me that boycotting was beginning to be very troublesome in the south of Ireland, & I impressed upon Harrington the importance of curbing so dangerous a propensity. He told me that the most troublesome County in Ireland at present is Wexford & that in that County men who, when agitation involved personal risk had slunk away, were now endeavouring to earn a cheap popularity by encouraging, if not outrage, at least a violation of the law by boycotting, holding of Land League Courts &c., and that he, Harrington, was so profoundly impressed with the danger of such disorders spreading that he had written to Parnell saying he would resign his post as Organiser & Secretary of the National League, & that in consequence of the representation made by him (Harrington) to Parnell, the latter had made his moderating speech on the Land Purchase Bill.

He said that when Parliament should have risen Parnell would come over to Ireland to exercise his personal influence in repressing not alone outrage, but all violation of the law.

6 Augt.

I saw Reed,[216] the Divisional Magistrate, today. He is stationed at Athlone but his duties recently have called him down to Clare. He says that Clare is greatly disturbed & that outrages of an aggravated character have recently increased in that County & he fears there will be a disturbed winter in that part of the Country.[217]

7 Augt

I saw Edmund Dwyer Gray MP today at the *Freeman* Office. He told me what is the accepted version among Parliamentary men in

Mayo and the Irish National Land League (1879), Nat. MP for Cork North-East (1893) and for Mayo South (1895–1899).

[215] John Monroe (1839–1899), Solicitor-General for Ireland (1885), justice of the Landed Estate Court, Ireland (1885–1895).

[216] Andrew Reed (1837–1914), Sub-Inspector of the Irish Constabulary (1860), private secretary to the Inspector-General (1868–1879), CI of Donegal (1879–1881), head of Crime Division (1881–1884), Assistant IG (1882), DM for Western Division (1884–1885), IG of RIC (1885–1900).

[217] See MCRs (W), for July and August 1885: CSO RPs 1885/16982, 16945.

London as to the scandal which has overwhelmed Sir Charles Dilke. It appears that Dilke has for some time past been unduly intimate with Mrs. Donald Crawford whose husband[218] was Secretary to the Lord Advocate for Scotland under Gladstone's Government.[219] This Mrs. Crawford is sister to the widow of the late Ashton Dilke,[220] the brother of Sir Charles.

The liaison was, it is said, discovered owing to Mrs. Crawford having recently gone home with Sir Charles Dilke for the indulgence of their illicit intercourse, & having when in his bedroom perceived that another woman, also his lover, was there, a revelation which gave Mrs. Crawford such a shock that she rushed from the house, drove home to her husband's house, fell into a violent fit of hysterics & then confessed all. The injured husband has instituted proceedings for a divorce and Sir Charles Dilke is for the moment at all events shunned by all his associates in the House of Commons. He has broken down in health under the strain & it is openly stated by the *Pall Mall Gazette* that he will retire altogether from public life.[221] It is some confirmation of my view as to Chamberlain's pluck to find that while all other friends seem for the moment to have deserted Sir Charles Dilke, he, Chamberlain, has stuck to him, has had him down at his home near Birmingham to recruit his health, & when Dilke a few days since reappeared for an hour or so in the House of Commons, Chamberlain in the most marked manner was friendly & cordial with him while the rest of his associates slunk away from him.

Dilke & Chamberlain have abandoned their intended visit to Ireland.[222]

Gray mentioned that Chamberlain had been very badly treated by some members of the Irish party. I asked in what way had he been badly treated. Gray replied that before Chamberlain wrote the article for the *Fortnightly Review* he had been assured that if he made a pronouncement on those lines he should have the support of the Irish party, & that now he finds that their support is given not to him but

---

[218]Donald Crawford (1837–1919), legal secretary to the Lord Advocate (1880–1885), Commissioner for Parliamentary Boundaries (1885), Lib. MP for Lanarkshire N.E. Division (1885–1895); he married Virginia Smith in 1881.

[219]John Blair Balfour (1837–1905), first Baron Kinross (1902), Lib. MP for Clackmannan and Kinross (1880–1899), Lord Advocate (1881–1885, 1886, 1892–1895).

[220]Ashton Dilke (1850–1883), Lib. MP for Newcastle upon Tyne (1880–1883), editor of the *Weekly Dispatch*; he was survived by his widow, Margaret Mary (née Smith).

[221]See 'The break-up of the Liberal Party', *PMG*, 3 August 1885, p. 1. For the Crawford divorce, see Roy Jenkins, *Sir Charles Dilke: a Victorian tragedy* (London, 1958), pp. 215–370.

[222]Their plan to visit Ireland was sabotaged by Parnell, who instigated a nationalist press campaign against them, and the withdrawal of offers of hospitality from the Catholic hierarchy: F.S.L. Lyons, *Charles Stewart Parnell* (London, 1977), pp. 288–290.

to the Tories. This tallies with what Chamberlain himself told me in London.

11 Sep.

I have not written any notes for over a month during about one half of which time I was absent on vacation. The campaign of the General election will soon open and it will be interesting to watch the effect of the events which have occurred during the past few months.

Parliament rose about the 11th of August. The Land Purchase Bill & the Labourers (Ireland) Bill, 1885 & also the Endowed Schools Bill passed into law.[223] The Land Purchase Bill authorises the Land Commission to advance the entire purchase money to Irish Tenants purchasing their holdings, the advance being repayable by instalments at the rate of £4 per cent during 49 years. The Labourers Act 1885 extends & simplifies the operation of the Labourers Act of 1883 – the Endowed Schools Act establishes a Commission to control & divide for the benefit of all denominations in Ireland the endowment for intermediate education hitherto exclusively enjoyed by Protestants. These Acts represent a substantial gain for the Irish people.[224]

The Tory Government still holds its popularity in Ireland & the English Liberals are visibly nettled at such a result.

On Parnell's return to Ireland he made two important speeches, the first of which was delivered by him at Arklow about the middle of August. In this he spoke of the difficulties which Irish manufacturers have [to] contend with owing to the English manufacturers being so well equipped that they are able always to undersell the manufacturer till they break him, & then they recoup themselves by raising their prices. He declared that in his opinion it was necessary for the success of Irish manufactures that the Irish people should be able to impose protective duties for a time at least.

His next speech was delivered at a dinner given to him at the Imperial Hotel, Dublin by the members of the Irish Parliamentary Party. This was about the 25th August.[225] In this speech he said that

---

[223]Bill to amend Labourers (Ireland) Act, 1883, and for other purposes connected with Labourers' Dwellings in Ireland: *PP* 1884–5, II, 187. Bill to Re-organise Educational Endowments of Ireland: *PP* 1884–5, I, 445. Parliament was prorogued on 14 August.

[224]Purchase of Land (Ireland) Act, 1885 (48 & 49 Vic., c. 73); Labourers (Ireland) Act, 1883 (46 & 47 Vic., c. 60); Labourers (Ireland) Act, 1885 (48 & 49 Vic., c. 77); and Educational Endowments (Ireland) Act, 1885 (48 & 49 Vic., c. 78), which diverted £140,000 of endowment funds to Catholic schools and colleges.

[225]Parnell spoke at Arklow on 20 August and at Dublin on 24 August: *The Times*, 22 August 1885, p. 6; 25 August 1885, p. 4.

hitherto the Irish party had purposely abstained from pushing in Parliament directly the question of self government for Ireland but still that this course of action had been dictated by a resolve to impress upon England the necessity of granting Self Government to Ireland & that their efforts had not been unsuccessful, but that in this next session of Parliament the efforts of the party would be concentrated upon a determined effort to win for Ireland a freedom fully as great as she enjoyed under Grattan's Parliament but without a House of Lords.

On the following day the Irish Parliamentary Party held a meeting at which they passed resolutions declaring that the best way of selecting candidates for Irish constituencies would be by holding County Conventions to decide on the selection, & that Mr. Parnell & the Irish Party were entitled to be taken into consultation in reference to such selections.[226]

The members then agreed to take the following pledge individually & collectively and recommended that no Irish constituency should elect any candidate who would refuse in writing to bind himself by the same pledge. The pledge was to the following effect –

"I promise to sit, act, and vote with the Irish party led by Mr. Parnell and in the event of a majority of the party convened by notice for the purpose deciding that I have violated the pledge I undertake to resign my seat."[227]

Meanwhile, Mr. Chamberlain had made, or else made a few days after Parnell's pronouncement, a strong radical speech in which he confined himself to English affairs but sketched out for England a very advanced radical programme.[228]

A few days afterwards Lord Hartington at Waterfoot made a Whig speech in which he plainly dissented from Chamberlain's policy & as regards Ireland, he alluded to Parnell's speech & said that Parnell's policy of wringing from Parliament freedom for Ireland was impossible.[229]

Parnell was a few nights afterward entertained at a dinner by the Lord Mayor at the Mansion House and in his speech there he alluded to Lord Hartington's statement somewhat in the following terms –

"There are politicians in England who tell us that to win freedom for Ireland is impossible. It may be that they are right, but if we are

---

[226]The meeting took place at the offices of the Irish National League in Sackville St, Dublin, on 25 August 1885: *The Times*, 26 August 1885, p. 7.

[227]See Lawrence W. MacBride, *The Greening of Dublin Castle: the transformation of bureaucratic and judicial personnel in Ireland, 1892–1922* (Washington, DC, 1991), pp. 46–47.

[228]Chamberlain spoke at Hull on 5 August 1885: *The Times*, 6 August 1885, p. 6.

[229]Hartington spoke on 29 August 1885: *The Times*, 31 August 1885, p. 8.

prevented from obtaining freedom for Ireland we can at least make all things impossible for those who seek to prevent us."

This sentiment was received with rapturous applause. Parnell then alluded to the rumours of some outrages having recently taken place in Kerry & he very emphatically & earnestly exhorted the Irish tenants to abstain from all outrage & he warned the Irish landlords to be moderate in their demand for rent as this season was a very bad one.[230]

On the 8 September 1885 Chamberlain attended a meeting at Warrington & made a big speech in which he stuck to his guns as regards to the radical programme.[231]

Lord Randolph Churchill early in September 1885 made a speech at Sheffield in which he confined himself to lauding the success of his Government in putting foreign affairs to rights & his only allusion to Ireland was a short one defending the Government for having allowed the Crimes Act to lapse. He did not mention Parnell's name.[232]

On the 8th Sep 1885 Chamberlain spoke at Warrington. He reiterated the radical programme & he then launched out into a discussion of Parnell's speeches. He said in effect that there was an alliance between Parnell & the Tories & he used the following words, "Well now what is Mr. Parnell's programme. He says that in his opinion the time has come to abandon altogether attempts to obtain remedial measures or subsidiary reforms and to concentrate the efforts of the Irish representatives upon the securing of a separate and independent Parliament which is to consist of a single chamber and whose first object it is to be to put a protection duty against all English manufacturers. Then he says in the second place that he expects Whig & Tory will vie with one another in helping him to a settlement on his own terms; and he says in the last place that if any party seeks to make this object impossible that he and his party will make all things impossible for them. Well, gentlemen, I am not a Whig and I certainly am not a Tory but speaking for myself I say that if these and these alone are the terms on which Mr. Parnell's support is to be obtained I will not enter into the compact."

I think it well to keep a copy of all the portions of Chamberlain's speech which relate to Ireland & therefore I have taken the following cutting from the *Freeman's Journal*.[233]

---

[230]'Moonlight' raids were carried out in north Kerry on 18 and 27 August, and Parnell delivered his speech on 1 September: *The Times*, 28 August 1885, p. 4; 2 September 1885, p. 6.

[231]See *The Times*, 9 September 1885, p. 6.

[232]Churchill spoke on 4 September 1885: *The Times*, 5 September 1885, p. 6.

[233]Cutting inserted into journal: see *FJ*, 9 September 1885, p. 4.

The commentaries of both the *Freeman's Journal* & of almost all shades of the English press on this speech are to the effect that Mr. Chamberlain has pledged himself against any separate legislature for Ireland, but I think that he has been far too astute to do anything of the kind. He has pledged himself against allowing an Irish legislature to impose a protection tariff against English goods, but this is the extent of his pledge as I read the speech.

Dr. Walsh, the new Archbishop of Dublin, entered Dublin about a week ago. He met with a very enthusiastic reception from the people but the absence of the richer class of Catholics was most marked. In reply to an address presented to the Archbishop on his arrival he emphatically stated his opinion that peace & content could never reign in Ireland until she had won a separate legislature.[234]

This is, I believe, the first instance in History on which a Roman Catholic Archbishop of Dublin openly expressed himself in favour of an Irish Parliament. Dr. Walsh's declaration renders it certain that the Irish Bishops to a man may now be counted among Mr. Parnell's followers. I doubt if the same could at any time after 1829 have been said of O'Connell.

Charles Russell QC MP came to Dublin a couple of days ago. I had a long chat with him today. He told me that he met Dr. McEvilly,[235] the Roman Catholic Archbishop of Tuam, on the day before yesterday & that the latter told him there was considerable political apathy in the West of Ireland & that he accounted for it by the fact that the farmers believe they have got from politics nearly all the personal benefit they are likely to receive, & that they object to the prospect of men of a low social position being almost the only candidates for parliamentary honours owing to the imposition of the 'pledge' formulated by Parnell; the ground for that objection is not however their dislike of being represented by men of a comparatively low social position, but is their belief that they, the farmers, will be called upon to contribute to the support of members who have not means of their own to support them.

---

[234]Walsh spoke on his arrival at Kingstown and in reply to an address from the Corporation of Dublin at Westland-row station on 4 September 1885: *The Times*, 5 September 1885, p. 7; Patrick J. Walsh, *William J. Walsh, Archbishop of Dublin* (Dublin, 1928), pp. 179–181.

[235]John MacEvilly (1816–1902), Archbishop of Tuam (1881–1902), a powerful advocate of tenant right and home rule.

This may be true. I doubt its accuracy & I venture to predict that west of the Shannon there will not be a candidate returned who will not take the Parnell pledge.

18 Sep.

Mr. Chamberlain has made another speech. His audience on this occasion being the Liberals of Glasgow.[236] His language regarding Ireland & Mr. Parnell's demands was much more conciliatory than were his utterances at Warrington.

John Morley MP made a speech at Hackney on the 16[th] inst in support of Charles Russell's candidature.[237] It was a manly, outspoken speech. Regarding Ireland he said "there was not anything very terrible and shocking in Mr. Parnell's views about a protective tariff for Ireland – at least it ought not to be to a Tory Government who had appointed a Commission to elicit opinion in favour of a protective tariff for England. Of course, the Liberal party could give no countenance to such questions and would do their best to persuade the Irish people that they would be doing themselves a great mischief if they resorted to such a course, but there were other demands which Mr. Parnell had made & they should go to meet these views &." Short of separation, he would go as far as he could and he hoped his party would go as far as they could to meet the views of the Irish nation, as soon as they were quite sure what the views of the Irish nation were. "In my opinion no solution would be adequate which did not recognize & attract to itself the indestructible national sentiment of the Irish people".

I dined on the 15[th] inst. with Fr. Thomas Finlay SJ,[238] the Rector of Belvedere College Dublin, to meet the Archbishop. Our party included the Archbishop, the Provincial of the Jesuits, several priests of the order & the following MPs, Wm. O'Brien, E. Dwyer Gray, T. Harrington & C. Dawson. Besides Wm. O'Brien was Sir Thomas Grattan Esmonde Bart.,[239] a young man of about 22 years of age who, as Fr. Finlay told me, is a very strong Parnellite. I asked Fr. Finlay was Sir Thomas's Parnellism acquired with a view to securing a seat in Parliament. He said no, that the young man had become an Irish Nationalist from sincere conviction.

[236]Chamberlain addressed the Glasgow Liberal Association on 15 September 1885: *The Times*, 16 September 1885, p. 7.

[237]Morley spoke at Clapton on 16 September 1885: *The Times*, 17 September 1885, p. 4.

[238]Thomas Aloysius Finlay (1848–1940), Rector of Belvedere College, Dublin (1882–1887), professor of philosophy and political economy, Royal University of Ireland (1883–1930).

[239]Sir Thomas Henry Grattan Esmonde (1862–1935), Nat. MP for Dublin South (1885–1892), later a senator of the Irish Free State and Chairman of the National Bank.

I spoke to O'Brien after dinner. He seemed struck with young Esmonde & said that if Esmonde asked him his opinion he would counsel him to remain out of Parliament because he perhaps did not know how painful a position he might be taking up by entering Parliament as an Irish Nationalist, but that if Esmonde was determined on his course he thought that he would make a good candidate for the dangerous division of Dublin City.

18 Sep.

Mr. Gladstone has broken silence by issuing a manifesto of 6 columns in length, in which he proclaims that he is ready to lead his party at the General election. The manifesto is published in this evening's papers & it deals with every branch of politics both domestic & foreign.[240] His allusions to Ireland occupy about a column. The principal sentence in the Irish portion runs as follows,

"In my opinion not now for the first time delivered the line is clear within which any desires of Ireland constitutionally ascertained may, & beyond which they cannot, receive the assent of Parliament. To maintain the supremacy of the Crown, the unity of the Empire and all the authority of Parliament necessary for the conservation of that unity is the first duty of every representative of the people, but subject to the governing principle every grant to portions of the Country of enlarged powers for the management of their own affairs is in my view not a source of danger but a means of averting it and is in the nature of a new guarantee for increased cohesion, happiness and strength. I believe that history & posterity will consign to disgrace the name and memory of every man be he whom he may and on whichever side of the Channel he may dwell that having the power to aid in an equitable settlement between Great Britain and Ireland shall use that power not to aid but to prevent or retard it."

I wrote a couple of days ago to Sir Rowland Blennerhassett, sending him the two articles of Sir C. Gavan Duffy which have already appeared on the subject of 'Colonial Constitutions'[241] and asking him (Sir Rowland) to write an article or two in a similar style on the subject of the constitution of Bavaria, shewing the degree of dependence and of independence which that Country enjoys in relation to the German Empire.

[240]See *The Times*, 19 September 1885, p. 8.
[241]For Duffy's proposals for an Irish parliament, see 'Appeal to the Conservative Party', *National Review*, 4 (February 1885), pp. 142–144.

24 Sep.

On yesterday I received a letter from Sir Robert Hamilton's private secretary saying that the Lord Lieutenant (Lord Carnarvon) would be glad to see me today at the Viceregal Lodge. I went out and saw him and we had a long conversation on the present state of affairs in Ireland.[242] His Excellency asked me could I give him any information as to the ability or inability of the tenants to pay their rents this winter and as to the course which the landlords would take in reference to such rents. I replied that I believed the Irish tenant was not dishonest, that he would pay his rent if he could do so, firstly because he was well disposed to pay his rent if he could pay & next because he had a mortal dread of law costs. Lord Carnarvon said he shared this opinion. I then remarked that as far as I could learn the majority of Irish tenants this year would not be able out of the year's harvest to pay their rents in full, and that if the landlords as a body pressed for the full rents & proceeded to evict in the case of non-payment there would be an organised resistance on the part of the tenants, which I feared would lead to very bad work. He said he also shared this opinion. He asked me to get him any information I could quietly obtain on these points & I promised to do so. He then discussed the question of Home Rule. I told him that I was a determined nationalist & that I was so because I believed that it was hopeless to expect peace until the people began to feel responsibility all round, & that they would never feel this until they became aware that practical effect would be given to the doctrines which they might support with their voices & votes. Lord Carnarvon said "the great difficulty is of course the Land Question, no English party can consent to abolish all safeguards for landlords' property". I replied that I should be sorry to see Irish landlords left without safeguards. Lord C., "what then would you do to give safeguards." I replied that I thought the plan suggested by Sir C. Gavan Duffy in his conversation with Sir R. Hamilton & myself would answer, viz. to have two chambers. One containing say 100 members of whom each of the 32 Counties should return 3, each voter being entitled to vote only for 2 & each voter being if so minded allowed to give his 2 votes for one candidate. This would give to property a representation of $^1/_3$ at the start. The second chamber or Senate to consist of say 60 members, all in the first instance nominated by the Crown so as to fairly represent all different interests, & of this Senate a certain proportion, say $^1/_3$, to be recruited every 5 years by election by County Boards on some restricted franchise. Furthermore, I said give a guarantee by inserting

---

[242]See **Document 14** and Alan O'Day, *Parnell and the First Home Rule Episode* (Dublin, 1986), p. 97.

in the Constitution a provision that compulsory expropriation should never be resorted to.

Lord C., "that is very good so far as it goes, but how would you prevent the landlords being ruined by a tax being put on their property of such an oppressive nature as virtually to deprive them of their property." I replied that it was hard off-hand to devise a safeguard of absolute demonstrable efficacy but that I believed there was a large element of latent conservatism in Ireland which I believed would come into play when we had an Irish responsible Parliament.

Lord Carnarvon, "well, probably you are correct."

## 28 Sep.

I saw Sir Robert Hamilton today & I asked him how stood the Crime Statistics. He said that the record of outrage was not increasing but that boycotting was in many places prevalent,[243] & he observed that *United Ireland* most injudiciously had for weeks past been setting forth a string of reports from local branches of the National League detailing most circumstantially the particulars of boycotting, & that it was from *United Ireland* that the *Standard* had culled its couple of columns of Irish intelligence on which that paper based its demand for renewed coercion for Ireland.[244] I said I would do my best to put a stop both to boycotting & to the reports of it by speaking to the prominent nationalist members.

I called on T. Harrington MP at the National League rooms & I spoke to him on the subject of boycotting & of the reports thereof. I found him fully as strong as myself in his condemnation of the folly of the League branches in allowing boycotting & in the sub editor of *United Ireland* [245] in publishing the reports. He told me he had already written peremptorily to some of the branches demanding the expulsion of their Secretaries for aiding and abetting in unjustifiable boycotting proceedings, & that if his demand was not complied with he would get the offending branches cut off entirely from the League. He also promised to write to William O'Brien MP, the Editor of *United Ireland*, calling his attention to the importance of omitting the boycotting reports.

[243]Between June and September 1885, the number of persons boycotted in Ireland increased fourfold to 885: Stephen Ball, 'Policing the Land War: official responses to political protest and agrarian crime in Ireland, 1879–91' (unpublished PhD thesis, University of London, 2000), p. 255.

[244]See *United Ireland*, 19 September 1885, p. 3, and 26 September 1885, p. 2; *Standard*, 24 September 1885, p. 4. For Carnarvon's response to the latter article, see Carnavon to Hicks Beach, 25 September 1885: CP Add MS 60825, fo. 91.

[245]James O'Connor (1836–1910), journalist and long-time member of the IRB, sub-editor of *United Ireland* (1881–1890), Nat. MP for Wicklow West (1892–1910).

3 Oct.

*United Ireland* of this week is admirable in tone. It discounternances boycotting in a succession of short articles very well written & I observe that in the branch reports there is no mention of boycotting save to condemn it.

5 Oct.

A few days ago a long letter appeared in the Irish papers addressed by Mr. John Ferguson[246] of Glasgow to Mr. Chamberlain. The letter was an appeal in Ferguson's bombastic style to 'Joe Chamberlain' to side with Parnell in his demand for a separate Parliament in Ireland.[247] A couple of days afterwards Chamberlain's answer appeared & it was as follows –

> "To John Ferguson Esq.
> "Highbury Moor, Birmingham
> September 21, 1885

"DEAR SIR – I have only time to acknowledge briefly your letter of the 15[th] inst. as regards the Irish question. You will do me the justice to acknowledge that in writing to you some time ago, and before any idea had got abroad of Mr. Parnell's recent manifesto, I stated that I was conscientiously opposed to a separate Parliament for Ireland, believing as I did, and do, that it would be absolutely ruinous to the best interests of Ireland, as well as dangerous to the security of England. I hope you will carefully consider the terms in which I made my statement at Warrington, and that you will see that they are full of sympathy for Irish grievances and respect for Irish leaders; but I cannot alter my conviction upon the main point. – I am yours truly,

J. CHAMBERLAIN"[248]

I was very sorry to see this letter of Chamberlain's & I wrote to tell him so & to tell him, furthermore, that from close observation of public opinion in Ireland I had become satisfied that during the past couple of months the idea of a separate legislature for Ireland with full legislative power in Ireland, save as regards control of the forces military & militia & save as to the imposition of a tariff, had made surprising progress even among the richer people in Ireland,

---

[246]John Ferguson (1836–1906), Irish nationalist and co-founder of the Scottish Labour Party (1888).
[247]See *FJ*, 18 September 1885, p. 6.
[248]See *The Times*, 29 September 1885, p. 6.

& I earnestly asked him not to pledge himself publicly against such a legislature.[249]

He wrote me a friendly letter asking me whenever I should be in London to call on him to discuss Irish affairs with him, but adding that nothing could in his opinion alter his view that a separate parliament would [not] at present be desirable or possible, that he hoped the 'National Council' referred to in the *Fortnightly Review* article would in course of time acquire very important powers, but that he was himself surprised at the vehemence of the English feeling against further concessions to Ireland, & that he believed it would be probably more easy to arouse a strong anti-Irish feeling throughout England than to carry at present a measure even so advanced as that sketched in the *Fortnightly Review* article.[250]

19 Oct.
A few days ago a speech was made in Pontefract by the Right Honble Mr. Childers, the Ex Chancellor of the Exchequer, in which he formulated a detailed scheme of Home Rule for Ireland.[251] He declared that the Imperial Parliament should have control of foreign affairs, Customs, Post Office & the army & navy but as for anything else it could be left to the national assemblies of Ireland & of Scotland, if it were deemed desirable to set up such an assembly for Scotland.

John Dillon spent yesterday with me & we discussed the present position & prospects of politics in Ireland. I was amused at hearing from him that when he & Parnell were in the train a few days ago on their way to the Cork Convention,[252] Parnell read Childers' speech & turning round to Dillon said to him without a smile "I really think that after all we shall find that we ought to deal with the Liberals. I fear that the Tories will not be able to do for us all we want".

Parnell is certainly a thorough politician. He cajoled Chamberlain into publishing the *Fortnightly Review* article – he then turned over to the Tories so as to get them well into his net, & now he is quite ready to join the Liberals in dishing the Tories.

I asked John Dillon had Parnell made up his mind whether it would be better to have a Parliament in Dublin and at the same time send members to the Imperial Parliament or whether it would be preferable

---

[249]See **Document 16**.
[250]See **Document 17**.
[251]Childers spoke on 12 October 1885: *The Times*, 13 October 1885, p. 12.
[252]The convention, held on 12 October 1885, was the most significant county assembly to be held prior to the general election: *The Times*, 13 October 1885, p. 6; *FJ*, 13 October 1885, p. 5.

to have only the Irish Parliament & for Ireland to have no share in the Imperial Parliament.

Dillon said that he believed Parnell had not made his mind up on the point, that Parnell's theory was to get whatever he could get most easily, that he had no bigoted view in favour of one plan as against the other.

John Dillon's own view is that we must continue to send members to the Imperial Parliament. I asked him did he expect that members of popular politics could be maintained in the Imperial Parliament after Home Rule had been obtained, because it would not be then likely that popular enthusiasm in Ireland would continue at fever heat, & without great popular enthusiasm it would be certain that rich men able to support themselves in London would be sure to monopolise the representation of Ireland in the Imperial Parliament. His opinion is that within a very few years, probably 5 years, the Radical party in England will have carried a measure for paying all members of Parliament.

I got a letter from Sir Robert Hamilton asking me to call to the Castle to see him. I went up & found that Sir Robert had been reading an article in the *Nineteenth Century* of November 1882 by John Morley entitled "Irish Revolution and English Liberals". The article was one for which I remember I furnished most of the materials to Morley.[253]

In reference to this note, Sir Robert asked me to find out does Davitt still approve of the Constitution sketched in it & can he give me a copy of the speech referred to in the note.[254]

The fact of Sir Robert Hamilton asking me to get this information tends to shew that the Government are really considering the question of what form of Home Rule can be granted at once.

I said that all parties were agreed that there should be two chambers. Sir R. said, "no, Parnell is opposed to a second chamber". I said not at all – he is opposed to a House of Peers but not to a Senate.

I have been looking over some pages of this diary and I find in them an account of an interview which I had on the 28 May at the Castle with Sir Robert Hamilton & John Morley, at which Sir Robert astounded

[253]John Morley, 'Irish revolution and English liberalism', *Nineteenth Century*, 12 (November 1882), pp. 647–666. Hamilton directed Fottrell to a passage in the article that considered Michael Davitt's views on the subject and advocated a constitution for Ireland based on the Canadian model.

[254]Davitt spoke at the New York Academy of Music on 19 June 1882: *Irish World*, 1 July 1882.

me by telling me that the Legal Adviser of the Castle had advised the Lord Spencer that the Conspiracy Act of 1875 did not apply to Ireland.

It is a curious commentary on this statement that I have now to mention I was with Sir Robert at the Castle about 10 days ago and we [were] discussing the question of boycotting & Sir Robert pulled out of his private dispatch box a print of the confidential instructions issued by him to Reed, the new Inspector General of Constabulary, on the occasion of his taking office about a month ago.[255] In these instructions Reed's attention is specially called to the provision of the Conspiracy Act of 1875 & he is told that this Act gives ample powers for dealing with boycotting and, as a matter of fact, it is under this Act that the boycotting prosecutions now taking place in Ireland have been instituted.[256]

28 Oct.

I was not able to see Davitt until today as he had been absent on a lecturing tour in Scotland.[257] He returned this morning and I saw him at the Imperial Hotel.[258] I told him I had been reading Morley's article in which the allusion was made to the speech which he (Davitt) had delivered in New York in 1882 in which he had advocated the establishment of two chambers in Ireland, and I asked him was he of the same opinion still.

Davitt – Not at all, I have quite changed my opinion. When I spoke in New York I thought that the Irish landlords would shew some sense & would settle with the tenants on reasonable terms for the sale of their holdings, but I have since seen that it is hopeless to expect any common sense or any justice from the Irish landlords and therefore I shall be no party to bringing about a scheme which would establish, in the shape of a second chamber, a landlord anti-Irish & pro-British assembly which would strive to thwart the Irish chamber of representatives at every step.

[255]See Hamilton to Reed, 30 September 1885: CSO RP 1885/17947.

[256]Between August and December 1885, 425 persons were prosecuted under this act: 'Summary of cases in which boycotting and intimidation have been prosecuted under the ordinary law from the expiration of Prevention of Crime Act 1882 to 31st December 1885': CSO, RP 1888/26523.

[257]Between 25 October and 8 November 1885, Davitt delivered lectures at Glasgow, Greenock, Aberdeen, Edinburgh, Dundee, Inverness, and Coatbridge: 'Land nationalization; or, national peasant proprietary', in Carla King (ed.), *Michael Davitt: collected writings, 1868–1906*, I (Bristol, 2001).

[258]Situated in Sackville (O'Connell) Street, Dublin, it was destroyed during the Easter Rising of 1916.

GF – I am sorry to hear that you are opposed to a second chamber. I for one regard it as inevitable & as eminently desirable. I should be sorry to see a second chamber set up composed of such elements as would make it likely that they would persistently thwart the action of the lower chamber, but I can see enormous advantages in the establishment of a second chamber which would, for example, by its veto postpone for a year the consideration of a measure which the lower chamber might have adopted in a gust of passion. Of course the Senate or second chamber would have to be so composed as fairly to represent all interests.

Davitt – Your view is an intelligible one. I am a social democrat & therefore I am opposed to the establishment of a second chamber which I believe will mainly represent landlords and capitalists, you are in favour of a second chamber because you are an Irish national conservative.

GF – I admit I am in many respects a conservative.

Davitt – So is Parnell, & if the Irish landlords had any sense they would see that in an Irish Parliament Parnell must be a conservative leader. He is no revolutionist. He was originally a conservative – events have thrown upon him the task of rousing the nation & at present short sighted people regard him as a revolutionary force. He is eminently constitutional & in an Irish Parliament he must be a conservative – most of his Parliamentary companions will side with him [–] there will be in Ireland a strong conservative party & my party, viz. that of social democrats will be in a hopeless minority for many years to come.

I have from time to time met some landlords to whom I have opined this view, & they have said that if they were certain that Parnell was not aiming at total separation from England they would throw in their lot with him. You know I am in favour of total separation but I recognise its impossibility, & recognising it I for one would give a fair trial even to Chamberlain's *Fortnightly Review* scheme of Irish government.

GF. We shall get more than Chamberlain's scheme, but we cannot expect that English statesmen would consent to grant autonomy to Ireland without providing safeguards against the confiscation of property of any class in Ireland, & therefore I consider that the second chamber is inevitable.

Davitt – No – it will be much easier to get a scheme carried for a single chamber than for two chambers. Parnell is opposed to the scheme of two chambers.

GF – No, I do not believe he is. He is pledged against a House of Peers but not against a Senate.

Davitt – I have the best reason for believing that Gladstone is quite prepared to concede at once an Irish legislature. He wants only to know what is Parnell's minimum. The Liberals are going to win at the General election by an overwhelming majority & Parnell will make a huge mistake if he asks the Irish voters in England to vote for the Tories. In the first place he will not succeed in inducing them to do so, and in the next place even if he did succeed he would be allying himself with a losing party.

GF. Anyway, he seems to have acted judiciously up to the present. He has left the Liberals to expect that he will throw in his lot with the Tories & he has thereby forced the Liberals to make a bid for his support, as witness Childers' speech.

After I had spoken to Davitt I went to the Castle to see Sir Robert Hamilton & I told him in general terms Davitt's opinion.[259]

Sir Robert. I am sorry to hear that he is opposed to a second chamber. I regard it as essential.

GF. So do I, I regard it as inevitable & also as eminently desirable.

Sir Robert. I shall now read for you a document which I have just roughly finished & which I must ask you to regard as absolutely confidential. No one save myself has yet seen it & I have not spoken of it to anyone save yourself.

Sir Robert then read for me a voluminous report which he has drawn up for the Lord Lieutenant to be laid before the Cabinet. It is a very able document & it marks a wonderful advance in opinion on the part of Sir Robert Hamilton. Indeed it represents a complete reversal of some of his former opinions a reversal which I believe has been to a great extent brought about by the discussions which he & I had with Sir Charles Gavan Duffy in last July.[260]

Sir Robert then read for me a second document which contained a scheme for the separation of the Exchequers of Great Britain & Ireland.

It was impossible for me to commit to memory the exact figures given in this document but its argument was somewhat to the following effect –

(a) that the national debt of Great Britain & Ireland should be divided between the two countries in the proportion at which the debts of the two countries respectively stood at the date of the Union (1801).

(b) that for a certain period at all events the portion of the debt allocated to Ireland should be guaranteed by the Imperial Exchequer

---

[259]See **Document 19**.

[260]Fottrell outlined the main arguments of the report: see **Document 20**.

& that such Exchequer should also guarantee whatever money would have to be raised for buying out the Irish landlords.

(c) that the Imperial Exchequer should defray the cost of maintaining the Constabulary until that force should be disbanded.

(d) that Ireland should defray the cost of maintaining in Ireland 12,000 troops, such cost would represent about £1,300,000 per annum, but that in order to avoid the unpleasantness & irritation which the annual discussion of a vote for the purpose might entail, that instead of making this an annual charge there should be added to the Irish debt a bulk sum of £40,000,000 & that therefore the entire vote for the army should be by the Imperial Exchequer.

(e) the result of the foregoing arrangement would be to leave Ireland with a debt of about 88 millions – made up as follows,

| | |
|---|---|
| proportion of National Debt – | 37 millions |
| added to cover the Army expenses – | 40 " |
| outstanding Treasury loans in Ireland – | 11 " |
| total – | 88 " |

(f) the estimated annual sum now raised by Irish taxation is about £7,800,000, which the expenditure in Ireland out of the Imperial Exchequer is about £700,000 less per annum.

(g) that after allowing for the annual sum payable for interest on the debt of 86 million, the revenue of Ireland would under the foregoing arrangement shew a surplus of about £1,300,000 per annum.

It is certainly instructive to compare these official reports of Sir Robert Hamilton of the 28 October 1885 with that which he told me of on the 27 June 1885.[261] The intervening four months have produced a wondrous change.

9 Dec.

The General election is nearly over. It has been perhaps the most remarkable election of this century. At the last General election, viz. that of 1880, the Liberal Party was returned to power with a majority of [54].[262] The election almost now concluded will leave the two English parties, Tory & Liberal, neck & neck. There will probably not be more than two votes difference between the members who <u>may</u> support the Tories & those who <u>may</u> support the Liberals, but (and here comes the interest of the position) there are 86 Parnellites among the new

---

[261] See **Document 9**.

[262] In the general election of 1880, the Liberals won 353 seats, the Conservatives 238, and the Irish Nationalists 61.

members, and into which scale will their votes be thrown? If into the Tory scale then the Tories will exactly number man for man the Liberals. If with the Liberals then the latter party will have a majority of about 172 over their opponents.

Parnell has managed either with consummate skill and foresight or with marvellous luck to place his party in the position of arbiters of the destiny of the two great parties in the state.

At the opening of the election he put forth a manifesto to the Irish electors in Great Britain calling down their vengeance on the Liberal party and asking the Irish electors in England & Scotland to vote solid for the Tory candidates.[263] The result of the manifesto was astounding. Even in places where there was a very strong local prejudice among the Irish voters in favour of the Liberal candidate they marched with the discipline of an army to vote for the Tory. All sides admit that about 25 seats (all or almost all in boroughs) were thereby transferred from the Liberals to the Tories. At first it seemed as if even in the counties the Tories were about to win, but after the first couple of days of County elections the Liberals in England, Scotland & Wales drew steadily ahead & they now bid fair to command 333 or even 335 seats out of 670. The Parnellites number 86.

In Ireland, Parnell has as regards Leinster, Munster & Connaught simply swept all before him. There is not in the entire of these three Provinces a single Liberal or Conservative member. In Ulster, the Parnellites offered to the Whigs there a compromise by which the latter might have won 3 or 4 seats in exchange for their support to the Parnellites in 3 or 4 other seats. But Lord Hartington came over to Belfast to a Liberal demonstration and his advice to the Ulster Liberals was to coalesce with the Ulster Tories against the Parnellites.[264] He must feel very satisfied now of the wisdom of his advice. The Liberals have been swept out of every single seat in Ulster, Munster, Leinster and Connaught. They have not a solitary representative in Ireland.

In Ulster, the Tories have won 16 seats & the Parnellites have captured 17 so that even in the sturdy north the national Party has a majority in the representation.

There was intense interest felt in the results of the elections for West Belfast & for the City of Derry. In the latter Justin McCarthy[265] as a Nationalist opposed Lewis, the sitting member, a strong reactionary

---

[263]The manifesto was drawn up by Parnell on 21 November and subsequently issued by T.P. O'Connor: see *The Nation*, 28 November 1885, repr. Grenfell Morton (ed.), *Home Rule and the Irish Question* (London, 1980), pp. 91–92.

[264]Hartington addressed the Belfast Liberal Club and later spoke at the Ulster Hall on 5 November 1885: *The Times*, 6 November 1885, p. 6.

[265]Justin McCarthy (1830–1912), Nat. MP for Co. Longford (1879–1885) and for Londonderry city (1886–1892), chairman of the anti-Parnellite party (1890–1896).

Conservative. The Presbyterian Liberals in the city were numerous enough to be an important factor in the election, and a bargain was struck between the Nationalists and them by which it was agreed that the Liberal Presbyterians should abstain from voting in the election for Derry City, and that in consideration of such abstention the Nationalist voters in North Derry should support Sam Walker, the late Liberal Attorney General, against his Tory opponent Mulholland.[266] At the last moment the Liberal Presbyterians in Derry City broke their word & voted for Lewis. As a result, Justin McCarthy was beaten by 30 votes & Derry City was lost to the National party. But if it was lost, its loss was promptly revenged for the nationalist voters in North Derry rallied with absolute unanimity around Mulholland & defeated Walker by about 2 to 1.[267]

In West Belfast, Sexton was the National candidate. The Presbyterian Liberals acted in the same way in West Belfast as they did in Derry City & Sexton was defeated in West Belfast.[268] This double defeat & as the nationalists believed, double treachery of the Liberals in the North cost the Liberal party dear. Dickson, Lea,[269] Barbour,[270] Walker, Shillington,[271] Shaw Brown,[272] Findlater,[273] one and all have been defeated with great slaughter & there are now in Ireland only two parties – the Irish Party numbering 85 Irish members & 1 English member (T.P. O'Connor[274] who was returned for Scotland Ward Division of Liverpool) – and the English party or Constitutional

---

[266]Henry Lyle Mulholland (1854–1931), second Baron Dunleith (1895), Con. MP for Londonderry North (1885–1895).

[267]McCarthy polled 1792 votes and Lewis 1824. At the election for Londonderry North (30 November 1885), Mulholland defeated Samuel Walker by 5180 : 3017.

[268]At the election for Belfast West (26 November 1885), James Horner Haslett (Con.) defeated Thomas Sexton by 3780 : 3743.

[269]Thomas Lea (1841–1902), Lib. MP for Donegal (1879–1885), Lib. U. MP for Londonderry South (1886–1900), lost the contest for Donegal East to Arthur O'Connor (Nat.) by 4089 : 2992.

[270]John Doherty Barbour, Lib. MP for Lisburn (1863) but unseated on petition, lost the contest for Antrim South to W.G. Ellison Macartney (Con.) by 5047 : 3680.

[271]Thomas Shillington (1835–1925), linen manufacturer and member of the Ulster Land Committee, lost the contest for Armagh North to Major E.J. Saunderson (Con.) by 4192 : 2373.

[272]John Shaw Brown (b. 1823), linen manufacturer, lost the contest for Down North to Colonel Thomas Waring (Con.) by 4315 : 2841.

[273]Sir William Huffington Findlater (1824–1906), Lib. MP for Co. Monaghan (1880–1885), President of the Incorporated Law Society and the Statistical Society of Ireland, finished third in the contest for Londonderry South behind Timothy Healy (Nat.) and Colonel Hugh McCalmont (Con.).

[274]Timothy Power O'Connor (1848–1929), Nat. MP for Liverpool, Scotland Division (1880–1929) and a vital link between Irish and Liberal parliamentarians; see his *The Parnell Movement* (London, 1886).

party or Tory party numbering in Ulster 16 & with the two members for Dublin University making up a grand total of 18.

4 Jany. 1886

The House of Commons now elected consists of Liberals – 335
Tories – 249
Nationalists – 86

Thus the Tories & the Nationalists exactly balance the Liberals.

Since I last wrote in this diary, now nearly a month ago, several events of great importance have taken place. On the 17th December the *Pall Mall Gazette* & the *Standard* published what purported to be the heads of a Home Rule scheme which Mr. Gladstone had matured. These heads were

1. A Parliament in Dublin.

2. A veto by the Crown on the advice of the Irish ministry.

3. Representation from Ireland in the Imperial Parliament.

4. The control of the police to be vested in the Irish Parliament.

5. Guarantees by Mr. Parnell for the protection of the Protestant minority in Ireland [and] for the recognition of the due rights of Irish landlords.

The publication of these heads of course excited a furious controversy in the press. The London press, except the *Daily News* & *Pall Mall Gazette*, denounced the project, while many of the provincial papers, e.g. the *Scotsman* & *Liverpool Daily Post*, supported it. Gladstone sent a carefully worded telegram denying that he had any hand in publishing the heads but not denying that they represented in the main his views. In fact, the contradiction left it open to him to adopt the heads or repudiate [them] at any future time according as he should see fit.[275]

Chamberlain & Dilke at once began to sulk & to say that it would probably be better not to oust the Tory party from office for the present. Chamberlain's speech was very sulky & in the worst grace. He said let the Irish party now see what they can get from the Tories, their friends, & when they find that they cannot get anything they

---

[275] Articles concerning Gladstone's position on home rule were published in the *Daily News* and the *Pall Mall Gazette* on 12 December and expanded upon in the *Standard* and the *Pall Mall Gazette* on 17 December: Herbert Gladstone to Lucy Cavendish, 31 December 1885: GP, Add MS 56445, fos 144–154.

will be glad enough to take [from] the Liberals anything which the Liberals may choose to give them.[276]

John Morley made a fine manly speech at Newcastle on Tyne insisting that Ireland should be allowed to get whatever measure of self government she required.[277]

Lord Hartington sent a carefully worded letter to one of his supporters in which he apparently protested against the heads but leaving [sic] himself a loophole for retreat.[278]

Mr. Forster denounced the scheme as revolutionary.[279]

A couple of days after the publication of the heads I saw Sir Robert Hamilton who said with glee, "did I not tell you that Gladstone was the man & the one man in England who would have the courage and foresight to concede Home Rule to Ireland & to carry it through Parliament". Sir Robert is now more eager and enthusiastic than I am myself for the speedy attainment of full legislative independence for Ireland. It is a marvellous change. By reference to my entries in this diary under the date of 27 June 1885 I see that at that time Sir Robert had not advanced beyond the notion of a Central Board elected partly by ratepayers & partly by the managers of National Schools, & which Board should not have any more extended powers than the management of the funds for primary education in Ireland,[280] & now within six months he has not alone considered as possible a complete scheme of Home Rule, but he is feverishly anxious for its immediate accomplishment.

We talked over the heads & we both agreed that a scheme which would give Ireland a separate parliament and also representation at Westminster would be less feasible than one which would cut Ireland adrift from all interference in the Imperial Parliament.

On the morning of 26th Dec. 1885 I went to London, mainly with the view of seeing John Morley and talking over the situation with him. I went out to his house, Berkeley Lodge, West Hill, Putney on Sunday the 27 Dec. and the first person whom I met there was my

---

[276]Chamberlain spoke at Birmingham on 17 December and Dilke at Chelsea on the following day: *The Times*, 18 December 1885, p. 7; 19 December 1885, p. 9.

[277]Morley addressed a meeting of the Liberal Five Hundred in the Northumberland Hall on 21 December: *The Times*, 22 December 1885, p. 6; John Morley, *Recollections*, 2 vols (London, 1923), I, p. 204.

[278]See *The Times*, 21 December 1885, p. 9.

[279]William Edward Forster (1818–1886), Lib. MP for Bradford (1861–1885) and for Bradford Central (1885–1886), Vice-President of the Council (1868–1874), Chief Secretary for Ireland (1880–1882). On 21 December, Forster wrote to *The Times* stating that home rule would not solve the Irish question and posed a danger to both Great Britain and Ireland: *The Times*, 23 December 1885, p. 4.

[280]See **Document 9**.

friend John Dillon MP. We had a long chat about Home Rule &c. & I found to my astonishment that Morley believed the Liberal party to be hopelessly broken up & if the Tories were put out, that Gladstone would not be able to form a Cabinet. Mr. Frederick [*sic*] Harrison,[281] the well known review writer, who joined us agreed in this opinion.

After John Dillon & Mr. Harrison had left, I continued with Morley & he told me then the reason why he believed the Liberal party to be disintegrated. He said that a couple of days after he had made his speech in Newcastle he had received a furious letter from Chamberlain, abusing him through all the moods and tenses for having in that speech given any encouragement to Gladstone in his Home Rule projects, & saying that he, Chamberlain, & Dilke were determined not to advance an inch beyond the National Council proposal in the *Fortnightly Review* article. The situation therefore is this. Gladstone & Morley are sound on the Irish question, Hartington is more than doubtful, Lord Spencer's views are not known & Dilke & Chamberlain are in a sulky revolt. The outlook is certainly blue enough.

I said to Morley that if he thought I could do any good I would go to Birmingham to see Chamberlain & try to talk him over. Morley jumped at this proposal & said he would write to Chamberlain telling him of my visit to London & asking would he wish to see me.

Two days afterward, Morley called at the National Liberal Club & told me that Chamberlain had written asking me to go down to his place Highbury, Moor Green near Birmingham, to stay with him for a day or two & talk matters over with him.

On the 31st December I went down to Chamberlain's house & at once plunged into a discussion of the situation. I found Chamberlain personally polite, but shewing palpable signs of suppressed rage at the turn which things had taken. For an hour or so his every observation was directed to shew the impossibility of any scheme of Home Rule, & he even went so far as to say, "have you ever considered the contingency of the English people making up their minds that their legislative business must & shall be attended to, & then promptly suspending the constitution of Ireland for say ten years." I replied very calmly, "yes I have considered that contingency & with great respect it strikes me that it is a contingency which an Irish Nationalist can view with less concern than can an English Radical".

---

[281] Frederic Harrison (1831–1923), President of the English Positivist Committee (1880–1895), professor of jurisprudence, constitutional, and international law for the Council of Legal Education (1877–1889), defeated Liberal home rule candidate for London University (1886).

"Why", said he.

"Because", I replied, "in the first place the process of carrying such a measure as the disenfranchisement of the Irish Nation is one which will occupy some considerable time, next when carried it will have placed in Ireland before the World with [*sic*] a grievance the comparison with which all grievances of which she has hitherto complained will be as nothing, & lastly the ink with which the Queen will have signed her name to the disenfranchising Act will not be dry before whatever English party happens at the moment to be out of power will forthwith begin intriguing to repeal or amend the Act."

He paused for a few moments & said then, with more quietness than he had shewn, "I believe you are right". "Now", said I, "let us calmly look at the question of Home Rule to see how even for England the advantages & disadvantages balance each other" & we then began our discussion with Chamberlain in the frame of mind which seeks to overcome, instead of raise, difficulties. By the way, I should mention that all this time his daughter was present and in the course of our discussion she occasionally interjected an observation. One of them amused me very much because it was such a delightfully clear proof of the belief which English people have at the bottom of their minds, that Irish members are not really citizens of the Empire with rights exactly equal to those of Englishmen. We were discussing the question of obstruction & Chamberlain had said that if obstruction were tried it would be promptly suppressed by the suspension of the Irish members. I replied, "certainly it would be suppressed if it were perceived, but with so many members as 86 to work it it would not be perceived because it would take the shape not of persistent opposition to any one proposal, but rather that of a criticism on all affairs of the Empire". "But", said Miss Chamberlain, "if the Irish members began discussing & criticising affairs of the Empire which did not concern them surely that would be obstruction". I smiled & said quietly, "I think Miss Chamberlain that you are laying down a somewhat inconvenient doctrine. I thought the theory of your father's to be that Irishmen are citizens of the Empire with responsibilities & rights equal to those of Englishmen & if so surely they are entitled to interest themselves in all affairs of the Empire".

The upshot of the discussion was that Chamberlain admitted there were fewer objections to the following scheme than to any other

1. A Parliament in Ireland with two houses, an assembly & a senate.

2. No representation of Ireland in the Imperial Parliament.

3. Ireland to pay for the maintenance of say 10,000 or 12,000 Imperial troops in Ireland.

4. Ireland to take over her share of the National Debt.

He declined to pledge himself to support this, but before I left for Ireland I felt satisfied that I had succeeded in seriously modifying the views which he held before our discussion began, & I now believe that there is not so much danger as there was of the Liberal party being disrupted by Chamberlain. Dilke will follow Chamberlain.

I returned to Dublin on the morning of the 1st January & on the 2nd I saw Sir Robert Hamilton & told him what I had done. He was greatly pleased & said that I had [done] a very useful & important work in speaking to Chamberlain as I had done.

He said that Lord Spencer would be sound on the Irish question. After I had left I began to think that it would be very important to convey to Lord Spencer the fact of Sir Robert Hamilton having come round to the opinions which he now holds as regards Home Rule for Ireland, & on yesterday I went out to the Under Secretary's Lodge to tell Sir Robert what I wished to do & to ask him whether he would prohibit me from writing to Lord Spencer informing him of his (Hamilton's) opinion. Sir Robert then told me in strict confidence that he himself had written fully to Lord Spencer giving his opinion, & that in doing so he considered he was not violating any official secret but that he was merely giving his own individual opinion.[282]

I was very much pleased to hear that Sir Robert's opinions had been communicated to Lord Spencer, for I know how much Lord Spencer relies on Hamilton's judgement. If Spencer comes round he will be a potent factor in bringing round Hartington. All may still be well.

I dined last evening at the Jesuit College, Belvedere & met T.D. Sullivan MP,[283] William O'Brien MP, Dr. Kenny MP, Tim Healy MP, Mr. Clancy MP[284] & Sir Thomas Esmonde MP, the youthful member for Dublin County. He is only 22 or 23 years of age. I had a long chat with him & I was greatly pleased with him. He is a very intelligent &

---

[282]See **Documents 32** and **37**.

[283]Timothy Daniel Sullivan (1827–1914), Nat. MP for Co. Westmeath (1880–1885) and for College Green Division, Dublin (1885–1892), editor and proprietor of *The Nation, Dublin Weekly News*, and *Young Ireland*, Lord Mayor of Dublin (1886–1887).

[284]John Joseph Clancy (1847–1928), Nat. MP for Dublin North (1885–1918), member of the editorial staff of *The Nation* newspaper.

thoughtful young man and unless I [am] much mistaken he will make a good figure in political life.

17 Jany.

In the second last issue of the *Statist* there appeared a letter signed 'Economist'. It is believed to have been written by Mr. Giffen[285] of the Board of Trade. It suggests as a preliminary to Home Rule for Ireland that all the landlords' interest in Irish land should be bought out on the following terms. The agricultural rental of Ireland is assumed to be about £8,000,000, which at 20 years['] purchase would represent 160 million sterling. This sum should be advanced to the Irish nation by means of consols, the annual interest on which would then belong to the Irish State who would be entitled to receive all the rent payable by the tenants. England would be paid this interest not by any cash payment from Ireland, but merely by the fact of England ceasing to contribute to local expenditure in Ireland what she now contributes & which contributions the writer estimates at 4 millions a year. England would thus lose on the transaction only £800,000 a year, which the writer thinks the [*illegible*] will be satisfied to lose for such a purpose.[286]

The Irish State would then have the rental of Ireland for its revenue & the writer maintains that the Irish Exchequer could then afford to reduce very materially the rent payable by Irish tenants. The *Statist* & the *Pall Mall Gazette* back up this proposal.[287]

I discussed it with Sir Robert Hamilton. He believes that Giffen is the author of the proposal. He thinks that Giffen underrates the agricultural rental of Ireland. Sir Robert says that the rental is about 12 millions a year of which about 3 millions represent demesnes & farms in the owners' possession, leaving the rental payable by tenants to be about 9 million. It is somewhat strange to find how many people by different processes of reasoning are coming round to the notion that if public money is to be advanced for the purpose of buying out the landlord, it is the Irish Exchequer & not the Irish tenant who should become the owner of the land.

---

[285]Robert Giffen (1837–1910), assistant editor of *The Economist* (1868–1876), Assistant Secretary of the Board of Trade and Controller-General of the Commercial, Labour and Statistical Departments (1882–1897), President of the Statistical Society (1882–1884), KCB (1886).

[286]See 'Home rule – a suggestion', *The Economist*, 9 January 1886, reprinted in *The 'Statist' on Ireland: reprint of 'Economist's' letters to the Statist on the Irish land and home rule questions, and of editorial comments thereon* (London, 1886).

[287]The scheme was lauded as 'a way in which the Irish difficulty can be settled with justice to all parties': *PMG*, 16 January 1886, p. 6.

I had a letter from John Dillon MP on yesterday. He is in London. He believes that Home Rule is still a long way off.

I have been reading the life of Francis Deak[288] by the daughter of Mr. Forster's wife, a very interesting book at any time but especially at present.[289] Deak was born in 1803 & he was therefore 64 years of age when Hungarian independence was won in 1867. The contest for her rights lasted in Hungary from 1849. In 1861 an attempt was made by the Emperor of Austria to come to terms with Hungary but the attempt failed. On this occasion Deak prepared an address to the Emperor in the course of which he made the following observation, which might with advantage be taken to heart by many of the writers who now flood the columns of the *Times* with letters denouncing any concession of legislative freedom to Ireland.

"A forced unity will never make the Empire strong; the outraged feeling of the individual states and the bitterness arising from the pressure of force awaken the desire for separation, and therefore the Empire would be weakest just at the moment when it would be in want of its united strength and the full enthusiasm of its peoples. The position of an empire as a great Power whose unity can only be maintained by force of arms is precarious and least safe in the moment of danger . . .[290] Feelings and ideas will extend themselves; and because a 'centralised unity' is in opposition to the past of the individual lands to which they look back with pious recollection, and because it is opposed to the hopes they nourish for the future, the practical carrying out of 'centralised unity' will have to contend not only with hostile feelings; but in the course of open deliberations, with opposition and considerable difficulties. If therefore your majesty wishes your Empire to be free and really strong, your majesty cannot attain that object by a compulsory unity but by a mutual understanding arrived at through the free consent of the nation".

Commenting on this observation, the author says that it "is based not only on the opinion of a Hungarian patriot as to the form of administration best suited to his own country but on a broad principle of Government applicable to all states and in all times".[291]

[288]Ferenc Deák (1803–1876), Hungarian statesman and chief organizer of the *Ausgleich* or compromise with the Austrian crown in 1867.

[289]Florence Vere O'Brien (née Arnold-Forster) (1854–1936), adopted niece of William Forster and author of *Francis Deak* (London, 1880): see T.W. Moody and R.A.J. Hawkins, with Margaret Moody (eds), *Florence Arnold-Forster's Irish Journal* (Oxford, 1988), pp. xx–xxii.

[290]Ellipsis in original.

[291]Fottrell reproduced a passage from pages 260–261 of the book, which outlined the constitution of the Austro-Hungarian monarchy (1867).

27 Jany.

I went to London on the night of the 22<sup>nd</sup> inst. While there I had
interviews with Charles Russell QC, John Morley MP, Mr. Giffen of
the Board of Trade & John Dillon MP.

Russell has been on a tour in the south of Europe during which
he spent a few days with Sir Charles Gavan Duffy. The effect of
this conference is very manifest. Russell has learned something about
Home Rule. He has been as a rule too busy to learn much about it.
His notions have been crude, and while he has been very radical on
the subject of Irish law I have always found that he had very erroneous
views on the subject of Home Rule. For example, he has kept on for
years telling me that Home Rule was steadily declining as a cause.
Duffy has, I think, convinced him of some of his errors & on the whole
I am disposed to think that Russell has now some grasp of the subject,
but he is out of touch with Irish sentiment. For example, he was
quite astonished when I told him that the Irish party would be quite
satisfied to have Home Rule without any representation in the Imperial Parliament.

John Dillon is in good spirits. The Queen's Speech was delivered
on Wednesday the 20<sup>th</sup> inst. For several days previously there were
all kinds of wild 'blood & thunder' statements in the London press
in reference to the intentions of the Government regarding Ireland.
Martial law, suppression of the National League & all kinds of stringent
coercion were put forward as being the policy of the Government.
In Ireland, we nationalists of the moderate type were in low spirits.
We found that the old weary round of coercion & retaliation was
about to be travelled. The Queen's Speech came. It was a curious
pronouncement. It said that serious crime had <u>not</u> materially increased
in Ireland, but that intimidation had been resorted to prevent people
from carrying out their contracts and that organised opposition to the
payment of full rents had been manifested in parts of the Country, &
it added some words to the following effect

"If, as the information at my disposal would lead me to believe,
the forces of the existing law shall prove inadequate to cope with the
increasing evils I rely upon my Parliament to arm the executive with
ample powers to deal with them". [292]

Sir Michael Hicks-Beach made a speech on the address in which he
shewed that the state of the Country as regards crime was not serious,
but he dwelt upon the boycotting & similar evils which he deplored

---

[292]The speech read, 'If, as my information leads me to apprehend, the existing provisions
of the law should prove to be inadequate to cope with these growing evils, I look with
confidence to your willingness to invest my Government with all necessary powers':
*Hansard*, CCCII, cols 32–36.

but still he did not urge that coercive measures should be at once adopted.[293]

Gladstone made a very adroit speech in which he did not commit himself to any definite scheme of Home Rule but plainly enough left the impression that Home Rule & nothing else could render Ireland what she ought to be.[294]

Parnell also spoke very adroitly & with great moderation shewing that Home Rule did not mean separation but quite the opposite, shewing that ample guarantees would be given if demanded for the protection of the minority in Ireland & that as regards the land question some such scheme as Giffen's would be supported by the Irish party.[295]

Neither Gladstone nor any of the Irish members moved an amendment to the address. The Tories were quite deceived in the tactics of both Gladstone & Parnell. They were certain that either of them would move a Home Rule amendment and that they, the Tories, would have had an opportunity of going out on the cry of 'the integrity of the Empire'.

On Friday the 22nd inst., it was announced to the astonishment of everyone that Mr. W.H. Smith has been appointed Chief Secretary for Ireland.[296] Lord Carnarvon had previously stated publicly his intention of resigning the Vice Royalty.

The object of Mr. Smith's appointment it was not easy to see. On Monday the 25th inst., Lord Salisbury announced portentously that Mr. Smith, who had crossed over to Ireland on Saturday, would at once make a report to the Cabinet about the state of the Country, & that the Government would be prepared within 24 or 48 hours to state their intentions as to repressive legislation. On Tuesday the 26th inst., Sir Michael Hicks Beach announced in the House of Commons that the ministry would ask to have the discussion of the address to the Queen's Speech adjourned in order that they might introduce a bill proclaiming the National League to be an illegal association & enacting the boycotting provision of the Crimes Act.[297] Mr. Jesse Collings's amendment as to the importance of compulsory powers given to local bodies to enable them to obtain allotments for labourers was moved, & on it the ministry was defeated by a majority of 79.

[293]Ibid., cols 120–130.
[294]Ibid., cols 100–120.
[295]Ibid., cols 151–160.
[296]Ibid., col. 68; *The Times*, 22 January 1886, p. 6.
[297]See *Hansard*, CCCII, cols 300–301, 416.

With the ministry voted Lord Hartington, Sir Henry James,[298] Leonard Courtney[299] & Goschen.[300]

Now to go back to my interview with John Dillon. I saw him on Sunday the 24[th] inst. He therefore did not know of the intended coercion move of the Tories. He considered that Gladstone had outwitted the Tories & that his attitude was a clear confession of his intention to work up to Home Rule. Dillon praised Giffen's scheme, said Parnell was quite taken with it and expressed his opinion that probably a scheme on the lines of Giffen would be carried this session & that it would lead next session to Home Rule.

On Saturday the 23[rd] inst. I had an interview of about an hour's duration with Mr. Giffen. I found him a most interesting man. A canny Scotchman with plenty of shrewd sense but also with remarkable boldness of mind. He explained his scheme fully to me. He told me it was produced owing to several conversations at the Athenaeum Club with many politicians. I told him that Sir Robert Hamilton considered that he, Giffen, underestimated the agricultural rental of Ireland. Giffen said that this was not his opinion. I said that Hamilton estimated the gross agricultural product of Ireland at 60 millions & that the rental was probably one fifth of this. Giffen said that Sir Robert was quite out in his calculation; that the gross products were only 40 millions & that if the rental was really 12 millions it was one which could not be paid by the agriculturalists. Giffen said that in the *Economist* of this week there is a letter from a Mr. Harris who is a good authority on the subject & in his letter he contended that the gross product of Ireland was only 36 millions.[301]

I told Giffen what were Sir Robert's views about the necessity of granting Home Rule & of beginning not by County Boards but by conceding the central Parliament. Giffen was greatly interested at hearing that Sir Robert had come around to this view & plainly he is himself quite prepared to acquiesce in the wisdom of Sir Robert's view.

[298]Sir Henry James (1828–1911), first Baron James of Hereford (1895), Lib. MP for Taunton (1869–1885), Lib. U. MP for Bury (1885–1895), Attorney-General (1873–1874, 1880–1885).
[299]Leonard Henry Courtney (1832–1918), first Baron Courtney of Penwith (1906), Lib. MP for Liskeard (1876–1885), Lib. U. MP for Bodmin (1885–1900), Financial Secretary to the Treasury (1882–1885).
[300]George Joachim Goschen (1831–1907), first Viscount Goschen (1900), Lib. MP for Ripon (1880–1885) and for Edinburgh East (1885–1886), Lib. U. MP for St George's (1887–1890), Chancellor of the Exchequer (1887–1892).
[301]William James Harris (1835–1911), Con. MP for Poole (1884–1885); see *The Economist*, 23 January 1886, pp. 112–113.

On Sunday the 24[th] inst. I lunched with John Morley at his home at Putney. We had a long chat about the political situation. He told me that Chamberlain kept straight for about a week after my interview with him but that he had then relapsed into his sulks & kept swearing that the Home Rule scheme would ruin the Liberal Party. It appears that he even went so far as to contemplate & feel his way for the establishment of a Hartington–Chamberlain alliance against Home Rule but that his radical friends plainly told him that such an alliance would mean his absolute ruin and effacement as a politician.

Morley praised Giffen's scheme & he said he had heard that Chamberlain was writing an article in the *Fortnightly Review* in support of it. Morley mentioned that in the course of the debate on the address to the Queen's Speech he believed Goschen would speak on Ireland & that if so he Morley would answer him. I suggested certain topics for Morley's speech & when we were walking down to the station Morley said with a laugh "I wish Fottrell you would come over here about once every ten days and coach me for a speech". He had no inkling of the ministry being so near their death as the event proved them to be. I spoke to him about the Irish Chief Secretaryship & I said that if Gladstone did come into office & if he Morley believed that Gladstone was really about to face the Irish problem in a bold way, it would be of great service to have him (Morley) accept the post of Chief Secretary.

## 3[rd] February

On Thurday the 28[th] Jany. Sir Michael Hicks Beach announced that Lord Salisbury had gone to the Queen but that he was not in a position to state what statement he would make to her Majesty. The House adjourned then to Monday 1[st] Feb. On Monday 1[st] Feb. Sir M. H. Beach announced that Lord Salisbury had resigned & that the Queen had sent for Mr. Gladstone.[302]

On Sunday the 31[st] Jan. I had a long chat with Sir Robt. Hamilton. We discussed the situation. He is quite hopeful of Gladstone's will & power to carry Home Rule. We discussed the Chief Secretaryship & spoke about the rumour that either Chamberlain or Childers would be the man selected. Morley had written to me to this effect. Sir Robert agreed with me that neither one nor other of these men would suit. Chamberlain he does not personally know but from my account of him he distrusts him & as regards Childers he has the poorest opinion of his ability, manliness or generosity & he went so far as to tell me that he had written to Lord Spencer, not quite to the effect that he, Hamilton, would not serve under Childers, but intimating that his service under

[302] *Hansard*, CCCII, cols 532–533, 534–535.

Childers would be so unsatisfactory that he should probably ask to be removed from the Under Secretaryship.[303] Hamilton said as regards Giffen's scheme that a further examination of the figures led him, Hamilton, to put the gross agricultural return of Ireland at about 50 millions per annum instead of 60 millions. Later in the day I saw Davitt & John Dillon & I discussed with them the question of the Chief Secretaryship. They both scouted the idea of either Chamberlain or Childers being sent over. I asked their opinion as to the wisdom of selecting John Morley for the post & they both replied almost in the same terms that they would be sorry to see Morley come here because they had too great a respect and love for him to wish that he should run any risk of losing his popularity in Ireland, or be subjected to the pain of feeling that he was ostracised from the friendship of the Nationalist members who are now friends of his. Both Dillon & Davitt seemed to think that Mr. Fowler[304] would be a good selection for the Secretaryship. By the same post I wrote to Morley telling him what Davitt & Dillon said & on this morning I recd. from him a pathetic letter telling me he had accepted the Secretaryship & that my letter had made him very sad. It is the letter of an honest man. He marked it private but added that I might show it to John Dillon, of whom he speaks in terms of great esteem and affection.

I forgot to note in its place a fact of some significance. On the 27[th] ultimo, the day after the defeat of the Conservative Government, I was at the Castle & in the course of conversation with Sir Robert Hamilton he mentioned to me that there had been some serious cases resulting from boycotting and as an instance he read for me the report of Major Butler,[305] RM for the Mallow District of Cork, a case of which the following were the facts.

A, a farmer, had six years ago taken a farm from which B had been evicted. B recently claimed the farm as his. A naturally demurred & pleaded that he had been six years in undisturbed possession, but yielding to local National League pressure or advice he offered to give to B £25 as compensation for his supposed claim, B agreed & was paid £5 on a/c but afterwards he repudiated this bargain & claimed the farm itself. A of course defied him & held possession. Some few days ago A proceeded to a forge to get his horse shod & when coming home from the blacksmiths he was violently assaulted by B. A promptly summonsed B before the magistrates who thereupon summoned as

---

[303]See **Document 40**.

[304]Henry Hartley Fowler (1830–1911), first Viscount Wolverhampton (1908), Lib. MP for Wolverhampton East (1880–1908), Under-Secretary of the Home Office (1884–1885).

[305]Thomas Butler (1837–1920), RM for Mallow, advocate of Irish administrative reform.

a witness the blacksmith, who gave his evidence very reluctantly. B was sentenced to a short imprisonment & was bound over to keep the peace. The next step was the summoning of the blacksmith before the Freemount Branch of the National League to give an explanation of why he had given evidence in favour of A, a boycotted person. On this state of facts Major Butler reported & urged that notice should be taken by the Executive of this attempt to override the lawfully constituted courts of the Country. I expressed my opinion that the case was outrageous & Sir Robt. told me he was sending it down to Captain Plunkett,[306] the RM of Cork, for prompt investigation.[307] I said that probably I could get the case dealt with in a more summary & effective way than Capt. Plunkett could & I straight away went off to T. Harrington MP, the Secretary of the Central National League, & I told him all the circumstances. Harrington at once promised to look into the case & that if the facts were as I stated he would at once dissolve the Freemount branch of the League. Two days afterwards an announcement appeared in the *Freeman* stating that the branch had been dissolved.[308]

I then told Sir Robt. Hamilton what had been done & I suggested that Capt. Plunkett should be told to let the matter drop & Sir Robt. promised he would send word to him to this effect.[309] Sir Robert was greatly pleased at the result of my intervention & said that if I could succeed in getting a few similar things done I would probably be the means of accelerating Home Rule by a year or two.

16 Feby.

The principal members of the new Liberal Administration whose seats have been contested on their seeking for re-election are Charles Russell & John Morley. Russell as Attorney General for England, Morley as Chief Secretary for Ireland. Both men were pronounced in their Home Rule declarations. Russell has been returned by an increased majority of 253 over that which he obtained at the General election, his majority now being 1195 against 942 then. Morley has won by a majority of 2661 against his former majority of 629. The exact numbers at the General election were as follows,

---

[306]Thomas Oliver Westenra Plunkett (1838–1889), son of the twelfth Baron Louth, RM (1866–1881), SRM and DM for South-Western Division (1881–1889).

[307]Butler to Hamilton, 26 January 1886; Hamilton to Plunkett, 27 January 1886: CSO RP 1886/1707 in RP 1886/2602; *Cork Examiner*, 26 January 1886.

[308]See *FJ*, 29 January 1886, p. 5.

[309]It was reported that this action was met 'by the farming class with great satisfaction': Hamilton to Plunkett, 29 January 1886; Plunkett to Hamilton, 9 February 1886: CSO RP 1886/2602.

| | | | | |
|---|---|---|---|---|
| Cowen[310] | – | 10489 | His recent election shewed the | |
| Morley | – | 10129 | following result, | |
| Hammond [sic][311] | – | 9500 | Morley | – 11110 |
| | | | Hammond [sic] | – 8449 |

The result of the Newcastle election shews that Morley got all the Liberal votes which he had at the General election & in addition got all the Irish vote & probably some few extra Liberal votes.[312] The Irish strength is variously estimated at from 1500 to 2000.

Two days before the election Morley came over to Dublin to be sworn in as Chief Secretary.[313] I saw him at the Castle for a few minutes. He was anxious & nervous. I tried to cheer him up & told him that the National party would give him every fair play. He said he felt sure they would treat him generously but he was appalled at the magnitude of the task which had been laid upon him, a task which he said would have been heavy for a Napoleon or Frederick the Great, and in carrying out which he felt so hampered by the fact that almost all Englishmen were so ignorant of the affairs of Ireland that it was difficult to convince them of the wisdom of any step which he as Chief Secretary might take.

He asked me did I think that Parnell would be satisfied to let the Government deal first with the Land Question & leave Home Rule in abeyance till the Land Question should have been settled.

I replied that I thought not but that I would make careful enquiries. Subsequently I did make careful enquiries from John Dillon, Dwyer Gray, Harrington & Leamy[314] & I felt satisfied from these enquiries that Parnell had made up his mind to oppose most determinedly any proposal for giving the Land Question precedence of Home Rule. His view is I think a sound one. He considers that the Land Question has reached such a pass that it must be settled & that no matter what ministry may be in power they must deal with that question, but he also considers that no statesman except Gladstone could carry Home Rule, that Gladstone is 76 years of age & therefore a precarious life & that ergo it behoves the Irish party to insist upon Gladstone at once forcing the Home Rule problem.

---

[310]Joseph Cowen (1831–1900), coal-owner and newspaper proprietor, Lib. MP for Newcastle upon Tyne (1874–1886), radical reformer and home ruler.

[311]Charles Frederic Hamond (1817–1905), Con. MP for Newcastle upon Tyne (1874–1880, 1892–1900).

[312]See *The Times*, 12 February 1886, p. 6; 13 February 1886, p. 6.

[313]He was sworn in on 10 February 1886: *The Times*, 11 February 1886, p. 10.

[314]Edmund Leamy (1848–1904), Nat. MP for Waterford city (1880–1885) and for Cork North East (1885–1887).

Accordingly I wrote very fully to Morley urging that the Cabinet ought to deal with the Land Question & with Home Rule in the one bill, & saying that in my opinion a bill dealing with both questions would for the purpose of commanding Tory support be better balanced than if it dealt with only Home Rule, & would for the purpose of commanding Irish national support be better balanced than if it deal [*sic*] exclusively with the Land Question.

A few days ago I had a characteristic letter from Charles Russell in which he said that if Home Rule were to be pushed forward now its fate would be sealed for years, because there is a strong feeling in England against any such measure & that nothing but time & discussion could remove this feeling &c. &c. I replied pointing out that his election & Morley's seemed rather to demolish his theory about the strong anti-Irish feeling in England & I added that while there might be some risk in Gladstone straightaway formulating his Home Rule plans, I was satisfied the risk was one which he would have to face, because if he did not face it he would have to face the bigger risk of losing the Irish vote. On today I got a letter from Charley Russell, his son, written by direction of Charles Russell himself in which he repeats his observation about the anti-Irish feeling in England, says that it may become less "six months hence" & says that with the exception [of] Gladstone & Morley all the members of the Cabinet are opposed to the Parnellites. This shews an ignorance of the state of affairs in London which is to my mind simply astounding.

I have it on what I consider to be the very best authority that Lord Spencer is as keen for Home Rule as Parnell himself, that Mundella[315] professed himself converted to the urgent necessity for Home Rule – that Childers is of the same opinion & so is Campbell Bannerman, and that the only really determined opponent of Gladstone in the Cabinet is Chamberlain.

I saw Sir Robert Hamilton today. He has been in London for the past 3 or 4 days. He has discussed the situation with every member of the Cabinet save Trevelyan, Childers & Lord Rosebury,[316] and after the discussion he is satisfied that the state of affairs is hopeful. I told him Russell's view & he simply laughed at his want of knowledge of the views of the Cabinet. He is enthusiastic in his admiration of the thorough way in which Lord Spencer has thrown himself into the

---

[315] Anthony John Mundella (1825–1897), Lib. MP for Sheffield (1868–1885) and for Sheffield Brightside (1885–1897), advanced Liberal and supporter of home rule.

[316] Archibald Philip Primrose (1847–1929), fifth Earl of Rosebery (1868), Lord Privy Seal (1885), Foreign Secretary (1886, 1892–1894), Prime Minister (1894–1895).

fight in favour of Home Rule. He said that Lord Spencer's views are as advanced as his own.

I told him what I had written to Morley about Parnell's resolve & he said "Parnell is quite right. If I were in his place I would oppose any dealing with the Land Question in priority to Home Rule. They ought to be both taken up together".

He said he had in London spoken to both Giffen & Fowler of the Board of Trade & that Giffen had admitted he had not fully thought out the details of his scheme. Hamilton considers that John Dillon's plan of naming a fixed number of years['] purchase at which every Irish landlord would be entitled to demand from the Irish state the purchase of his estate is more likely to be carried out than a plan like Giffen's for the compulsory expropriation of all landlords. Hamilton thinks that 15 years['] purchase for all holdings over £10 valuation, & 7 years['] purchase for all holdings under £10 valuation, would be a reasonable price to fix as that at which the Irish state could be compelled to buy. I said that the Irish people ought to give the landlords more than the commercial value of the land so as to settle the question. Yes said Sir Robert, but remember that the English people are to guarantee the price & England is so depressed at present that she will not tamely submit to guaranteeing any exorbitant price. He read for me a letter to him from Sir Thomas Farrer[317] giving the strictly economic view of the value of small holdings in Ireland. Farrer says that the rent should be arrived at by deducting from the gross produce of the land the amount necessary for the subsistence of the tenants or the amount necessary for the eviction & emigration of the tenants. Either deduction would I fear shew that a large proportion of the land in the west of Ireland can produce no rent & that therefore strictly speaking it has absolutely no purchase value.

The Irish party has during the past ten days gone through a crisis which went near to breaking up the party. Parnell without consultation with or notice to his colleagues sent Captain O'Shea[318] down to Galway City with a recommendation to the Electors to return him for their borough. O'Shea was a Whig and is – well no one knows what he is – except that he is the husband of Mrs. O'Shea.[319] The news reached Dublin on the night of last Thursday week. It was kept a secret till

[317]Sir Thomas Farrer (1819–1899), first Baron Farrer of Abinger (1893), Permanent Secretary to the Board of Trade (1865–1886).
[318]William O'Shea (1840–1905), Nat. MP for Co. Clare (1880–1885) and for Galway town (1886), facilitated communication between leading Liberal politicians and Parnell during 1880–1885.
[319]Katherine O'Shea (1845–1921) married William O'Shea in 1867 and, as Parnell's mistress, acted as go-between in his dealings with Gladstone. Divorced in 1890, she married Parnell in 1891.

Saturday morning when an announcement of the fact appeared in the *Freeman*. On this Friday night, as Edmund Dwyer Gray told me, there was a meeting of some of the Irish members including Timothy Healy which lasted till 4 am. To the consternation of the Irish party Healy & Biggar,[320] without any mandate from the party, rushed down to Galway on Saturday morning & forthwith publicly denounced O'Shea & supported Lynch,[321] a local nationalist. There was at once a private meeting held of all or most of the nationalist members in Dublin & they resolved that Parnell's authority should be upheld even although they hated O'Shea & finally a declaration to the effect was signed by over 50 of the members & published in the *Freeman*.[322] The morning on which this declaration appeared Parnell turned up in Dublin from London & went down to Galway where he met Healy & Biggar, & forthwith their candidate was withdrawn & two days later O'Shea was returned. Parnell produced a document purporting to have been signed by O'Shea a fortnight before the election in which he bound himself by the pledge taken by all the Nationalist candidates at the General election.

The anxiety throughout Ireland during the period which elapsed between Healy's arrival in Galway & Parnell's appearance there was simply electric, for there was a dread that the party was about to be hopelessly split up.

Three or four evenings afterward I met at the National League rooms Healy, Harrington, Leamy, Deasy[323] & T.P. O'Connor. The storm had then blown over.

The Divorce Case of Crawford & Crawford & Dilke was tried on last Friday.[324] It resulted in the dismissal of the bill as against Dilke but it also, in my opinion, resulted in his irretrievable ruin. Crawford, the husband, was examined & he detailed the confession made to him by his wife which justified all even the wildest rumours which were current in London when the Dilke scandal was first mentioned. Mrs. Crawford did not appear & the hearsay evidence of the husband detailing the wife's confession was not technically evidence against Dilke, although it was evidence against Mrs. Crawford herself & therefore the judge pronounced a decree of divorce against Mrs. Crawford but dismissed the bill as against Dilke. Dilke was represented by Charles Russell &

---

[320]Joseph Gillis Biggar (1828–1890), Nat. MP for Co. Cavan (1874–1885), pioneer of 'obstruction' in the House of Commons.

[321]Arthur Alfred Lynch (1861–1934), colonel of the 2nd Irish Brigade, South Africa (1899–1902), Nat. MP for Galway city (1901–1903) and for Clare West (1909–1918).

[322]See *FJ*, 10 February 1886, p. 6; Lyons, *Parnell*, pp. 314–340.

[323]John Deasy (1856–1896), Nat. MP for Cork city (1884–1885) and for Mayo West (1885–1893), prominent member of the Irish National League.

[324]See *The Times*, 13 February 1886, p. 12.

Sir Henry James & Russell, who as Attorney General 'led' in the case, made the astounding statement that after anxious consultation as there was no legal evidence against Dilke he had resolved not to put Dilke in the witness box to be cross examined about all the indiscretions of his previous life – needless to say that everyone must after this believe Dilke either guilty of the horrible transaction which Mrs. Crawford confessed to her husband, or guilty of the unspeakable meanness of abstaining from getting into the witness box to clear the character of a woman who, in a moment of phrenzy, had invented against herself and him a tale which blasted her reputation. On the whole it would have been as well if Chamberlain had not (as he told me he had) prevented Sir Charles Dilke from emigrating to the Antipodes when the scandal was first broached.

March 1st

About a week ago I got a letter from Charles Russell saying that he still adhered to his own view as to the desirability of dealing first with the Land Question & leaving Home Rule in abeyance, but he added "as you & Mr. Parnell have arranged that a different course is to be followed this puts an end to discussion". I thought that this sneer was quite uncalled for & I wrote a pretty tart reply to the Attorney General which brought from him a letter of explanation denying any intention of sneering & saying that he valued very highly my opinion, & in this letter he asked me to write for him a memorandum putting forth my views as strongly as I could & that he would bring my views before Mr. Gladstone.

I prepared this memorandum[325] & sent it to Russell a few days ago & I have received from him a letter in which he says "I think the order will be (a) a big land scheme but (b) dependent upon and of non effect without Home Rule, for the working it out will be the [?] new Irish Authority. If you ponder over this you will I think see it is very cleverly devised. Whether the whole thing will come out at once, i.e. in April, I don't know, but you may rely upon it the several parts will be independent".

I wrote saying that this line of policy met my difficulty in as much at it withheld from the landlords in Ireland a settlement of the Land Question until they swallow Home Rule. My whole contention was that the desire of the landlords for the settlement of one question should be used as a lever for securing the settlement of the other.

[325] See **Journal (12, 21 March 1886)**.

When I was in London last I, in speaking to Mr. Giffen, incidentally mentioned that Alderman Dillon,[326] the father of John Dillon MP, had some years ago written for the Dublin Corporation a report upon the taxation of Ireland in which he shewed that Ireland was too heavily taxed in proportion to her resources.[327] Giffen replied that he had never heard this alleged but he said he would look carefully into the question of Ireland's contribution. In the *Nineteenth Century* of this month there is a very important article by Giffen in which he states that Ireland contributes annually three millions more in taxes than she ought to pay & that England loses three millions more in useless expenses in Ireland, i.e. the expenses of an over grown military & police establishment &c.[328] The article is a very remarkable one & will I have no doubt have a great effect on the English view. A new election has taken place in Cardiff where Sir E.J. Reed,[329] who got some small office under Gladstone had to seek re-election. The Irish vote was cast for him. The result is encouraging. At the General election he won by about 100, he has now won by about 950 which would tend to show that Wales is not frightened by the bug bear of Home Rule for Ireland.[330] We are marching steadily on.

## March 12

On Saturday last, the 6th inst., I received a telegram from Charles Russell, the Attorney General, asking me to go over that night to London as it was important he should have a conversation with me. I went over & found that what he wanted to speak to me about was the Land Purchase Bill, which is in course of preparation by the Cabinet. He told me that he had been consulted by Gladstone & that he had been present at some official Cabinet meetings at which Mr. Stanislaus Lynch,[331] the Land Purchase Commissioner, was also present, but that

[326]John Blake Dillon (1814–1866), staff member of *The Nation* and *Young Ireland*, alderman of the city of Dublin, founder of the National Association, Lib. MP for Co. Tipperary (1865–1866).

[327]*Report on the State of the Public Accounts between Ireland and Great Britain* (1863, published Dublin, 1882).

[328]Robert Giffen, 'The economic value of Ireland to Great Britain', *Nineteenth Century*, 19 (March 1886), pp. 329–345.

[329]Sir Edward James Reed (1830–1906), Chairman of Milford Haven Shipbuilding & Engineering Company, Lib. MP for Cardiff (1880–1895, 1900–1906), Junior Lord of the Treasury (1886).

[330]Reed beat the Conservative candidate by 5708 : 4845 (see *The Times*, 1 March 1886, p. 7).

[331]John Stanislaus Lynch (1831–1915), Registrar of the Landed Estates Court and land purchase commissioner; see his 'Suggestions for the simplification of the procedure in relation to the sale of land in Ireland', presented to the Statistical and Social Inquiry Society of Ireland, 28 April 1885, and *The Times*, 11 May 1885, p. 7.

at none of the consultations had Gladstone opened his entire scheme & that he (Charles Russell) found it difficult to advise on any point without having before him the entire scheme for land purchase & Home Rule. He asked me to draft for him a memorandum, which he could forward to Mr. Gladstone, embodying his views on the land purchase scheme & on its dependence upon Home Rule. He gave me a sheet of note paper on which he had jotted down a few heads.

I went to work & drafted a portion of the memorandum.

On Sunday 7th inst. this conversation took place. On that day we had at lunch at 86 Harley St (Russell's house) Stanislaus Lynch, Samuel Walker (Attorney General for Ireland), The MacDermot (Solicitor General for Ireland), Thomas A. Dickson & myself. After lunch the Land Question was discussed. I was amused to find that both Lynch & MacDermot started by assuming that the basis of purchase was not what the tenant could be expected to pay as rent or annual instalments but what the landlord might expect to receive as purchase. Their argument was: Buy out the landlord by giving him a certain number of years' purchase of the existing rent and then reduce the tenant's rent by charging him interest at the rate of £3.10.0 per cent on the amount of purchase money & charge him no sum as a sinking fund. I ventured to ask who was to collect the interest & they said the Irish Exchequer, "but", said I, "what interest will the Irish Exchequer have in collecting the interest if you start by giving out & out to the landlord the highest sum you can screw up his compensation to by reducing, as you propose to do, the tenant's instalments to £3.10.0 per cent on the purchase money, a reduction which will have no possible margin of profit for the Irish Exchequer".

In addition to the persons whom I mentioned as being present at lunch there was a Mr. Henniger Heaton,[332] MP for Canterbury, a Conservative. I think he must have gone straight to some Conservative club & told all that he heard at Stanley St. because next day there appeared in the *St. James Gazette* a paragraph stating that several gentlemen who had lunched at Russell's were in London to be consulted by the Cabinet on the Irish Question. I was described as "Mr. George Fottrell late solicitor to Mr. Parnell and the Irish Land Commission."[333] After lunch Russell & I took a walk & called on John Morley, & Chamberlain, neither of whom happened to be at home.

---

[332] John Henniker Heaton (1848–1914), landowner and newspaper proprietor, Con. MP for Canterbury (1885–1910).

[333] *St. James's Gazette*, 8 March 1886, p. 8.

Next morning, Monday 9th March, I had a post card from Morley appointing an hour to see me at the Irish Office. I called and found him in good spirits. He is hopeful. I explained my views as to land purchase & I found he agreed with me in the main. He then asked my opinion as to whether or not Ireland should in the event of Home Rule being granted send members still to Westminster. I replied that as far as the Irish people were concerned they cared very little whether members would still be sent to Westminster or not, but that I fancied it would be easier in England to carry a scheme which would contemplate Ireland continuing to send representatives (very much reduced in number) to Westminster than to carry a scheme which would cut Ireland adrift from the Imperial Parliament. I also urged Morley to insist upon there being two chambers in Ireland.

I asked him about Chamberlain. He believes that Chamberlain is casting about to see could he carry a party with him if he abandoned the Cabinet. I asked did he, Morley, think I could do any good by speaking with Chamberlain & he said he thought it might be useful for me to do so, but he had not much hope I should be able to influence him.

Late in the day I was at the House of Commons & I had a long chat with John Dillon MP & with Wm. O'Brien MP. I found that O'Brien had very shadowy notions on the subject of land purchase. He seemed in some vague way to suppose that the circumstances of every estate would have to be investigated by a Commission who would fix the price at which the landlord was to be compulsorily bought out. I said that if this plan was to be followed it would take 50 years to make any impression. I said that there must be a uniform rate of purchase laid down in the Act of Parliament & that there should be no compulsory powers sought for purchasing out the landlords; because compulsion would not be necessary & because it would involve too high a price being fixed as the rate for purchase. But, said O'Brien, if there be no compulsory provision obliging Irish landlords to sell, how are we to make them sell. "Simply enough" I replied. "Landlords in Ireland will have the choice of selling or of abiding by such legislation as an Irish Parliament will pass & I think that the alternative open to them will induce a large number to sell quickly enough." O'Brien said that the Imperial Parliament would never deal in this fashion with the Irish landlords. John Dillon took a different view & said that he believed my view was sound.

While standing in the lobby of the House of Commons I met Lord Spencer who chatted with me for a few minutes & asked me to call on him at Spencer House on the following morning so that he might have a conversation with me.

I had a long talk with Thomas Sexton MP. He too is very hopeful. I did not discuss details with him.

I went to hunt up Mr. Chamberlain. I found him in a room at the foot of the staircase which leads to the Strangers Gallery. The ministers have each a private room within the precincts of the House of Commons.

Chamberlain was at work with some papers & was smoking a cigar. We plunged at once into a discussion of the 'situation'. "We are in an eddy at present" said he with a smile. "Yes", said I, "there is a strange sensation among public men at present. A kind of suppressed excitement & a vague expectation. What is it to come to". "Well", said he, "I have not changed the opinion which as I told you I had formed when last I saw you. We English people may possibly grant Home Rule to get rid of the Irish members, but I think they are not such fools as to grant Home Rule and at the same time pledge their credit for an enormous sum to buy out Irish landlords." "Well", said I, "in the first place I don't think the sum for which their credit would have to be pledged is as large as you suppose for I don't see any necessity of adopting such a gigantic scheme as Giffen's, & in the next place I think that the chances of loss to the English taxpayer if a proper scheme of land purchase be adopted is extremely remote. Giffen says that Ireland has been overtaxed. I do not pretend to be a financier but I believe that those who are financiers agree that something would have to be returned each year to Ireland by England out of the Customs & Excise duties. If by any chance Ireland, i.e. the Irish Exchequer not the Irish tenants, failed in any year to pay up the full amount due upon the land purchase transaction for interest & sinking fund surely it would not be very difficult for England to pay herself the deficit by simply abstaining from sending over so much of the rebate out of customs duties to Ireland."

Chamberlain shook his head, said I might be right but he feared that the English taxpayer would be hostile &c. &c. "Well", said I, "I have been hearing a deal about this hostility of the British taxpayer, you yourself Mr. Chamberlain will remember that you wrote to me saying that a bitter anti-Irish feeling might at any moment be aroused in England but I confess I don't yet see any evidence of it. The elections since the General election certainly lend no support to the theory that the anti Irish feeling is rampant in England." "My dear Sir", said Chamberlain, "these elections do not prove anything. Nothing was explained to the Electors." I replied, "you are correct if you mean to convey that the sharp details of a definite scheme were not explained but surely the very fact of Mr. Gladstone having spoken as he spoke in

Midlothian,[334] followed as his speeches were by the 'Hawarden Kite' on the subject of Home Rule & followed as this again was by persistent paragraphs in the newspapers to the effect that Mr. Gladstone was engaged in elaborating a scheme of land purchase & of Home Rule for Ireland, was quite sufficient to arouse the anti-Irish feeling if it had any existence in England & yet we find that all the re-elections have been favourable to Gladstonian candidates."

Chamberlain pooh-poohed my view, said he was persuaded that Englishmen would never agree to pledge their credit for buying out Irish landlords & said he believed he would have to leave the Cabinet.

"But", said I, "if you go where will you go?". Chamberlain replied, "I don't conceal from myself that if I do go I must work with the Whigs." "Well Mr. Chamberlain", said I, "I don't pretend to understand your affairs as well as you do but I must say that if you elect to stable your horses in the Whig stalls I think you will find that the atmosphere will not agree with them. The motive power of your political mind is diametrically opposite to that which moves the Whigs & I cannot see how an alliance between you & the Whigs can last long with advantage or comfort to you. Don't create a big line of cleavage in the Liberal party merely for the sake of theorectic danger which you apprehend in the financial part of the Gladstone policy. At least satisfy yourself that there is a real practical risk before you take so serious a step as to resign."

Chamberlain smiled again, said he would not do anything rash & then we parted, he asking me at any time I happened to be in the House of Commons to come down to his room to discuss matters with him.

On Tuesday morning (9th March) I called on Lord Spencer. He at once entered upon a discussion of details of land purchase schemes & asked my opinion on several points, for example as to whether I thought a voluntary or a compulsory scheme would be more satisfactory & workable, as to what could be done to deal with the head rents to which landlords' estates in Ireland were frequently subject, as to whether the gross or the nett rent should be taken as the basis for purchase &c. I gave him my views on these several points and I think he was disposed to agree with them. Incidentally he mentioned that as regards his own estates in England he had not got his accounts checked over for 20 years and he found that the average annual deduction from

[334] The speech was delivered at the Music Hall, Edinburgh: *The Times*, 25 November 1885, pp. 11, 12.

his gross rental was 34 per cent, of which only 4 $^3/_4$ per cent was for agency fees, the bulk of the deduction was for money paid for erecting or repairing farm buildings on the estate. The average deduction on Irish estates is only about 15 per cent.

He said that his views as to Home Rule had undergone great changes since he left Ireland & that some two or three months ago, finding that such was the case, he thought it right to send a letter to Sir Robert Hamilton telling him of his altered views & that he did so because he had while in Ireland worked so cordially with Hamilton & their views had always agreed. To his surprise he received a letter in reply from Sir Robert Hamilton which shewed that while his, Lord Spencer's, views had undergone modification, Sir Robert had without any communication with him come round to just the same opinion as Lord Spencer had arrived at.[335]

After a talk of about an hour's duration Lord Spencer asked me to write for him a memorandum on land purchase embodying what I had said to him. I said that I would gladly do so but that it was right he should know I was drawing up a memorandum on the subject for Sir Charles Russell, the Attorney General, which he (Sir C. R.) intended to forward to Mr. Gladstone & that therefore he, Lord Spencer, should not be surprised at the similarity of the views expressed in the two documents.

Late in this day I saw the Attorney General & told him about Lord Spencer's request that I should write the memorandum & the Attorney then said that under these circumstances my best plan would be [to] write the memorandum for Lord Spencer & let him submit it to Mr. Gladstone.[336]

I saw John Morley & told him the result of my interview with Chamberlain & he expressed himself not surprised –

Morley, "I shall tell you now sub sigillo what occurred last evening. Chamberlain tried to pump one after another three subordinate members of the Government to see whether he would be likely to detach them from the ministry if he should resign. His query was, "If Mr. Gladstone should bring in a Home Rule bill what will you do", & it appears that each of the three made the same answer, "I shall stick by Gladstone." I said that my own view is that Chamberlain will not resign & Morley said "I think so too".

[335] See **Document 32**; Spencer to Carnarvon, 5 August 1886: CP, Add MS 60830, fos 60–61.

[336] See Fottrell to Spencer, 10 March 1886: AP, Add MS 77152.

21 March

I prepared the memorandum for Lord Spencer & forwarded it to him on the 11<sup>th</sup> inst. It was a rather elaborate document.[337]

I received from Lord Spencer the following reply,

14 March 86

Dear Mr. Fottrell

I have read over your paper carefully and sent it on to Mr. Gladstone.

I was so busy yesterday that I had not time to read it. It is a valuable paper and tackles several of the most difficult problems.

I shall not now go into it at length. The immediate reduction to the tenant is very large. At the same time you give the Irish Authority a large benefit for 66 years and after that an immense fund.

Your proposals for dealing with Head rents, Crown rents &c. are very well worthy of consideration.

The paper will be very useful and gives a new mode of handling the subject.

There are two others[338] already under discussion.

yours truly
Spencer.

I wrote to John Morley telling him of the memorandum & saying that if it was not [to] be printed for the Cabinet I could let him have a manuscript copy if he wished for one. He replied,

17 March 86

My dear Fottrell

The memo is now in the press.[339] I understand that it has excited much interest in high places. I have told Lord Spencer that you would like a proof of it & will certainly send you one if it be possible.

---

[337] Fottrell listed the fourteen points made in his paper: see 'Confidential. Land Purchase. Memorandum of G.F.', 11 March 1886: GP, Add MS 44632, fos 177–184. For original manuscript, see AP, Add MS 77324, and Fottrell to Spencer, 11 March 1886: AP, Add MS 77152.

[338] For schemes proposed by Chamberlain and Gladstone, see CAB 37/18/22, CAB 37/18/27.

[339] 'Confidential. Ireland. Land Purchase Scheme. Summary of Memorandum dated March 11 1886', 16 March 1886: CAB 37/18/29. See also his 'Confidential. Landed Estates Court. – Report and Memorandum of G.F.', 17 March 1886: AP, Add MS 77324.

We have plenty of trouble on hand & ahead. Hav'nt we?

yours truly
John Morley.

1 April

Chamberlain & Trevelyan's resignations were accepted a few days ago. Chamberlain is replaced by Mr. Stansfield[340] – Trevelyan by Lord Dalhousie.[341]

Gladstone has announced that on the 8th instant he will move for leave to introduce a bill for the future government of Ireland, i.e. the Home Rule Bill & that on the 15th inst. he will move for leave to introduce a bill for land purchase in Ireland, so that not alone has it come to pass that land purchase will not be dealt with in priority to Home Rule, but it has dropped into a secondary place while Home Rule occupies the post of honour. I have been looking over the note which I wrote in this diary on 16 February last as to the relative positions of Home Rule & land purchase as measures to be dealt with promptly & I see that my forecast was not very wide of the mark.

11 April

Poor old Forster, late Chief Secretary for Ireland, died on last Monday. His death has not caused even a ripple on the political waters. It is strange how fast we live. Seven or eight years ago he was a possible Prime Minister. Then in an evil moment for himself he took the post of Irish Chief Secretary. He shewed doggedness &, in my opinion, stupidity in his action as Chief Secretary. He imprisoned Parnell & John Dillon & about 1300 'suspects'[342] or as he called them 'village ruffians' & at the end of about a year England found that the game was not worth the candle, Forster was recalled and in spite of all the predictions that he would ruin the Liberal Government by reason of his recall, he seems poor fellow to have ruined only himself. I have no reason to love him for indeed he did not treat me too well as he, in the House of Commons, to save himself invented a conversation between me & him which never took place, & yet I believe the poor old fellow to have been in the main honest.[343] He was pigheaded &,

---

[340]Sir James Stansfield (1820–1898), Lib. MP for Halifax (1859–1895), President of the Local Government Board (1871–1874, 1886), radical and home ruler.

[341]John William Ramsay (1847–1887), thirteenth Earl of Dalhousie (1874), Lord-in-Waiting in ordinary to Queen Victoria (1880–1885), Secretary of State for Scotland (1886).

[342]Between March 1881 and July 1882, 955 persons were arrested and imprisoned under the Protection of Person and Property (Ireland) Act (44 & 45 Vict., c. 4): Ball, 'Policing the Land War', p. 22.

[343]See appendix, pp. 323–324.

like most Englishmen who come over here, he assumed as an axiom that he knew more about Ireland than any of us who had lived in Ireland during all our lives.

## 15 April

Gladstone on the 8[th] instant introduced his Home Rule Bill.[344] The scene was one of wild excitement. The Irish members arranged on the previous night that in order to make a goodly show of their strength they would go to the House very early in the morning so as to secure seats. They began to arrive at half past five o'clock in the morning and before 9 o'c they had practically all secured their seats. The members of the House number 670, while the House is constructed to accommodate only about 430. The eagerness to secure seats was such that the hitherto unprecedented course was followed of placing chairs on the floor of the House for members.

Gladstone was received outside the House with marvellous enthusiasm. The newspapers state that: Crowd between Downing St and the House of Commons was the largest ever seen & that even the house tops were filled with people. A deafening cheer was raised as Gladstone drove through the mass of people assembled. On his entrance into the House of Commons the Irish members rose en masse and the Liberals caught the contagion & a mighty cheer such as is said was never before heard in St Stephens greeted the veteran statesman who was about to unfold his scheme for conferring legislative freedom upon Ireland. He spoke for 3 hours & 25 minutes and at the end he was fresh as a May morning.[345]

Gladstone was followed by Colonel Waring,[346] one of the rag-tag of the Orange faction, & the contrast afforded by the two men set the House of Commons into a roar of laughter & consequent good humour. Trevelyan spoke against the Bill & unfolded his own plan, which is to establish County Boards in Ireland instead of a Central Legislative body. His speech was rather viperish & it reflected upon Lord Spencer for sticking to the Cabinet. Parnell followed Trevelyan & gave him a very rough handling, contrasting Lord Spencer's dogged pluck in remaining at his post with Trevelyan's pusillanimity in running away from his.[347]

---

[344]Bill to Amend Provision for Future Govt. of Ireland: *PP* 1886, II, 461.

[345]See *Hansard*, CCCIV, cols 1036–1085. Fottrell listed the forty provisions of the bill.

[346]Colonel Thomas Waring (1828–1898), Con. MP for Down North (1885–1898), Grand Master of the Loyal Orange Institute of England (1892–1898); *Hansard*, CCCIV, cols 1085–1089.

[347]Ibid., cols 1104–1134.

Chamberlain moved the adjournment of the debate & on the 9[th] April he spoke. His speech opened badly. He tried in explaining his reasons for leaving the Cabinet to disclose not only what had taken place in the Cabinet in relation to the Home Rule Bill but also what had occurred in relation to the Land Purchase Bill, a bill which had not yet been introduced. Gladstone at once pounced on him & stated that he had no permission from Her Majesty to allow Mr. Chamberlain to divulge Cabinet secrets relating to a bill not yet drawn. Chamberlain was plainly quite put out & his speech was in my opinion a disjointed one. His object was to do as much damage as he could to the Home Rule Bill. His criticisms were in the main a declaration against the removal of Irish members from Westminster, & a declaration that such removal would lead the Irish Legislature to repudiate the obligation of contributions for Imperial purposes provided for by the Bill. So far, he made a tolerably effective speech but he then proceeded to develop his own plan which was certainly a sufficiently comical one. He proposed to pass an act staying all evictions in Ireland for 6 months & thereupon to establish a Commission to enquire into the relations between England & Ireland with a view to further legislation. Meanwhile he proposed to saddle the Irish landlords on the Imperial Treasury for their rents.

There were just a few initial objections to these proposals. First, that the Right Honl. gentleman could not possibly pass through the House of Lords, & probably not through the House of Commons, a bill suspending evictions for 6 months. Secondly, if he did succeed in doing so & in starting his Commission of enquiry that of course no one in Ireland would allow the Commission ever to finish its labours, the Irish landlords would receive their rents from the Imperial Exchequer while the Irish tenants would pay no rents at all.

Healy followed Chamberlain & made an extremely able speech in support of the Bill.

The Marquis of Hartington opposed the Bill with tooth & nail. His argument was that the strict maintenance of law & order was the only panacea for Ireland & that it was most dangerous to concede any extension of local freedom. He said that Gladstone had brought a disaster upon the Empire by bringing forward his Bill because it was now impossible to undo the mischief & Gladstone's scheme would be henceforth the irreducible minimum of the Irish demand.

John Morley followed Hartington & made a strong speech in favour of the Bill. Lord Randolph Churchill opposed the Bill but confined himself to a criticism of details & did not pledge himself against Home Rule.[348] Sir Charles Russell, the Attorney General, supported

---

[348]Ibid., cols 1181–1222, 1238–1278, 1317–1344.

the Bill and in doing so quoted Lord Grey,[349] Charles Fox,[350] & other Whig statesmen of the Union period to shew that the leading Whig politicians of that day were opposed to the Union.[351]

The House was greatly impressed by a speech in favour of the Bill by Mr. Whitbread,[352] a member of the Whig section & who is greatly respected & trusted by the Whigs. His speech was a very able & dignified one.

Sir W. Harcourt, Chancellor of the Exchequer, made a rattling speech which threw great ridicule on the alternative proposals put forward by Trevelyan, Chamberlain & Lord Hartington, all of whom agreed in opposing the Bill but no two of whom agreed as to the scheme which ought to be substituted for that put forward by the Government.[353]

Mr. Goschen bitterly attacked the Government proposals. Sir Mich. Hicks Beach also assailed the Bill but his speech was rather weak.

Gladstone wound up the debate with a speech which it was admitted on all hands was a most brilliant reply and then at five minutes past one o'clock on Wednesday morning the 14 April 1886 the Home Rule Bill for Ireland was read a first time, no division having been challenged on Gladstone's motion for leave to introduce it.[354]

Now I wish to chronicle the state of public opinion which followed Gladstone's speech. For the first two days there was undoubted despondency among Liberals & it was freely said that the Government was certain to be defeated at a very early stage of the Bill. Gradually opinion began to veer round and after a few days the date of the disaster prognosticated for the Government was shifted from the first reading to the second reading of the Bill. Now the date seems to be again adjourned, for most men say it will be carried by a substantial majority. In example, Healy laid me one sovereign to two sovereigns that the Bill will go through its second reading with a majority of 50.

[349]Charles Grey (1764–1845), second Earl Grey (1807), Whig MP for Northumberland (1786–1807), First Lord of the Admiralty (1806), Foreign Secretary (1806–1807), Prime Minister (1831–1834).

[350]Charles James Fox (1749–1806), Whig MP for Midhurst (1768–1780), for Westminster (1780–1783, 1785–1806), and for Kirkwall (1784–1785), a lord of the Treasury (1772–1774), joint Secretary of State (1783), Foreign Secretary (1782, 1806).

[351]*Hansard*, CCCIV, cols 1344–1364. Russell drew particular attention to Chamberlain's views as articulated by Fottrell in the *Fortnightly Review*: *Hansard*, col. 1352.

[352]Samuel Whitbread (1830–1915), Chairman of Whitbread Brewery, Lib. MP for Bedford (1852–1895), home ruler; *Hansard*, CCCIV, cols 1396–1406.

[353]Ibid., cols 1439–1458. Harcourt also forced Chamberlain to admit that he had not written the *Fortnightly Review* article.

[354]Ibid., cols 1458–1482, 1518–1550, and see Bill to make amended provision for Sale and Purchase of Land in Ireland: *PP* 1886, V, 193.

I do not find that many men are so sanguine on the subject as Healy, usually the number spoken of as a probable majority is between 5 & 15.

On Friday the 16[th] April 1886 Gladstone introduced his Land Sales & Purchase Bill in a speech which was considered a more eloquent effort than that which he put forth when introducing the Home Rule Bill.[355] It was mainly a historical retrospect with the object of shewing that England had for centuries bolstered up the system of Irish landlordism, & that therefore she had contracted obligations towards existing landlords in Ireland which she ought to recognise by allowing her credit to be used to raise money for the purpose of buying them out.

He states that the sum to be borrowed on such credit was not without further sanction to exceed 50 millions sterling.

The essence of the Land Bill is that every Irish landlord can compel the Irish State to buy him out, the rate of purchase being usually 20 years' purchase of the nett rent, in some exceptional cases 22 years' purchase of the nett rent, while power is reserved to the Land Commission to reduce these rates if on investigation they consider such rates excessive. On a sale being effected, the tenants are to become owners of their holdings subject to their paying for 49 years instalments, representing four per cent on the purchase money of the gross rent, thus giving them usually a reduction of 20 per cent less by the additional taxes which the tenant as owner would become liable to, while the Irish State would be liable to the Imperial Exchequer for the instalments for 49 years, representing only 4 per cent on the purchase money of the nett rent, so that the Irish State would have a premium of 20 per cent on the annual instalments less by the cost of collection.

In my opinion the Land Purchase Bill is not at all as satisfactory a measure as might have been devised and I find that both John Dillon & E. Dwyer Gray both consider that my plan of making the tenant pay a perpetual, & the Irish State a terminable rent charge of £4 per cent on the purchase money of the nett rent would have been better both for the Irish tenants and for the Irish State.

Sir Robert Hamilton is of the same opinion. I hear that the reason why the Cabinet did not adopt my suggestion was that it was strongly represented to them by certain northern Liberals that the Ulster tenants would very much prefer a system which would at the end of a certain number of years leave them free of rent, even although their immediate reduction of rent might be less.

[355] *Hansard*, CCCIV, cols 1778–1811.

Both Gray and John Dillon consider that the real explanation of Gladstone's plan is that he wants to show that the Irish State will have a good revenue, so as to satisfy Englishmen that the Irish State will fulfil its financial engagements to England. Gray considers that Gladstone's proposed contribution from Ireland to England under the Home Rule Bill is more than Ireland could possibly continue to pay.

John Dillon tells me that Parnell's *mot d'ordre* as regards the Land Purchase Bill is for the Irish party neither to praise nor to condemn it, but to leave it to the Tories to oppose its second reading if they are foolish enough to do so & that then the English politicians of every shade would become disgusted with the unreasonableness of the Irish landlords. I think that this is prudent on Parnell's part.

Dillon also told me that Parnell is quite resolved that either the provision in the Home Rule Bill declaring that no members shall be sent from Ireland to Westminster shall be adhered to, or else that the full present number (103) of Irish members must have seats in the Imperial Parliament, in which case he believes that the struggle in Westminster would continue for 3 or 4 years more & that then Mr. Chamberlain & his friends would insist upon that which they now oppose, viz. the retirement of Irish members from the Imperial Parliament.

Sir Robert Hamilton said to me on yesterday that he believed every day was improving the chances of the Home Rule Bill & that every day was lessening those of the Land Purchase Bill.

27 April

John Morley, the Chief Secretary, came to Dublin this morning and he sent me a letter stating he would wish to see me at the Castle. I went up to him and had an hour's chat. Dr. Patton[356] of the *Daily Express* was with him when I arrived & I waited till he left.

We discussed the Land Purchase Bill of which he asked me my opinion. I told him that I considered it was not in its present shape a workable measure because I had reason to believe that the tenants would not consent to the Irish State deriving such an income as 20 per cent from every purchase & that Dillon & Dwyer Gray took the same view. He admitted that the reason for adopting the line laid down in the Bill was partly information received from the north of Ireland that the Presbyterian farmers would resent being made not proprietors but tenants of the Irish State, & partly because Gladstone wished to show that the Irish state would derive a good revenue from the land. He

---

[356]George Valentine Patton (1836–1898), editor of the Dublin *Daily Express* (1873–1898) and Dublin correspondent for *The Times* (1866–1898).

seemed to think however that if the Bill ever reached the Committee stage it might be altered to my plan.

He considers that the Home Rule Bill will pass not only a second reading but that it will in all probability pass through all its stages in the House of Commons; that it will then go up to the Lords where it will be at once rejected, that then the probable course will be an Autumn Session in which both the Home Rule Bill & the Land Bill both (probably considerably modified) would be again considered & both sent up to the Lords, & if then rejected that a dissolution would most likely take place. All this however he said was problematical as nothing had yet been definitely decided.

We discussed Chamberlain's attitude. He said that all politicians were surprised to find what a small following Chamberlain had. I said it seemed that Chamberlain's probable course would be to concentrate his strength upon opposing the Land Purchase Bill & relax his opposition to the Home Rule Bill. This view, Morley said, he thought would probably prove to be correct.

Morley expects the Home Rule Bill to pass its second reading by a majority of between 20 & 30.

We spoke about the big meeting at Newcastle. He told me that when Lord Spencer saw the dense crowd which filled the building in which the meeting was held, he turned quite pale & was very nervous & turning to Morley that he said "I don't know what to do. This is a scene such as I have never witnessed. I have spoken in the House of Lords & I have spoken at agricultural meetings after a farmers' dinner but I never spoke to a crowd like this & I am quite put out." Morley said "Don't be alarmed Lord Spencer, you will find it far easier to speak to an enthusiastic crowd like this than to address the House of Lords or the House of Commons", & added Morley, "he then went on to the platform & he was cool as a cucumber & spoke with great dignity & self possession. His speech had & will have very great weight."[357]

Morley asked me what answer I would give to several points which Chamberlain had made against the Home Rule Bill & he took note of the answers so as to use them in a speech which he is to deliver in Glasgow on next Friday.[358] He is much more cheery than when I last saw him which is a good omen. He tells me that the brunt of the work preparing the Home Rule & the Land Purchase Bills fell on him & on Gladstone & Lord Spencer. The latter is, he says, a capital man at 'collar work', that he can sit down & work hour after hour. He has a

---

[357] The meeting was held at Newcastle Town Hall on 21 April 1886: *The Times*, 22 April 1886, p. 6.

[358] It was addressed to the National Liberal Federation of Scotland at St Andrew's Hall, Glasgow, on 30 April 1886: *The Times*, 1 May 1886, p. 9.

very high opinion of Lord Spencer's high character & pluck. "Believe me", said he, "it needs a deal more pluck for Lord Spencer to do as he is now doing, setting defiance to all the opinions of his own caste & of his social friends, than it did to run the risk of his life over here from the knife or bullet of the assassin."

## 3rd May

On last Friday morning (30 April 1886) I received from Thomas A. Dickson, formerly MP for Tyrone, a letter stating that Mr. Shaw Lefevre,[359] the newly returned MP for Bradford & formerly Postmaster General in Gladstone's last Administration, had just arrived in Dublin & that he would call on me at my office at 12 o'c.

Both Shaw Lefevre & Dickson came at the appointed hour & we had an hour's conversation mainly about the Home Rule Bill.

Shaw Lefevre's opinion is that a delegation of 20 or 25 members from the Irish Legislature, as suggested by me, would obviate the difficulty raised by many of the radicals to the provision in the Bill which enacts that Ireland shall not send members to Westminster, but he considers that even this delegation should not be sent until the expiration of 5 years & not even then unless the Irish Legislature by a majority decided in favour of sending them. He argues with Mr. Whitbread MP in thinking that both for Ireland & for England it would be better to have a few years of separation during which Irish statesmen could devote all their energies to the work of 'constructing' in Ireland a proper system of government.

He told me with what I regarded as somewhat unusual frankness in a Cabinet Minister of what occurred in the Cabinet in last May & June. For example, he told me that when Gladstone on the 15 May 1885 announced in Parliament the resolve of the Cabinet to reintroduce "some valuable and equitable provisions contained in the Crimes Act" there had not up to that moment been any resolve arrived at, and also that in the division which took place in the Cabinet on the question of whether or not any provisions of the Crimes Act should be renewed all the Peers in the Cabinet voted for the renewal & all the Commoners against.

He thinks that the Land Purchase Bill may pass but that the English people will need to be satisfied that not more than 50 millions will be needed. I suggested that all farms over £100 rental might be excluded from the Act. This would afford some limit.

John Dillon MP spent last Saturday evening (1 May 1886) with me. We discussed the Home Rule & Land Purchase Bills. He approves

---

[359] George Shaw-Lefevre (1831–1928), first Baron Eversley (1906), Lib. MP for Reading (1863–1885) and for Bradford Central (1886–1895), Postmaster-General (1884–1885).

of Shaw Lefevre's suggestion that there should be a period of some years during which no representation of any kind should be sent by Ireland to Westminster. He is not in favour of reducing the number of representatives in the Irish Legislature to 103 of the second order & 50 of the first order. He thinks that the numbers contained in the Home Rule Bill [are] on the whole preferable. At first he was disposed to think that the smaller number would be better, but Wⁱⁱⁱ. O'Brien MP pointed out to him that a House numbering 153 in all would rarely have in attendance more than one half of this number & that with so few a number of members present as 80 or 90 the assembly would scarcely command respect as a deliberative body.

He would not vote for an alteration in the Bill providing for an immediate dissolution on the passing of the Act.

As regards the Land Purchase Bill, he thinks that on the whole the proposal to leave to the Irish Land Commission the power of fixing the price to be paid in every case would be best for the Country.

He would allow Judge O'Hagan[360] & Mr. Litton[361] to continue as Commissioners & even to allow Mr. Lynch & Mr. MacCarthy[362] to continue as such if the Irish party were allowed to nominate 3 others. As two of these three he suggested myself & Thomas A. Dickson.

3 June

The division on the second reading of the Home Rule Bill is now at hand. It may take place tonight or possibly it may not be taken till next week. The debate began on the 10th May. The fluctuations of opinion as to the chances of the Bill passing a second reading have been remarkable. A few days before the debate began Timothy Healy MP took from me a bet of 2 sovereigns to one that the Bill would not pass by a majority of 50. A week after the debate began odds were freely laid that the Bill would not pass a second reading at all. At the end of another ten days or fortnight 5 to 2 were quoted as the odds in favour of the Bill & now its defeat seems almost certain.

At first the Conservative party kept a prudent silence, leaving it to Lord Hartington to lead the opposition to the Bill & egging on Mr. Chamberlain & his following to support Lord Hartington. Suddenly

---

[360]John O'Hagan (1822–1890), Judicial Commissioner of the Irish Land Commission (1881–1889), nationalist poet and supporter of Irish home rule.

[361]Edward Falconer Litton (1827–1890), Lib. MP for Co. Tyrone (1880–1881), land commissioner (1881–1889), Judicial Commissioner of the Irish Land Commission (1889–1890).

[362]John George MacCarthy (1829–1892), Lib. MP for Mallow (1874–1880), sub-commissioner of the Land Act (1881–1885), land purchase commissioner (1885–1892), author of works on Irish history and the land question, advocate of 'tenant-right'.

Lord Salisbury made a pronouncement outside of Parliament shewing that if the Bill were defeated it was the Conservatives & not the Whig or Radical malcontents who would seize the spoils of victory & declaring as the Conservative policy "20 years of firm & resolute government for Ireland" and the deportation of a million of the Irish population to Manitoba.[363]

This pronouncement exercised a damping effect upon the courage of Lord Hartington's followers & more thoroughly damped the ardour of Mr. Chamberlain's supporters, & the prospects of the Bill rose. Lord Hartington objects to the Bill *in toto*. Mr. Chamberlain objects to the provision contained in its 24[th] clause which enacts that Ireland shall not send members to Westminster, rather a strange objection coming from the man who so late as the 12 March regarded the getting rid of the Irish members as the main reason which would induce the English people to consent to Home Rule. Notwithstanding the opposition of Hartington & Chamberlain it seemed very probable that the Bill would pass its second reading, but a couple of days ago a meeting of Chamberlain's followers was held in Committee room no. 15 and Chamberlain had provided himself with a letter from John Bright announcing the intention of that old Tribune of voting against the second reading.[364] The effect of this letter was immediate & striking. Men who had been shivering on the brink of opposition made up their minds to take the plunge when they found that they would have John Bright as a fellow plunger and by a majority of the meeting it was decided that they should vote against the second reading.

June 9

On Monday night, the 7[th] inst., the division took place & the Bill was defeated by a majority of 30. For the second reading there voted 311 including 85 Parnellites. Against it there voted 341 which number included 93 nominal Liberals & radicals. The majority comprised among others Chamberlain, Lord Hartington, Sir Henry James, Trevelyan, Leonard Courtney, Goschen & John Bright.

I saw Sir Robert Hamilton today. He was summoned to London on Saturday last. He told me that he spent Sunday with Mr. Gladstone &

---

[363]On 15 May, Salisbury told the National Union of Conservative Associations at St James's Hall that the effect of sending 'a large proportion of the inhabitants of the congested districts to Manitoba ... would be magical upon the social condition of the Irish people': *The Times*, 17 May 1885, p. 6.

[364]John Bright (1811–1889), Leader of the Anti-Corn Law League (1838–1846), Lib. MP for Durham (1843–1847), for Manchester (1847–1857), and for Birmingham (1858–1885). For Bright's letter to Peter Rylands MP, the Liberal Unionist candidate for Burnley, see *The Times*, 26 June 1886, p. 9.

that the old man was firm as a rock & resolved to budge not an inch but to fight to the bitter end for his plan of Home Rule. Gladstone is thoroughly master of all the details of the Irish question & Sir Robert said that he found he had next to nothing to post the veteran statesman on. Sir Robert was present in the House of Commons during the debate on Monday night. He said he would not for an extra year of life have missed being present. Parnell's speech was in his opinion a masterly statement & he says that if Parnell had spoken a couple of nights sooner he (Sir Robert) believes that the Bill would have passed its second reading. Gladstone's speech was in Sir Robert's opinion a splendid effort. He tells me that Chamberlain looks anything but comfortable. He writhed under Gladstone's contemptuous allusions to him.[365] A dissolution is inevitable. The ministerialists are badly off for money & candidates. Sir Robert mentioned that he could not have believed what bitterness now exists in London 'Society', & all the hangers on of Society are absolutely savage in their denunciation of Gladstone & Home Rule & any man who ventures to support Home Rule is ostracised from London Society life. This I regard as a good sign. It marks the cleavage between classes, & when a measure comes in England to be regarded as 'the people's cause' it is sure to win.

Terrible riots took place last night in Belfast. They read like the Gordon riots. I think that the police in Belfast were not well handled. 150 extra men have been sent down today.[366]

## Dec. 5[th]

I have not written a line in this diary since the day after the defeat of Gladstone's Home Rule and yet I ought to have done so for the events of the past few months have been interesting and highly instructive.

The General election took place in [July] and it resulted in the return of

| Conservatives | / | Gladstonians |
| Liberal Unionists | / | Parnellites[367] |

Gladstone at once resigned and Lord Salisbury took office as Prime Minister. His Chancellor of the Exchequer & leader of the House of Commons being Lord Randolph Churchill while Sir Michael Hicks Beach was relegated to the post of Chief Secretary for Ireland. As soon as the Conservative Government was installed in office a savage

---

[365]*Hansard*, CCCVI, cols 1168–1184, 1215–1240.

[366]For an account of the policing of the riots, see Mark Radford, '"Closely akin to actual warfare": the Belfast Riots of 1886 and the RIC', *History Ireland*, 7, no. 4 (1999), pp. 27–31.

[367]The Conservatives won 317 seats, the Liberal Unionists 77, the Liberals 191, and the Irish Nationalists 85.

onslaught was made in the *Times* and *St James Gazette* on Sir Robert Hamilton and his dismissal or transference from the office of Under Secretary for Ireland was loudly called for.[368] The reason alleged by the *Times* for this attack on Sir Robert was the fact of his having assisted Mr. Gladstone in framing his Home Rule Bill, while the *St James Gazette* put forward as one of their main arguments against him that he was known to be very intimate with me, a fact which that journal stated to be a conclusive proof of his unfitness for the post of Under Secretary for Ireland.[369] Under the circumstances I considered it fairer to Sir Robert to avoid his society for a while at least & during four months I saw him only twice.

Immediately after Gladstone's resignation Parnell came over to Ireland for a few days. I called to see him at Morrison's Hotel[370] and in the course of conversation I said that I thought the Conservative Government would disappoint expectation by working along very quietly in Ireland instead of adopting a retrograde policy or one of an Orange complexion. Parnell replied with his soft voice & quiet smile "my dear sir the Conservative Government cannot govern Ireland without a coercion act", "but", said I, "I feel sure they will try to avoid anything like coercion", to which Parnell's only reply was a still softer tone of voice & a still more pronounced smile as he said "oh they cannot govern Ireland with a coercion act", & from this little conversation I saw that Parnell's game was to render government by the Conservatives without a coercion act an impossibility. He laid his plans with quiet astuteness. He opened the new session, which began immediately on the re-election of the Conservative ministers, by laying great and prolonged stress upon the agricultural depression which undoubtedly existed in Ireland, a depression which rendered the payment of full rents, even of judicial rents almost impossible. He next introduced a bill for staying evictions by referring it to the Land Commission or County Court judges to decide whether or not the tenant was able to pay his full rent this year & if he were proved to be able to pay in full & if he lodged a certain proportion, I think 50

---

[368]Those defending Hamilton included Sir Ralph Lingen, Sir Thomas Farrer, Henry Jephson, and John Morley who, under the signature 'M', argued that, while Hamilton was not the author of the Home Rule Bill, he had been duty-bound to lay opinions formed upon the subject of his daily work before his political chiefs: *The Times*, 27 July 1886, p. 8; Morley to Spencer, 10 August 1886: AP, Add MS 76938. See also *The Times*, 22 July 1886, p. 10; 24 July 1886, p. 9; 29 July 1886, p. 8; 30 July 1886, p. 5; 31 July 1886, p. 5; 4 August 1886, p. 12; 5 August 1886, p. 6; 7 August 1886, p. 10.

[369]Hamilton was accused of having 'taken a leading part in forming the party policy of Mr. Gladstone's Irish Governments': *St. James's Gazette*, 24 July 1886, p. 4; and see 21, 29, and 31 July.

[370]Situated at the junction of Nassau and Dawson Streets, Dublin. Parnell was a regular guest and his party met there frequently to select parliamentary candidates.

[per] cent of the rent due, the tribunal was to have power to stay the eviction on such terms as it should consider reasonable.[371] The bill received the support of Gladstone & the Liberals but it was defeated by the Conservative and Liberal Unionist vote. In the course of the debate on the second reading Sir Michael Hicks Beach threw out some hint of coercion whereupon he was replied to by John Dillon, who made [a] most impassioned speech in which he defied the ministry to do their worst and told them that they had now thrown the tenants of Ireland upon their own resources and that he would go back to Ireland to urge the Irish tenants by their own combination & pluck to win the safety from landlord rapacity & cruelty which the Government had denied them by opposing Parnell's bill. The speech created a most profound impression, Lord Randolph Churchill who sat on the Treasury Bench grew livid with excitement and all the newspapers agreed that the scene was one of the most dramatic ever witnessed in the House.[372]

John Dillon came back to Ireland & forthwith a series of public meetings began at which the inability of the tenants to pay their rents in full was again & again insisted. Meanwhile the Government had appointed General Sir Redvers Buller[373] as a kind of Magisterial Dictator in Kerry so as to put an end to a horrible system of moonlighting outrages which had increased to an intolerable extent. The hopes of the landlord party were high that Buller would pacify Kerry by capturing the moonlighters and thus assist materially in [the] collection of the landlords' rent. Buller drove all over the County, a couple of parties of suspected moonlighters were captured, but soon rumours began to spread among the landlord clubs that, anxious as Buller was to capture moonlighters, he seemed to be almost still more anxious to compel the Kerry landlords to accept reasonable rents for their land instead of exacting their full demand. Gradually the rumours reached the press and it was openly said that Buller had insisted upon having ample notice sent to him whether any landlord required police aid for carrying out evictions, and that on such notice being given the General investigated the facts of the case so as to see whether the rent demanded was reasonable, and if he found that the demand was not fair he plainly told the landlord that no police aid would be given to him to enforce payment of a

[371] Bill for Temporary Relief of Agricultural Tenants in Ireland, and for Admission of Certain Leaseholders to Land Act, 1881: *PP* 1886 (Sess. 2), VI, 3.

[372] *Hansard*, CCCIX, cols 1191–1207, 1223–1247.

[373] Sir Redvers Henry Buller (1839–1908), chief of staff for Khartoum expedition (1884), Special Commissioner for Cork and Kerry (1886), Under-Secretary for Ireland (1886–1887), Commander-in-Chief in South Africa (1899–1900).

rent which the tenant could not afford to pay.[374] These statements caused great alarm among the Irish landlords who opened their eyes with amazement when they found that a revolution was quietly being carried out by the Conservative Government itself, upon which they had relied for protection of all their interests. Their alarm was not lessened when *United Ireland* published what purported to be a portion of a letter written by one of the members of the Royal Commission on the working of the Land Act[375] to a friend of his in England, in which letter it was stated that Buller had given evidence before the Royal Commission and that in this evidence he had lauded the Land League as the sole protection which the unfortunate Kerry tenants had had against oppression, & that in short his evidence was wildly revolutionary.

This announcement appeared in *United Ireland* about three weeks ago.[376] About the same time Sir Robert Hamilton went over to London for a few days and again the abuse of him began in the *Times* & *St James Gazette*, & it was kept up so persistently for several days that it was plain that it was being done to order.[377] On Sir Robert's return I called on him and he then told me that he had been offered & has accepted the post of Governor of Tasmania, a post worth £5000 a year. He regarded the offer as being virtually a dismissal from his office. He was not offered the option of a pension. If he had been offered it, he said, he would have accepted it & would have tried to get into Parliament. Sir Robert admitted that my intimacy with him had been the real cause of his unpopularity with the Conservatives, but he said that if all that he had done with me had to be done again he would pursue exactly the same course as he had followed. He said that it was a strange commentary on the strictures which had been made in relation to his intimacy with me that as soon as the Conservatives had come in to office I was one of the first men whom they had selected for an important post, he referred to the Royal Commission of Enquiry on the working of the Land Act. My connection with the body was as follows.

---

[374] For Buller's service in Ireland, see Geoffrey Powell, *Buller: a scapegoat? A life of Sir Redvers Buller 1839–1908* (London, 1994), pp. 81–96.

[375] The Royal Commission on the Land Law (Ireland) Act, 1881, and the Purchase of Land (Ireland) Act, 1885 was appointed on 29 September 1886. For its reports, see *PP* 1887, XXVI, 1, 25, 1109.

[376] See 'General Buller against the landlords', *United Ireland* , 20 November 1886, p. 2.

[377] It was claimed that Hamilton's 'speedy departure from the Castle is indispensable to the restoration of "social order" in Ireland': *St. James's Gazette*, 18 November 1886, pp. 3–4. See also *The Times*, 18 November 1886, p. 9; 20 November 1886, p. 11; 23 November 1886, p. 6.

In August last I went for my vacation trip to Bavaria & Lord Ashbourne, the Lord Chancellor, hearing that I was at Innsbruck addressed a letter to me there asking me to accept the post of Royal Commissioner on the Commission above named. I did not receive this letter and on my return to Ireland early in September I was met at the landing pier by Dunbar Barton[378] (Lord Ashbourne's private secretary) who handed me a letter from Lord Ashbourne enclosing a copy of the former letter written about a fortnight before and urging me to accept the post of Commissioner. I went to the Castle next day & on Lord Ashbourne's assurance that the Commission would not occupy much of my time I accepted the post.

My colleagues on the Commission were shortly after nominated & their names were announced in the House of Commons as follows,

Lord Cowper[379]      J. Chute Neligan QC[380]
Sir James Caird[381]     & Lord Miltown[382]

As a matter of fact I did not act upon the Commission because my brother[383] having fallen ill, & Lord Cowper having written to me to say that the sittings of the Commission would be continuous, and the nationalists having shewn unmistakeable signs of boycotting the Commission, I found it necessary for me to resign & I accordingly did so.[384]

Sir Robert Hamilton in reply to an enquiry of mine said that he would not leave Ireland until next spring.

A few days after this interview the Irish public were mystified by the extraordinary announcement that General Sir Redvers Buller had

---

[378]Dunbar Plunket Barton (1853–1937), private secretary to Lord Ashbourne (1885–1886), justice of King's Bench and Chancery, Ireland (1900–1918).

[379]Francis Thomas de Grey (1834–1905), seventh Earl Cowper (1856), Lord Lieutenant of Ireland (1880–1882), Chairman of the Royal Commission on Irish Land Legislation (1886), opponent of home rule.

[380]John Chute Neligan (1826–1911), county court judge for King's County (1882–1890), recorder of the cities of Londonderry and Cork (1890–1908).

[381]Sir James Key Caird (1837–1916), entrepreneur and philanthropist, owner of the Ashton and Craigie jute mills near Dundee.

[382]Edward Nugent (1835–1890), sixth Earl of Milltown (1871), Lord Lieutenant of Co. Wicklow, owner of land in counties Wicklow, Queens, Kings, Dublin, and Tipperary.

[383]John George Fottrell (1857–1940), crown and state solicitor for Co. Meath (c.1904–1935) and co-author, with his brother, of several publications on land law.

[384]See The Times, 1 October 1886, p. 7; 4 October 1886, p. 6; and John J. Clancy, Six Months of 'Unionist' Rule (London, 1887), pp. 36–37.

been appointed Under Secretary for Ireland.[385] Surprise was expressed on all sides at this announcement. The national press bandied the Government on their selection of a man whose opinions were more pronounced against Irish landlords than Sir Robert's had ever been, & the Conservative press, *Daily Express* &c., seemed shamefaced & unable to give any plausible explanation of why Redvers Buller was to be Under Secy.[386]

Either of two explanations must I think be correct. Either the Government, not knowing how to get Redvers Buller out of Kerry, has adopted this course of temporarily putting him into office as Under Secy., or else, feeling that the only chance of the Conservatives keeping in office is the avoidance of coercion & that the only chance of the avoidance of coercion is official repression of the landlords, the ministers have put Buller into office in the hope that he will frighten the Irish landlords into mitigating their demands.

John Dillon has been served with a summons to appear before the Court of Queen's Bench under the Act of Edward the 3rd to give bail for his good behaviour.[387]

This is in consequence of his proceedings under the *United Ireland* 'Plan of Campaign'. As this plan is likely to be historic I may as well shortly describe what it is. It appeared in *United Ireland* about three weeks ago.[388] Its authors are Timothy Harrington MP & William O'Brien MP. The object is to enable tenants to whom their landlords refuse a reasonable abatement of rent to combine together to defeat any proceedings which the landlords may adopt against the tenant or any of them. Under the plan the tenants would meet together & resolve first upon what percentage of reduction it would be fair to demand. This being done, if the demand be acceded to well & good, the tenants pay. If the reduction be refused the tenants again meet & appoint a managing Committee from among themselves & they then arrange to pay to some one or two trusted persons the amount of their rent less by the reduction demanded & this money, when collected, is then handed by the one or two persons who collected it to some person unknown to the tenants & unknown to any one save to the person so handing it over. The money so collected is then available for the support of any tenant whom the landlord may seek to evict

[385]See *The Times*, 30 November 1886, p. 6.

[386]See *FJ*, 1 December 1886, pp. 4–5.

[387]34 Ed. III, c. 1. Normally used to deal with vagrancy, this statute enabled the Crown to prosecute defendants without need of complainant or opportunity of appeal. It was revived, after a lapse of 300 years, for use against political agitators in 1883: Thomas Gerrard to William Lane Joynt (Crown and Treasury Solicitor), 30 March 1883: CSO RP 1883/11555.

[388]See *United Ireland*, 23 October 1886, repr. Laurence Geary, *The Plan of Campaign, 1886–1891* (Cork, 1986), pp. 144–150.

and it will not be paid to the landlord until he comes to terms with the tenant, & if any tenant behind the back of the others pays his rent to his landlord he forfeits at once all right to the contribution which he made to the tenants' collected fund.

John Dillon had under this plan collected rents on Lord Clanrickarde's estate & on Lord Dillon's estate. The plan has been put in operation on several other estates, among others on the Ponsonby estate in the County of Cork.[389] The adoption of the plan threw the Cork Property Defence Association[390] into a panic & they promptly called upon Captain Plunkett, the Divisional Magistrate in Cork, to arrest Mr. Lane MP[391] while actually collecting the rents on the Ponsonby estate. Captain Plunkett was too cautious to accede to this request but he sent a memorandum up to the Castle stating the particulars of the case & asking for the opinion of Mr. Hugh Holmes,[392] the Attorney General. The opinion given was as follows,

"There is a mode by which the landlord might get hold of the money which of course is not a matter for the Government; & I dare say the landlord will have good advice. I do not see how any action can be taken by the Executive.

Hugh Holmes<br>Attorney General"

This opinion was by some mysterious means conveyed to the Editor of *United Ireland* who published it in the issue of the paper dated yesterday and the result is consternation.[393] The publication must embarrass the ministry terribly because the opinion practically cuts the ground from under their feet in relation to the seizure of *United Ireland*, which John Dillon assures me was certainly determined on in Dublin Castle early in last week.[394] The National League seem to know almost as soon as

---

[389]The Marquis of Clanricarde owned 56,826 acres at Portumna, Co. Galway; Viscount Dillon owned 83,749 acres in County Mayo; and Charles Talbot-Ponsonby held 10,367 acres near Youghal, Co. Cork.

[390]The Cork Defence Union was established in October 1885, under the presidency of the Earl of Bandon, to assist landowners, merchants, farmers, and labourers boycotted by the National League.

[391]William John Lane (b. 1849), Nat. MP for Cork East (1885–1892), trustee of Cork Savings' Bank.

[392]Hugh Holmes (1840–1916), Con. MP for Dublin University (1885–1887), Solicitor- and Attorney-General for Ireland (1878–1880, 1885–1886, 1886–1887), justice of Common Pleas and Queen's Bench, and Lord Justice of Appeal for Ireland (1887–1915).

[393]See *United Ireland*, 4 December 1886, p. 5.

[394]In fact, the Chief Secretary, on the advice of his law officers, abandoned the idea of prosecuting *United Ireland* for publishing the Plan of Campaign: Hicks Beach to Salisbury, 30 November 1886: SAP, D2445, PCC/31.

the Law Officers themselves everything which transpires in the secret councils at Dublin Castle.

Friday Dec. 17.

On last Thursday I had a farewell dinner for Sir Robert Hamilton. He, the Most Rev. Dr. Donnelly, E.D. Gray MP, Mr. Commissioner Lynch & others were present. Sir Robert devoted most of his time to an earnest talk with Gray. On last Monday I met Sir Robert at dinner at Father Healy's of Little Bray,[395] and in the course of a conversation which I had with him on our way up from the train he told me that in his opinion Sir Redvers Buller was not an advocate for Home Rule, but that his (Sir Redvers Buller's) view was that the Irish people had hitherto seen the law used altogether in favour of the landlords & that consequently they were disaffected, but that if they could once realise that the law would not be put in force to aid bad landlords in cruel oppression the Irish people would come to have not alone a respect for the law but also an indifference towards Home Rule. I laughed at this estimate of the Irish situation & Sir Robert agreed that it was a very shallow one. At Father Healy's was Mr. John Mulhall,[396] the private secretary of Lord Londonderry,[397] the Lord Lieutenant. Mr. Mulhall was introduced to me by Sir Robert Hamilton & we had a friendly chat on our way home & in the course of it he promised to introduce me to Sir Redvers Buller.

On last Tuesday I dined at the house of Samuel Walker QC, formerly Attorney General for Ireland under the Gladstone Government. Sir Robert Hamilton was present & among others Thos. A. Dickson, formerly MP for Tyrone. In the course of the evening I remarked to Sir Robert that I thought Sir George Otto Trevelyan had shewn a great want of foresight when he did not avail himself of Sir Robert's practical dismissal from the Under Secretaryship to sever his connection with the Liberal Unionists, because as Trevelyan had brought Sir Robert over from the Admiralty to Ireland & as they were most intimate friends & connections, the bad treatment of Sir Robert would have enabled Trevelyan to pose as a chivalrous man in resenting that treatment & making it an excuse for abandoning his

---

[395]Rev. James Healy (1824–1894), curate and administrator of Bray (1858–1893), parish priest of Ballybrack (1893), member of the FitzGibbon–Churchill circle: Foster, *Lord Randolph Churchill*, p. 42, and see W.J. Fitzpatrick, *Memories of Father Healy of Little Bray* (3rd edition, London, 1898).

[396]John Mulhall (b. 1856), private secretary to Lord Londonderry and the Earl of Zetland (1886–1892), Vice-Chairman of the General Prisons Board (1892–1912).

[397]Charles Stewart Vane-Tempest-Stewart (1852–1915), sixth Marquess of Londonderry (1884), Con. MP for Co. Down (1878–1884), Lord Lieutenant of Ireland (1886–1889), Chairman of the Ulster Unionist Council (1912–1914).

untenable position as a Liberal Unionist. Sir Robert then told me that Trevelyan had not written him one single line for several months past & had not sent any message of sympathy or any expression of regret or resentment at the treatment which he, Sir Robert, had met with. He also said that he was aware that Sir George Trevelyan did feel that the Liberal Unionists were fighting a losing game.

Dickson came to me to tell me that Mr. Knipe,[398] the tenant farmer who had been put on the Royal Commission in my place, had been with him (Dickson) & had said that he was very anxious to draw a separate report & had asked Dickson for help to do it. Dickson evidently wanted me to draw it, but I said I not alone could not draw it but that I could not even give any hints about it unless I saw the evidence. Dickson promised to get me the evidence.[399] Dickson also told me that he had been examined the day before by the Royal Commission & that in the course of the examination Lord Cowper, the Chairman, asked him would it not be a good plan to enact that in every proceeding for ejectment the judge should be bound to enquire into the ability of the tenant to pay the rent sued for, & that a decree in ejectment should not be granted if it was proved that the tenant was unable to pay.[400] I smiled & asked how this differed from Mr. Parnell's Bill, which Lord Cowper's friends had aided in rejecting. Dickson said that Lord Cowper & the other Royal Commissioners seemed quite to admit that the judicial rents of 1881 & 1882 could not possibly be maintained.

On the morning of Wednesday the 15 Dec. 86 I saw Sir Robert Hamilton at the North Wall & bid [sic] him goodbye on his leaving Ireland. No one was there to see him off except Harrel,[401] the Commissioner of the Metropolitan Police, Reed, the Inspector General of the Constabulary, Sir William Kaye,[402] Assistant Under Secretary, & myself.

---

[398]A Presbyterian farmer holding 500 acres at Ballaghy, Co. Armagh: *The Times*, 4 October 1886, p. 6.

[399]Dissenting from the Commission's findings, Knipe recommended that the Land Commission be empowered to lower rents: Report by Mr. Thomas Knipe on the Land Law Act 1881, and the Purchase of Land Act 1885: *PP* 1887, XXVI, 1241.

[400]See *PP* 1887, XXVI, 25, pp. 906–910.

[401]David Harrel (1841–1939), RIC officer (1859–1879), RM for Co. Mayo (1879–1883), Chief Commissioner of the Dublin Metropolitan Police (1883–1893), Under-Secretary for Ireland (1893–1902).

[402]Sir William Squire Baker Kaye (1831–1901), Assistant Under-Secretary for Ireland (1878–1895), private secretary to the Lord Lieutenant of Ireland (1895–1900).

On Wednesday morning John Dillon MP dined with me and we had a chat about the Plan of Campaign. He told me that he & his staff had collected already about £7000, & that he expected to collect altogether about £20000 which he thought would be enough to enable the Irish party to fight the battle of the tenants. His belief is that when the English people come to realise the enormous expense, trouble & disgrace involved in a contest to enable a man like Lord Clanrickarde[403] to screw impossible rents out of his tenantry they will speedily throw Lord Clanrickarde & his like overboard & will insist upon some settlement being come to. John Dillon told me he was going down on the following morning to Loughrea to continue the rent collection on Lord Clanrickarde's estate.

On yesterday (Thursday) morning I went down to Newcastle West, Co. Limerick to meet Lord Devon's[404] tenants in order to see if I could arrange terms of sale. I travelled home by the night train & on arriving home at 5 am I learned that John Dillon had been arrested in Loughrea during the day.[405] It appears that the magistrate there granted a warrant for his arrest on the charge of conspiracy. I should have mentioned that on last Saturday John Dillon's case was resumed before the Court of Queen's Bench & in the course of the proceedings the Attorney General (Holmes) stated that the Plan of Campaign was distinctly a conspiracy, & the Judges (Judge O'Brien[406] & Judge Johnson[407]) in pronouncing judgement & ordering John Dillon to find bail himself in £1000 & two sureties in £500 each for his good behaviour likewise said that the plan was a conspiracy.

In Loughrea John Dillon was collecting rents along with Mr. Matthew Harris MP,[408] Wm. O'Brien & Mr. Sheehy MP[409] when the police broke into the house, seized all the books & money (about £100) which John Dillon had before him, [and] marched all the aforesaid

---

[403]Hubert George de Burgh-Canning (1832–1916), second Marquess of Clanricarde (1874), Con. MP for Co. Galway (1867–1871).

[404]William Reginald Courtenay (1807–1888), eleventh Earl of Devon (1849), Con. MP for Devon South (1841–1849), Chancellor of the Duchy of Lancaster (1866–1867), owner of 33,026 acres in Co. Limerick.

[405]See *The Times*, 17 December 1886, p. 5.

[406]William O'Brien (1832–1899), justice of Common Pleas and Queen's Bench, Ireland (1882–1899).

[407]William Moore Johnson (1828–1918), Lib. MP for Mallow (1880–1883), Solicitor- and Attorney-General for Ireland (1880–1881, 1881–1883), justice of Queen's Bench, Ireland (1883–1909).

[408]Matthew Harris (1826–1890), Land League organizer, representative for Connaught on Supreme Council of the IRB (1878), Nat. MP for Galway East (1885–1890).

[409]David Sheehy (1844–1932), Nat. MP for Galway South (1885–1900) and for Waterford city (1903–1918).

gentlemen before a magistrate who remanded them for a week taking bail for each in £100 for himself & two sureties of £50 each.

On this morning I saw John Dillon in bed. He came up last night. On his way to the train he was thrown from his car & he has severely bruised his side so that he must rest for a couple of days.[410]

I asked what would he & his friends now do & he told me in confidence that if they could not collect the rents openly they would do it by sending collectors round quietly to the tenants' houses.

Dec. 25.

A day or two after I had seen John Dillon, he & his co-defendants were served with a summons to appear before the magistrates at Dublin to answer for their conduct & simultaneously, or immediately after, they were served with a notice by Sub Inspector Davis[411] (their Loughrea prosecutor) that he would not proceed any further with his prosecution. I saw John Dillon on the evening of notice being served on him & he told me that he had not made up his mind which course he & his friends would pursue, but that his belief was that they would go down to Loughrea on the day named in the remand (which by a curious piece of stupidity on behalf of the Crown was the same day as that named in the Dublin summons) and demand a dismissal of the Loughrea proceedings or a prosecution of them.

On Thursday last, accordingly, the proceedings at the Police Court in Dublin ended in a fiasco because the Defendants did not appear & Mr. Healy, Counsel for one of them, mentioned that the charge being one of conspiracy, & therefore the evidence against one Deft being evidence against all, it would be singularly inconvenient to go on with the case in the absence of some of the Defts. who were in Loughrea. Accordingly the Dublin proceedings were adjourned for a week.

Meanwhile Dillon, O'Brien & Harris had gone down to Loughrea & a message had been sent to the supposed national magistrates to attend the Loughrea bench. Col. Nolan MP[412] & Mr. McDonagh attended, & Mr. Radford & Mr. Townsend,[413] representing the other side of politics. Nolan, who was Chairman of the Bench by virtue of seniority, seems to have acted rather weakly. The Bench were evenly divided as to whether the case should be entered as 'dismissed' or as 'no rule' & therefore the ruling entered was "no rule the prosecution being withdrawn",

[410] See *The Times*, 17 December 1886, p. 5.

[411] William Davis (b. 1834), RIC District Inspector for Loughrea.

[412] Colonel John Philip Nolan (1838–1912), Nat. MP for Co. Galway (1872, 1874–1885) and for Galway North (1885–1895, 1900–1906).

[413] Norman Lionel Townsend (b. 1846), Sub-Inspector of RIC (1866–1886), RM (1886–1911).

but on an application being made for an order to restore to Dillon the money & book seized Nolan alleged that the Court had no jurisdiction & refused to make any order.[414] I am not much of a lawyer but I should have supposed that the money & book having been ostensibly seized as evidence for a prosecution which was withdrawn, he ought to have decided that on the withdrawal the money &c. should be restored to the persons from whom they had been taken.

One the same day a thunderbolt fell in the political world. Lord Randolph Churchill resigned his post as Chancellor of the Exchequer. Of course, the surmises as to his reasons were various. The alleged reason was his inability as Chancellor to acquiesce in certain large increases of expenditure on the army & navy which were demanded by Lord George Hamilton[415] on behalf of the navy & by W.H. Smith on behalf of the army. The general impression is that he resigned partly because he could not get the Cabinet to agree in putting forward a tolerably democratic scheme of County government & partly because he did not like the Irish outlook.[416] I had a letter today from Mr. Labouchere MP[417] in which he says that the opinion in London is that Lord Hartington will now join the ministry, or failing him that Mr. Goschen will be put forward.

On the day of the announcement of Lord Randolph's resignation Chamberlain made a speech in Birmingham which I think evidences a decision on his part to get back into the Liberal ranks.[418] It said that he & his friends were agreed with the Liberals on 99 per cent of their programme.

1887

Jany. 3.

On Christmas Eve my Father met with an accident to which I did not at the moment attach so much importance as I ought to have

---

[414] See *The Times*, 18 December 1886, p. 6; 21 December 1886, p. 6; 24 December 1886, p. 4.

[415] Lord George Francis Hamilton (1845–1927), Con. MP for Middlesex (1868–1885) and for Ealing (1885–1906), First Lord of the Admiralty (1885–1886, 1886–1892), Secretary of State for India (1895–1903).

[416] See Foster, *Lord Randolph Churchill*, pp. 301–310.

[417] Henry Du Pré Labouchere (1831–1912), Lib. MP for Northampton (1880–1906), proprietor of *Truth*, radical reformer and home ruler. Earlier, Labouchere had transmitted news of Gladstone's position on home rule to Churchill, as revealed to him in a recent letter from 'go-between' (presumably Fottrell): Labouchere to Churchill, 1 January 1886: RCHL, 1/11. 1238.

[418] Chamberlain addressed a private meeting of the Liberal Divisional Council of West Birmingham on 23 December 1886: *The Times*, 24 December 1886, p. 4.

done but which has since developed very seriously. He was thrown down by a car in Sackville St and his forehead was cut across. For a few days he shewed no serious symptoms but for the last two days he has been delirious & his condition is critical. I had arranged to be in London on Monday morning the 27 Dec. but in consequence of my father's accident I delayed leaving Dublin until that evening, when the Doctors told me that I might safely go without apprehension of any bad result during my absence.[419]

On Tuesday morning the 28[th] Dec. I called at Gardiner Place, by appointment, on Lord Stanhope[420] (whose estate I was engaged in selling to his tenants) so that he might execute the conveyances to complete the sale. I did not remember ever having met Lord Stanhope before but he reminded me that he had been a member of the House of Lords Committee in 1882 which sat to enquire into the working of the Land Act of 1881 & before which Committee I was examined.[421]

I chatted with him on various topics, political and other, but I could not gather from him that he knew anything more of political prospects than what we all knew. His brother, the Hon. Edward Stanhope MP,[422] is the Colonial Secretary & a member of the Cabinet. Lord Stanhope asked me to call on his brother who is also his trustee & who was up in London on that day attending the Cabinet Council which had been summoned to consider what the ministry should do consequent upon the resignation of Lord Randolph Churchill. Unfortunately, when I called at the Colonial Office Mr. Stanhope had gone to his County seat & therefore I had no chance of learning his views.

On Wednesday the 29 Dec John Morley, Sir Robert Hamilton, Mr. Labouchere MP, Captain Waldron[423] & young Charles Russell dined with me at the National Liberal Club. Labouchere was in his most entertaining mood. He is I think almost the best if not the very best dinner companion I have ever met. He is almost more exhilarating in this capacity than poor Isaac Butt,[424] than whom it would be impossible to name a more genial companion. Butt of course

---

[419]See *FJ*, 28 December 1886, p. 6.

[420]Arthur Philip Stanhope (1838–1905), sixth Earl Stanhope (1875), Con. MP for Nottingham (1860–1866), owner of 2,129 acres in Queen's County.

[421]Land Law (Ireland): First Report from the Select Committee of the House of Lords: *PP* 1882, XI, 1. For Fottrell's evidence (24 March 1882), see pp. 219–264, and for his report as solicitor to the Land Commission (11 February 1882), see pp. 441–448.

[422]Edward Stanhope (1840–1893), Con. MP for Mid-Lincolnshire (1874–1885) and for Lincolnshire, Horncastle Division (1885–1893), President of the Board of Trade (1885–1886), Secretary of State for the Colonies (1886) and for War (1887–1892).

[423]Francis Waldron (1853–1932), captain of Royal Artillery, brother of Laurence Waldron.

[424]Isaac Butt (1813–1879), Con./Lib. MP for Youghal (1852–1865), Nat. MP for Limerick (1871–1879), founder of the Home Government Association (1870) and the Home Rule League (1873).

was infinitely a greater man & gave vastly more information in his sallies of humour than Labouchere could contribute, but the cynical playfulness of Labouchere it would be hard to beat. For four hours he kept us all in a roar of merriment. With him no man is sacred. He would scalp his grandmother for the sake of a joke & yet it would be unjust to say that he is hard hearted or cruel. Indeed, he jokes at himself as much as he does at other people. Some of his stories about the election for Windsor, for which place he was years ago returned as member & after which election he was by an Election Committee of the House of Commons unseated for bribery, made Hamilton stare in dazed amazement. Hamilton takes a serious view of life & it was most amusing to watch his perplexity while Labouchere rattled away in the most audacious fashion telling how he bribed & how he cajoled electors first, & how he endeavoured afterwards to cajole the Commons Committee.[425] Of course, Labouchere if his statements about himself were to be taken as *grand serieux* would be worthy of the dock, but as was truly said of him by a newspaper correspondent (I think T.P. O'Connor MP) some time ago he takes more pains to make himself out infinitely worse than he is, than most men take to make themselves appear better than they are. In truth, he is a very strong, earnest politician keenly anxious for the triumph of radical principles of government & anxious to improve the condition of the people, but to listen to himself one would suppose he was a mere 'flaneur'. Some of his descriptions struck me as very racy. Waldron, *à propos* of some mention of the Duke of Marlborough[426] asked him – "Is not the Duke a clever man". "Yes", said Labouchere, "very clever & a charming fellow. I have known him & Randolph since they were boys & they are both charming fellows – very interesting – they are among my dearest friends – they are both members of the criminal classes – I mean that if one did not happen to be a Duke & the other a leading statesman they would be picking pockets at the corner of a street".

He described the scene in the House of Commons in 1881 when the Gladstone ministry was engaged in passing the Coercion Bill for Ireland – "Harcourt & Parnell gave me great pleasure at that time. Parnell thought that Harcourt would lock him up in prison & Harcourt thought that Parnell's friends would blow him (Harcourt) up with dynamite. Parnell used to ask me with a long face whether I thought the Government really meant to pounce on him when the Bill would have passed, & Harcourt used to enquire eagerly whether I really thought there was a danger of a dynamite attack on himself

---

[425]Labouchere was elected on 12 July 1865 but unseated by a committee of the House of Commons on 25 April 1866: *The Times*, 13 July 1865, p. 10; 26 April 1866, p. 7.

[426]George Charles Spencer-Churchill (1844–1892), eighth Duke of Marlborough (1883).

personally. I used to say 'thank God another 24 hours have passed without any fresh outrage I really thought there would have been worse work before now', & when Harcourt one day asked me home to dine with him I said 'oh no my dear Sir William I am much obliged but I really should be afraid that your cellar may be filled up with dynamite'. Harcourt got such a fright at that time that if he were now to waver in his new born faith in Home Rule I believe that the explosion of a cracker would promptly bring him to heel".[427]

Turning to more serious conversation, I found that Labouchere very strongly urged upon Morley that the Liberals, leaders & followers, should not alone drop the land purchase scheme for Ireland, but that they should go for Home Rule alone as the work of the next Parliament, & pledge themselves not to use Tory votes to carry a purchase scheme until after the passage of a Home Rule bill [or] a new Parliament should have been summoned.

Morley did not express a decided opinion, nor did any of the rest of us & when Morley had gone Labouchere came up to me to have a few private words with me & he urged me very strongly to use my influence with Morley to get him to fall in with the opinion which he, Labouchere, had expressed. He said, "if you can bring Morley round don't be afraid, we shall get the old man (Gladstone) to go for the plan. He will throw Catherine in", some slang expression which I had never heard before,[428] but the plain meaning was that Gladstone would be able & willing to shew that he was not bound by any declaration of his to couple land purchase & Home Rule together.

On yesterday I wrote [to] Morley urging him not to pledge himself as Labouchere suggested, but simply to allow land purchase to fade gradually out of the Liberal programme – to go straight for Home Rule & to allow all the pressure in favour of a purchase scheme to come from the Tories or from their Liberal Unionist allies.

On Thursday the 30 Dec. I saw Mr. Stead,[429] the Editor of the *Pall Mall Gazette* & remained with him for some quarter of an hour or so. He told me with a great air of mystery that since he had seen me in Dublin Parnell had sent for him & that in his interview he (Stead) had mentioned that Captain O'Shea had called on him a few days previously & had told him that he (O'Shea) had discovered among his letters a couple of letters from Parnell in which Parnell acknowledged that he was the originator of Chamberlain's

---

[427]'Was there ever', Labouchere asked Churchill, 'such a timorous Jumbo?': Labouchere to Churchill, 23 December 1885: RCHL 1/10. 1199.

[428]Presumably a reference to Gladstone's wife, Catherine.

[429]William Thomas Stead (1849–1912), editor of the *Pall Mall Gazette* (1883–1890), founder of the *Review of Reviews* (1890).

'National Council Scheme', which I had developed for Chamberlain in the *Fortnightly Review*. He said that Parnell replied there were no letters of his he was afraid of even although they had been given to Chamberlain, that it was quite true he, Parnell, had in starting the National League in 1881 shadowed forth such a Council, but that he never intended it as a substitute for a legislative assembly.[430] I incidentally mentioned that Chamberlain in speaking to me had distinctly told me he had in writing Parnell's approval of the 'heads' which Chamberlain, or rather Escott had given me as the basis of the article which I was asked to write. To my astonishment I found in the *Pall Mall Gazette* of the 1st inst. the statement on the opposite page.[431]

Mr. Goschen has accepted the post of Chancellor of the Exchequer under Lord Salisbury.

It was announced in Saturday's (1 Jany. 87) evening papers that Morley had had an interview with Chamberlain on the previous day at the Devonshire Club & had then gone together to the Lyceum Theatre to see Henry Irving in Faust.[432] I wrote in my letter to Morley asking what the meeting portends the more especially as it is stated that a conference is to take place between Morley, Chamberlain, Harcourt, Lord Herschell[433] & Trevelyan.

Jany. 6

I received a letter today from John Morley in which he says "I am much obliged for your letter & will lay it to heart all the more as I was already of the same mind. Be sure that there is not the slightest fear of my selling the fort. I wish you could find time to jot down ever so roughly any points which you think might be useful to me in our disputation with the opponents of next week."

Jany. 7

On this morning at a quarter to 12 o'c. noon my poor father breathed his last. God rest his soul. A more kindly, innocent, unselfish man never breathed. He had not an enemy in the world.[434]

[430] The Irish National League was founded on 17 October 1882.

[431] Cutting inserted into journal: see *PMG*, 1 January 1887, p. 8.

[432] Sir Henry Irving (1838–1905), actor credited with reviving popular interest in the plays of Shakespeare; during 1885–1887 he appeared as Mephistopheles in Wills's *Faust*. See also *PMG*, 1 January 1887, p. 3.

[433] Sir Farrer Herschell (1837–1889), first Baron Herschell (1886), Lib. MP for Durham city (1874–1885), Solicitor-General (1880–1885), Lord Chancellor (1886).

[434] See *FJ*, 8 January 1887, p. 4. Following an inquest, the car driver responsible for the incident was charged with manslaughter: *FJ*, 10 January 1887, p. 2; 15 January 1887, p. 6.

Jany. 24

Monday

On last Friday I got a sudden summons to London on business connected with the sale of a large Irish estate. I let John Morley know that I was going over & he asked me to go to him to lunch to have a quiet chat alone on the political situation.

I was with him on last Saturday for a couple of hours. I did not point blank ask him the result of the 'round table conference' nor did he in turn mention the result, but it was plain from his observations & from his questions that the result might be summed up by saying that Chamberlain had seen the error of his ways & that he would by successive & gradual feats of oratorical gymnastics get back into the Gladstone fold & show that in doing so he had all along been consistent.

Chamberlain was the first to make overtures for the meeting of himself & Morley at the Devonshire Club. Morley at first refused the meeting but Chamberlain asked him to go to the Lyceum Theatre with him & Morley fought shy of this proposal but yielded after a while.[435] He has since received many letters from Liberals abusing him for going so ostentatiously with Chamberlain.

Morley asked me a number of questions as to my opinion on certain points, always saying "remember I don't say that the suggestion which I put before you is my own or whether it is not".

For example, he asked me did I believe it possible to frame a scheme of purchase from Irish landlords which would be compulsory & which would not involve pledging Imperial credit. I replied "certainly not". A successful scheme of purchase involves a reduction in the annual sum payable by Irish tenants. A reduction in such sum involves either the borrowing of money on cheap terms or the purchase on the basis of a small number of years' purchase of the rental. If the Irish bonds in which the Irish landlord is to be compelled to accept payment be bonds bearing a low rate of interest, say 3 or $3^1/_2$ per cent, they will not stand at par & therefore the landlord will be paid in a depreciated currency, if on the other hand they bear interest at a rate which will secure that the bonds shall stand at par then the tenant cannot get a reduction in his annual payment unless the purchase be at a very low number of years of the rental.

---

[435] Morley informed Spencer that Chamberlain had pressed Hartington to join them but the latter declined, fearing that his presence might kindle distrust in the Conservative Party: Morley to Spencer, 1 January 1887: AP, Add MS 76938; and see Michael Hurst, *Joseph Chamberlain and Liberal Reunion: the Round Table Conference of 1887* (London, 1967), pp. 152–156.

# DOCUMENTS AND CORRESPONDENCE

**1.** E.G. Jenkinson to Lord Spencer, 18 April 1884; 'Secret'; AP, Add MS 77033.

I am very glad Your Excellency is coming over to England.

I am much disappointed about Col: Butler.[1] He has wasted all his time in Canada. He wrote last from Ottawa under date 30[th] March, and up to that time had not succeeded in finding any one for our work. He was then going to start for New York, and intended to sail on the 12[th] April in the "Alaska" – so that we may expect him back next week! New York is by far the most important place, and yet he gives only a few days to it. But it will be fairer to judge of him when we hear what he has to say.[2] Meanwhile I am not entirely dependent on him, for since his departure I have sent out an agent to New York who will, I hope, be of great use. Mr Hoare[3] too is doing fairly well.

I have heard from Chicago that at the late Convention of the V.C. (United Brotherhood)[4] the delegates received private instructions from the Executive (F.C.) to pick out & recommend to the F.C. men able to be sent off for active work at a moments notice – a determined effort is to be made before June to leave a mark which will redound to the credit of the present administration. The exact secret instructions issued to the Chief officers of the V.C. organization are "To diligently enquire without informing the parties or any one else the names & addresses of the men best fitted for private work of a conf[dl] & dangerous character". So that there can be no doubt, the V.C. are going in for Dynamite work. If we have only one set of men to contend with the work would be much easier. But the number of sections each working independently of the other makes the work very difficult.

---

[1] William Francis Butler (1838–1910), assistant adjutant-general, Western district (1880–1884), ADC to Queen Victoria (1882–1892), KCB (1886), later commanded the Cape and Western districts.

[2] Butler travelled to North America on 24 January to develop an intelligence network for Jenkinson: Sir William Harcourt to Spencer, 19 January 1884; Jenkinson to Spencer, 22 April 1884: AP, Add MSS 76932, 77033.

[3] William Robert Hoare, British Vice-Consul and Consul-General for New York (1883–1886, 1886–1891).

[4] See **Document 8**.

I suppose Your Excellency read Parnell's recent speech at Drogheda?[5] I thought it very good. But then you know I am a Home Ruler at heart!

Did you read "A plea for an Anglo-Roman Alliance" in the last *Fortnightly Review*?[6] There is a great deal in it I think and the opinions expressed in the concluding para: tally exactly with my own. The suppression of outrage and the vigorous administration of the present exceptional laws are necessary now, but only as a means to an end. We cannot always go on fighting Dynamiters & Secret Societies, and keeping people down by force. No country can ever be really prosperous under such a system of Govt. It is forced upon us now by circumstances. But hand in hand with it should go on the work of "removing the causes of Irish disaffection, and of that demoralization which produces periodical disturbances of law and order". It is only the hope that this is being and will be done that reconciles me to the work on which I am at present engaged and which is, as Your Excellency knows, so distasteful to me.

I suppose Your Excellency has seen the 2nd number of the *Dynamite Monthly*?[7]

A kind of preliminary answer to the despatch of the 13$^{th}$ March came from Washington the other day, and was rather more favourable than I expected.[8] But it must await the formal reply of the U. States Gov$^{t}$. I fear they won't do much, judging from the tone of the American Press.

**2.** E.G. Jenkinson to Lord Spencer, 14 September 1884;[9] AP, Add MS 77034.

It is rather a long time since I wrote to Your Excellency, but I have not had very much to say about my own particular work

---

[5] On being presented with the freedom of the city, Parnell lauded the recent election of a nationalist city council, stating that local self-government would be 'the cradle and precursor of national self-government': *The Times*, 16 April 1884, p. 7.

[6] W. Maziere Brady, 'A plea for an Anglo-Roman alliance', *Fortnightly Review*, 41 (April 1884), pp. 453–462.

[7] An American journal published during 1884–1885 by Patrick Rellihan, a former employee of Patrick Ford: see James Paul Rodchenko, *Patrick Ford and His Search for America: a case study of Irish-American journalism, 1870–1913* (New York, 1976), p. 43.

[8] Possibly referring to diplomatic correspondence with the US Government concerning the movements of Fenians in Iowa and Minnesota and a rumoured invasion of Manitoba: TNA, FO 5/1929, fos 20–34, 158–179.

[9] It seems likely that the letter was sent on 16 September 1884, as Jenkinson's letter to Spencer of 15 September states that a longer letter had been begun but not finished, and his letter of 17 September refers to 'the long letter of yesterday': AP, Add MS 77034.

and I have also been waiting for your return to Dublin from the South.[10]

At the present moment the only place from which danger is to be expected is Paris. The dynamiters there have of late been very active. They have received some money from America, and there can be no doubt that they are planning some outrage, and any day we may expect to hear of some explosion. I know the men in Paris who are engaged in this work, and they are all, as far as possible, under observation. But, I believe it to be next to impossible, under the present system of working to find out beforehand what their plans are. Two or three men at the most are in the secret and even they do not, till the last moment, make up their minds as to what is to be done. Dynamite is smuggled over to England, and then just before the outrage is to come off workers, who are probably unknown to each other, and who are not in the secrets of the leaders, are sent over. Unless the men are detected in the act, or recognized by some persons on the spot they escape and there is no possibility of obtaining any proof against them. They get off to France or America, and we cannot make a case for extradition. In fact the conditions are all in their favour and all against us. If men are determined to bring Dynamite into England, and to blow up buildings, merely for the sake of creating a scare as in the case of the last explosions, no precautions that we can take can stop them. We cannot possibly guard every point of attack, and we cannot be by any means sure of finding out their places before hand. Still we can do, and I believe have done, a great deal to prevent these outrages. I am quite sure that we should have had a great many more serious explosions and much more injury to property would have been done, and more lives lost, but for the great and continual precautions which have been taken to protect public buildings in England and Ireland, for the successes we have had against the different groups of Dynamiters since the beginning of 1883, and for the fear, and distrust of each other, arising out of our successes, and our system of working. They work no doubt much more quietly than they did before, and their arrangements are better but they are very distrustful of each other. No man feels sure that his most intimate friend is not a traitor, and they find it exceedingly difficult to get workers. On both sides men are hanging back. In America they are ready to supply the money, if workers can be found on this side, but the men over here though very ready to sympathize and assist are very loathe to act. I do not believe that the desire or even the intention is to destroy property on a large

[10] During 5–11 September, Spencer toured counties Cork and Kerry, visiting Mallow, Killarney, Millstreet, Listowel, Castleisland, Ardfert, and Tralee: *The Times*, 6, 8, and 9 September 1884.

scale or to take life. The object is to create a scare: To keep the agitation going, and to let Englishmen feel that there is a strong and desperate party of Force behind the constitutional agitators. In England, and also I am told among very many of the most influential Fenians in America, there is a strong feeling against the Dynamite policy, so that the Dynamiters must act to a great extent under restraint. A very serious outrage causing much destruction to property and much loss of life might change the feeling against them to one of active hostility and they might have to retire from the field altogether.

I believe too that the Parliamentary Party are just now against this Dynamite work, and are, as far as they dare, using their influence against it. They feel that they are playing a winning game, and that any serious outrage would probably give them a check, and injure their cause. One of them, T.P. O'Connor in his recent paper "The Irish Question, Present and Prospective" published in the *American Catholic Quarterly Review*, when speaking of the necessity of union among themselves and of the danger of getting the English people against them does actually protest against the use of dynamite. He says "There is one thing, and one thing only that can unite all Englishmen against Ireland, and that is the destruction of life in some of these outrages by which London is occasionally shaken. These outrages bring terror to the Irish minority whose lives & property are at the mercy of the English majority around them: and to the Irish representatives appear one of the gravest obstacles to the early success of the national cause." Then he instances the check they received from the Phoenix Park murders, and says "Those who passed through that bitter trial may well have sinking of heart in their hours of most sanguine hope, lest once again a successful crime should change the eve of overwhelming victory to an hour of disastrous defeat."[11] But they dare not break with the Extremist party altogether, *Fini*, because they are dependent on the National League, and what is the same thing (the Fenian organization in America) for funds, & because they know that it is an advantage to have a party of force behind them. It supports them and gives them greater weight both in Parliament and in the Country, and they do not know that the day may not come when they may not want again to use it. They do not object to Dynamite and outrage on principle, but on grounds of expediency. If they thought that Dynamite would give them what they want they would not hesitate to encourage outrages and to induce organizers of outrages through the country as they did in 1881–82.

---

[11] T.P. O'Connor, 'The Irish question, present and prospective', *American Catholic Quarterly Review*, 9, no. 2 (July 1884).

What they all feel, both the men who do not want to go beyond constitutional agitation, and the Fenians who look forward some day to an appeal to arms, is that the movement cannot go on without money, and that without supplies which come to them from America both the National League organization and the Fenian organization would be broken up. The Parliamentary Party want money for payment of members and for election expenses, the Fenians want it for payment of organizers and officers and for the purchase of arms, while many, who have not a spark of patriotism about them, look to these organizations as a means of livelihoods and sooner than lose the money on which they have so long lived would abandon the principles they have so long professed and would join the Dynamite party.

I believe that at the present moment certainly in England, and very probably also in Ireland, the majority is against Dynamite outrages and assassinations. But very many of them feel that it is now "Dynamite or nothing". They are being urged to join the Clan-na-gael or Party of Force in America, and they feel that if they refuse to do so the Fenian organization will cease to exist, and their occupations and income will be gone. A short time ago the question was discussed at a meeting of prominent Fenians at Boulogne. They had been talking about the man who they believe gave the information which led to the arrest of J. Daly[12] and when John O'Connor[13] the President told them what Daly's intentions were, how he meant to throw one of the bombs on to the Treasury Bench in the House of Commons,[14] one of them, the delegate from Leeds, said boldly "Well if he did inform I think he was quite right, and I shall defend him". The majority was against the proposed union with Clan-na-gael, and even John O'Connor, who is their agent, seemed to be of the same mind for he said "I believe in my heart it is a mistake, but if we refuse to join how are we to carry on, how are we to live d—n them if they will try it let them."

In America they are obliged to listen to the Extreme Party and to send money and emissaries over for the commission of outrages, for there the chief contributors to the Emergency and other Funds[15] are

[12] John Daly (1845–1916), representative for Connaught and Ulster on the Supreme Council of the IRB (1875), imprisoned for planning explosions at the House of Commons (1884–1896), Mayor of Limerick city (1899–1901).

[13] John O'Connor (1850–1928), Nat. MP for Co. Tipperary (1885–1892), Secretary of the Supreme Council of the IRB, assisted Parnell in fashioning the New Departure.

[14] See 'Case of John Daly: Fenian convicted of treason', 23 January 1885: CAB 37/14/5; Owen Magee, *The IRB: the Irish Republican Brotherhood from the Land League to Sinn Fein* (Dublin, 2005), pp. 119–121.

[15] The *Irish World*, founded by Patrick Ford in New York (1870), established the Skirmishing Fund (1876) to undermine British rule in Ireland and the Emergency Fund (1880) to support the Land League.

men who believe in Dynamite, and who complain if "active work" is not carried on. At present the subscriptions are falling off because sufficient work has not been done, so in order to keep the game going and to bring fresh subscriptions the leaders will soon have to organize fresh outrages.

In New York there are three different Parties who have money at their disposal for Dynamite work. First Rossa and his council of 18 men.[16] Second The Clan-na-gael. Third The Fords,[17] with who is associated F. Byrne[18] one of the Invincibles.

The first are not at present very dangerous for they have very little money, and cannot do much unless supplied with funds by the Fords or Clan-na-gael. Still they are very bitter against us and have the worst intentions. They have Agents in Paris and Rossa corresponds with Eugene Davis[19] and Patrick Casey,[20] both of whom are leading Dynamiters in Paris. At the moment Rossa and his council are very angry with Patrick Ford and are putting great pressure upon him to hand over to them some of the Emergency Fund for "active work". They accuse him of appropriating some of the money for the purpose of paying off a mortgage on the *Irish World*, and are preparing a pamphlet in which they mean to expose his dishonesty. Ford is very close with the money which he has received, and is no doubt using some, though very little, of it, in conjunction with F. Byrne, on the payment of Agents over on this side, and is naturally very distrustful, especially with men of the Rossa stamp. But very strong pressure is being put upon him by many of the most violent and influential men of the Extreme Party, and also by the subscribers who complain that he has not shown work for their money, and before very long he will be obliged either to carry out some explosions on a very large scale, or will have to hand over money to those who will work.

[16] Jeremiah O'Donovan Rossa (1831–1915), founder of the Phoenix Society (1858), business manager of *Irish People* (1863), imprisoned for treason felony (1865–1871), head centre (i.e. leader) of the Fenian Brotherhood (1877) and administrator of the Skirmishing Fund (1876–1880).

[17] Patrick Ford (1837–1913), editor of *Irish World* (1870–1913) and fundraiser for the Fenians and the Land League; Austin Ford (1840–1933), assistant editor of *Irish World*, editor of *New York Freeman's Journal* (1888).

[18] Frank Byrne (d. 1894), Secretary of the Land League of Great Britain (1879–1882), fled to the US after being implicated in the Phoenix Park murders.

[19] Eugene Davis (1857–1897), contributor to *The Irishman* and *Shamrock*, settled in Paris and became acting editor for *United Ireland* (1881) and a member of the editorial staff of *The Nation* (1887): see Magee, *The IRB*, p. 92.

[20] Patrick Casey, journalist and Fenian exile in Paris, believed to have been involved with the British secret service: see Christy Campbell, *The Maharajah's Box: an imperial story of conspiracy, love and a guru's prophesy* (London, 2001).

Ford has to my knowledge already sent three agents over here, but these men have been discovered, and brought over by me, and two of them are now working for me.

Both Ford and the Clan-na-gael say that they mean to go to work in earnest after the Presidential Election (on Nov. 4) but that they do not intend to do anything big till then.

The proceedings at the Boston Convention (Aug 13/84) were entirely controlled by the V.C. or Clan-na-gael men.[21] Their programme was carried out in its entirety. Everything was done in the interest of the V.C. or United Brotherhood of Fenians. The National League as now constituted is only a cloak for Fenianism. Patrick Egan,[22] the newly elected President is a Fenian, and a Clan-na-gael man, and all the officers just elected are V.C. men. It was arranged beforehand that A. Sullivan[23] should retire from the Presidency, and Patk. Egan should be elected. There was much dissatisfaction with Sullivan. It was believed he used the organization for Political purposes, and they hoped that Egan, who has not been long in America, and is not much mixed up in politics would look more to the interests of the League, and would preserve the independence of the organization. At the convention all the influential & prominent Fenians were present, and among them were Frank Byrne, Tynan no. 1,[24] Capt. J. McCafferty[25] & Desmond[26] of San Francisco. At secret meetings the Dynamite Policy was freely discussed. The Executive's action in the past was approved, and it was determined to go on with the active work. But no definite plan of action was decided on. Money was to be freely given to Dynamite work, as need for it might arise. But the feeling generally was that it would be wisest to watch the course of events, and to let the F.C. (or the Executive) organize outrages at the most fitting time according to their own judgement. The Parliamentary Party have been so successful of late, and have made such good & unexpected progress that it was determined to give them a fair trial & a good

[21] See **Document 8**.

[22] Patrick Egan (1841–1919), managing director of North City Milling Company and member of the Supreme Council of the IRB, Treasurer of the Land League (1879–1881) and suspected of financing the Invincibles, co-founder and President of the Irish National League of America (1884–1886), US ambassador to Chile (1888).

[23] Alexander Sullivan (1847–1913), Chairman of Clan-na-Gael (1881–1885), President of the Irish National League of America (1883–1884), active in Chicago politics and founded the 'Triangle' to support the dynamite campaign in Great Britain.

[24] Patrick J.P. Tynan was (wrongly) identified at the trial of the Dublin Invincibles as 'No. 1' in the conspiracy: see his *The Irish National Invincibles and Their Times* (London, 1894).

[25] John McCafferty (b. 1838), organizer of the Fenian raid on Chester Castle and subsequently imprisoned (1867–1871), fled to the US following the Phoenix Park murders.

[26] Thomas Desmond (1838–1910), Sheriff of San Francisco (1880), an organizer of the Catalpa expedition to rescue Fenian prisoners from Fremantle, Western Australia (1876).

chance. A large sum of money was to be given to the Parliamentary Party, and they are to have the full support of the League, and should constitutional agitation fail, then more active measures will be taken, and more violent councils will prevail. No doubt Sexton & Redmond were both aware of all that was going on, and I have it on good authority that Redmond is on terms of intimacy with the leading V.C. men in America and is a sworn Fenian. Patrick Egan as President of the League will be in favour of helping his old friends and colleagues of the Parnell Party over on this side and will supply them with funds as far as he is able. But he is heart and soul in the Dynamite movement and we may be sure that the man who supplied nearly £5000 out of the Land League Fund for the organization of the Dublin Invincibles for the purpose of murdering Govt. officials in 1881–82, and who is the colleague of F. Byrne, P.J. Sheridan,[27] Capt. McCafferty and Tynan, will not hesitate to give money again for outrages & murder out of the National League & V.C. Funds which are now placed practically at his disposal. He is also too much in F. Byrne's power to break with him, or to refuse to give him money, and F. Byrne wants money and would do anything for money.

The above is, I believe, a fair picture of the present situation, as far as regards the Party of Force on this side and in America. I could of course go a great deal more into detail, but I doubt whether I should convey a clearer idea of affairs to Your Excellency's mind and I should probably write more than you would care to read.

Shortly the situation is this. There is a Parliamentary Party, seemingly at the present moment holding winning cards, supported by and in sympathy with all nationalists and Fenians of every shade of opinion, but for the moment against outrages and the use of Dynamite. And behind the Parliamentary Party a large and increasing body of men in favour of Dynamite and active work, which has considerable funds at its disposal, which is impatient of restraint, and whose members keep putting great pressure on the leaders to carry out outrages and explosions on a large scale.

There are some few Dynamite agents over here and in Paris, these are violent men who are in constant communication with New York, and who have some money at their disposal, and from these men we may any day expect a scare on a large scale, but nothing of real importance will be undertaken either by Patk. Ford or the Clanna-gael immediately. They will watch the course of events and act accordingly.

---

[27] Patrick Joseph Sheridan (c.1844–1918), IRB county centre (i.e. leader) for Sligo and Land League organizer, implicated in the Phoenix Park murders and fled to the US to become an advocate of the dynamite campaign.

The work of watching the movements of these parties and of obtaining information about them occupies me incessantly and is the cause of great anxiety to me. I feel that so much depends on me, and yet that I am able to accomplish so little. It is almost a single handed fight between me and a set of ruffians who now work on such a secret system that it is next to impossible to find out who their agents are and what their plans are. I feel always as if I were a man beating against the air, and as if my work could not have any lasting or beneficial result. For what I am doing does not go to the root of the matter. I may succeed in preventing many outrages, and in deterring many of the plans of these men, and all sorts of difficulties have been placed in their way. But our successes only exasperate them and make them more bitter against England. We do not do anything to remove the bitter feeling which there is against us, on the contrary all that we do, unfortunately, intensifies that feeling. No one can deny that the hatred of England and the desire to be rid of us is much stronger than it was and goes on increasing in strength, and that the leaders in Parliament have now much more influence in Parliament & more power in the country than they perhaps ever had before. And is there to be no end to all this? Are we to go on without a well defined policy, trying to do that which is impossible, trying to reconcile the people of Ireland to our rule under our present system, and to govern on Constitutional lines, and on Liberal principles when in point of fact our administration is not really Constitutional, and when we cannot, or rather do not, carry out those principles to the logical conclusions?

I wish I could persuade you to take up seriously and with all the weight of your position the great and pressing question of the future Government of Ireland. In England the greatest ignorance about Ireland prevails. The facts of the case are not known, and consequently there is no such thing as intelligent comprehension of the Irish question, and no sound opinion as to what should be done. The faith in our administration has, I think, been shaken. There is a feeling that something is wrong, and that some remedy is required. And I believe there is a growing opinion in favour of Home Rule which before very long will have to be recognized. At the same time, if any bad outrage were to take place in England attended by great destruction of property & loss of life a very strong feeling would be aroused against the Irish, which would be followed by deplorable results, and which would postpone for a very long time the settlement of our Irish difficulties.

We are in my opinion passing through a very critical time. I need not give my reasons now for this, because Your Excellency knows better than I do what has lately taken place during the past four years, what the present situation is and what we have to look forward to in the immediate future. But I mention it because I feel very strongly that it behoves all English statesmen and above all Your Excellency to ponder deeply over the present condition of things, and to consider earnestly whether it be not possible to take a new departure, and to initiate a policy which in the end may rid us of this troublesome Irish question, may raise Ireland out of her present demoralized and backward condition, and may bind the hearts of her people with bonds of affection and loyalty to England. Surely the matter is serious enough and of large enough dimensions? We cannot honestly say that Ireland is now well governed, that the people are contented, and that the country prospers under our Rule. We are not in touch with the people, the Castle is held up to ridicule and hatred, agriculture deteriorates, the population decreases, capital is not drawn into the country, recruits have almost ceased to enter our army,[28] and if ever bad times were to come for England, and we were hard pressed in a large European War, Ireland would be a weakness to us, instead as she should be a strength, and a thorn in our side.

The knowledge of all this imposes an enormous responsibility upon Your Excellency, there is no man in the world whose opinion about Ireland could carry with it a hundredth part of the weight of Your Excellency's opinion. No statesman has such knowledge of Ireland as Your Excellency. You have a great reputation for ability, honesty, independence of judgement, fearlessness, and freedom from narrow and dogmatic views, and I believe that it is in your power at the present time to lead England on the Irish question, to lay the foundation of a healthy and sound opinion in England, and so to pave the way for incalculable benefit for Ireland.

Will Your Excellency accept the obligations which this great responsibility imposes on you? Will you, putting aside all party considerations, proclaim to the world what your convictions are about the Government and the future of Ireland, and say exactly what the present state of affairs is, what the dangers before us are and what in your opinion should be done?

I am not an enthusiast, or a dreamer as Your Excellency knows. I am, I flatter myself, a practical man. I see that our present system is bad, and I believe that we require a system which could bring with it a continuity of policy, and a consequent settlement of all our difficulties and I urge you to take up the matter earnestly and seriously, not only for the sake of England and Ireland, but also for the sake of your own reputation as a statesman and as a Viceroy of Ireland.

---

[28] In 1880, 15% of British Army recruits came from Ireland; by 1882 the figure had fallen to 10%: Sir John Ross to Courtney Boyle, 29 November 1882: AP, Add MS 76914.

I have worked so much under you and have so much reason to admire your many great qualities that your reputation is dear to me, and I am jealous of it. When the History of the present time comes to be written what will be said of a Viceroy who mistook the times, who missed his opportunities, who was content with a policy of watching events from day to day, and did not attempt to solve the greatest and most difficult problem of the time?

For some time I believed, or rather hoped, that it might be possible to steer a middle course. To go on as we are, ruling firmly and justly, endeavouring to reconcile the people to our rule, and so gradually to improve the country, and to live down the present agitation and the present bad feeling against us. But now I believe this to be impossible. The feeling against us is too strong and too deep. It is kept alive by men and money from America and Australia, and above all it is hopeless and impossible because under our present system of Party Government, as applied to Ireland, we cannot have any continuity of policy. We cannot go on governing Ireland on one settled system and on the same line of policy through a course of years.

Therefore it seems to me that a middle course is out of the question. We must either make up our minds to establish a more despotic form of Government, and firmly to suppress all agitation, all outrages, all speeches and writing which could poison the minds of the people & demoralize them, or we must prepare ourselves for Home Rule. In present times and in the present state of public feeling I doubt very much whether the former system could be established and personally I should be against it because it would only perpetuate the feeling against us, and could not last for long. It would not settle the Irish question. English Liberals would not tolerate such a system long. I have for long leaned towards a form of Home Rule, and the more I know about Ireland, and the more I think the matter over, the more am I convinced that Home Rule is the true solution of the difficulty. Our policy at the present time is I say neither wise nor honest. It is not true to say that the land question has been finally settled, and that no more concessions will be made to the Parliamentary Party when we know that we have not arrived at the final settlement of the land question, and that further concessions are sure to be made on many points in Parliament. And if we do mean what we say, if no further concessions are to be made, it is not honest to the people to allow agitators and Members of Parliament to poison their minds, to keep them in an unsettled state, and to hold out hope to them which, as far as our intentions go, are never to be realized. Let us crush all such hopes with a strong hand, or let us give the people what they want. For my own part I would boldly avow the principle of Home Rule. I would not grant it at once, but

I should tell the Irish that they should have it, when events are ripe for it, and when they are fit for it. I would change the system of administration at the Castle. I would appoint a Viceroy (if possible one of the Queen's sons) who would not belong to a Party, and who would not therefore retire on the change of Gov.<sup>t</sup> in England. I would form an executive council on which Irishmen of all opinions would be represented, I would decentralize the finances, I would leave as much as possible the management of domestic affairs to the Viceroy and his council, and I would gradually give the people political education and fit them for self-government, by developing municipal, & local Government in the counties. At the same time I would insist strongly on the maintenance of the Union with England. Ireland must remain part of the English Empire. The local Parliament would deal with domestic and internal affairs, and where common action might be required in the common interest the Imperial Parliament would have control.

I should not fear the result of such a policy in the least. Notwithstanding the many, and, to some people's minds, the insuperable, objections in the way, I believe it would succeed. I believe it to be the true & only remedy for Fenianism and Dynamite outrages. In time the Irish will be quite able to manage their own affairs. And it is my firm opinion that if we do not admit this now we shall be forced to admit it some day, and that a not very distant one. As sure as I am writing this letter Home Rule in some form or other will come. Public opinion is all moving towards decentralization and towards local Gov.<sup>t</sup> everywhere. And surely it would be far wiser, even if we look at the matter from a purely English, a selfish point of view, to let the Irish have Home Rule as a gift from the wisdom, generosity and foresight of our statesmen, than to have it wrung from us by force, and under pressure in times of trouble and difficulty?

And now I have finished this long letter. There is much more I should like to say, there are many more details into which I should like to enter if it were only to show that I understand the many difficulties in the way and have thought over the question in all its bearings. But I should weary Your Excellency if I were to write more.

Whatever conclusions Your Excellency may come to; Whether you agree with me or not, I beg you, now that you have the opportunity, to write a long state paper reviewing the past, describing the present situation and fearlessly stating your opinions, and proposing a line of policy for the future. In doing so I am sure you will be rendering real & lasting service to England and Ireland, and will increase your own reputation as a statesman and as an administrator.

If in the course of this letter I have been too outspoken, or have said anything which is unpleasant I hope Your Excellency will forgive me.

**3.** Lord Spencer to E.G. Jenkinson, 18 September 1884; Vice Regal Lodge, Dublin; AP, Add MS 77034.

Your letter was not too long & every word of it interested me very much.[29]

I shall not now answer it at length or finally. I have not time to do so thoroughly & it is a letter I should like to ponder even before answering. I will only write generally.

It is known that great revolutions and changes are followed by a period of crime. It has been specially so in Ireland, after Catholic Emancipation such an outburst took place, after the disestablishment of the Church the same thing occurred, & lately we have witnessed the same thing.

When a people have been dependent and submissive to the rule of others they cannot bear with prudence and moderation the severing of old conditions. They have their leaders and have none but agitators to guide them.

Just now it is the landlords who have lost their power, there has risen no class or body of moderate men to take their place, probably many landlords will gradually regain their influence but just now we are passing through the most dangerous period for a nation, a transition state. We must be patient, it is possible that extreme measures of Home Rule may become necessary, but just now it will be impossible to attempt it. The North would never agree to it, we should at once have civil war between Ulster and the South and West, nowhere then should we find the elements for Government. We shall need a development of Local Institutions before we could, if it were desirable, carry Home Rule.

We must not act prematurely. The duty of Government to keep up law and order is essential and must be done.

It may be my fate only to have this duty though I have taken part in the Land Legislation, which I trust is already telling in a healing sense.

I quite agree with you that simple repression is not sufficient. We must win the people over to our side, we could not go on with force alone.

We have begun with the Land Act, we go on with the Franchise, we must carry a large & wide measure of Local Govt.

We must however wait for this: next session will be occupied with Parliamentary Reform after that a comprehensive reform of Local Govt. which should educate Irishmen to govern will be necessary, I

[29] See **Document 2**.

would make it very wide. If that be carried and failed then we may require to go further.

To announce such a scheme before we have made it & see what we can propose would not be possible, nor do I think that a transition government which I understand you suggest would be practicable. I think it very probable that we shall eventually come to something very like Home Rule called for by the best Nationalists.

I do not know that you differ in your views really from what I write now.

My letter has run on to more length than I intended. You overrate my ability & power to settle this question, I may & must try to be of use in dealing with a large plan for self govt. & among my reasons for holding on to my post is that I may yet do this. Your friendliness towards me makes you exaggerate what I could do.

What you tell me in your last letter as to [the] trial of the Daly matter[30] is interesting.

**4.** E.G. Jenkinson to Lord Spencer, 24 September 1884; Secretary of State, Home Department; AP, Add MS 77034.

I am delighted to see from Your Excellency's letter[31] in reply to my long one of the [1]4th September[32] that your views are so much in accord with mine on the future Government of Ireland, but I am sorry that you are of opinion that nothing can be done at the present time, and that we must be content with a waiting policy.

I said particularly that Home Rule could not possibly be granted now. Under present circumstances it would be impracticable. The land question must first be finally settled and the present animosity between landlords & tenants and between the two parties must have time to subside. But I would boldly acknowledge the principle of Home Rule, and by my words and by my acts would show that Ireland should have self Government in time when her people are politically fitted for it. I think this should have been our policy at the end of 1883 when we had suppressed outrage, and were strong, and I said so at the time. We are not so strong now and I am afraid we are getting weaker and the weaker we become, and the more our administration is discredited, the more difficult it will be, morally speaking, to make concessions and to do that which we know to be right.

---

[30] Referring to the trial (in absentia) in Manchester of the informer who gave evidence against John Daly: see **Document 2** and Jenkinson to Spencer, 17 September 1884: AP, Add MS 77034.
[31] See **Document 3**.
[32] See **Document 2**.

Your Excellency says rightly that our aim should be to win the people over to our side, but is it possible to do this under our present system? Our administration, as I said before, is not in sympathy with them, we do little to benefit their material condition, we allow their leaders to vilify & abuse us, to discredit our administration in every possible way, and to hold up our Viceroy to ridicule and hatred, and we say publicly that the land question is finally settled, that no more concessions will be made, and that England will never grant Home Rule.

If we were to acknowledge the <u>principle</u> of Home Rule, and to show by our acts that we are working up to it we should have the majority of the people with us instead of against us, we should create disunion among the Nationalist leaders, and all practical and sensible ones among them would come over to our side and would help us to work out a <u>practical</u> solution of the Home Rule question.

I know we all learn from History that great revolutions and changes, as Your Excellency remarks, are often followed by a period of crime. But the remark hardly applies to the Ireland of 1881 & 82. Immediately preceding 1881 there had not been a great change of any kind. The feeling which had been in existence for centuries had been growing more intense, secret organization of the people had been going on, and crime broke out all over the country not as the result of a revolution but for the purpose of obtaining a great and radical change. The people did not break out into crime because suddenly they felt relief from an unbearable yolk, but because they were urged to commit outrages by their leaders, and because secret societies were organized for that purpose.

At the present moment the people are under control. Our strong measures have for the time frightened them and their leaders who have great influence and control over them discourage the commission of outrages. But the feelings which prompted them to commit outrages still exist, indeed I believe them to be stronger than ever, and it is quite possible, even probable, that unless we take wise & timely precautions against it we may have again to face a state of affairs such as existed in 1881–82.

I think there is a tendency to overrate the good effects of the Land Act. That it was a good measure & a just one I firmly believe, and that it has done good, & will do more good I do not doubt, but as it stands it will not satisfy the people, nor can I believe that under it the landlords (I am not speaking of individuals) will ever, as Your Excellency hopes, regain their influence. It hardly touches the poverty stricken tracts in the West, where the people are most demoralized and degraded, and where the worst outrages take place.

The measures which Your Excellency foreshadows, and hopes some day to have in hand are excellent, and are all I believe in the right direction, but <u>when</u> can we hope for their introduction, or if the Conservatives come in to power will they be introduced at all? Meanwhile none of the Nationalists know what our intentions are, and to what end we are working. What they believe is that Your Excellency is a hard and cruel Viceroy, who will do all in his power to have the Prevention of Crime Act renewed and who has no sympathy with, or love for the people he governs. I know that it is not so, but they are taught to believe it. And I say that we are not only acting wrongly but also foolishly if we do not do something to remove this impression, and to change the feelings of the people towards us.

I believe that every day we wait it will be more difficult to act. But if we will act now it is not too late.

As a question of Party Policy too would it not be wise & prudent to bring over the Nationalists to our side? Look to the picture, too true I fear, which Mr. Trevelyan drew in his speech the other day of the future.[33] With the Irish Members on our side how strong we should be, and how much good we should be able to do in Ireland! We might then hope for some continuity in our Policy, a thing which is now impossible, and must continue to be so, unless some new Policy be adopted.

At any time we may be involved in great difficulties abroad. The horizon at the present moment is anything but clear, and in the event of such difficulties who will pay any attention to Ireland? What will become of all our good intentions? And at such a time what a trouble and danger Ireland may be to us!

It is these thoughts which lead me to urge Your Excellency to take some steps which may help to form in England a sound & intelligent opinion on the Irish question, may satisfy the Irish people, and may be the means of averting the great danger and difficulties which await us, I believe, in the future, if we now remain content with a timid and a waiting Policy.

My scheme for a "transition" Gov$^t$, as Your Excellency terms it may be faulty in detail, but it is I am sure right in principle. It would help to take Irish affairs beyond the range of Party strife, it would render Castle Rule popular, and it would draw to our side the greater part of the able and earnest Irishmen who now bitterly oppose us, and who do all in their power to make the Government of the Country impossible.

Think what an enormous benefit both to England and Ireland would be the solution of the troublesome Irish question, and to what gratitude the statesman who should solve it would be entitled!

---

[33] He addressed constituents in the Exchange Hall, Hawick, on 19 September, and spoke in support of the franchise bill on the following day: *The Times*, 20 September 1884, p. 10; 22 September 1884, p. 7.

**5.** Lord Spencer to E.G. Jenkinson, 28 September 1884; AP, Add MS 77034.

I told Dunsterville to tell you my plans, but it is well to repeat what they are.

[*Spencer planned to discuss the Crimes Act with the Divisional Magistrates on 8 October and hoped that Jenkinson would be able to attend. He was to visit Balmoral between 13 and 18 October before going on to London or Althorp and returning to Dublin on 23 October.*]

Touching your letter about the future of Ireland,[34] I should like to say this, that I am not sure whether you are referring to my speech at Gowan when you speak of the impolicy of saying that no more Land Reform is possible.[35] If you are you probably read the comments on it & not the words I spoke.

I carefully guarded myself against absolutely closing all legislation, but I felt & feel strongly that the Tenants should not be deluded as to the likelihood that large changes are to be offered in the occupation clauses of the Land Acts: some small changes may be necessary in these clauses, but great harm is done by the farmers being led to expect large further reductions of rent etc. They will not settle down to their occupations.

I spoke favourably of the importance of increasing proprietors.

If you differ from these views, or differ very substantially. [*sic*]

You allude to the miserable holdings in the West, which no land law legislation will touch.

The only chance for them is to increase facilities for communication, & encourage voluntary emigration or if it were practicable (which it isn't) migration.

Directly people see that their only chance is to move from these miserable holdings, they will use the power of sale given under the Land Act. This indeed is the only clause of the Act relating to land which really may help such districts.

They would not live comfortably if their holdings were given to them.

As to a transition government that will give no satisfaction, & I see no practical method of carrying out the idea.

---

[34] See **Document 4**.

[35] Delivered at Lord Clifden's residence in Co. Kilkenny on 2 September, it provoked a defiant response from T.P. O'Connor at the annual convention of the Irish National League of Great Britain: *The Times*, 3 September 1884, p. 6; 8 September 1884, p. 6. For the text of the speech, see AP, Add MS 77326.

I have never made any secret of my desire to develop Local Government. I have more than once spoken in this sense, and Mr. Gladstone, whose utterances are far more important, has repeatedly been attacked for saying too much in this direction.

To adopt the cant phrase 'Home Rule' on account of these views would be ridiculous.

What I said as to going further in case those changes which we hope to carry out are [in]sufficient, should certainly not be propounded prematurely.

There is no such false step in politics as to announce a general policy or move before you are sure of the details. You are accused of bribery and treachery if what you propose falls far short of what you have led men to expect.

As to the period of crime in 1880–81, it may be true that no great change immediately preceded it, but the Land Act of 1870 & the Church Act of 69 had not been very long passed, & one reason for the appearance of crime after a great change in the laws as there has been made in Ireland, [is] that men believe in "the Chapel Bell", "the Clerkenwell Explosion" argument.[36] They agree that concession is wrung from England by outrages.

Another lesson may be derived from recent Irish events, that the Land Act of 1870 was not thorough enough.

I think that I told you before that Lord Carlingford, then C. Fortescue,[37] who was Chief Sec. & chiefly formed the Act of 1870, & I, who was Ld Lt & had a good deal to say to the original Bill, each of us proposed a change in the Law; so that the tenants all over Ireland shd have the right to sell their tenant right, that rents shd be subject to a decision of a Land Court, we did not agree on these at the time & there is no doubt that Parliament would not have adopted them, but had those two changes been in the Bill of 1870 as they were in the Bill of 1881 the latter Bill would not I believe have been necessary.

I am more sanguine as to the effect of the Land Laws than you are, in many places present Landlords will never regain their influence, but those who do their duty, remain in their houses & take part in local public life will gain the influence which men of character & superior education must always exercise among the poorer & less educated class.

As to getting on terms with the National Leaders I shall not despair of that, & should indeed desire it.

[36] After an explosion killed twelve people during an attempt to free Fenian prisoners from Clerkenwell jail in December 1867, Gladstone stated at Oldham that the enormity of the crime should not prevent the English people asking themselves 'whether the condition of Ireland is such as it ought to be': *The Times*, 19 December 1867, p. 7.

[37] Chichester Parkinson-Fortescue (1823–1898), first Baron Carlingford (1874), Chief Secretary for Ireland (1865–1866, 1868–1871), Lord Privy Seal (1881–1885), Lord President of the Council (1883–1885).

But it will not be possible to act with men who have openly abetted organized crime, or do fight with unfair weapons.

You say in your first long letter that 5,000£ was given to "the Invincibles" from Land League funds. On what does that assertion rest?

As far as I recollect in the evidence of the Phoenix Park murders, it was shown that small sums like 10£ etc. were enough for these men. It was not clear where Tynan no.1 or others got their money from.

What part do you yourself think it can be proved that Parnell took in payments of this sort?

The evidence against Egan was very weak.

Certainly since he went to the U.S. he has openly spoken for & supported the party of violence, is that not so? But that is not conclusive as to his having taken the same part in Ireland.

It is serious that we have not advanced a peg towards tracing upward the Invincible organization, Tynan no.1 is the highest man mentioned, & perhaps Capt. McCafferty, but we do not know what people or organization they represented.

When you can we must have a good talk over this.

Have you thought again if my hope that without doing away with precautions I could do with less ostentatious protection, say fall back on 2 cavalry orderlies when I ride about, having escorts for night, or journey home for hunting.


**6.** E.G. Jenkinson to Lord Spencer, 2 October 1884; Secretary of State, Home Department; 'Private'; AP, Add MS 77034.

I am much obliged to Your Excellency for your last long letter.[38] I hope to be over in Dublin early next week so I will not trouble you with another long letter. I shall only say that I am disappointed that Your Excellency holding as you do such liberal and enlightened views about Ireland should come to the conclusion that nothing can be done at present. However if Your Excellency can persuade the other members of the Cabinet to agree with your views a great step will have been gained. In his last letter to me Sir W. Harcourt writes

"I have always been a pessimist in Irish affairs. I believe the policy of conciliation has failed and will fail against the inveterate hatred of race. A separation is impossible. There remains therefore only one resource, and that is the strong arm and the time is fast coming when it must be used."[39]

---

[38] See **Document 5**.
[39] Harcourt voiced similar concerns to Spencer: Harcourt to Spencer, 21 September 1884: AP, Add MS 76933.

When I hear a statesman of his ability and position speak like that I almost despair of the future of Ireland. But I feel that he is in one sense speaking the truth. I do not believe that the policy of conciliation would fail, but if we do nothing now, if we let the time pass by, a policy of conciliation will be impossible, and then the "strong arm" policy will be forced upon us. The time for conciliation and making concessions and doing justice is when we are strong, not when we are weak and in difficulties. The present state of affairs is, I think, most unsatisfactory and we are only preparing in my opinion troubles and difficulties in the future both for England & Ireland. I do not ask that any violent change should be made. I would work gradually up to Home Rule, and having laid down the lines of my policy would work patiently & resolutely on those lines. But perhaps under our system in which Party with the majority is the first consideration, and in which great questions are not treated on their merits, but according to the political necessities of the hour, such a policy would be almost impossible. However Your Excellency can I am sure much more than any man living help to form, as I said in my first letter, a right and sound opinion about Irish affairs, and can do much to make the Irish believe that we look forward to a different and better system of Government in the future, and that we have other resources than that of the "strong arm". And I wish I could persuade Your Excellency to take some steps in that direction.

**7.** George Fottrell,[40] 'Memorandum in relation to Irish business in the Session of 1885', 10 January 1885; AP, Add MS 77338.

The political creed of the English Liberal party and that held by the Irish party led by Mr. Parnell are both based on the same principle. This principle is that the true aim of enlightened Politicians should be to vest in the governed an effective control over the several Departments of Government.

In the absence of disturbing causes it may therefore be hoped that the tendency of political forces will be to attract towards each other the Irish popular party and the English Liberal party, and to bring about not alone a modus vivendi between them but even to establish an alliance honourable and useful to both.

Whether such an alliance is to be rendered likely, or whether it is to be indefinitely postponed will greatly depend upon the course of events in Parliament during the Session of 1885.

[40] Though unsigned, notes on the document state that the memorandum was 'forwarded to H.J.G[ladstone] by Mr. C. Russell M.P.', the author being identified as 'an Irish official not connected with the Castle': see **Journal (23 January 1885)**.

This Parliament elected in 1880 has now nearly run its race. The judgements of men are affected as their vision is by perspective and in arriving at a conclusion as to their proper action in any great emergency peoples are influenced far more by those events which have just transpired than by those whose details have by time become blurred and indistinct.

It is probably no exaggeration to say that upon the next general election in Ireland the transactions of the Session of 1885 will exercise a more powerful influence than the events which have taken place in Parliament during the past 4 years.

The Irish party in Parliament is composed of men whose political opinions are anything but homogeneous. The same description would be true in reference to the English Liberal party comprising as it does men of views so moderate as to be almost conservative and men whose radicalism is of a very pronounced type, but there is a marked distinction between the English Liberal party and the Irish popular party which must be borne in mind by anyone who hopes to form a correct estimate of the effect of [sic] measures of any particular tendency are likely to have upon the next general election in Ireland.

The entire [sic] of the English Liberal party from the most moderate whig element to the most uncompromising of the radical adherents comprise[d] within its fold is animated by a thorough reliance upon the efficacy of constitutional methods for the redress of grievances, constitutional not only in the sense in which the word is used as opposed to methods of physical violence outside of Parliament but also as opposed to that form of pressure with which Parliament itself has during recent years become familiar. From the disbelief in the efficacy of any method other than constitutional as above described it follows that every measure of radical tendency in England is regarded as an absolute gain by advanced radical English members and at the best as a negation of loss by those members whose opinions tend towards whiggery as distinguished from radicalism.

But in judging of the Irish popular party any such view as to the effect produced by measures having a tendency to give to the people of Ireland an increased control over the departments of government would be erroneous. A measure extending such control would strengthen not the extreme but the moderate element in the Irish party for the extreme men hope for future great results in the direction of freedom by making present government in Ireland impossible while the moderate men seek to impress upon the people that in politics as in most other human affairs it is wise to seek for the whole in the future by securing part in the present.

In illustration of my meaning I can recall a conversation which took place in my presence about 18 months ago between a very advanced Irish Politician then a member of Parliament and a Gentleman also an Irish member with popular sympathies but of views which would be styled moderate. They were both typical men of influence. The moderate man propounded to the other this query – "If you had now the nomination of the Irish Chief Secretary whom would you select?" To which query the reply of the nationalist was "Clifford Lloyd"[41] and he explained his answer by saying that with his nominee as Chief Secretary Government would soon become impossible in Ireland and that the result must be the concession of absolute freedom in Ireland within a comparatively short time.

In relation to the next general election in Ireland it may be predicted with confidence that if the constituencies can be persuaded that Parliamentary action has produced little or no results in the direction of extending the control of the Irish people over their own affairs the chances of extreme in preference to moderate nationalists being returned in Ireland will be materially increased but that if the constituencies are satisfied substantial progress has been made towards the attainment of practical control over their local affairs moderate candidates will secure a large share of popular support. By this statement I do not mean that the majority of the members returned for Ireland will not be pledged "to sit at and vote with the Irish party led by Mr. Parnell" but anyone who recalls the opinion and modes of action of the different men who at present comprise the Irish party will see that the result of the party as a political force would be materially modified according as the majority of the new members would conform to one or other of the types which at present exist in the party.

But outside of those constituencies which will return members pledged to follow Mr. Parnell there are constituencies in Ireland numerous enough to be important in which the question as to whether the future member is to be a liberal or a tory will to a great extent depend upon whether between this time and the date of the general election such measures shall have been brought forward as will enable the Irish party in Parliament to cooperate in the main with the Government or whether the ministerial programme will be such as will drive Mr. Parnell's followers into adopting in Parliament a course of bitter and angry hostility towards the Liberal party.

If the cooperation of Mr. Parnell's party could be secured only on the terms of the Liberal Ministry abandoning any measure which they consider necessary for the peace of the country or proposing any measure which they believe likely to be prejudicial to the true interests of Ireland or of the Empire no honourable man could suggest the advisability of paying such a price even for a beneficial result.

[41] Charles Dalton Clifford Lloyd (1844–1891), SRM for Western Division (1881–1883), Inspector-General of Reforms, Egypt (1883–1885), RM for Londonderry (1885), Governor of Mauritius (1885–1886); see his *Ireland Under the Land League* (Edinburgh and London, 1891).

The position of affairs is shortly this.

A Crimes Act the passage of which was fiercely contested by the Irish Parliamentary party will shortly expire, it was passed at a crisis where men were horrified at the deeds of blood which had shortly before been enacted. A renewal of the Act if such renewal be now sought for will take place under very different circumstances. The country so far as non-official people can judge is almost crimeless save as regards the ordinary offences which occur in every community. I have implicit confidence that the Irish Executive will not ask for a renewal of the Crimes Act or of any portion of it which they honestly believe they can dispense with consistently with their duty as guardians of the peace of the Country but if the Ministry seek to renew any portion of the Act the Irish people will regard the measure as one of repression and if it be unbalanced by any striking measure of Emancipation there is little doubt the opposition of the Irish party to the measure will be so angry so protracted and so determined as to lead to scenes in the House unfortunate for the Government discreditable to the House and which will effectively result in fixing the attention of the Irish people on the measure of repression as the main feature of the programme put forward for Ireland by the Liberal party in the last year of the expiring Parliament. Such a result would I submit be most unfortunate for moderate politicians in Ireland. It would launch the Country into a general election in a fever of indignation against the Liberal party; it would in some doubtful Northern seats secure the return of Conservatives instead of Liberals while in National Constituencies it would render impossible the return of any save very advanced men.

Now is there any reason why a repressive measure should be the main feature of the Liberal programme for Ireland in the Session of 1885. The Redistribution Bill will probably not occupy much time in passing through the House of Commons. Cannot time be found for some striking Bill of Emancipation for Ireland. I respectfully submit that even in point of time the introduction of such a Bill to counterbalance the repressive measure would probably effect a saving.

If a measure of Emancipation is to be introduced the next question is what is the measure which would best combine the elements of attractiveness to the Irish people; opportuneness for the purposes of good government in Ireland and accordance with the true principles of the Liberal party.

Without hesitation I say that the measure which in the greatest degree would combine the desiderata is one establishing elective County Boards in Ireland. No one who has not lived in Ireland can realise how completely the people of Ireland are shut out from any influence direct or indirect upon the management of the affairs of their Districts.

So long as the peasantry were mere serfs in most of the relations of life this exclusion from power in the control of local affairs was not felt as it is now for now the people thanks to the change in the land laws are no longer serfs. They are in many respects freemen and to freemen the denial of influence in the management of the public affairs of their district is a galling insult while to serfs it would have seemed a natural result of their condition. The sturdiness of the people of Ireland is of recent but it is also of very rapid growth and a prudent statesman who understands Ireland will seek without a moment's unnecessary delay to divert the rising flood of popular activity into numerous small channels in which being distributed it may run with safety and advantage instead of swelling into one great torrent which might only too soon menace the safety of much which wise men would wish to preserve or at least to change but slowly.

It may be said with truth that at present every man in Ireland is a politician. The Irish peasant discusses National or Imperial politics because he has no local politics to discuss. Give him a voice in determining the conduct of local affairs in his district and his interest will then be divided between them and the larger politics, and this division will make him less keen in throwing blame upon the central authority, less apt to believe that every misfortune which occurs in any part of Ireland is traceable to "the Government", in a word it will sober him by responsibility and experience of the difficulties of managing even small public affairs.

There is scarcely any reform which Ireland needs that will not be rendered less difficult by the establishment of a representative system of County Government as a preliminary. I am personally aware that the best and most clear headed men among the Irish Parliamentary party attach the greatest importance to the rapid establishment of such system, the writings and speeches of the leading Liberal statesmen shew that the desirability of such system is a prime article in the creed of the Liberal party and earnestly wishing as I do the success of liberal principles in Ireland I venture to express an anxious hope that the session of 1885 will see a County Government Bill for Ireland carried by a Liberal Ministry.

**8.** E.G. Jenkinson, 'Memorandum on the organization of the United Brotherhood, or Clan-na-Gael in the United States', 22 January 1885; 'Secret'; Printed for the use of the Cabinet, January 26, 1885; CAB 37/14/4.

Fenianism at the present time is represented by two powerful secret organizations, one in Great Britain and Ireland, called the I.R.B., or

Irish Republican Brotherhood, the other in North America, called the V.C., or United Brotherhood.

I do not purpose in this paper to give any detailed description of the organization of the I.R.B. But it is necessary to take some notice of it, because the two organizations have a common object, and are, as I shall hereafter show, closely connected.

The I.R.B. exists "for the purpose of overthrowing English power in Ireland, and of establishing an independent Irish Republic, and is governed by a Council entitled, 'The Supreme Council of the Irish Republican Brotherhood and Government of the Irish Republic.'"

For the purposes of organization and administration, the United Kingdom is divided into seven electoral divisions, namely, Leinster, Munster, Ulster, Connaught, North of England, South of England, and Scotland.

The S.C., or Supreme Council, is composed of eleven members, seven of whom are elected by the seven electoral divisions, as above, and four are honorary members elected by the seven. The Executive of the S.C. consists of the President, Secretary, and Treasurer; the decision of any two of whom shall be binding on all.

A Report which was drawn up about a year ago, and sent to America, shows that the number of members was 47,500, thus distributed –

| Ireland – | | | |
|---|---|---|---|
| Ulster | .. .. .. | 10,000 | |
| Munster | .. .. .. | 12,000 | |
| Leinster | .. .. .. | 9,000 | |
| Connaught | .. .. .. | 5,000 | |
| | | ——— | 36,000 |

| Great Britain – | | | |
|---|---|---|---|
| North of England | .. .. | 6,000 | |
| South of England | .. .. | 2,500 | |
| Scotland | .. .. .. | 3,000 | |
| | | ——— | 11,500 |

| Total | .. .. | 47,500[42] |
|---|---|---|

In the event of an armed rising, which might take place if England were engaged in a war with any European Power, these numbers would no doubt be largely increased.

[42] This figure has been strongly disputed, see Magee, *The IRB*, p. 133.

The V.C., or United Brotherhood, known also very generally as the Clan-na-Gaels, is the corresponding organization to the I.R.B. in the United States. But though not numerically so strong as the latter, it is a much more powerful organization. It is an Oath-bound Secret Society, modelled originally upon the plan of the Masonic Fraternity, the members of which all pledge themselves by the most solemn oath to take up arms to establish an Irish Republic when called upon to do so by the chiefs of the organization.

The Society originated in 1869, on the disruption of the F.B. and other smaller Fenian organizations, and was first known as "the Knights of the Inner Circle." The first branch or club established was the "Napper Tandy," in New York, and this club still exists, and is known as D. No.1. The leading men then were P.K. Walsh, now of Cleveland, Ohio; Dr. Carroll,[43] now of Philadelphia, and for several years President of the Executive Body; Dr. Wallace, of New York; John D. Carroll, of Brooklyn; Michael Steady, of New York; Thomas F. Burke,[44] of New York; Alexander Morrison and William Clingen, of Chicago. But it was not till 1873 that much progress was made. In that year the first Convention was held in Providence, R.I., and since then there have been biennial Conventions.

The organization is not supposed to interfere in any way with politics, but in practice it does. The leaders are nearly all professional politicians; and during the recent Presidential election some of the most influential of them supported Mr. Blaine,[45] and used, it is said, not only the organization, but its finances for political purposes.

According to the Constitution of the V.C., printed in 1881, "Its object is the complete political independence of Ireland under a Republican form of government, with full civil and religious liberty guaranteed to all her inhabitants; and the only policy which it believes will attain this end is by force of arms."

The Executive Body, or, as it is always called, the F.C. of the V.C., used to consist of five members, but at the last Convention, held at Boston in August 1884, the number, for purposes of greater secrecy was reduced to three. One of these is the Treasurer, and there is besides a Secretary to the F.C., but he has neither voice nor vote.

There are altogether sixteen Districts distinguished by letters of the alphabet. Letters A to O represent the fifteen districts in the United

[43] William Carroll (1835–1926), Chairman of Clan-na-Gael (1875–1880); he established a Revolutionary Council within the IRB and opposed the 'New Departure'.

[44] Thomas Francis Bourke (b. 1840), leader of a column in Co. Tipperary during the Fenian rising and subsequently imprisoned (1867–1873), elected to Council of Fenians (1876).

[45] James Gillespie Blaine (1830–1893), Republican Senator for Maine (1876–1881), US Secretary of State (1881, 1889–1892), defeated at the presidential election of 1884 by Grover Cleveland.

States, and P represents Canada. The districts in the United States are thus divided: –

A. New York City and City of Yonkers.
B. New Jersey.
C. Long Island and Staten Island.
D. New York State (except as above) and Vermont.
E. Connecticut and Rhode Island.
F. Massachusetts, Maine, and New Hampshire.
G. Pennsylvania.
H. Delaware, District of Columbia, Maryland, Virginia, West Virginia, North Carolina, South Carolina, Alabama, Georgia, and Florida.
I. Kentucky, Tennessee, Arkansas, Texas, Louisiana, and Mississippi.
J. Ohio and Indiana.
K. Illinois and Michigan.
L. Iowa, Minnesota, and Wisconsin.
M. Missouri, Kansas, Arizona, and New Mexico.
N. Colorado, Nebraska, Dacotah, Wyoming, and Montana.
O. California, Oregon, Utah, and Nevada.

Over each of these districts is an E.N., or District Member. The members of the F.C. and the E.N.'s are selected by the Convention biennially. The Secretary is also chosen at the same time, and he is the Secretary not only of the F.C., but also of the E.N.'s.

The districts are divided into Camps or D.'s; each having its own officers, Treasurer, and Trustees. The principal officers are the Senior Guardian (S.G.) and the Junior Guardian (J.G.). To these two officers are made known the names of the Treasurer and Secretary of the F.C., and the name of their E.N.; but the names of the other members of the F.C. are kept secret. The members of the organization in each D. know only their own officers. They do not know who the members of the F.C. or who the E.N.'s are. The management and inner working of the Society are a secret to 95 per cent of its members.

The initiation fees must not be less than 1 dollar, and the weekly dues not less than 10 cents. The Treasurer of each D. keeps in his possession a sum not exceeding 25 per cent. for contingent expenses, and the remainder is deposited in the bank in the name of the Trustees.

Numerical and Financial Term Reports are forwarded from each D. to the Secretary of the F.C. in October, February, and June, and the S.G. has to forward with his Report 10 per cent. of all the money received during the term for the purpose of organizing and other expenses. This is called the Percentage Fund.

On receipt of these Reports the Secretary of the F.C. has to compile and to furnish to each D. within thirty days after the expiration of each term detailed statements of membership, receipts, and expenditure of the Society, and a balance account of all funds remaining in the hands of the F.C. These statements are printed, and from them most valuable information as to the strength and financial condition of the V.C. can be obtained. But it is exceedingly difficult to get copies, for only one copy is sent to each D., and the S.G. is directly and personally responsible for the safety of all documents pertaining to his office.

From these statements it appears that the number of members in the fifteen districts of the United States was, at the end of 1884, about 20,000, and the balance of the Percentage Fund in the hands of the Treasurer of the F.C. amounted to 5,000 dollars. There are other funds besides this Percentage Fund, to which I shall allude later on.

Under the constitution of the V.C., provision is also made for the establishment of a Secret Military Department, and of a Revolutionary Directory, known by the letters R.D.

The Military Department is a special organization under the direct and supreme control of the F.C., who appoint the necessary officers, and make rules for their guidance. At the present moment there is no such department. It is only in time of war, that is, of a rising against England, that it would be organized.

The Revolutionary Directory consists of seven members. Three of these are named by the F.C. of the V.C. in America, and three by the S.C. of the I.R.B. in the United Kingdom. And these six men elect a seventh, who may reside either in Europe or America. These six men hold office for three years, one retiring annually, and a new man being elected in his place. The names of the R.D. are known only to members of the F.C. in America and of the S.C. in the United Kingdom.

The R.D. so constituted "has charge of all preparations for a struggle with England; it has power to declare war; to negotiate with foreign Powers hostile to England, and to assume all the powers, functions, and authority of a Provisional Government in Ireland when war has been declared." It may "make requisitions on the V.C. for any funds it may require for revolutionary purposes," and "it is recognized as the supreme authority in all Irish revolutionary matters, directing the policy of the whole movement, and must be obeyed so long as in the judgment of the F.C. and the S.C. its action is directed solely to the complete independence of Ireland."

The plans and operations of the R.D. must be first approved of by the F.C. and the S.C., and the purposes for which money, material, or men are required must be stated. But beyond that there is no control over the action of the R.D. Their operations are conducted with the utmost secrecy. When the general policy has been approved, the R.D.

select men for the particular work in hand, and manage all details. Money is supplied as they want it, and no questions are asked.

It is to this Revolutionary Directory that the planning and execution of all "active work" against the enemy is entrusted. According to the original principles of the organization such work meant a rising in arms, and the "removal" of informers and traitors; but during the last two years more violent opinions have prevailed, and the Extreme Party has obtained the upper hand. Any means are now considered justifiable. An armed insurrection is known to be hopeless unless England is engaged in a great foreign war. Dynamite outrages and even assassinations are justified on the ground that the Irish race is at war with England, and are therefore looked upon as acts of war. If life is lost no crime has been committed, as every war is unavoidably attended with loss of life.

[*Jenkinson lists the names of the members of the Executive Body, the Revolutionary Directory and other leading figures in the United Brotherhood, including James Reynolds,[46] J.J. Breslin,[47] William Mackey Lomasney,[48] P.H. Cronin,[49] Thomas Brennan[50] and T.V. Powderly.[51]*]

It is impossible to speak of the I.R.B. in the United Kingdom and of the V.C. in the United States without mentioning the National League. The two organizations – the secret and the open constitutional movement – are so closely connected, and so intimately blended and associated are they in their membership, that it is very difficult indeed to draw the line between the two.

Under the banner of the National League in America are ranged all the Irish Societies without distinction, so as to give the idea that all Irishmen are united in the National cause, and that the League is the dominant Society. The National League in America and in Great Britain and Ireland, the Parliamentary party under the leadership of

---

[46] James Reynolds, trustee of the Skirmishing Fund and chief planner of Catalpa expedition, Chairman of the Executive Committee of Clan-na-Gael (1880).

[47] John J. Breslin (c.1836–1888), accomplice in the escape of James Stephens from Richmond Prison, Dublin (1865) and in the Catalpa expedition, prominent member of Clan-na-Gael and business manager of the *Irish Nation*.

[48] William Francis Mackey Lomasney (1841–1884), participant in Fenian rising, subsequently conducted arms raids in Co. Cork and was imprisoned (1868–1871), killed attempting to destroy London Bridge in December 1884.

[49] Patrick Henry Cronin (d. 1889), an opponent of Alexander Sullivan's 'Triangle'; he was abducted and murdered in 1889: Terry Golway, *Irish Rebel: John Devoy and America's fight for Ireland's freedom* (New York, 1998), pp. 167–168.

[50] Thomas Brennan (1842–1915), Secretary to the Land League (1879–1882) and early promoter of 'boycotting', fled to the US following the Phoenix Park murders.

[51] Terence V. Powderly (1849–1924), Mayor of Scranton, Pennsylvania (1878–1884), Grand Master of the Knights of Labour (1879–1893), Treasurer of Clan-na-Gael.

Mr. Parnell, the I.R.B. and the V.C., are all working together with one common object in view, and the policy *publicly* set forth is to aid the Parliamentary Party in its efforts to secure the independence of Ireland by constitutional means. But those who are working openly and on constitutional lines know perfectly well that they have secret organizations and a party of force at their backs. The mainspring of the whole movement is the V.C. This Society does all it can to assist the Constitutional Party, though it is careful not to do anything openly which would compromise any of its leaders. It is the most powerful among all the organizations, and makes its influence felt more than any other Society, because through its members, who are the most influential officers of the National League, it can control and direct the policy of the Nationalists and of the Constitutional Party in the United Kingdom, and because it can supply or withhold funds, without which the Parliamentary Party would be nearly powerless, and the I.R.B. would cease to exist.

In April 1883 a Convention, which was attended by Delegates from all parts of the United States was held in Philadelphia for the purpose of abolishing the Land League,[52] which had played so prominent a part in the agitation in Ireland of 1880, 1881, and 1882, and of establishing the National League. This League was to be a great public agency, under cloak of which the V.C. could carry out its secret operations. At the Convention most of the Delegates were V.C. men. The programme put forward by the V.C. was adopted, and Alexander Sullivan, the President of the F.C., was elected President of the new National League; and nearly all the members of the Executive and the principle officers were selected from members of the V.C.

At the same time, secret meetings under cover of the Convention were held. The dynamite policy was discussed, and finally adopted by a large majority; and it was decided that funds should be devoted for the purpose of carrying on "active work." The approval of the F.C. was also given to all that the Revolutionary Directory had done, or might do in the future.

At the commencement of May a Secret Circular, dated 12[th] May (a copy of which is now before me), was issued by the F.C. of the V.C. to all the D.'s in the United States, in which all were urged to join the National League, and assurances were given that "active work" was being carried on.

---

[52] The League's fourth and largest annual convention in America. The body was dissolved on 25 April 1883 and superseded by the National League: see Clyde E. Reeves, 'Philadelphia's maternal link with the Land League Fathers', *Pennsylvania Speech Annual*, 22 (September 1965).

In the Circular the F.C. say: "We urge immediate action to secure universal assent to the action of the Philadelphia Convention. Set every Society to which you belong to affiliate with the new public organization ...[53] Any two brothers not officers of the D. can be designated as President and Secretary, and those brothers can conduct any correspondence that may be necessary with the officers of the public organization. Publicly we must not be identified with the organization, and the names of the real D. officials must not be sent. ... We give you brothers the assurance of the R.D. that the most important measures are being organized and put in progress, and we believe their work will be both significant and effective." At the end of this Circular a call of money was made from the V.C., by request of the R.D.

At the same time money was furnished for the defence of Dr. Gallagher,[54] a leading member of the V.C., who had been with others arrested in London with explosives in his possession.

In September 1883 another Secret Circular was issued by the V.C., from which the following is an extract: "Nor are we idle. Other movements are being pushed, both in instructing men and securing war material. Even our disappointments are not regarded by us as failures. We believe that while agitation and public organization are necessary, these would not have been effective in securing conversions from our enemy had not the courage, the capacity, and the great scientific skill of the secret organization brought them to the very doors of the oppressor. ... Though the efforts of your Executive have not been fully realized, or rather were marred by the informers' treason, yet those brothers (with one solitary exception) entrusted with the work did nobly, and were at the very threshold of deeds that would have startled the world, and put the fear of the organization in the hearts of the enemy. These brothers have with heroic faith carried your secrets to the dungeon under a fate and torture worse than death. They did nobly. It was by no fault of theirs they failed. They have settled the legal status of a new mode of warfare. By a solemn decision of the highest authority in England, presided over by the Chief Justice, we have compelled her to recognize a new epoch in the art of war. ... We cannot see our way for an armed insurrection in Ireland this side of some great foreign war with England. But in the meantime, we shall carry on an incessant and perpetual warfare with the Power of

---

[53] Ellipsis in original (both here and in all quotations given in this document).

[54] Thomas Gallagher (1851–1925), director of training for the dynamite campaign, arrested on a mission in England in April 1883 and sentenced to life imprisonment, released in 1896 and died in a New York asylum.

England in public and in secret. . . . You will note with pleasure that the informer is foredoomed, and that no man can betray and live."

The meaning of the language here used is unmistakable, and the Circular, without disguise, acknowledges the services of Dr. Gallagher and his colleagues, who, there can be no question, worked under the direction of the R.D., and were supplied with funds by the F.C.

In August 1884 another large Convention was held in Boston for the purpose of reviewing the work of the past year, and of electing officers of the National League for the coming year. This Convention was attended by Mr. Sexton, M.P., and Mr. W. Redmond, M.P., and the proceedings were a mere repetition of what took place in April 1883 at Philadelphia.[55] The V.C. men had it all their own way. Alexander Sullivan, who had become unpopular because he had interfered in politics, and had used both the organization of the National League and of the V.C. for electioneering purposes, was forced to resign the Presidentship, and Patrick Egan, an active member of the V.C., and formerly Treasurer of the Irish Land League, a close ally of the Irish Parliamentary Party, was elected President of the National League.

At the same time, at a Secret Convention, the policy of the past and of the future was considered. Politics were altogether thrown out. Dynamite business was discussed and settled. And a new F.C., consisting this time of three instead of five members, was elected.

Immediately after this Convention in September 1884 the new F.C. issued its first Circular. After alluding to some amendments in the Constitution of the Society, and to the fact that the "active" policy adopted by the "late F.C. had been deliberately and unanimously adopted by the Convention as the rule of future operations," the Circular says: "To enter into a detailed review of the operations of the last three years as detailed before your Convention would be to take chances of disclosing the methods of future operations to the enemy, and every one will see the great weakness of disclosing the future by revealing the past. We are aware that the false claims of others are well calculated to make our brothers restive when they know the means of denying such claims exist in their possession, but to deny in each case would be to affirm, which we cannot do and succeed in the work before us. Besides, these false claims afford us the means of diverting the attention of the enemy from our work, and in that the false claims render us most valuable assistance."

The "false claims" refer of course to the claims set up by Rossa, Ford, and other independent men to the authorship of the dynamite outrages in England.

[55] See *The Times*, 8 September 1884, p. 6.

The Circular then directs attention to the necessity for extending and strengthening the organization, to the great importance of silence and secrecy, and adds: "As the present and future policy of the organization will, from prudential reasons, prevent a publication or allusion of any kind to the work on hand, the F.C. will publish but few, if any, Circulars alluding to the work in course of progress. For the progress of the work we refer you to the statements of the enemy through the press. In conclusion, we instruct you peremptorily henceforth not to talk outside your halls of the business transacted there, or of anything concerning the organization. Men talk in the streets, on their way home, in saloons, and elsewhere about our business. Some men think that loyalty to the organization compels them to talk about and defend it in the presence of outsiders and of expelled members. This is wrong. The organization needs no defence. What it does need is silence. This *must* be secured. It must be remembered that we are all sworn not only to obey the Constitution, but also to obey orders from the Executive. Those who disobey this order must be expelled. We ask that each and all make the next two years a period of the most active work in gathering the resources and extending the numbers and power of the organization. The light of a great hope is breaking through the cloud of centuries. Work and organize with all the genius of the race."

This Circular, like all others emanating from the F.C., is signed by the President, Treasurer, and Secretary.

In addition to the Percentage Fund, which has already been alluded to, and which is required for the ordinary expenses of the organization, there have been since the spring of 1883 two other funds, one called the "Special" Fund, and the other supplied from the money paid in by the D.'s in response to the call in the Circular of the 12$^{th}$ May, 1883. These two funds have been devoted to the work carried on under the direction of the R.D., and to contributions to the Treasury of the I.R.B. in Great Britain and Ireland.

From information received, and from printed statements before me, it is calculated that, exclusive of other balances in hand, and of the remains of the "Skirmishing Fund"[56] (the Trustees of which are under the control of the V.C.), amounting to 37,000 dollars, the money received for these two funds up to October 1884 was about 89,000 dollars, and that the balance in hand at the close of 1884 was about 26,000 dollars. The call for this large sum was, it should be remembered, made at the request of the R.D. and was therefore intended to be used entirely for revolutionary purposes.

[56] Established at the suggestion of Jeremiah O'Donovan Rossa in 1875, it was used by Clan-na-Gael to finance the 'New Departure' and the dynamite campaign in Great Britain.

The amount sent over to the Executive of the I.R.B. for work in Great Britain and Ireland during 1884 was about 40,000 dollars.

We thus see clearly what an important position is held by the V.C. in the movement against England, and how, having the command of the finances, it is able to support and control the sister organization in the United Kingdom.

I firmly believe that if it were possible to take the opinions of the members of the I.R.B. in Great Britain and Ireland, it would be found that very few of them are in favour of explosions and outrages. They know too well that such work can in the end only injure their cause, and must do great harm to the Irish working population in Great Britain. But the funds of the I.R.B. are low. There is hardly money enough to pay the ordinary working expenses of the organization. If the Society is to be kept alive, if work is to be done, money must come from the richer organization in America; and during the past two years the leaders of the I.R.B. have been compelled to give their approval to the policy adopted by the V.C. in America, because, had they not done so, the supplies, as was threatened, would have been stopped.

Thus we see the great power and importance of the Secret Society in the United States, whose organization and policy I have in this paper attempted to describe. This Society and the I.R.B. in the United Kingdom are separate in their organization, and in the management of their finances; but the latter, being poor, is dependent on the former to carry on any active operations, and in pursuing their revolutionary projects the two act as one body through the Revolutionary Directory, which is a secret Committee, formed of men chosen from both Societies by the F.C. of the V.C. and the S.C. of the I.R.B.

Our efforts, then, in this country, against the operations of the I.R.B., cannot be really effective unless measures are taken to check the influence and to thwart the designs of the V.C. in the United States of America.

I have very strong reasons for believing that the explosions at Scotland Yard in May and at London Bridge in December 1884[57] were the work of the Revolutionary Directory, and that funds were in both cases supplied by the V.C.

The V.C. disapprove of independent work by Societies, or individuals who are not members of it. Their object is to unite all Irishmen under one Executive, and to get into their own hands the direction of all operations against the common enemy, England. And they therefore give no support to men like Patrick Ford and O'Donovan Rossa, who keep open subscription lists in their own

[57] The explosions occurred on 30 May and 13 December 1884.

papers, and have secret agents of their own working for them in the United Kingdom.

Since I wrote the above the explosions in the Tower of London and the Houses of Parliament have occurred. These, I am confident, were the work of the Clan-na-Gaels, for at the end of December 1884 I received reliable information that this Society intended very shortly to attempt an explosion in the House of Commons, and I wrote to the Chief Commissioner of the Metropolitan Police warning him, and asking him to take precautionary measures.[58]

**9.** Sir Robert Hamilton to Lord Spencer, 26 April 1885; Chief Secretary's Office, Dublin Castle; AP, Add MS 77060.

The estimation in the popular mind of the attitude of the Liberal Government to Ireland will depend at the next elections more upon the policy announced now than upon what has actually been done legislatively or administratively in the last few years, whether that be viewed in a favourable or an unfavourable light.

The extreme Parliamentary party seek to make Government in Ireland impossible. Disturbance is the only atmosphere in which they thrive. I therefore not only regard with extreme distrust their bona fides in putting forward any propositions which do not involve absolute and complete separation from England, but I feel sure that they will oppose any changes which they regard as calculated to render the bulk of the people in Ireland more contented. I do not look forward therefore, by any measures we may propose with this object, that we shall be able to conciliate the extreme members of the party, and I am aware that the Parliamentary difficulties to be faced from their opposition and obstruction will be extremely formidable. Formidable however as these may be they ought not for a moment be allowed to weigh against the real interests of Ireland, or to lead to any line being taken with the view of lessening them which would involve the risk of a state of serious disturbance arising in the Country and its progress towards contentment & prosperity being retarded.

But altho' you can't conciliate the extremists there is a moderate section in the country who have hitherto gone with them, and this section can, and I believe by the introduction of judicious measures will, be formed into a party, who, altho' perhaps going somewhat in

[58] See Jenkinson to James Monro, 26 December 1884: MEPO 3/3070; Jenkinson to Spencer, 25 and 26 January 1885: AP, Add MS 77035.

advance, will work with and not against those who are striving for the better Government of the Country. These are the people who will be influenced by the policy now to be adopted & announced for Ireland, and their state of feeling will be reflected to some extent in the new Parliamentary representatives who tho' they will be followers of Mr. Parnell will exercise a moderating influence on the councils of the party.

Now the first duty of any Government is to maintain order & enforce obedience to the law, while removing all real grievances to which the people are subject.

To enforce the law we must have as perfect a police organization as possible, and the experience of the last few years shows that it is absolutely necessary that we should be able to maintain the decentralization effected by the creation of Divisional Magistrates. The police bill therefore legalizing the position of these magistrates must without fail be passed.[59]

We must also have power to secure a fair trial by change of venue & we must have power to deal with intimidation. Certain other powers now conferred by the Prevention of Crimes Act would be useful but are not in my view indispensable.

Then as regards grievances, that connected with the land, which in an agricultural country like Ireland touches the great bulk of the people, has been dealt with, and now only requires to be completed by a workable scheme of purchase, but this I do not regard as so pressing as to be absolutely necessary at the present moment. It is only the landlords who are pressing for it.

The real existing grievance is that there is no local government.

Let representative County Boards be at once established in Ireland elected jointly by occupiers and owners, and let it be boldly announced that this is only the commencement and necessary foundation of local government which will be carried further if the powers conferred are properly used. This will be accepted by the moderate people as an earnest of confidence in them. It will afford employment for them and give them some idea of responsibility in matters of government.

Then abolish the Vice Royalty & have a Royal residence in Ireland. The people will understand by this that they are no longer to be governed by the will of one man, but that they are to [be]

---

[59] Divisional magistrates were temporarily appointed in December 1881 to supervise policing in the twelve most disturbed counties of Ireland. Their powers were later limited as the scheme was extended to the whole country. This was the third legislative attempt to make the positions permanent ones: see Stephen Ball, 'Policing the Land War: official responses to political protest and agrarian crime in Ireland, 1879–91' (unpublished PhD thesis, University of London, 2000), pp. 161–164, 300–304.

constitutionally governed like other subjects of the Queen in England
& Scotland. The recent visit of the Prince of Wales has prepared the
Country for this change. They accept their position as subjects of the
Crown, while they strongly object to be [sic] governed by a minister
whom they regard as the head of the Castle. The Extreme party are
wise enough to see that such a change will not suit their views and
they will oppose it now altho' they have often advocated it before.

Lastly let an experiment be tried of entrusting Primary Education
in Ireland to an Irish representative body elected jointly by the
managers of schools & the guardians of the poor as representing
the educational & financial interests respectively.[60] This would be
an important experiment of local control over a large branch of
administration & ample justification exists for selecting this branch in
the fact that Imperial aid to Education has reached its utmost limits,
& the necessary further support for its maintenance and development
must be raised locally, & should be locally controlled.

Some advocate the granting at once of what for the want of a better
word may be called Home Rule, but this I think would be disastrous.
If it were done, the whole energy of the local Parliament would be
directed to securing separation from England & the establishment of
the machinery of local government would be neglected. A state of
chaos would supervene, and England which would never tolerate the
existence of a Hayti on her borders, would be obliged to withdraw
the concession, and establish a reign of repression under which the
progress of the country towards contentment and prosperity would be
indefinitely retarded.

Another suggestion is that an elected body should manage all
the Administrative Depts. in the Country, leaving legislation with
the Imperial Parliament. This course would lead to the gravest
difficulties. Such a body, with some show of reason, would be held
to be representative of the whole country for all purposes and entitled
to express their opinion on every subject. This would be an intense
embarrassment to the Government of the day. They would never
confine themselves to their legitimate functions which it would be very
difficult to define, and the conflict between them and the Treasury, as
Guardians of the Imperial Exchequer would from a political point of
view intensify the difficulties of Irish Administration.

This in my view would be a too hazardous experiment to make. The
experiment I propose as regards Education gets rid of both classes of
difficulties, (1) the body not being elected by the ratepayers generally
could not assume to represent with authority the views of the people
on other subjects than Education, and (2) by allowing no discretion to

[60] See Hamilton to Spencer, 19 April 1885: AP, Add MS 77060.

this body as to the amount of the grant from the Imperial Exchequer, the dangerous conflict which I foresee in the other case with the Treasury would be avoided.

**10.** George Fottrell to Joseph Chamberlain, 3 July 1885; Geo. D. Fottrell & Sons, 46 Fleet St., Dublin; JCP, JC8/4/1/2.

You must excuse me for having so long delayed sending you the promised notes on the educational system and the municipal system in Ireland.[61]

It was only such time as I could snatch from my professional duties that I could [*illegible*] to making the necessary enquiries, & hence the delay.

I now send you,

1. Notes on municipal government in Ireland.
2. Notes on primary education in Ireland.
3. Rules of the Board of National Education.
4. Report just issued by the Board for the year 1884.
5. Form of application used by the Board.

I trust that these documents may give you some if not all of the information which you desire.

If you still require further information please let me know & I shall try to provide it for you.

I see that you have resolved not to visit Glasgow at the end of this month.

Have you definitely resolved when you will come to Ireland. I expect to leave Dublin on the 12th August for a month's vacation & I should like to be at home when you come.

*United Ireland* attacks the Local Government Scheme as quite incomplete.[62] I am glad of this. Less than your scheme would be of little use and I have learned enough of politics to know that a scheme has no chance of passing into law unless it be considered a middle term. If therefore the national press supported your scheme it would never get through, but with judicious apathy or even condemnation by them it may have a chance.

---

[61] See JCP, JC8/4/1/5 and JC8/4/1/6.
[62] See *United Ireland*, 27 June and 4 July 1885; Frank Callanan, *T.M. Healy* (Cork, 1996), pp. 119–120.

**11.** Sir Robert Hamilton to Lord Carnarvon, 1 August 1885; 'Very secret'; CP/TNA, PRO 30/6/67 (1).

I have just returned from breakfasting at the Shelbourne with Sir Charles Gavan Duffy and while the conversation is fresh in my mind I will endeavour to put it upon paper as exactly as I can. Mr. Fottrell of whom I have spoken to Your Excellency as enjoying the confidence of the best of the national party was present.[63]

I should premise that the conversation was strictly confidential, and that Sir Charles more than once said that the identification of his own or of any other name with any particular scheme would be most undesirable and that the only chance of success was that the Govt. should enunciate a scheme after having perfected it in all its detail. That portions of such a scheme however defensible as part of a whole, would be carped at and perhaps discredited if they came out separately as the suggestions of any individual. He told me he had never opened his mind on the subject to any one to the extent he had confided his views this morning to me.

First, he put on one side altogether any scheme of mere County Government, while quite admitting the necessity for establishing this upon a sound basis, on the two grounds, (1) that it would go no way whatever in satisfying national aspirations, and (2) that it would bring to the front quite second rate and inferior men.

He said nothing short of an Irish Parliament would set at rest the Irish Question, & he told me a curious fact that Michael Davitt & John O'Leary[64] both stated solemnly to him that if this were conceded they would bind themselves to accept it, and in no way to use it for going further in the direction of separation from England.

With the view of securing the rights of the minority and of property he thinks the Irish Parliament should be elected on the basis of minority representation. Taking for example a Parliament of 100 members he thinks one third might be taken to represent the property & monied & Protestant population. He further assumes that there would be a contingent of moderate representatives which together would make a pretty close balance of parties, and prevent any wild or extreme measure being brought forward.

Then he would have a second chamber, a Senate composed of say 60 members, whose names should in the first instance be stated in the

---

[63] See **Journal (30 July, 5 August 1885)**.

[64] John O'Leary (1830–1907), Young Irelander and Fenian, President of the Supreme Council of the IRB (1874–1885), opponent of parliamentary nationalism, returned to Ireland from exile in Paris in 1885 and influenced a generation of literary nationalists; see Marcus Bourke, *John O'Leary: a study in Irish separatism* (Dublin, 1967).

bill, to be re-elected afterwards by Provinces say every 6 years from certain specified classes, and by the rate or tax payers with certain property qualifications.

He would give to the Irish Parliament the fullest powers of taxation and, after a settlement of accounts with England, he would leave the Irish Parliament free to raise its revenues as it thought best. He would not allow any local forces to be raised in Ireland, & such troops as England might station in Ireland should be paid for out of the Irish Exchequer.

He would withdraw altogether the Irish representatives from the House of Commons, but he looks forward to a grand union of all dependencies of the Empire in an Imperial Parliament in London in which Ireland should be represented, and if this were done he then believes that Ireland in common with other outlying parts of the Empire would readily contribute to the expense of foreign wars approved by this Central Parliament. In the absence of such a federal assembly he thinks Ireland should not be called upon to pay any part of the cost of foreign wars.

He strongly advises that Mr. Parnell who represents so largely the opinion of Ireland on these matters should be taken into council by the Government, and that a Committee or Commission of six or seven members should be appointed of whom about half should be men with knowledge of official administration, & the remainder the most distinguished members of the national party. This Committee should draw up a constitution for Ireland which should be submitted to the Government. The Government should then determine how far they are prepared to take action in the matter, and should announce to the leaders of the national party what they are prepared to do, and carry, if they should come into power with a majority after the general election; or to announce it as their policy for the future if they should be in a minority.

He would then retain the office of Lord Lieutenant; but would make it like the office of Governor General of India a time appointment.

I did not feel at liberty to suggest the idea of a council partly nominated and partly elected, but I feel pretty sure that this would not have found acceptance with him.

I pointed out the great objection that would be raised in England to English manufactured goods being subjected to taxes on importation into Ireland, but he said he thought this would be done only to a limited extent, and not directly, but [by] means of bounties given out of the Irish Exchequer to foster individual industries in Ireland. I cannot say that my free trade views favour this idea but I quite think Ireland will never be satisfied that she has got power over her own affairs unless she possesses the power to raise her own revenue as she thinks best.

It is of course conceivable that the great Imperial Parliament of the future might deal with such matters for the Empire as a whole, in which case Ireland would fall in with the rest.

He was very strong about keeping the gentry & men of culture in the Country, and lamented the present position of the Irish gentleman with no possibility before him of taking any part in the Govt. of his Country. The establishment of a Parliament would he felt sure bring the best of these men to the front again, while a measure restricted to County Govt. would probably drive them out of the Country.

I think I have faithfully reported what he said as regards what he considers alone will satisfy the Country & put an end to agitation. He spoke in the highest terms of Your Excellency, and said it augured well for the cause of Ireland that you should have accepted the post of Lord Lieutenant, and for himself he said that having realized a competence for his declining years and while he would not take the most lucrative appointment that might be offered to him, he would gladly serve in an Irish Parliament, even at the certain cost of shortening the few remaining years of life that he may hope to live.

**12.** E.G. Jenkinson to Sir Richard Cross, 2 September 1885; 'Private'; CP/TNA, PRO 30/6/62 (21).

I received your note in reply to mine of Friday last on my return from Dublin yesterday. Mr. Monro[65] will return from leave on the 4[th] and I propose to go away on Saturday or Monday, but as I said before I shall go on with my work just the same. Being away from town will not make any difference whatever, and really things are so quiet just now, that I could not choose a better time for going away.

Everything about the Irish Police administration has now been settled. Colonel Bruce[66] is to retire immediately. Mr. Reed has been appointed his successor and all the arrangements proposed by me in the memorandum which you read will be carried out at once. When I was over in Dublin the manner in which my particular branch of the work should be carried on was discussed, and I drew up a memorandum on the subject to which Mr. Reed agreed, and which was approved of by Lord Carnarvon.[67] Practically there is no real difference. The Irish work of the "Special" Department will come to

[65] James Monro (1838–1920), Assistant Commissioner and head of CID (1884–1888), Commissioner of the Metropolitan Police (1888–1890).

[66] Lieutenant-Colonel Robert Bruce (1825–1899), Chief Constable of Lancashire (1868–1877), Deputy and Inspector-General of the RIC (1877–1882, 1882–1885).

[67] For details of these arrangements, see Jenkinson to Carnarvon, 18 September 1885: CP/TNA, PRO 30/6/62 (23); Hamilton to Secretary of Treasury, 25 September 1885: NAI, Government Letter Books, CSO LB 283.

me as usual, but my minutes will in future be addressed to the Inspector General instead of to the Divisional Magistrates.[68] The arrangement is I think a very good one, and will work well.

As regards myself nothing was settled. Indeed Lord Carnarvon told me that it was not in his power to settle anything, but said he was writing to you on the subject, and desired me to write also on my return to London. He promised me however that until something is definitely settled here, I should retain my appointment as Assistant Under Secretary, and even if there be some delay in giving me an appointment over here, there will be no difficulty as regards my appointment in Ireland because my pay has been voted up till February next, and there cannot therefore be any trouble in Parliament about it.

I feel however that there are so many difficulties attending the settlement of the matter that I should like very much before any final decision is come to to have the opportunity of talking it over with you. I know that it would be inadvisable to make a permanent appointment in connection with the special kind of work on which I am engaged. I always live in hope that some solution of the Irish question may be found, and that all this Fenianism and Dynamite work may cease. At present the situation is this – Nationalists and Fenians of all sections have fallen into line with Parnell. They are all determined to wait, and watch the result of the General Election and of the next Session. Meanwhile a truce has been declared; all the influence of the Parnellites and leading Nationalists and moderate Fenians will be exercised to prevent outrages both in Ireland and in Great Britain, and I feel confident that no outrages will be attempted by any of the organizations either in Ireland or in America: Some wild individuals might perhaps break away and attempt something, but they would not be acting under the direction of any organization, and anything they might do would be comparatively insignificant. If before the close of the next session the Parnellites succeed in obtaining some form of Home Rule we should probably hear no more of Dynamite or outrages, but should they fail then Fenians of all ranks both in Great Britain and Ireland and in America will be up again and we shall have a repetition of what happened in 1881 and 1882 in Ireland and Dynamite outrages and murders in London and other parts of Great Britain. On this I know they are determined, and they are even now collecting money, organizing, and making preparations in Great Britain and in America. Agents have lately been over discussing the question with the Parliamentary Party, and with the leading Nationalists and Fenians in Ireland and settling plans for the future.

[68] For a discussion of the departmental reform of the Irish police force in this period, see Ball, 'Policing the Land War', pp. 293–305.

Much as I should like to do so, I could not under these circumstances advise you to make any change in my position or in the arrangements connected with my work. We must keep on collecting information, and watching all National and Fenian organizations during the next year, and beyond that one cannot look at the present moment. If the hopes of the Nationalists are realized, as I hope they will be, you will not have any further need for my services, but if not it will be time enough to decide what to do at the end of the year.

So I can see how difficult it must be to look forward in my case, and to give me any assurances of settled employment – yet if anything could be settled it would be a great comfort and convenience to me for in the present state of uncertainty I cannot take a house or settle down anywhere and such a condition of things entails a great deal of expense, and discomfort to my family. Besides not feeling sure what is in the future, and not having any appointment which carries any pension with it I naturally cannot be free from anxiety. If I could be certain that I should remain in doing my present work in the Home Office for another year from this time, and after that should obtain some other appointment at London I could take a house somewhere and get all my things together. Would it be impossible to make me with the sanction of the Treasury an Assistant Under Secretary in the Home Office in the same way as I was made Ass. U. Secretary in Dublin in 1882? However as I said before I should very much like to speak to you about all this before anything is settled and meanwhile there is no immediate hurry because I still hold my appointment in Dublin, and I cannot do anything about taking a house till my return from the seaside towards the end of October.[69]

**13.** Sir Robert Hamilton to Lord Carnarvon, 23 September 1885; Chief Secretary's Office, Dublin Castle; 'Secret'; CP/TNA, PRO 30/6/67 (11).

I have had a very interesting conversation with Mr Harrel the Commissioner of the Dublin Police on the feeling of the country respecting Your Excellency. Mr Harrel has means of ascertaining such feeling, & I entirely rely upon his information on the subject.[70]

He tells me the feeling is undoubtedly most friendly, and that what may be called the national party would be prepared to accept from you measures relating to the government of the country which would

[69] See Jenkinson to Cross, 11 August 1885: TNA, HO 144/721/110757.
[70] See Harrel to Carnarvon, 19 September 1885: CP/TNA, PRO 30/6/67 (10).

have no chance of acceptance if proposed by another. He says that the friendly disposition you have evinced in all matters in which they are interested has gained their affections, & that they trust you as a real friend of the Country.

Your presence on a recent occasion in the Cathedral of Armagh, and the few kind words you said there, have greatly touched them, and while at first they were disposed to regard your friendly words as more or less put on, they now recognize them as genuine and real.[71]

It would be a thousand pities that this attitude of the country should not be taken advantage of to the fullest extent, & bearing in mind how the history of Ireland shows that everything in the nature of amelioration has come too late, & instead of being received with gratitude has borne the appearance of having been wrung by pressure, I would strongly urge the importance of avoiding delay in dealing with the great subject of the government of this country.

We have arrived at a point that no half measures will succeed. You must either govern the country in all details of government or let them govern themselves under sufficient safeguards against confiscation & separation.

I write with the fullest appreciation of the gravity of the situation, and without being prepared with any cut & dried scheme to lay before you, on this most difficult problem, which has arisen probably in this generation, but simply to urge upon you with all the force I can that the consideration of the whole subject should be undertaken at once.


**14.** Lord Carnarvon, 'Conversation with Fottrell', 24 September 1885; Vice Regal Lodge, Dublin; CP/TNA, PRO 30/6/67 (21).

(1) He anticipates trouble this autumn from lowness of prices. If only prices were high all wd be quiet and well. The Irish labourer will pay if he is able. He fears & has recollection of the legal costs to w$^{\underline{h}}$ he was put during the years of agitation.

Landlords are very poor – & some are hard & tenants if they cannot pay will fight.

(2) Land now is difficult to sell, but if once a commencement is made, though at first tenants will get it at very low prices speculators will soon come in & raise the price.

Vernon[72] told Fottrell that he remembered in 1853 a property selling at 7 years' purchase.

[71] See *The Times*, 17 September 1885, p. 7.
[72] John Edward Vernon (1816–1887), landowner and agent to the Earl of Pembroke and Montgomery, Irish Land Commissioner (1881–1887), Governor of the Bank of Ireland (1885).

(3) Some landlords and agents are angry with me: because they consider me too liberal.

(4) He admits that in any future constitutional changes the real difficulty wd. be the absence of a police to collect rent etc. He is not afraid of the people's general temper wh. is loyal & conservative. He believes there has been a gt. change towards conservative views among the more responsible Irish leaders. The prospect of coming change is exercising a sobering effect on them.

**15.** E.G. Jenkinson, 'Memorandum on the present situation in Ireland'; 26 September 1885; 'Secret'; Printed for the use of the Cabinet, 2 November 1885; CAB 37/16/52.[73]

The present time, when we are on the eve of a General Election, and when affairs in Ireland demand such earnest attention, seems to be a fitting one in which to consider the condition and probable policy of the National League, and of the different Fenian organizations which are closely connected with it, and to endeavour to draw some conclusions which may be of use in the solution of the very difficult and intricate problem which lies before us.

In my printed memorandum of 22nd January 1885,[74] I described the organization of the V.C., or Clan-na-Gael, in the United States of America, and showed how intimately the I.R.B. of the United Kingdom, the Irish Parliamentary Party, and the National League, both in America and the United Kingdom, were connected with that powerful organization, and how they were all working together with one common object.

Since then events have marched rapidly, and great changes have taken place. The National League in America, of which Patrick Egan, former Treasurer to the Irish Land League, is President, still remains under the influence of the V.C. organization, and is in close alliance with the National League in the United Kingdom and with Mr. Parnell and his party; but there has been an estrangement, amounting almost to a rupture, between the V.C. and the I.R.B., and the consequence of which is that, for the moment, the latter organization is not nearly so powerful or so influential as it used to be. The members are as numerous as ever, but the organization, from want of funds and recognized leaders, has fallen to pieces, and the Supreme Council, which should consist of eleven, has now only five members.

---

[73] For original letter, see Jenkinson to Carnarvon, 26 September 1885: CP/TNA, PRO 30/6/62 (24).
[74] See **Document 8**.

The estrangement between these two organizations commenced in the summer of 1884. The Executive Council of the V.C., which had begun to take the direction of operations in England into its own hands, complained that the men in Great Britain and Ireland were not active enough, that no sufficient results were shown for funds supplied from America, and that secrecy was not maintained; while the Supreme Council of the I.R.B. objected to the blowing up of railway trains and buildings in London, and to the manner in which operations were being carried on. They contended that they, on the spot, were the best judges of the time and mode of action, and that there was no reason for a departure from the old arrangement under which money was sent to them from America, and their wishes were consulted and their advice taken before any plan of operations was decided on.

They were told, in reply to these protests, that unless they were willing to fall in with the views and policy of the V.C. no more money would be sent to them, and that the intimate relations between the two organizations must cease. Since then no supplies have been received by the I.R.B., and the V.C. has been acting independently. We now know for certain that the explosions in London at the end of 1884, and in the House of Commons and the Tower of London in January 1885, were the work of the V.C., acting independently, and even against the wishes of the I.R.B.

At the Convention which was held at Boston in August 1884 the Extremists had everything their own way. Patrick Egan was elected President of the National League in succession to Alexander Sullivan, of Chicago, and the constitution of the V.C. was revised and amended. In order to ensure secrecy, the mode of election of members of the Executive was altered, the number of the Executive was reduced from seven to three, and the Article under which the R.D., or Revolutionary Directory, was composed of seven members belonging to the I.R.B. and the V.C., was cancelled, and the number was limited to three men, all members of the V.C.

In consequence of these proceedings, John O'Connor, the Acting President of the I.R.B., went, at the request of the other members of the Supreme Council to America in the end of February 1885, to endeavour to bring about a reconciliation with the V.C., but he does not seem to have met with much success.

Negotiations are still going on which may end in the re-establishment of a close intimacy between the two organizations on the terms offered, and on the conditions laid down by the V.C. On the other hand, signs are not wanting that the I.R.B. will become extinct, the more moderate members joining the ranks of the National League, and the Extremists, or those who are in favour of violent measures, becoming members of a new revolutionary organization, which will be worked on very secret lines, and will be in close connection with a similar organization, or with the V.C. in the United States. Very much, however, depends upon the course of events during the next few months, and on the policy of the English Government towards Ireland after the General Election.

It is clear that nothing was settled during John O'Connor's stay in America, for last week (September 13th to 17th) a most important meeting of the Supreme Council was held in France with the object of receiving Patrick Kiernan Walsh, the paid delegate of the V.C., and one of the oldest and most trusted members of the organization in the United States. At this meeting P.K. Walsh read a long paper, in the nature of an ultimatum from the Executive of the V.C. to the Supreme Council of the I.R.B., in which the latter were asked to account for or to refund the sum of 12,000l., which had been remitted to them, and were plainly told that if they should refuse to join in a policy of action the V.C. would have nothing more to say to them, and would continue to work in the United Kingdom independently of them.

After this paper had been read, various methods of action were discussed. Among these were the blowing up of buildings and English men-of-war, and the assassination of myself and Major Gosselin,[75] and of leading statesmen who might show hostility to the "Irish cause." Finally, a reply was drawn up in which the Supreme Council declared against dynamite in every way, and, without committing themselves to any particular measures, stated that they were willing to join the V.C. in a policy of action. The Delegate left Havre for New York with this reply on the 18th August,[76] and within a short time we ought to know the result. Meanwhile, measures will be taken to elect a full Council of eleven members, of which in all probability John O'Leary or Michael Davitt will be made President, and efforts will be made to put new life and vigour into the organization.

This is how matters stand for the present as regards the relations between the two large sister Fenian organizations, and I have entered this much into detail about them because an understanding of them is necessary if we wish to have a correct knowledge of the present situation, and to be able to form some estimate of the future.

The recent successes of the Irish Parliamentary Party under the leadership of Mr. Parnell, the non-renewal of the Prevention of Crimes Act, the change of policy in Ireland following upon a change of

---

[75] Nicholas Gosselin (1839–1917), Adjutant of the Cavan Militia (1877–1882), RM for Sligo (1882–1888), deputy to Jenkinson with responsibility for the north of England (1884–1887), head of the 'Secret Department' of the Home Office (1888–1901).

[76] Should read 'September'.

Government, and the hope that in the next Parliament Mr. Parnell, with his eighty or ninety followers, will succeed in obtaining Home Rule for Ireland, have, for the time being, quieted the Extremists, and led to a cessation of active hostilities against England. All, with the exception of some of the more violent spirits and irreconcilables, are willing to give the Parliamentary Party a chance. Mr. Parnell, they think, is riding the winning horse, and just now the enthusiasm about him is unbounded, and his will is law. In America the National League, under the Presidentship of Patrick Egan, is giving Mr. Parnell all the support it can, and is sending money wherewith to carry on the Parliamentary campaign. The Clan-na-Gaels have decided to stop all active work until next year, and are engaged in organizing and raising money and making preparations for revolutionary work in the future; and in many of the States money is being subscribed for the purpose of paying Irish Members of Parliament, the State of New York (excluding the cities of New York and Brooklyn) alone having guaranteed the salaries of six members; while in Ireland the National League, under the direction of Mr. Parnell, is all-powerful, and Fenians and Nationalists are working together on the same lines, united and confident of success.

Not many weeks ago it looked as if Michael Davitt might succeed in renewing the fight against landlords and rent on the lines of the Land League. He argued that such an agitation would be joined by all classes, and that it would help Mr. Parnell. But Mr. Parnell's counsels of prudence and moderation happily prevailed, and Michael Davitt's "fighting policy" does not for the moment meet with approval. We should, however, remember that he represents the opinions of a very large number of Irishmen. There are many who with him believe that "nothing is to be got by reason, by entreaty, by patient endurance, but everything by intimidation;" that as O'Connell failed, so will Parnell fail; and that, "though diplomacy may avail something in Westminster, it never has achieved, and never will achieve, anything but defeat for the popular cause in Ireland." All these men will be ready to adopt a "fighting policy" the moment they see that Parnell's policy is not going to succeed.

It is not necessary to lengthen this Memorandum by describing in detail the present condition of affairs in Ireland. So far the determination to rule Ireland under the ordinary law has met with success. It is true that the National League has increased in power and influence, and that the practice of "boycotting" has not only extended, but is being abused. There has also been a slight increase in agrarian outrages. But there are not at present any signs of a renewal of agitation and outrages such as we had in 1881 and 1882. Mr. Parnell and his lieutenants are doing all they can to keep down outrages, and have even condemned the indiscriminate use of "boycotting." At the same time, the feeling against the English Government and against the landlords was never worse than it is now, and I do not hesitate to say that were it not for the faith which the people have in Mr. Parnell, and for the influence which he and his party exercise over them, there would be an outbreak of serious outrages in all the worst and most distressed parts of Ireland.

At present there is, as the Fenians themselves describe it, a truce. All are waiting to see the result of the General Election and of the action of the Parliamentary Party during the next Session. All are prepared to fight to the bitter end, and the Parliamentary Party are determined in the next Parliament to take an active interest, as they put it, in all English questions, and to worry the English Legislature into a concession of Home Rule. They are not attached to one party more than another, neither have they faith in either party. The Irish vote, it is true, is to be given to the Conservatives; but this is not because they love the Conservatives any more than they do the Liberals, but because they hope to weaken the Liberal majority, and so hold the balance between both parties in Parliament.

It is therefore clear that we have arrived at a most critical time in Irish history. It is a most serious consideration that the peace of Ireland depends upon the influence and position of Mr. Parnell, and upon the forbearance of the Extremists, and it is a consideration which should, I think, have great weight with the leaders of both parties in their public utterances. Any words which may lessen Mr. Parnell's influence, or dash hopes which at the present time fill the hearts of the Irish people, might lead to an outbreak of crime and to the renewal of dynamite outrages. And there can be no doubt that in this sense some recent speeches, in which it was declared that it would be impossible to grant an independent Parliament to Ireland, had an injurious effect.[77] They confirmed the fears and the opinions of the Fenians and Extremists, and encouraged them to break away from Mr. Parnell, and to set the organization for the commission of outrages into motion again.

We may be quite sure of this: unless Mr. Parnell succeeds in obtaining during this next year Home Rule, or a promise of Home Rule, for Ireland, he will either fall from power and lose all control over the Irish people, or he will have to place himself at the head of a revolutionary movement. In America they firmly believe that when the times comes he will not hesitate to adopt the latter course. The leading Fenians in New York and Chicago say that, in the event of failure in Parliament, he has given his word to adopt revolutionary measures, and though this may be an exaggeration, yet it is not without some

[77] See **Journal** (**11 September 1885**).

support from some of Mr. Parnell's recent speeches. It was in his speech at the banquet to General Collins[78] on the 22nd July last that he said: "Speaking for myself, and without consulting my colleagues, as one who has never shrunk from any risk, from any sacrifice in the times of the Land League, as one who may be willing to go much further than any of us went in the times of the Land League, if occasion required, I will say that I consider our movement of this winter should be one distinguished by its judgment, its prudence, and its moderation."[79]

There was a great outcry in the English newspapers against Mr. Parnell's declaration of his policy in his August speeches in Dublin, and all jumped to the conclusion that nothing less than separation from England would satisfy the demands of the Irish.[80] But I do not understand that Mr. Parnell asked for more than he ever asked for before, and I think that Mr. Parnell's peculiar position at the time, and the necessity for making such speeches, were not properly appreciated by the English press. Mr. Parnell had a double purpose in view; he had to destroy Michael Davitt's influence, and to say something which would satisfy the Extremists and prevent them from committing outrages; and he had also to unite under his banner, and to bring into harmony with his policy, Fenians, and Nationalists of all classes and opinions, in order that he might secure the return of his nominees for Parliament at his proposed County Conventions. In this he has succeeded. He spoke, may be, in rather bold and exaggerated language, but he never demanded absolute separation. What he says is, that nothing but legislative independence will satisfy the demands and aspirations of Ireland, and that does not imply separation. He knows that is impossible. "Separation from Great Britain," as Mr. O'Kelly, M.P.,[81] one of the most extreme men in the Parliamentary Party, said in his speech at Leeds on the 21st September, "could only be achieved by force."[82]

To hope that the Parliamentary Party may become disunited, or that "Mr Parnell's influence will melt away," and that there will be

[78] Patrick Andrew Collins (1844–1905), US Representative for Massachusetts, 4th District (1883–1889), President of the American Land League (1881), and leader of the moderate wing of Irish nationalism in the US.

[79] The dinner was held at the Café Royal, London: F.S.L. Lyons, *Charles Stewart Parnell* (London, 1977), pp. 292–293.

[80] Speaking at the Parliamentary Party banquet at the Imperial Hotel, Dublin, Parnell declared that national independence would henceforth be the party's sole platform: *The Times*, 25 August 1885, p. 4.

[81] James J. O'Kelly (1845–1916), Nat. MP for Co. Roscommon (1880–1885) and for Roscommon North (1885–1892, 1895–1916), IRB organizer in England and correspondent for the *New York Herald*, played a significant role in developing the 'New Departure' and was imprisoned for his part in the land agitation (1881–1882).

[82] Kelly addressed the local branch of the Irish National League at the Albert Hall, Leeds, on 20 September 1885: *The Times*, 22 September 1885, p. 6.

"an end of the crusade," if the demand for legislative independence be firmly met, is to take a most foolish and short-sighted view of the situation. Ireland is passing through a revolution, and we hope that it may be a bloodless one, resulting in the establishment of good government, and in the ultimate welfare and prosperity of the people. We have to deal now with a united party under the leadership of a man who deserves the name of a statesman, and who is looked up to and followed by the Irish people in Ireland and in all parts of the world. Are we likely to come to a peaceful and satisfactory solution of this very difficult question when we are face to face with Separatists and Dynamitards, and when Mr. Parnell no longer retains his influence? Should we not rather endeavour to keep him in his present position, and to attempt to settle the question while his party is still united, and before moderate counsels give way to agitation and active revolution?

There never was a time in which the "Irish question" so urgently pressed for solution.

The only fear is that we may be too late (as, alas! is too frequently the case in our dealings with Ireland) in doing what is wise and just and right. We missed, in my opinion, a great opportunity at the end of 1883, when we were strong, and had repressed all outrage in Ireland. We might have done then what it may be impossible to do now; and if we neglect the present opportunity, we may not be able to do a year hence what we could do now. Two years ago a large measure of local self government, leading gradually up to Home Rule, would have satisfied Ireland. A year hence, perhaps, the Extremists will have got the upper hand, and then nothing but absolute separation will content them.

I have always held that our policy in Ireland during the last three years could only make matters grow worse and worse, and was not an honest one towards the people of Ireland. Our Government of the country was neither one thing nor the other. It had the pretence of being a constitutional Government, but we only kept the country in order by suspending the Constitution; and we were not honest, because, while we set our faces against Home Rule, we gave free licence to the press, and allowed it to vilify and abuse our administration, and to educate the people to believe that Ireland never can be prosperous except it has a Parliament of its own. We also allowed the National League to rise up on the ashes of the Land League, and to cover Ireland with its branches and its organization. Depend upon it that the time has now come when the present state of things can no longer continue, when we must make up our minds to the adoption of one of two courses. We must either have recourse to what is called the "strong arm" policy, or we must boldly acknowledge the principle of Home Rule, and give Ireland, gradually if possible, a separate Parliament for the management of its own internal affairs.

I think it would be a mistake before the General Election to make any declaration of policy. It would not be taken in good faith by the Irish, and would only be construed into a bid for the Irish vote. But would not the return of eighty or ninety Home Rulers to Parliament give us an opportunity for acknowledging frankly and generously that the large majority of the Irish people were in favour of Home Rule, and for trying, in consultation with the leaders, to find some practical solution of the difficulty, and to ascertain whether a separate Parliament could not be granted to Ireland without endangering the supremacy of the Crown, and without disintegration of the Empire?

I will not say more about the first of the two courses which I have mentioned than that I believe the "strong arm" policy to be simply impracticable and impossible. The people of England would not for long consent to see Ireland ruled under a despotic form of Government, and it certainly would not satisfy the people of Ireland, and restore wealth and prosperity to the country.

The advantages of Home Rule, if it can be introduced without violent disturbances and great injustice to any class of the community, and without separation from England, are so obvious that I need not here enumerate them. I prefer rather to note the principal objections which are now raised against Home Rule, and to deal in detail with each separately.

These objections are –

1. That Home Rule means separation from England and the disintegration of the Empire.

2. That it would entail civil war between the north and the rest of Ireland.

3. That if it be introduced before the Land question is settled great injustice will be done to the landlords.

4. That there would be a persecution of the Protestants by the Roman Catholics.

5. That Irish industries would be protected.

6. That there would be an unjust, dishonest, and corrupt Administration.

7. That it would be impossible to make terms or come to an understanding with men like Mr. Parnell and his followers who, to gain their own ends, have not hesitated to associate themselves with Fenians and men who have organized and committed outrages.

As to the first objection, that

*Home Rule means Separation from Great Britain,*

I do not know why this should be assumed. In my opinion, no sane Irishman desires separation. What the Irish people ask for is the right to regulate their own internal affairs, the right to preserve their revenues for their own advantage, and to make their own laws. Mr Parnell has never demanded separation, and, I feel sure, does not desire it. There is a world of difference between legislative independence, or Home Rule, and a total separation; and I cannot understand how legislative independence is incompatible with the sovereignty of the Crown and the integrity and safety of the Empire. Arrangements could, I take it, be made under which the direction of the foreign policy of the Empire would be in the hands of the Imperial Parliament, and just a quota from the Irish revenues would be contributed for Imperial purposes. We should also have to keep for some time to come an army in Ireland, and to hold certain strong places on the sea coast. But in all other respects the Irish Legislative [*sic*] would be independent of the Imperial Parliament, and would be left to manage its own affairs. Mr Parnell is not asking for more than Franz Deak asked for Hungary, and if what was granted to Hungary be granted to Ireland, the English will, as in the case of the Hungarians, satisfy the aspirations of the Irish people, and Ireland will become contented and therefore a strength to the Empire, instead of being, as she is now, a constant danger and a standing menace.

*2. Home Rule would entail Civil War between the North and the rest of Ireland.*

I do not believe in this for a moment. Five, perhaps even only three, years ago the Orangemen and Protestants of Ulster would have been ready to fight the south and west of Ireland on the subject of Home Rule. But there has been an immense change since then. The North has been invaded by the Nationalists, and at the coming election a great many of the constituencies in the north will return Home Rulers to Parliament. I could give the names of Orangemen in support of what I allege. Not many weeks ago I sent one of my best and most intelligent agents on a visit to Ulster, and in his Report he says:–
"I went freely about the country, and came to the conclusion that Fenianism is no more, but that the national spirit survives in the National League, stronger than I had any idea of. The Orangemen are joining the Nationalists everywhere, and in one village I found an Orangeman who had been elected as a Nationalist to the Board of Guardians, and was leading the National Conservative party on the Board.

\*          \*          \*          \*

"I had an introduction from a leading Nationalist and Fenian in Dublin to Mr. Roddy, of the Roddy Hotel, Derry, and the editor of the *Derry Journal*, and was introduced by him to a number of persons, many of them Orangeman. Amongst these was the capitalist and speculator, McCarter, a leading Orangeman, and a proprietor of the above-named journal. As a sign of the times, I may hear a remark that this journal, owned by an extreme Orangeman, is 'run' on Nationalist principles by Roddy, the Local President of the League, and a late extreme Fenian Centre. More than this even; Roddy told me that at one time they dare[d] not issue a National publication in Derry, that their house and hotel had been wrecked because it was known to be a rendezvous for Nationalists, but that now their principal customers were Orangemen, farmers, and commercial travellers and the local Protestant gentry. Before leaving Derry I was introduced by McCarter to a very clever English engineer, named —, who has lived in the north of Ireland many years. This man thought I was English, and in the course of conversation gave me his views on the situation. He said that the Orangemen would hold out to the last in the outlying towns, where they are to a certain extent independent, but that intelligent Protestant farmers and the shopkeepers in the large centres of population would have eventually to cast in their lot with the Nationalists, and that this was already going on."

I believe this to be a correct view of the situation. The Nationalist movement in recent years has differed from all former agitations in Ireland, in that it has appealed to the material interests of the farmers. The farmers of the north are an astute, canny set of people, and are only too ready to join a party which obtains for them a reduction of their rents and holds out to them hopes of a still further reduction. They are loyal to the Crown, and will remain so; but they care for their land and their profits more than they do for their landlords, and will not hesitate to join hands with those who can give them greater profits and greater security of tenure. If they see that Mr. Parnell is sure of victory and that Home Rule is inevitable, they will most certainly join the winning side.

*3. If Home Rule is introduced before the Land Question is settled great Injustice will be done to the Landlords.*

This is the most serious and important objection of all. Indeed, it is the only one to which I attach any real importance. The Land question must be settled before Home Rule can be granted to Ireland. Even nationalists to whom I have spoken allow that on establishment of an Irish Parliament the Land question would be the one with which they would first have to deal, and that having regard to the events of the last four years and to the existing feeling against landlords as a class, it would be far better if the Land question were settled by the English Parliament before the introduction of Home Rule.

The Land Act of 1881 sounded the death-knell of the present race of Irish landlords, and their own folly and want of foresight is bringing them to ruin. Two years ago, when I was using the same arguments as I am doing now, I was told that the influence of the landlords was reviving, and that they would soon be again on good relations with their tenants. But this was a dream destined never to come true. The estrangement between landlords and tenants (I speak of the class, not of individuals) is greater than ever, and it is patent to everyone that the landlords of Ireland are, as a class, politically extinct. The tenants have no affection for them. It would take very little trouble to get up a strong agitation against them. They have no power in the country. In the greater part of Ireland they cannot command more than very few votes, and they are of no use to the Irish Administration, or to the political party in England to which they may belong. I confess that, for my own part, I have not much sympathy with the landlords of Ireland. As a class they have neglected their duties as landlords, and they have never shown any sympathy with their tenants, or with the aspirations of the Irish people. They have been both short-sighted and selfish, and during the troublous times of 1881 and 1882 I was myself a witness of their helplessness. They did not combine among themselves to protect their own lives and property. They were of no assistance to the Government. Mr. Forster tried to put some spirit into them, and to induce them to take a firm stand on the side of law and order. But he failed. They either left the country, or remained shut up in their houses in terror of their lives, and neglecting[*sic*] their duties as Justices of the Peace, in the exercise of which they might have rendered such assistance to the Government. They have always been short-sighted, and I am afraid will be so to the last, even in matters in which their own interests are most concerned. When Isaac Butt foresaw the contest between the landlords and the people he tried to save the former, but they would not listen to him. How much better terms would they have obtained had they joined the National movement then than they will now! They might have been the leaders of the people, but now they are hated by the people, and run a great chance of being abandoned by England, in whom they trusted. What Michael Davitt said about them in his speech in Dublin on the 28th July 1885, is very true; he said: "Had they joined the Home Rule movement under Isaac Butt their social salvation was secured. National gratitude would have gone out to them from the Irish heart, and they would have been saved from the defeat which has since overtaken them . . ."[83] *Even yet*, if they helped Mr. Parnell to obtain an Irish Parliament, they would be surer of far

---

[83] Ellipsis in original.

more generous terms at his hands than they are likely to obtain from a democracy which will win legislative rights without their assistance, and build up an Irish nation on the ruins of their power."[84]

It would be unsafe now to leave the settlement of the Land question to an Irish Parliament. But why could not a settlement be come to; why could not the best terms possible be made for the landlords before the introduction of Home Rule? The Land Purchase Act[85] recently passed is a step in this direction. But its success will be but partial, and its operation slow, because the landlords, with their usual want of foresight, will, I am afraid, hold out for higher prices than they can get, and because the tenants will not dare to purchase without obtaining the sanction of the National League to the transaction. If the landlords were wise they would now gladly accept eighteen years' purchase for their lands, instead of holding out for twenty and twenty-two years' purchase. I believe that the only chance of bringing them to their senses is to acknowledge the principle of Home Rule, to let them understand England does intend to give a Parliament in Dublin to the Irish. Seeing, then, that they have nothing further to hope from England, they will, in all probability, join the National side, and make the best terms possible for themselves; and if the principle of Home Rule were acknowledged, as I suggest, we should have the Irish leaders with us instead of against us. They would assist us in carrying into operation the remedial measures which in late years have been passed for Ireland, instead of throwing every obstacle in the way, and it would not, I believe, be difficult to come to some understanding with them on the Irish Land question, and to come to terms which, under existing circumstances, would be just to the landlords. I am sure that the latter have nothing to gain by holding out and waiting.

They are much more likely to obtain good terms now than two years, even one year, hence. But, as I said before, it is absolutely necessary that the Land question should be finally settled, and that terms should be made for the landlords before Home Rule is granted to Ireland. To obtain this result, we should try to get the Irish leaders to work with us instead of against us, and this is only to be done by promising them Home Rule. Home Rule must come; it is inevitable. Why, then, should we continue to fight against it, and to go on crying out, "Never, never?"

---

[84] The lecture, entitled 'Twenty years of Irish history – 1865 to 1885', was delivered at the Rotunda, Dublin: *The Times*, 29 July 1885, p. 9.
[85] See **Journal (11 September 1885)**.

*4. There would be a persecution of the Protestants by the Catholics.*

I do not believe this. The feeling between the Protestants and Roman Catholics is not what it was in past years. "The poison of religious ascendancy," as Mr. Gladstone says in his recent Manifesto,[86] "in its various forms, has been expelled from the country," and there is no reason to suppose that the Roman Catholics will be intolerant, and show any animosity towards the Protestants. If there were any fear of this, how is it that both in the past and in the present Protestants have joined the National ranks, and that the leaders have been and are Protestants?

*5. That the Irish Industries would be protected.*

And what if they are?

Supposing that protective duties are imposed, or that a system of bounties is established, what great harm would be done to English trade and commerce? Why is it absolutely necessary that there should be a common tariff? If the Irish think that Irish industries will be encouraged by the imposition of protective duties, why not let them try the experiment? By our selfishness in years past we destroyed the manufactures and industries of Ireland, under our administration nothing has been done to revive them. We have not even succeeded in establishing security for the introduction of capital. There is no continuity in our Irish policy. For a few years the unruly are kept under subjection and order is maintained, and then follows a violent agitation, in which there is little or no security for life or property. Are we always to remain selfish? Cannot we afford to be liberal and generous? Even if we were to lose something by the abolition of a common tariff, what would the loss be when put in the balance against the political and financial loss arising out of our present relations with Ireland. If we cannot ourselves do anything towards the revival of Irish industries, we should let the Irish try what they can do themselves, and let them succeed if they can.

*6. That there would be an unjust, dishonest, and corrupt Administration.*

I daresay there would be a great deal of corruption and political immorality. But this is more the concern of the Irish than the English. It will not do England any harm. We cannot expect perfection at once.

---

[86] Gladstone's 'Address to the electors of Midlothian' was circulated by the National Press Agency on 18 September 1885: Richard Shannon, *Gladstone: heroic minister, 1865–1898* (London, 2000), p. 381.

It is impossible to sail at once from the middle of a revolution into smooth and settled waters. Every nation must pass through the fire, and must learn by experience. Could there have been greater political immorality and corruption than in England in the last century, and yet look at England of to-day?

If England has come pure out of the furnace why should not Ireland? And with the experience of our own country before us, why should we be afraid to give Home Rule to Ireland? I do not believe that there would be an unjust or dishonest Administration in Ireland. I believe that in an Irish Parliament there would very speedily be formed, probably under the leadership of Mr. Parnell, a strong Conservative party, supported by the Roman Catholic Church with all its strength, the landlords, the newly-created peasant proprietors, the farmers and the professional classes, which would keep the Separatists, Socialists and Irreconcilables in check. Mr. Parnell has from the beginning kept on good terms with the Church, Archbishop Croke,[87] the leading Nationalist amongst the clergy, is his firm ally and supporter, and no one can doubt that the Roman Catholic Church is and must be conservative, and opposed to revolution.

Under such an administration we need not, I think, be afraid that any revolutionary measures will be passed, or that injustice will be done to any particular class.

Having got Home Rule, it will be in the interest of the Irish to prove that they are fit for self-government, and can manage their own affairs well, and with justice to all classes.

*7. That it would be impossible to make Terms with Men who, to gain their own ends, have not hesitated to associate themselves with Fenians and Men who organized and committed Outrages.*

This is a sentimental objection, and I would ask those who make it whether it is not better to try to settle the Irish difficulty in consultation with Mr. Parnell and his followers, than by keeping aloof from them on sentimental grounds to drive them to accept revolutionary measures, and so to plunge Ireland again into anarchy and disorder? If this question of Home Rule is not settled on a wise and generous basis during the coming year we shall have a renewal of agitation and of outrages in both Ireland and England. We have not now, it must be remembered, to deal only with Ireland, as was the case in former days. We have to reckon with millions of Irishmen in America and

---

[87] Thomas William Croke (1824–1902), Archbishop of Cashel (1875–1902), a leading supporter of home rule, the Land League, the Gaelic Athletic Association, and the Gaelic League.

Australia, and all over the world. At present all eyes are turned towards Mr. Parnell, but should he fail, the time of the Extremists will come, and all the machinery of the secret organizations will be again set in motion. The Parliamentary Party are well aware of this, and look forward to it as a very possible contingency. I have remarkable proof of this in a letter before me, in which there is an account of a dinner which was given secretly at the end of August in Dublin to P.S. Cassidy,[88] a member of O'Donovan Rossa's Council, and a leading Clan-na-Gael man, who came over from New York to see the Irish leaders, and to judge for himself of the state of affairs. He is an Extremist, and in favour of dynamite work. At this dinner Fenians, Nationalists, and Priests were present, and the Parliamentary Party were represented by John O'Connor, M.P., and Mr. McMahon, M.P.[89]

After dinner Mr. John O'Connor "opened the conversation by asking Cassidy to use all his influence on his return to New York with all parties to stop all further explosions." He added, "Do not think for a moment that I am a milk-and-water Irishman in thus addressing you. I am as hot a Fenian now as ever, and if there was only an opportunity, I, for one, would accept nothing from the English without fighting for it; but," he continued, "the wishes of the majority of our people at home and abroad should be respected; there has been a measure of success gained; it now remains to see what can be done in the next Parliament;" and concluding, he said, "I know I am speaking the sentiments of all here when I ask you to organize! organize! organize!, husband your resources, and if we cannot succeed legitimately, it must be war to the bitter end by all and every means in our power." Mr. John O'Connor was, as we know, one of the leading Fenians in Cork, and is therefore one of the most extreme men in the Irish Parliamentary Party. But he, like many other leading Fenians, has joined the Nationalists, and hopes that the battle may be won under Mr. Parnell's leadership in the English House of Commons. As regards Mr. Parnell himself and the more moderate of his followers, I think we should be just in our judgement of them. They have been playing for a great stake, and have had a very difficult game to play. It is true that they did not, except in the case of the Phoenix Park murders, denounce outrages, but we have no proof that they were a party to them. Mr. Parnell has been obliged from the first to carry with him Nationalists of all shades of opinion, Fenians, Extremists, and Irreconcilables in Ireland and in America. Had he denounced

---

[88] Patrick Sarsfield Cassidy (b. 1850), business editor of the *New York Sunday Mercury*, defected from Clan-na-Gael to head the Fenian Council in November 1886 and subsequently launched a press campaign against O'Donovan Rossa.

[89] Edward McMahon, manufacturer, Nat. MP for Limerick city (1883–1885).

outrages openly, or had he broken with the Extremists, he would not have been able for a moment to have retained his position as leader of the National movement, and he would not have received the supplies from America with which he was able to carry on the agitation both inside and outside Parliament. I think that this much should in fairness be said in his favour. Now, at any rate, he and his followers have spoken out against outrages and in favour of moderation, and if we, from want of wisdom, foresight, and generosity, or from any sentimental objection, render the prompt settlement of the Irish question impossible, and so drive the Irish to extreme measures, surely the responsibility will be ours.

I am afraid I have dwelt at great length on this subject; but it is one, to my mind, of such importance, and of such vast consequence to both England and Ireland, that I could not well deal with it in smaller compass. As it is, I have not said anything about the immense political difficulties which lie in the way of any Statesman who may earnestly wish to bring the question to a practical issue, and to carry his party and English public opinion with him, though these are difficulties of which I am well aware, and which I do not under-estimate.

But I feel more and more convinced that things cannot remain as they now are. Something must be done to satisfy the natural desire of the Irish people to legislate for themselves on matters of purely Irish concern.

If this something be done promptly agitation will cease; if not, then we will have a renewal of violent agitation, unseemly fighting, and obstruction in Parliament, a Session wasted, perhaps a Government overthrown, and another General Election this time next year; and in that case should we be any nearer a righteous and just settlement of the question than we are now? Would not the feeling against us in Ireland be stronger and more embittered? Would it not be more difficult to protect and do justice to the landlords, and would not the Extremists and the Irreconcilables make bolder and more impossible demands.

The problem immediately before us demanding solution is, how to steer Ireland through a Revolution without a renewal of bloodshed, and with the least possible amount of suffering and injustice to certain classes, and how to give the Irish full power to manage their own internal affairs, to give them, in fact, what they ask for – a separate Parliament, without separating Ireland from England, and without danger and without injury to the Empire and to England. And is this problem so impossible of solution? The first thing that we must try and do is to bring our Government in touch with the people. At the present moment, our administration in Ireland is isolated. No real reform can be carried out, Ireland cannot be made prosperous and happy as long as the Government is not in touch with the people, and as long as we look coldly on their aspirations, and are not in sympathy with the national sentiment. No honest and unprejudiced man can say that our administration, whatever our intentions may be, is popular, or that under it Ireland is well governed and prosperous. If we wish to place ourselves in touch with the people, we must practically show our sympathy with them by acknowledging that our present system of administration is not suited to the country, by joining hands with their leaders, and by acknowledging the principle of Home Rule. Having conceded that much we should not, I believe, have any real difficulty in coming to a satisfactory solution of the puzzling problem which is now before us, and which, in my opinion, cannot, in the interests of both England and Ireland, be too promptly solved.

**16.** George Fottrell to Joseph Chamberlain, 29 September 1885; Geo. D. Fottrell & Sons, 46 Fleet St., Dublin; 'Private'; JCP, JC8/4/1/3.

You were so frank in speaking to me when in London that I am sure you will not be annoyed at my speaking frankly to you. I therefore tell you that I was sorry to read your letter to Mr. Ferguson[90] because I think it went further than any former declaration of yours in pledging you against a separate parliament for Ireland by which I understand a parliament or assembly absolute in its own sphere and subject to no revision within its own sphere by any other legislative body.

Now I have watched very carefully for the past few months the signs of public opinion in Ireland & I feel satisfied that within the last few months a large number of people in Ireland who were either hostile or indifferent to the project of a separate legislature for Ireland have come to be convinced that even for the landlord interest it would be better to have a separate legislature here – a real legislature with absolute powers save on question of tariff & save that it should have no control of the military.

I wish I could have a chat with you to explain fully the change which has come over people's minds here even among the richer people meanwhile I earnestly impress upon you that the change has come & that it would be well not to pledge yourself against a scheme

[90] See **Journal (5 October 1885)**.

to which so large a proportion of Irishmen are turning as affording the only safe way out of a condition of danger doubt & difficulty.

**17.** Joseph Chamberlain to George Fottrell, 30 September 1885; 'Private'; JCP, JC8/4/1/4.

I should be at all times glad to have the opportunity of talking over Irish matters with you, & whenever you are in London while I am there I hope you will do me the favour of calling. I do not think that anything would change my opinion on the question of an independent parliament for Ireland. I have gone to the extreme limit in agreeing to a National Council. I have large ideas as to the possible development of such an institution, but this would only come gradually & would have to be justified by the experience of its working in its original form. The feeling in this country is stronger than I supposed possible. We have strained our supporters very much by what they think our excessive concessions to Mr. Parnell's demands, & it would be much easier now to get up an anti-Irish agitation than to propound & carry even such a scheme as that which was explained in the *Fortnightly Review*.[91]

**18.** E.G. Jenkinson to Lord Carnarvon, 5 October 1885; 'Confidential'; CP/TNA, PRO 30/6/62 (25).

In my letter to you of 26[th] Sepr[92] I mentioned that money was being raised in several states in the United States for the payment of salaries to Irish members of Parliament. Since writing that letter I have heard that great efforts are being made to raise money for the Parliamentary Fund, in order to give support to Parnell in the coming elections. They hope to raise $500,000 in the United States. At Chicago subscriptions are rapidly coming in and nearly $75,000 are expected. Wealthy Irishmen in New York and New Jersey have promised money freely for Parnell. St Louis, Mo., has guaranteed $5000, Cincinnati $5000, Milwaukee $1800 and further subscriptions are expected when Parnell or his delegates go over for the great National League Convention which will take place at Chicago in January 1886.[93]

---

[91] See **Journal (12, 27 June 1885)**.
[92] See **Document 15**.
[93] The convention took place on 18–19 August: *New York Times*, 6 August 1886, p. 8.

Vice President Hendrick's speech at a mass meeting of citizens in Indianapolis, Indiana (his own state) in which he openly expressed Parnell's cause, has stimulated Irish sympathizers, and has brought in further subscriptions to the Parliamentary Fund. The *New York Herald* thinks this speech was "in the worst possible taste".[94]

Everywhere in America there is the greatest enthusiasm about Parnell, but this enthusiasm would not be what it is were it not based on the firm belief that should the Parliamentary Party fail to get what the Irish want from the English Parliament, the time will come for the Extremists and Revolutionists to act, and that Parnell will place himself at the head of the Active Revolutionary Party. The money now coming in is being given for a double purpose. Part of it will go to the Parliamentary Fund, but part of it will be reserved by the V.C., the Fenian organization which practically has the control of the whole movement, for "active work" in the future. Everywhere there are signs of preparation for the future. The Extremists are quiet just now because they think it fair to give Parnell a chance, but they have no belief in his success, and they are consequently organizing and preparing for the future. The preparations are going on not only in the United States but in Great Britain and in Ireland. Lately a great many of the men who were engaged in the murders and outrages of 1881 and 1882 have returned to their houses in Ireland, and in Dublin there are at the present moment eight of the old Invincibles, most of whom have come back during the last few months.

Parnell is filling the offices in the National League both in Ireland and Great Britain with I.R.B. men, in order that he may have, as he says, "men who will be ready to go to prison, or be fit for any kind of work when the time comes". And in the United States the V.C. in order that it may have complete control over every move at the National League Convention in January next is expending money "to place in good standing every camp by its public name as a Branch of the National League". So it is quite clear that in the event of Parnell receiving a check, the whole movement and all the active policy of the future will be directed by the V.C. in the United States acting in conjunction with the sister organization the I.R.B., and the National League on this side, and in America they all firmly believe that Parnell will place himself at the head of the movement. But whether he does or not, we know what we have to expect should

---

[94] Thomas Andrews Hendricks (1819–1885), Democratic Senator and Governor of Indiana (1863–1869, 1872–1884), Vice-President of the United States (1884–1885). In his speech on 8 September, Hendricks 'expressed his belief that Mr. Parnell would lead Ireland to triumphant success': *The Times*, 10 September 1885, p. 3.

the moderates lose the game, and should the Extremists get their own way.

**19.** Lord Carnarvon, 'Davitt's views as to constitutional change'; *c.*29 October 1885;[95] CP/TNA, PRO 30/6/67 (34).

Sir R. Hamilton took an opportunity of learning through Fottrell whether Davitt's opinions on these subjects remained unaltered.

Davitt said he had changed his opinion as to a second Chamber & that he was in favour of only one.

He went on to say that there were now "many Tories in the Nationalist Party & that when an Irish Parlt. was given he expected to see Parnell at the head of the Tory Party in it".

**20.** [Sir Robert Hamilton], 31 October 1885; 'Very Secret'; Printed for the use of the Cabinet, 8 December 1885; CAB 37/6/57.

In the following Memorandum I endeavour briefly to sketch the present political and economic condition of Ireland, and to show the critical state in which the country is. I point out that, whatever difficulties may surround the obtaining of a true knowledge of the views of the country, these views will be constitutionally expressed at the coming elections on the plain issue raised in Mr. Parnell's programme. I proceed to discuss the advantages or disadvantages, and the risks, attending the acceptance or the non-acceptance of that programme, and I conclude by offering a practical suggestion as to the best way, in my judgment, of bringing the consideration of the Imperial Parliament to bear on this important subject. I submit my views with great diffidence, and with the humble hope that they may tend towards the elucidation of one of the most complicated problems which have [*sic*] ever engaged the attention of statesmen.

Ireland is passing through a great social revolution. Protestant ascendancy went with the disestablishment of the State Church; landlord ascendancy went with the introduction of the Land Act; but nothing has taken their place. These influences which worked, imperfectly enough, I admit, and often tyrannically, for the guidance

---

[95] See **Journal (28 October 1885)**.

of local affairs, have disappeared, and nothing has been substituted for them. While nominally under a free Constitution, Ireland's Representatives have no part in the administration of the Government of their country, and everything more and more falls on that much abused institution, Dublin Castle.

The desire for the recognition of Irish nationality has always been present in the country, but the education of the masses, which has made enormous strides in recent years, has turned what was a passive but deep-rooted discontent on their part with being governed by England into an active determination to assert their right to manage their own affairs. It is now so easy to cross the Atlantic that there are to be found in all parts of the country men who have been in America, and by means of intercourse with these, and by constant correspondence with their friends and relatives who, since the famine of 1846, have established an Ireland beyond the seas, they are familiar with American institutions, and with the part the people take in the government of the United States and Canada. They devour the newspaper literature both of Ireland and of America which now floods the country, of which the real or supposed wrongs of Ireland form so large a part, and their minds are kept at fever heat. Instead of a vent being found for their energies in allowing them to manage their own affairs, and so curbing the excesses which are almost inseparable accompaniments of emancipation from ignorance and serfdom these excesses have been curbed by enactments of a drastic repressive character.

Not only is the political state of Ireland, from the causes referred to above – some of which are due to legislation, others to advancing civilization – in a critical state, but the economic state of the country is also most serious. The great fall in the prices of all agricultural produce comes at a time when the way of living of the people has so improved that they regard as necessaries of life many comforts which only a relapse into something like barbarism would enable them to do without. There will be great difficulty in paying rents. Landlords will insist, in many instances, upon the judicial rents being paid without reference to the circumstances of their individual tenants, and those who can pay will use the position of those who cannot to help them to evade payment.

While such is the state of Ireland politically and economically, an organic change is made by the recent enormous extension of the franchise to the masses, and all exceptional legislation of a repressive character is abandoned. The masses feel their power, and use it unsparingly. They organize and combine to force the minority to join them on pain of being "Boycotted," and they establish Courts of their own, to whose Judgments they render more obedience than to the legally constituted Courts of the land. Mr. Parnell issues a programme merging all lesser objects in a demand for a separate Irish Parliament, to which the Catholic Hierarchy give their warm support, and by means of Conventions, jointly of priests and people, Members pledged to support this programme are being selected throughout the country with extraordinary unanimity.

The ignorance of England and Scotland of Irish matters, even on the part of Members of Parliament, is very great. This is cause for serious concern at the present moment. I believe the apathy too often displayed by them on the subject has disappeared, but the difficulty of obtaining a true knowledge of the situation and of the real views of the Irish people is very great. On the one hand, the landlords, and all who look at the matter from their point of view, cry out for coercion, and point to the excesses still vividly in the public memory as the justification for it. On the other hand, the extreme press denounce the English as foreign oppressors, and clearly point to, and indeed directly advocate, a policy of separation from England and of expoliation,[96] as the end and aim of the people being allowed to manage their own affairs. Then, again, the religious differences of opinion are much mixed up with the political differences. Many Protestants hold that the Church of Rome is at the bottom of the discontent, and is fomenting it to secure her own aggrandizement; while others assert that the Land question is the only matter really at issue, and that if this were satisfactorily settled the cry for an Irish Parliament would disappear.

Others contend, while admitting the great force and power of the present moment, that its true foundation is not in a desire for a recognition of nationality, but that it is merely an upheaval on the part of those who have not, against those who have, and they point to the absence of men of means from it in support of this view. They point also to the feeling in the North of Ireland, where, among the propertied classes, the desire to maintain the Union is very strong, and urge that something like a civil war would be the result of conceding a local Parliament to Ireland. These are grave considerations indeed; but, on the other hand, it is urged, first, that the propertied classes generally in Ireland are intimately connected with the land, and that their national feelings are overborne by their individual interests; and, second, that although the question of religion has an extraordinary power in the North, yet that community of interests in other respects would soon secure their co-operation, and that if they felt secure that they would not be subject to Catholic domination, much of their antagonism towards an Irish Parliament would cease.

---

[96] An archaic word meaning the act of stripping off or removal (definition from the *Oxford English Dictionary*).

The adhesion of the Catholic Church to the movement is pointed to as strong evidence that they who know the country well, and all whose interests in a normal state of society are Conservative, regard the movement as a genuine one, and not based on a policy of expoliation of which they themselves would eventually, if not immediately be sufferers. And while religious differences are matter of great regret, it is urged that it is more fair and just that the minority should give way to the majority rather than that the majority should give way to the minority, although it is, of course, essential in any well-governed community that there should be the utmost liberty and freedom for all.

But there is no ambiguity in Mr. Parnell's programme. There is no longer any possibility of doubt as to what is asked for. The issue is distinctly before the country, and if at the coming elections, as I believe will be the case, the great majority of the country (say, four-fifths) declare for an Irish Parliament, whatever may be the considerations that can fairly be discounted, it must be recognized that such constitutionally expressed view [*sic*] is the view of the great majority of the country.

Now, in that event, what is to be done? Have the statesmen who are responsible for the government of this country considered what the position of matters is, and what direction the future legislation for Ireland is to take? I do not stop to discuss whether the views of the Representatives of Parliament are to be ignored by Parliament for this I hold to be not only impossible in a free Assembly, but also inconsistent with the fundamental principles of constitutional government. Is it conceivable that if the great majority of the Scotch Members were unanimous in advocating some measure for Scotland, it would not be seriously considered by both parties, with the view of granting it if Imperial interests would allow? The more important the subject, the stronger is the call for such treatment of it; and surely the time has arrived for taking into consultation the Representatives of the Irish people in settling how they are to be governed.

It is urged by many Englishmen who are well-disposed to Ireland that the Irish members are a party of rebels, with whom no loyal man should enter into communication. But is this fair or just? Undoubtedly great violence of expression has been used by many members of the party, which is much to be regretted and condemned, but which is almost the inevitable consequent [*sic*] of strong excitement. Let us take care that we do not foster treason by refusing to listen to any demands, whatever they are, which were preferred in a constitutional way.

When Parliament reassembles, are the Representatives of Great Britain to combine to postpone indefinitely what Ireland asks, and, if so, what are they to do in the meantime; or are they to yield it accompanied by efficient safeguards (1) that the integrity of the Empire is maintained, and (2) that there shall be no undue interference with the liberties of the minority and the rights of property? The question is not one of "never," but of "when" and "how."

In dealing with this question the interests of the Empire as a whole are at stake as much as the interests of Ireland. The integrity of the Empire must be maintained, but whatever solution of the other relationships of Ireland to Great Britain is just and fair to Ireland must be best for the Empire. No solution of the matter which, from any cause whatever, withholds what it is just to concede to Ireland can be permanently advantageous to the Empire.

Now, let us consider what Mr. Parnell's programme involves, and what the effects of adopting it would be.

In the first place, it involves the power being conceded to the Irish Parliament to raise their own revenues as they see fit, and no settlement will be accepted as satisfactory to the Irish people which does not leave this power to Ireland. It can scarcely be urged that the concession of liberty in this respect will any more conflict with the integrity of the Empire than the exercise of it does in the case of our great self-governing Colonies. It no doubt would be inconvenient to have different Tariffs in Ireland and in Great Britain, but there are no Imperial interests involved in the matter. It is conceivable that some individual manufacturing interests in England or Scotland might to some extent suffer by the imposition of import duties in Ireland, or the granting of bounties on Irish manufactures, which is the most likely form protection would take. But, as England will always be the great market for Irish produce, the Irish are not likely to take any step which would destroy this market. In this relation, England can do without Ireland, but Ireland cannot do without England. To England an interruption of the Irish supply would be but a temporary inconvenience. To Ireland it would be fatal, and they are too keen not to see this. There would be little risk, therefore, in conceding this part of Mr. Parnell's programme.

The really serious issues we have to face in dealing with this matter are (1) that the concession of legislative independence is demanded, and might be accepted only as a step to absolute separation; and (2) that the rights of property and of the Protestant minority might not be secured, not withstanding any safeguards which might be introduced into any new Constitution for Ireland; and (3) that if (1) and (2) were successfully met, still the country, from the absence of any training or experience in matters of government, might be found unequal to the task of governing itself.

As regards (1), I do not think any real danger is to be apprehended. Ireland would have no power granted to her by her Constitution to raise local forces. Great Britain would keep such troops in Ireland as she saw fit, and would retain the entire control of these, and of the Irish militia. The granting of a separate Parliament would not put the country in a better position to take up arms against England, or to harbour an enemy's troops in Ireland; while there is at least the hope that the feeling in Ireland towards England would so improve by conceding to her the right to manage her own affairs, she would soon come to recognize that her best interests were bound up with those of England, instead of being in any way antagonistic to them.

The second point is the more difficult one. England is largely responsible for the present state of Ireland, under which there is great exasperation of classes, and she cannot shirk her responsibilities in the matter, and let the party who are now the weakest, but who by the bolstering-up of England have hitherto been the strongest, go to the wall. I believe in the innate sense of justice in the Irish people, and I should have no fear that an Irish Government, chosen by the people, would act unfairly to any class, were it not for the great excitement in which the country now is. Some moderating influence is required, and this might be provided for (a) by England retaining for the present the control of the Constabulary, and (b) by introducing into a carefully-devised Constitution for Ireland, which would find a place in the government of the country for all classes and interests, certain temporary provisions to meet the peculiar circumstances of the moment.

As regard[s] (a) there is nothing inconsistent in England retaining the control of the Constabulary, which is, at least, a *semi*-military force, being armed, drilled and capable of concentration on any given point. Under a Constitution to be granted for Ireland, provision might be made that as the local authorities supplied, at their own cost, local police, this general and semi-military force, maintained at Imperial charge, might be gradually disbanded.

As regards (b), I am not prepared with a cut and dried Constitution. This could only be devised after the utmost consideration of the subject in all its bearings; but it is manifest that weighty controlling influences could be secured by the creation of a second Chamber, which should sufficiently represent the propertied classes in the country; by requiring a majority of, say, two-thirds, before measures dealing with certain specified matters should become law; by adopting, so far as practicable, the plan of minority representation; and by retaining in the hands of the Crown, as is the case in some of the Colonies, the appointment of some [of] the superior Judges. Such provisions to meet the temporary difficulties of the situation might be devised, as an extension of purchase of landlord's interests, providing fair terms for persons who might be dispossessed of appointments under the Government, &c.

Into these details I do not propose to enter. The whole arrangement would be one of give and take. It should be dealt with in a liberal spirit by the Imperial Exchequer, and it surely ought not to be beyond the power of statesmen to establish such safeguards in granting a Constitution for Ireland, if they are honestly determined to create them, and the leaders of the Irish party are honestly determined to accept them and to carry them out.

The third point, viz., whether, if legislative independence were granted to Ireland, she would be able to govern herself, is also a very serious one. I am aware of the risks attending such a course. If failure should be the result, England, which could not tolerate the existence of a Haiti on her borders, would have to interfere, and the last state would be worse than the first. I attach no importance whatever to the suggestion sometimes made, that the necessary power and capacity for administering the affairs of Ireland does not exist in the country. The experience of our Colonies and of England itself negatives such a suggestion, but experience in matters of government is undoubtedly wanting on the part of those on whom its conduct would devolve, and grave mistakes might be made which would be criticized by no friendly eye by many. I assume, of course, that the safeguards referred to in (2) are introduced into the Constitution; but these could not provide for efficient administration, though they might prevent undue interference with certain rights. Many true well-wishers to Ireland say you should begin at the bottom and not at the top. Establish a good machinery of local government, by means of which you can build up a superstructure culminating in a local Parliament. If you grant a Parliament before you have the foundations of local government, the whole thing will go to pieces, and chaos will be the result. Now there is much to be said for this view; and had the step of creating the machinery for local government been adopted years ago, a less haza[r]dous course than is now required might have been possible; but we have to deal with matters as they are.

No mere creation of County Boards will be acceptable to the people now. If such a scheme were promulgated and worked, the present Board of Guardians element would dominate all the local Councils, and the upper classes would be forced out of the country, before a local Parliament, built up on such a foundation, could be granted. No real well-wisher of Ireland would desire to see the propertied classes forced out of the country; but by granting legislative independence in the way I have suggested, you find a place for the representation of the upper classes in the Government of the country, and you open to them a legitimate way of securing that their interests are attended to by making themselves felt in the councils of the nation, instead of their solely relying, as heretofore, on British bayonets to protect their rights.

Now assuming for the moment that it was possible to concede Mr. Parnell's programme with efficient safeguards, let us see what advantages would follow. At the present moment all classes of Nationalists, from the loyal Home Ruler, who would fight to maintain the connection with England, to the Separatist and Dynamitard, are united in making a great constitutional effort to secure it being carried out. Money from abroad, which used to go to create outrages, is all going to constitutional purposes; and this fact of itself is most significant, as showing that, once what is asked for is got, the supplies will cease, and as there can be no skilfully planned outrages on a large scale without money, that such outrages will cease also. Then again, the great body of the Catholic Hierarchy and of the priests have thrown themselves into the movement. It is only reasonable, therefore, to assume that the concession of Mr. Parnell's programme would satisfy the great majority in Ireland, including the Catholic Church, and would put an end to dynamite and other outrages. The Irish Members would no longer sit in the House of Commons, and the intolerable Parliamentary difficulty would disappear, and the public business of the Empire would go on in the old legitimate way. Another source of growing trouble and difficulty would also be removed. The present feeling of the Irish in America is very hostile to Great Britain, and might prove a serious danger in the event of complications arising with the United States. But the Irish in America have unanimously allied themselves with Mr. Parnell's programme, and it is only reasonable to hope that the concession of this would convert them into friends of Great Britain.

In a certain sense it may be said that the withdrawal of Irish Representatives from the Imperial House of Commons would be a derogation to Ireland, as she would then have no voice in Imperial questions, such as foreign policy, alliances, or wars. But these matters do not have the same interest with the Irish mind, certainly in its present temper, as they have with Englishmen. Moreover, sometimes it is necessary to take a step back as a preliminary to taking a step forward. A time must come before long when Imperial federation of all parts of the Empire will take place, and then Ireland will take her place with others. But until this occurs it is better that she should cease to take part altogether in Imperial questions than that, with the present condition of the Imperial Parliament, an attempt should be made to allow her Representatives only to take part in the discussion of Imperial questions. Without an entire remodelling of the Imperial Parliament as at present constituted, and the establishment of local Councils in England and Scotland to deal with purely local affairs, it would not be practicable to limit the interference of Irish Representatives to purely Imperial questions. Great as the Irish difficulty is, Britain will not be prepared to pay this price at present for solving it, while the irritation and embarrassment arising from the determination of what were Imperial questions, and what were not, would largely neutralize the advantages which should leave to Ireland the sole and undivided control of all those questions on which her mind is now set.

I am far from thinking that when this is done, if it should be done, the Irish Parliament would not have a very difficult task before them which would tax their utmost energies. The keen religious difference in their country and the complications arising therefrom, the different circumstances of the manufacturing industries in the north, and of the agricultural industries in the richer parts of the middle and south, and the terrible problem of the congested districts would always make the government of Ireland a matter of great difficulty. But surely there is more hope of these being satisfactorily dealt with by those who know the circumstances and represent the various interests at stake themselves directing the government of the country, than by a centralized system of government directed by a Lord Lieutenant and Chief Secretary, whose tenure of office is seldom sufficiently prolonged to enable them to acquire anything like a thorough knowledge of the complicated problems which surround the government of Ireland.

Now let us consider the effects of the alternative policy of waiting, and endeavouring to prepare the country for self-government by minor measures.

To begin with, nothing short of an Irish parliament will satisfy the aspirations of the National party. Whatever is done, therefore, will not be accepted with satisfaction or gratitude. It will not receive their co-operation or help, and will have to be done for the country by England, instead of being done by themselves. The Parliamentary Party will not help Parliament in devising beneficent measures, and with the best intentions these measures will largely fail in their objects. When passed, instead of trying to get all the advantage possible out of them, the people will exercise their ingenuity to make them abortive. The influence at present used with such effect by the Parliamentary party to keep down outrages will lose its heart and weight, and outrages will recommence. Repressive legislation will have to be re-enacted. The Parliamentary difficulty, already intolerable, will become more intolerable still, and even the extension of the objectionable plan of the "clôture"[97] will be powerless to prevent it. The people will be kept in a perpetual state of excitement, and will be unable to settle down to attend to their own affairs. The cry for separation, which is not a real sentiment at present, will gain immeasurably in force, and a few years

[97] A means of closing parliamentary debate with the consent of a majority of those voting, cloture was introduced in 1881 to overcome the obstructionist tactics of the Irish nationalists.

hence will certainly, in my view, not find Ireland in the least degree more prepared for self-government than it is at present.

It is true that the want of money, if the struggle is long protracted, may raise difficulties as regards many of the present Parliamentary party. They may more or less break up, but we should be living in a fool's paradise if we regarded this as a cause for congratulation, or thought that the intense longing on the part of the country for a recognition of its nationality had ceased, because she was too poor to continue to give expression to it in a constitutional way. Far less money than it takes to support the Parliamentary party would go a long way in promoting dynamite outrages both in England and Ireland, and undoubtedly much of it would go in this direction. But it is not upon this ground I would have the action of a great country like England based. Is it wise, is it generous, to exert the strong arm of power to curb a feeling which is laudable in the minds of any people, and which can, by just treatment, be made a source of strength instead of weakness to the Empire of which they form a part?

And now for a practical suggestion. Whatever party may be in power after the elections should, in my view, take up the Irish question as of the first and supremest importance. A Resolution should be proposed to the House of Commons that the fullest measure of legislative independence should be given to Ireland consistently with maintaining the integrity of the Empire and the supremacy of the Throne, and with efficient safeguards for the rights of property and the liberties of the minority; and a joint Committee of both Houses on which, of course, the Irish National party should be largely represented, should be appointed to draw up a Constitution for Ireland with this object, providing for a complete separation of the accounts and indebtedness of the two countries, on some such lines as are indicated in the Appendix to this Memorandum.[98]

This ought to be possible. I believe it would be found to be possible. Difficulties disappear when there is a common object in view, and that object is in itself definite and distinct. The sole danger to guard against is the disintegration of the Empire. The geographical position of the two countries, and their best interests, forbid it, and as in the Northern States of America, so in Great Britain, every man would fight to the last to prevent it, and the issue is undoubted, but after taking ample securities in this respect, let Great Britain give up the

---

[98] The paper includes an appendix entitled 'Separation of accounts between Great Britain and Ireland': see **Journal (28 October 1885)**. When the paper was reprinted on 29 January 1886, a second appendix entitled 'Land question' was added: see AP, Add MS 77328 and GP, Add MS 44631, fos 122–129.

impossible task of trying to govern an educated people from without, instead of allowing and aiding them to govern themselves.

Should this task prove impossible, and the interests of the Empire forbid the concession such as I have suggested, then, and then only, should we be justified in continuing to rule Ireland in a way which is opposed to the sentiments of the people as expressed by their constitutional Representatives, and forcing them, whether they will or not, to fall into line in all respects with England and Scotland, and in incurring the serious risks which such a policy would involve.

**21.** E.G. Jenkinson to Lord Rosebery, 4 November 1885; Home Office; NLS, MS 10084, fos 121–125.

In the summer I sent to you with Sir W. Harcourt['s] permission a printed memorandum of mine on the organization of the Clan-na-gael society in the United States,[99] and I now send you with Lord Carnarvon's permission a memorandum which I wrote in the end of September partly in continuation of the former memorandum, and partly expressing my views on the present situation in Ireland.[100] The immense importance of the Irish question not only from a local but also from an Imperial point of view must be my excuse for troubling you at this time when you must have so many engagements and so much to occupy your thoughts. Besides I think I should fail in my duty if having such special sources of information at my disposal I did not do all in my power to assist leading men in England in the solution of the Irish problem. Little is I fancy known of the under currents in the movement now going on in Ireland, and of the secret forces which are at work behind the Parliamentary Party. But if the situation is to be understood, and if we are to find a right solution of the problem a knowledge and appreciation of these is indispensable.

It should never be forgotten that we have not now to deal with Ireland only. If that were so we should not have such a very difficult task before us. We have to reckon with the Irish population in America and in our Colonies and we must bear in mind that the main spring of the movement is in the United States of America. I feel quite sure that there is no question of such pressing & vital importance at the present moment as the Irish one, and if I could only impress this upon English statesmen and at the same time help to dispel the ignorance which exists in England about Ireland & the Irish I should feel that I had done

[99] See **Document 8**.
[100] See **Document 15**.

something towards its solution. It is too late now for any half measures. We must deal with the question liberally, boldly and generously. We must either trust the Irish altogether or not trust them at all.

I need hardly say that this memorandum is secret, and nothing in it should be quoted publicly, but if your Lordship thinks that there is anything in it worthy of consideration you will be quite at liberty to show it to any one privately.

I doubt whether Mr. Gladstone himself is aware of the great power of the secret organizations which exist in America & the United Kingdom, and which at the present time are giving all the support they can to Mr. Parnell, but which will be ready to renew violent agitation directly Mr. Parnell's policy receives a check.

I suppose you have the former memorandum by you. If not I could send another copy should you desire it.

**22.** E.G. Jenkinson to Lord Carnarvon, 6 November 1885; 'Private'; CP, Add MS 60829, fos 136–139.

I saw Lord Salisbury yesterday, and had a long talk with him about Ireland. He takes a rather gloomy view of the future, and is inclined to think that it will be impossible in the present state of opinion in England about Ireland to do anything in the way of settling the Irish question early in the next session.[101] He thinks it must come to a head in the way we most dread. I am afraid it must be so, but it is so terrible and so lamentable I do not like to think of it. Lord Salisbury said that he was afraid Home Rule could not come from the Conservatives.

I sent a copy of my memorandum[102] to Sir R. Cross the same day as I sent a copy to Your Excellency because I thought that as my chief while over here, he ought to have one, and because I thought you would wish him to have it. The copy which Your Excellency received was sent off on the 2nd November and as no telegram or letter came on the 3rd or 4th November 1885 telling me not to send copies to the persons I had mentioned to you I sent off one copy to Lord Rosebury.[103] After I had dispatched it your telegram of the 4th reached me, and I immediately wrote to Lord Rosebury to keep the memorandum

---

[101] Salisbury spoke in similar vein to Spencer during a shooting party at Sandringham in mid-November: Spencer to Lord Granville, 22 November 1885, repr. *RE*, II, pp. 79–80.
[102] See **Document 15**.
[103] See **Document 21**.

strictly private.[104] I would not have done this had I not understood that I had received Your Excellency's permission to send copies to Lord Spencer, Lord Northbrook[105] & Lord Rosebery. I suppose I am to understand now that I am not to send copies to the Lord Spencer and Lord Northbrook?

**23.** Lord Carnarvon to E.G. Jenkinson, 8 November 1885; Vice Regal Lodge, Dublin. Copy; 'Private'; CP, Add MS 60829, fos 140–143.

Your letter of the 6[th] has taken me entirely by surprise.[106] I had, & could have, no idea that you wd. distribute copies of a very confidential mem. printed at the F.O. to any one except the Prime Minister without further communication. You will remember that I was very doubtful as to the printing of the mem. at all that when I finally agreed to it I said there must only be a very limited number of copies (I think I said six) – that I did not propose to circulate it even among my own colleagues & that it was therefore clearly impossible that I should desire its circulation outside the Cabinet and that I cannot therefore conceive how you could have so far misapprehended anything I said or did not say as to think yourself free to make a communication of this kind. For it must be remembered that though the mem. is drawn up by yourself, it was drawn for my information or use, and is printed at the F.O. and may seem to carry with it a certain amount of official authority.

I trust that your telegram to Ld Rosebury will be in time to assure his absolute & entire silence on the subject; but I have thought the matter of such great importance that I have myself [written] to him to ask him to treat the communication as entirely confidential.[107]

It is a matter much to be regretted; but I seriously hope that no mischief will come of it.

**24.** Sir Robert Hamilton to Lord Spencer, 3 December 1885; Chief Secretary's Office, Dublin Castle; 'Private'; AP, Add MS 77060.

I got your letter and its enclosures which I return. [*These dealt with an administrative matter concerning the Church of England.*]

---

[104]See Carnarvon to Jenkinson, 4 November 1885 (telegram): CP/TNA, PRO 30/6/62 (32).

[105]Thomas George Baring (1826–1904), first Earl of Northbrook (1866), Governor-General of India (1872–1876), First Lord of the Admiralty (1880–1885), opponent of home rule.

[106]See **Document 22**.

[107]See Carnarvon to Rosebery, 8 November 1885: CP/TNA, PRO 30/6/62 (33).

I certainly expected the Liberals to have a much larger majority than they are likely to have, but it is still possible that they may outnumber the Tories & Nationalists together.

I don't think the new Parliament can be a long lived one. I doubt if the issue even now as regards Ireland has been clearly before the minds of the English Voters.

I think the time has gone by for small measures, and that the risk must be run of passing a great one. But the future is very dark.

I am very glad that your brother is in.[108] My prediction that the extension of the franchise would result in the extinction of the Liberal representatives for Ireland is being completely fulfilled. It was the right course never the less.

I was not very sorry that Childers & Lefevre were defeated[109] for I always dreaded one or other of them coming here.

**25.** Lord Carnarvon, 'Remarkable report by Fottrell to Sir R. Hamilton', 7 December 1885; Vice Regal Lodge, Dublin; CP/TNA, PRO 30/6/67 (30).

Fottrell told Sir R. Hamilton these remarkable things.

1. Dillon & Gray had been during the last few days anxiously considering what measures could be taken to enforce the law for the collection of rents, where the rents were reasonable, & to relax it where they were impossible "fully appreciating the chaos which wd ensue if the rights of property were not maintained". All this was being considered with a view to the speedy obtaining of an Irish Parlt.

2. They also were in favour of a second Chamber of which a certain part should be Irish Peers: but they were inclined to provide that in the event of a difference between them & the Lower House the vote of the Upper Chamber cd be suspensive only, say two or even three times the power of a veto.

3. They were in addition considering the possibility of a minority representation.

---

[108]Hon. Charles Robert Spencer (1857–1922) sixth Earl Spencer (1910), Lib. MP for Northamptonshire North (1880–1885) and for Mid-Northamptonshire (1885–1895).

[109]Childers lost the seat for Pontefract but was returned as a Liberal Home Ruler for Edinburgh South in July 1886. Shaw-Lefevre lost the seat for Reading but was returned for the constituency of Bradford Central following the death of W.E. Forster in April 1886.

**26.** [Lord Carnarvon], 7 December 1885; 'Very Confidential'; Printed for the use of the Cabinet, 11 December 1885; CAB 37/16/64.

Whatever may be the decision of Cabinet in reference to the elections, I think it desirable to place before my colleagues, as shortly as I can, the present state of Ireland, and the opinion which I hold in regard to it. Those of them who remember what I said on a former occasion will scarcely be surprised at the purport of this paper.

1. As regards the condition of the country, agrarian crime and outrage have been, and continue, low. There has been only one agrarian murder since I have been in Ireland, if, indeed, this particular crime was not due to other causes. "Boycotting" has been held in check, as I said it would be, and has diminished, though it is still very mischievous and capable of development.

On the other hand, the National League has lost none of its power. It has, on the contrary, acquired a remarkable organization and force. The Roman Catholic Clergy, though with reluctance on the part of the Bishops and higher clergy, have been drawn more and more under the influence of the National League and into the ranks of the Nationalist party. The landlords seem in most districts hopelessly alienated from the tenants, and without influence. Everywhere, except in the Counties of Antrim, Armagh, Down, Londonderry, and Tyrone in the north, the Nationalist cry has swept all before it. At the last Dublin Municipal Election, not a single Conservative seat was retained,[110] and the history of the recent Electoral Conventions, and the defeat of Mr. Callan in Louth,[111] show that, at present, there is an unexampled organization and power at the disposal of Mr. Parnell.

To all this I must add that there is a great development of the Secret Societies in the United States, an abundance of money subscribed, the closest communication existing between them and kindred Societies in Ireland, which, though not active, are only waiting the signal to become so, and are every week growing more formidable.

Meanwhile, the Government in Ireland remains in a state of hopeless isolation, and with the means at its disposal is totally

---

[110] The four Conservatives seeking re-election were defeated by Nationalists: *FJ*, 26 November 1885, p. 7.

[111] Philip Callan (1837–1922), Home Rule MP for Dundalk (1868–1880) and for County Louth (1880–1885): see Gerard Moran, 'Philip Callan: the rise and fall of an Irish Nationalist MP, 1868–1885', *County Louth Archaeological and Historical Journal*, 22, no. 4 (1992), pp. 395–411.

unable to do more than for a very short time to keep things *in statu quo*.

2. Besides this, there are other most serious dangers immediately ahead. The position of trade and agriculture is very grave. On all sides there is a disposition to refuse rent in whole or in part. Fresh organizations – more difficult to deal with – are constantly being formed, and at any moment we may have to face a widespread agreement on the part of tenants to refuse rent. In many parts of the country this is due to a real absence of money; in other parts, advantage is taken of the agricultural depression. We are, in fact, enjoying a short truce.

3. If no settlement of this state of things is practicable, not only will the condition of Ireland become almost intolerable, but the difficulties outside it will be most grave. First and foremost a renewal of outrages, on a more extended scale than ever, will occur, having their base of operations in the United States. We know, indeed, that preparations are being made. Next, it is reasonable to expect a further disorganization of Parliament and public business, with all the discredit, difficulty, and danger to public institutions which are likely to follow in the play of factions; and last, the great danger from a hostile Ireland in America, and the risk in Canada, and even in Australia, where there is a considerable Irish element. To all this must be added the extraordinary, not to say discreditable, spectacle of a four-fifths representation in a nominally free Assembly, whom Parliament, if they cannot come to terms, will be compelled to silence or ignore.

4. The question then arises, what in these circumstances can be done. So far as the interests of Ireland, England, and the Empire generally are concerned – though I recognize the extreme dangers of any change whatever – I think the best chance of safety lies in the course which I will indicate.

I believe half-measures in this case are impracticable and dangerous, particularly to the landowners – that class whose interests are now threatened in Ireland. There is no real alternative now, I fear, between large concession and repression; and a very considerable number of men, of the greatest experience and capacity, and of undoubted Conservatism and loyalty, whose judgement I have been able to obtain, have not hesitated in confidence to avow themselves of this opinion. I do not think it right to state any names even in so secret a Memorandum as this, but the fact is so; and the reason why both they and I take this view, is that small instalments of change cannot be accompanied by any counter-balancing precautions or checks, and will only lead at no distant day to that which is the great present danger – the gradual or forcible expropriation of the landlords.

There are three burning questions at present – the land, the education [*sic*], and local self-government. And let me here say that by local self-government is not meant the establishment of County or District Boards, but some elective body, which shall have all the outward form and semblance of a Parliament. This is what is desired, and nothing less, as far as I can see, will be accepted; and when a nation has passionately, however irrationally, set its mind upon this, and when all the really influential classes (excepting, of course, a part of Ulster) are agreed, it will be found, under our Parliamentary system, practically impossible to refuse it.

All these three questions, then, will have to be faced before long, but probably the land is the most important, and must form an essential, if not the first part, of any scheme of settlement.

Difficult as it may be, I do not think that it would be impossible to frame such a scheme as might with comparative safety embrace these three subjects. I believe that there are one or two methods at least which might be attempted with some reasonable hope of success, and I do not see that even a Parliament, if duly balanced and guarded, need be so dangerous as at first sight it may appear. I feel, anyhow, convinced that it is less dangerous than the half-measures which are most in favour with both political parties. I will not, however, embarrass this Memorandum by going into these details. I could do so if necessary.

5. So far I have considered the matter in the general interests of England, and particularly of Ireland; but it remains to consider it in the light of Party possibilities, and if it is clear, as some think, that the Party will not endure such a course as I have indicated, then I admit that it is a paramount duty at this crisis not to split or divide it.

But it is worth considering whether there is any line of action which can solve the difficulty without creating discord in the Party.

I can see only three courses:—

(1.) To propose and do nothing, and wait till we are turned out by a combination of Liberals and Irish, which is a view I only mention to discard.

(2.) The adoption of some considerable, yet comparatively minor, measures in the hopes of tiding over the difficulty till the Irish party are disintegrated – which, by the way, let me say would not really settle the difficulty or, perhaps, much improve the case.

A larger scheme of higher education seemed, at one time, the most likely expedient in this direction. We have formally promised to deal with it; if we meet Parliament, we must allude to it in the Queen's

Speech; it was the question by which we trusted to satisfy and win to the side of order the Roman Catholic Bishops; it was one which separated them, in a religious point of view, from a large part of the Irish Parliamentary party; it was also one on which I thought we might see our way to deal broadly and successfully; and, lastly, if properly dealt with, we might safeguard that which is grievously threatened in the immediate future – the interests of Trinity College.

But events have moved too fast, and I am afraid that the attempt would be too late, mainly through the action of one man. The Archbishop of Dublin, it is clear, has made an alliance with Mr. Parnell; he has publicly declared against such a settlement as I think we ought to make, and he has within the last few weeks, strange to say, apparently won over a majority of the Bishops. It is not easy to suppose that he would go back from a public utterance such as this.

(3.) One last alternative remains, viz., to do something, without committing ourselves as a Government to any course which might divide the Party. I wish my colleagues to consider whether it might not be possible to propose a Joint Committee of both Houses to consider the relations of Ireland and England, or the better government of Ireland, or some such general proposition, subject to the two following conditions, expressed in the most distinct language:—

1. The supremacy and authority of the Crown.

2. The maintenance of the rights of minorities in religion and property.

This would gain time, would educate the party and the country to a knowledge of the case, in which they are extraordinarily ignorant; would be constitutionally a very defensible course; would give a chance of moderate councils prevailing; would secure the combined action of both parties; and would, if we failed to come to a conclusion through the fault of the Irish Party, leave us free to deal with the question in a much more decided manner, – and all without committing the Government to any definite proposals.

But such a course, if adopted, ought, I think, to have the preliminary concurrence of the Party. I do not overlook or underrate the objections which might be made; but in this extremely grave juncture, some risks may reasonably be run.

It would also, I think, be highly desirable, if possible, to ascertain by very private negotiation whether we should have the support of any or all of the leaders of the Opposition.

The first of these modes of proceeding appears to me necessary, the second not absolutely necessary, but very desirable. A very considerable number of people in England would, I believe, approve of a union of the leaders of parties in order to solve the problem.

**27.** E.G. Jenkinson to W.E. Gladstone, 11 December 1885; 14 St. James Square, London S.W.; 'Secret & Private'; GP, Add MS 56446, fos 170–179.

I hope you will not think that I am taking too great a liberty in writing to you a few lines about Irish questions. But it seems to me to be of such pressing importance and I have so intimate knowledge of what is going on behind the scenes both in Ireland and in America that I cannot refrain from putting before you what, I believe to be a true picture of the present situation.

Even at the risk of writing obscurely I will state what I have to say in the smallest compass possible.

I do not know whether you are aware of the existence of two powerful Fenian organizations, the one in America called the Clan-na-Gael and the other in the United Kingdom called the United [Irish] Revolutionary Brotherhood. There are also some smaller organizations the principal of which is the old Fenian Brotherhood headed by O'Donovan Rossa in New York, and by James Stephens[112] in Europe.

The Clan-na-Gael organization is however far more powerful than any other and has at its command large resources both in money and men. It really is the main spring of the whole movement. The Dynamite explosions in London in 1882 & 1884, as also the blowing up of the House of Commons this year were the work of its agents, and practically it controls and guides the Policy of the National League in America and in the United Kingdom, and to a large extent also the Policy of the Irish Parliamentary Party.[113]

At the present time this organization and also all other Irish organizations in America and the United Kingdom have determined

---

[112] James Stephens (1824–1901), Young Irelander and founder of the IRB (1858) and *Irish People* (1863), head centre (i.e. leader) of the Fenian movement until 1867, returned to Dublin from exile in Paris in 1885.

[113] The Fenian bombing campaign began in Salford in January 1881 and continued with attacks on Liverpool Town Hall, the Mansion House, and Local Government Board offices. The first attack thought to have been fomented by Clan-na-Gael occurred at Victoria underground station on 25 February 1884 and was followed by explosions at Scotland Yard and London Bridge: see K.R.M. Short, *The Dynamite War: Irish-American bombers in Victorian Britain* (Dublin, 1979); Bernard Porter, *The Origins of the Vigilant State: the London Metropolitan Police Special Branch before the First World War* (London, 1987), pp. 45–48, and Jenkinson, 'Confidential memorandum', 22 June 1885: CP, Add MS 60829, fos 57–61.

to hold their hand and to give Parnell as they say, a "chance". All Dynamite work and all violent measures have been stopped and large sums of money are being forwarded to Parnell to aid him in his electioneering campaign, and to provide salaries for some of the new Irish members. But at the same time Fenians generally do not believe much in Parnell's chances of success. They think what they want can only be wrung from England by force – and they are in consequence organizing and preparing everywhere, in London, in the large cities in England, in Ireland and in America for "active work" in the future. It is uncertain how long in time they will give Parnell. The extremists and the Irreconcilables are already beginning to show signs of impatience. But it is quite certain that should Parnell not meet with success or should he receive a check we shall have before next summer a renewal of violent agitation in Ireland. The outrages & murders of 1882 will be repeated, in Ireland, and in London & perhaps in other parts of England there will be Dynamite explosions, the murder of statesmen and officials, and other outrages. All are determined about this, and all are preparing for it.

We shall be able more clearly to see what is in contemplation after the Convention at Chicago which is fixed for the 20th & 21st January 1886 has taken place.[114] There will first be a Convention of the Irish National League the proceedings of which will be practically under the control of the Leaders of the Clan-na-Gael, and this will be followed by secret conventions of the Clan-na-Gael and other Irish secret organizations. Future prospects will there be discussed and the Policy of the coming year will be settled. The Extremists will urge the recommencement of active revolutionary work, but the probability is that they will be kept in check for some little time longer by the moderates who wish to give every possible chance to constitutional agitation.

We therefore seem to have arrived at a most critical time in Irish History. Ireland is passing through a great revolution, and the problem to be solved is how to guide her safely through that revolution without a renewal of violent agitation & horrible outrages, without additional suffering and injustice to the landlords, and without danger to the integrity of the Empire. *It is impossible to put off any longer the solution of this problem. The Irish question is so large that it not only overshadows, but it includes every other question of importance.*[115] It includes not only the reform in the procedure in the House of Commons, & all domestic legislation, but also matters connected with our Foreign and Colonial Policy. Neither

---

[114] See note 93 above.
[115] The passages in italics are those highlighted in the margin of the letter, presumably by Gladstone or a private secretary.

is it possible to put off the final settlement of the question by any half measures. It must be dealt with finally and boldly. *We must either meet the wishes and aspirations of the large majority of the Irish in Ireland and all parts of the world and give them a large & liberal measure of Home Rule, or we must make up our minds to adopt what is called the strong arm Policy, and to rule Ireland by force.* I cannot believe that any sensible man would think for a moment of adopting the latter course. The danger of delay is very great. If we are to give Home Rule to Ireland (and I feel firmly convinced that Home Rule is inevitable) *it is far better to give it generously and spontaneously than to allow the Irish to wring it from us by force.* I believe, and was of that opinion at the time, that we had a great opportunity at the end of 1883 when we had discovered the Invincible conspiracy and had put down all outrage in Ireland. We were strong then, and in our strength we might have been generous. Now it seems to me we have another opportunity and if we miss it, or if we fail to take advantage of it we shall find ourselves face to face with open revolution. Instead of having to deal with Parnell and his party we shall have to reckon with Extremists & Irreconcilables. *At the present time the moderate men among the nationalists & Fenians form the majority.* It is possible to make terms with them to keep the extremists and violent men in check. But let them see that Parnell is going to fail, that England is going to refuse Home Rule to Ireland and we shall have the present minority of Extremists converted into a majority and it will then be impossible for us to listen to the Leaders, or to make any concessions. The old miserable remedy of coercion will have to be applied again.

Now that so large a number of nationalists have been returned by such overwhelming majorities in Ireland, and Ulster for the first time is largely represented by Parnellites have we not a splendid opportunity for approaching a settlement of the Irish question? We may have thought before that the small band of men in Parliament did not truly represent the wishes & aspirations of the Irish people, that they were merely professional agitators working for their own selfish ends. But it is impossible any longer to think so. We have before us convincing proof of the strong feeling against our present system of Government and of an intense desire for Home Rule. Would it be right or wise to overlook this proof, and to tell the Irish people that we have no sympathy with them and cannot put any trust in them? Would it not be far wiser and more generous to acknowledge frankly our faults in the past, to admit the defects of our administrations, and before it is too late to grant Home Rule to Ireland in a form which would satisfy the people, and make Ireland a strength to England, and a loyal portion of the Empire?

*I firmly believe that if we do not grant Home Rule now we shall later on either have to agree to "Separation", or have to prevent Separation by force of arms.* The longer the settlement of the question is put off the more difficult will it be [to] satisfy the Irish, and to obtain good terms for the landlords. As time goes by the demands of the Irish will rise, and the landlords will be in a worse plight. We could have got much easier terms in 1883 than we can hope to get now. And a year hence the terms which would now be accepted would be refused.

By Home Rule the Irish mean the right to regulate their own internal affairs, the right to preserve their revenues for their own advantage, and to make their own laws. During the last three years I have frequently conversed with nationalists and Fenians of all shades of opinion – and with the exception of the violent extremists, mostly Irish Americans, these men do not want separation. Legislative independence does not mean total separation. To my mind the refusal of Home Rule now would much more probably lead to the disintegration of the Empire than would the granting of Home Rule. Arrangements which I need not specify here would have to be worked out in detail, and a settlement of the land question in the interests of the landlords would have to be made. *This latter is a very essential point, indeed in my opinion it is the only real difficulty standing in the way of Home Rule.* It would be impossible to give the Irish a Parliament of their own until either the landlords had been bought out or some sure guarantees have been taken for their protection. I do not fear in the least any persecution of the Protestants by the Roman Catholics, nor do I believe for a moment that on the introduction of Home Rule there would be a Civil War between Ulster and the rest of Ireland. There are many Protestants in the National Ranks, and in the recent Elections many Protestants & Presbyterians voted for Parnellites. Let the land question be settled and there would be no difficulty about Home Rule. If we trust the Irish at all, we should trust them altogether. They are a clever people well able to manage their own affairs – and if we are afraid of trusting them altogether it would be better not to trust them at all. A half measure of Self Government would not satisfy them, and would only be a platform from which they would continue their attacks upon us. The hostile feeling against England would if possible increase, and the Irish would not be satisfied with anything short of Separation.

The men to be feared are the Extremists who think that nothing but fear will induce England to make any concessions to Ireland, and who wish for the establishment of an Irish Republic. For the present these men are kept in check by Parnell, and I believe that in an Irish Parliament they would be a minority. *I believe that in that Parliament there would very speedily be formed, probably under the leadership of Parnell, a strong Nationalist Conservative Party supported by the whole strength of the Roman Catholic Church, the landlords, the newly created peasant proprietors, the farmers, and the professional classes, which would be much more than a match for the Separatists & Irreconcilables.* There would of course be considerable trouble, and opposition at first but in time things would settle down and all would go well.

I feel so sure that Home Rule is the only solution of the Irish question, and am so convinced that it must come some day that I long to see the subject taken up seriously by English statesmen. It would be most lamentable if with a correct knowledge of the present situation we were with our eyes open to allow blood to be spilt, and the country to be again given up to the mercies of Moonlighters and Secret Societies. *We never were so hated and our Government never was so powerless.* The National League rules Ireland, and our Government is isolated and completely out of touch and out of sympathy with the people. We cannot carry the people with us in anything, and even a measure passed entirely in their interest and for their benefit fails to do any good because its operation is met with obstruction on all sides. Under such conditions no administration can be carried on. It is absolutely necessary that we should get into touch with the people, and that can only be done through their Leaders. *Why should we be ashamed to consult and make terms with men who undoubtedly represent the national feeling,* and who recently have been behaving in a moderate manner, and have been doing their best to keep down outrages? Surely sentimental objections should not stand in the way of such a course, and the taunts of opponents about secret alliances should not prevent us from doing what is just and wise and right? A great step would be gained if the English would acknowledge the principle of Home Rule. Would it not be possible at the commencement of the next Session to pass a Resolution to the effect that Home Rule would be granted to Ireland provided the integrity of the Empire and the supremacy of the Crown could be maintained and sufficient protection could be afforded to the landlords and the minority?

If such a resolution was framed a Committee composed of able men from both Parties, & of Parnellites could be appointed to consider the question in a practical way, and to work out all the details – and with the Report of such a Committee before it Parliament would be able to come to some decisions. The matter would be brought to a head. If Home Rule could safely be granted to Ireland, then there would be legislation in that direction, if not then it would be necessary to put a stop to all agitation in favour of Home Rule, and to devise some other form of Government for Ireland. The advantage of such a course would be it seems to me that we should prove to the people of Ireland our anxiety if possible to meet their wishes as expressed at this last Election, we should keep the Extremists quiet for some months more (and every month so gained tells in our favour) and we should prevent a renewal of agitation, unseemly fighting and obstruction in Parliament, and perhaps a wasted Session. If the question is allowed to drift on for months shall we not be further off a righteous and just settlement of the question; will not the feeling against us in Ireland be stronger and more bitter, would it not be more difficult to protect and do justice to the landlords, and would not the Extremists make bolder and more impossible demands?

The subject is a very large one, and though I have written at greater length than I intended, I feel I have treated it very imperfectly.

I enclose a printed paper which will explain to you if you have time to read it *the details of the organization of the two large Fenian Societies, and will show their connection with the National League and the Parliamentary Party.*[116] There have been some slight changes since the paper was written but in all essential details it is correct.

Trusting that you will do me the favour of reading this letter, and hoping also that you will excuse me for addressing you at a time when you must be so much engaged and for expressing my views so plainly & frankly.

**28.** W.E. Gladstone to E.G. Jenkinson, 12 December 1885; Hawarden Castle, Chester; 'Secret'; GP, Add MS 44493, fos 212–213.

For long I have been mourning over the slowness with which the pupil of the political eye in many enlarges itself to take in the light. It certainly has not been so with you. I agree, very emphatically, in what appear to be the leading propositions of your letter.[117] But they are not abstractions. They call, in your view, for immediate action. I too am enraged when I hear people talking of waiting games. Time is indeed most precious.

But I am of opinion that it is the Government who ought to act: first because they are the Govt. & none but the Govt. of the day can act with effect or hope. Secondly because they are a Tory Government.

For my part, if they will not trifle with the subject but bring in a measure adequate & safe, I shall use them, as I have used them about Afghanistan and about Bulgaria. If they flinch, then it is a different affair.

Having explained myself thus freely I must ask you to explain in what capacity you address me – and what use I may make of your

---

[116] See **Document 8**.
[117] See **Document 27**.

letter. Particularly as to those of my late colleagues who stand foremost in responsibility as to Ireland.

By the wish of the Irish to retain their own revenues for their own use, I hope I am not to understand that they expect England & Scotland to pay their share of the National Debt, and to find an army and navy to defend them gratis.

**29.** E.G. Jenkinson to W.E. Gladstone, 14 December 1885; 14 St. James Square, London S.W.; 'Private & Secret'; GP, Add MS 56446, fos 180–181.

I thank you very much for your kind answer to my letter.[118] I am very much gratified that you should have thought what I said to be worthy of your attention and consideration.

You ask me in what capacity I addressed you, and what use you may make of my letter. Of course I need hardly say that I have in my possession information and papers which I could not give to any one outside the present Government without the express permission of Lord Carnarvon and Sir R. Cross, but I thought I might with perfect propriety write to you as I did in a private capacity merely expressing my own personal opinions, the more so as those opinions are not new, or based on information recently received, but have been held by me for some time past. Not knowing what might be the outcome of the Election, and thinking that you might have at any moment to come to some important decision on the Irish question I thought it my duty, as one who knows so much about Ireland, and has worked so much under Lord Spencer, to place before you my view of the situation and the conclusions I have come to.

Lord Spencer, Lord Northbrook, Lord Rosebury and Mr Trevelyan all know my views on the subject, and have all read the printed memorandum which I sent you[119] – and I can see no reason why they should not see my letter[120] if you think it worth their reading. It should however be clearly understood that it is a confidential letter not to be made public, and that it contains only an expression of my own personal views.

In so short a letter I could not go into arguments and details. I tried to make it as short as possible, and therefore, as I said, I dealt with the subject very imperfectly. Indeed I could not write comprehensively &

[118] See **Document 28**.
[119] See **Document 8**.
[120] See **Document 27**.

exhaustively without making use of papers which as an official in the Home Office I have to keep secret. The question of the Irish share of the National Debt, and of the cost of the Army and Navy are matters of detail (though exceedingly important detail) which would be settled after the principle of Home Rule had been acknowledged. *But I do not understand that the Irish expect to be let off their proper share of Imperial Expenditure.*[121] The quota which they would have to pay annually could, I should say, be fixed without very much difficulty.

I hope that if I have written too freely or frankly about this matter you will forgive me. My excuse must be the immense importance I attach to the Irish question. *It is just now, the question of questions. The settlement of it does not admit of delay. If we do not face it boldly, & settle it on broad and liberal lines now we shall have heavy trouble in the future.*

**30.** Lord Northbrook to Lord Spencer, 18 December 1885; 4, Hamilton Place, Piccadilly; 'Private'; AP, Add MS 76918.

After reading E. Jenkinson's letter[122] I wrote to him to say that the foundation of the proposal to concede Home Rule was the idea that by doing so the "Extremists" would be checked and a moderate party formed which would be against Separation.

The facts being (I said) that the Irish National League & the Parnellite Party have hitherto acted as the instruments of the Clan na Gael whose avowed object is the establishment of an Irish Republic by force, what reasonable probability is there that the connection will cease when Home Rule is given? Is it not more likely that the power which will be so gained will be used in furtherance of Separation and for the organization of the means of resistance to England if it should come to blows?

He came to see me yesterday afternoon & we had a long talk upon this and the question generally.

He said that all the information he has received for the last three years leads him to believe that the majority of the Nationalists, Fenians &c. in the United Kingdom are against Separation, but that they are forced to rely on the Clan-na-Gaels because their funds are derived from them. He believes that the whole of the R. Catholics headed by Archbishops Croke & Walsh would be against Separation.

I asked him whether it was likely that the Irish, hating us as they do, would not use Home Rule against England in any time of difficulty.

---

[121] The passages in italics are those highlighted in the margin of the letter, presumably by Gladstone or a private secretary.
[122] See **Document 27**.

His answer was by no means positive. In fact he recognizes that after all Home Rule cannot be said to be any more than perhaps the least bad of two alternatives, & that all that is to be said is that there is a reasonable probability of a party being formed against Separation & which would keep down outrage. I am disposed to agree with him that there is such a reasonable probability. But I am very doubtful how long it would last.

I asked his opinion upon the question as to which you expressed some doubts, viz. which is the strongest feeling in Ireland – the desire for Home Rule or the desire to get possession of the land. He said that among the older men the latter certainly, & also in Ulster. The younger men are more for Home Rule. He could not suggest any guarantee for the property of the Landlords except buying them out, and could not demur to my objection that the English people would never agree to such a scheme coupled with Home Rule.

I cannot help thinking that this difficulty is not insuperable, but I have as yet seen no solution of it.

He greatly regrets that Mr. Gladstone's opinions should have been made known – and is alarmed at the prospect of some grant of Home Rule being conceded without proper safeguards & the very careful consideration which ought to be given to it. In fact he thinks the announcement will put Parnell in the position of being able to hold off while the two parties are bidding one against the other. He does not know that any communications have taken place between Mr. G. & Parnell or his people.

I see that you have published that you have not agreed to a plan of Home Rule. Your position on the matter is the most important of that of any Englishman almost if not altogether, and I think you will do well to abstain from committing yourself until matters clear themselves in the legitimate way on the meeting of Parlt.

I wish I could say that further consideration has cleared my views. The alternatives are so detestable that it is very difficult to choose between them.

I met Lismore[123] at dinner last night, he is getting very old – his violence against Mr. G. is excessive, he says outrages are increasing. He said that the D. of Abercorn[124] just before he died estimated the Loyalists in Ireland at $2^1/_4$ millions or rather 2,400,000.

---

[123]George Ponsonby O'Callaghan (1815–1898), second Viscount Lismore (1857), landowner and Lord Lieutenant of Co. Tipperary (1857–1885).

[124]James Hamilton (1811–1885), second Marquess of Abercorn (1818) and first Duke (1868), Lord Lieutenant of Ireland (1866–1868, 1874–1876).

PS. If today's *Times* is correct that Mr. G. has written to the Queen who has communicated with Ld. Salisbury the explanation of the *Standard* paragraph of Thursday is simple.[125]

But I cannot understand how Mr. G. could have thought it right to take a step of such supreme importance without consulting Hartington, Chamberlain, yourself and others.

He is leader of the party and he cannot disassociate himself from that position.

I fear that what he has done will break up the party and seriously interfere with any satisfactory solution of the Irish question.

I do not see why because Mr. G. has been indiscreet others should follow his example & give vent to opinions somewhat hastily formed (I don't mean yours) without the advantage of discussion with others & when no further advantage can be gained from their publication.

Evelyn Baring[126] tells me that Mr. Errington[127] told him that the Pope was about to appoint Moran[128] archbishop, and had sent for him for the purpose when Manning[129] wrote to the Pope that Dilke & Chamberlain, who were the coming men, were in favour of Walsh, and therefore he was appointed!!!

I also hear that Lds. Ashbourne & Carnarvon brought forward a large measure at the Cabinet but it was rejected.

The last of my gossip is that Sir R. Hamilton is in favour of Home Rule.

**31.** E.G. Jenkinson to Lord Spencer, 20 December 1885; Woodcote, Walton-on-Thames; AP, Add MS 77036.

I have not written to you for some time, the reason being that up till quite lately there has been no real change in the situation, and also that not now being under you officially I cannot write freely as I

---

[125] On 17 December, *The Standard* had printed what purported to be Gladstone's home rule proposals, and Lord Salisbury had an audience with the Queen later that day: see *The Times*, 18 December 1885, p. 9.

[126] Evelyn Baring (1841–1917), first Earl of Cromer (1901), British agent and Consul-General in Egypt (1883–1907), leader of the Liberal free traders in the House of Lords.

[127] George Errington (1839–1920), Lib. MP for Co. Longford (1874–1885), responsible for efforts to establish diplomatic relations between the British Government and the Vatican: see Ambrose Macaulay, *The Holy See, British Policy and the Plan of Campaign in Ireland, 1885–93* (Dublin, 2002), pp. 4–11.

[128] Patrick Francis Moran (1830–1911), Archbishop of Sydney (1884–1911), historian of the Irish church and opponent of Fenianism.

[129] Henry Edward Manning (1808–1892), Catholic Archbishop of Westminster (1865–1892), sat with Dilke on the Royal Commission on the Housing of the Poor (1884–1885).

used to, and feel some delicacy about writing at all on matters which are closely connected with my work. A conversation which I had with Northbrook on Friday however induces me to write to you.[130] He told me that my two letters to Mr. Gladstone[131] were to be sent to you to read, and, although you know my view about Ireland well enough, I should like to add a few words by way of explanation.

Although I am a strong advocate for Home Rule, and believe that we must face the question now without loss of time, yet I am strongly against any precipitate or thoughtless action. What I fear is that the matter may be settled in too great a hurry, that in order to gain a Party triumph, or to clear the way for other legislation Home Rule may be granted without due deliberation, and without sufficient safeguards. It is no doubt the question of questions at the present time. Everything must give way to it, and no half measures will suffice. But never was there a time when there was more need that wise and cool heads should take counsel together and should see their way clearly before them before action is taken.

I know I need not say this to you. I only say it because I wish you to know that I see the enormous difficulties and objections in the way, and while I give my own opinions frankly I yet respect the opinions of others, and am anxious that the subject should be approached calmly and deliberately, and if possible as a question outside of Party altogether.

Cannot the Leaders on both sides sit down together and thresh out all the details thoroughly, and taking the Irish Leaders into counsel see whether it is possible to give a practical & workable measure of Home Rule to Ireland.

I am sure, as I said before, no half measure will be of any use whatever. We must trust the Irish altogether or not at all. That is the question which we have to settle.

In considering the subject the three great difficulties, (indeed to my mind they are the only real difficulties), which force themselves on one's attention are (1) The question of separatism (2) The Land question (3) The question whether supposing it were decided to give an independent Parliament to Ireland the people of Great Britain would consent to such a course.

The question of separation lies at the root of the whole matter, and it is one on which it is next to impossible to produce data or evidence. It is really a matter of opinion, of faith. I firmly believe that the people of Ireland do not want separation, and I found this belief on opinions which I have heard expressed by leading Nationalists, and Fenians,

[130] See **Document 30**.
[131] See **Documents 27** and **29**.

from letters which I have seen and on the principles of commonsense. The Irish are not fools, and they are led by men of ability. They must see that it will be to their advantage for a great many reasons to remain united to England. This is so obvious that I need not go into the details. We also know that the Roman Catholic Church is in favour of the Union, and is against separation. Such men as Archbishop Croke and Walsh though fervent Nationalists, and longing for an Irish Parliament in Dublin, are perhaps as strongly against the separation of Ireland from Great Britain, and against a measure which would lead to the dismemberment of the Empire. I attach great importance to the share which the Roman Catholic Church will take in the solution of the Irish question and to the great influence which it will exercise.

And I think it would be a wise thing to draw closer to that church, and to put ourselves in communication with such men as the two Archbishops I have named.

Still I feel that it is dangerous to prophesy, I may be quite wrong in my opinion, and men who say that Home Rule must lead to separation may be quite right. Let us then thresh it out: Hear what men most interested in the matter, and most competent to judge have to say, and then come to some definite conclusion.

It is easy to say that the Land question should be settled before Home Rule can be granted, but it is very difficult to say how it should be settled. The only way is to write different proposals and then decide which is the best. The Land Act of 1881 sounded the death knell of the Irish Landlords. They have been going from bad to worse, and really the only question now is how they can be protected from further suffering and loss. If they had been wise and long-sighted they would not be in their present plight. They might have got much better terms four years ago than they could get now and they will get better terms now than they can hope for a year hence. The longer the settlement of the question is postponed the worse will their position and chances be. Perhaps the best way would be to buy them out but that would mean a very large sum of money. However, nothing is to be gained by delay. The settlement of the Land question completely blocks the way to the introduction of Home Rule. In justice to the landlords it must first be taken up. The granting of Home Rule without its settlement would mean the immediate confiscation of the land and the ruin of the landlords.

The third question is one on which I hardly feel myself competent to give an opinion. There is great ignorance about Ireland, and the feeling against the Irish and their methods of agitation is no doubt very strong in London, and in the Home counties, and I believe also in the North and Scotland. Even if Mr. Gladstone were to propose a large measure of Home Rule it is a question whether he would be able to carry the people of England with him, more particularly if the scheme involved the payment of a large sum of money for the settlement of the Land question. If he were to propose such a measure and fail because the country was not with him, he would break up the Liberal Party, and enable the Conservatives to go to the country with the cry of "No Separation". This all points to the advisability of the settlement of the question by both Parties acting together as was done in the case of the Redistribution Bill. Public opinion in favour of some form of Home Rule has advanced very much during the last three years, and would no doubt come round altogether before very long if the people were educated to it, and were to see that the Leaders of the two Parties were in favour of it.

I am living now as you can see from the address at the top of this letter at Walton-on-Thames not far from St. George's Hill. It is a charming situation, and within easy reach of London. I suppose there is no chance of seeing you in town for some time. With kind regards to Lady Spencer.

**32.** Sir Robert Hamilton to Lord Spencer, 20 December 1885;[132] Chief Secretary's Office, Dublin Castle; 'Very Confidential'; AP, Add MS 77060.

Things have changed very much in Ireland in the past six months. (1) Exceptional legislation no longer exists, and except times of convulsion again arise it is practically impossible to revive it. Measures which were possible to a strong Government with its aid are impossible now.
(2) Mr. Parnell has issued a programme of one plank, viz. the legislative independence of Ireland, and to this five sixths of Ireland have given their adhesion, including the whole of the Catholic Hierarchy.
(3) This programme is not only accepted by the moderate Home Ruler, but by the Irish in the United States, in Canada, and Australia, and even by the dynamitard, and money that used to go for the promotion of outrages is now all going to the support of the Parliamentary party.
(4) The influence of the national party in keeping down the more serious class of outrages in Ireland is much more powerful than most well informed people thought it would be.

All this is matter of public notoriety. The situation is most critical. No half measures in my view now will do. Immense risks attend either

---

[132] The letter was written in reply to an untraced letter from Spencer (*c*.16 December): see **Document 33** and **Journal (12 March 1886)**.

alternative, but you much [*sic*] choose between allowing the country to try to govern itself, and ruling it with a rod of iron which will have to be forged.

I am in favour of the former alternative. The bolder the scheme now introduced, the more hope there is of introducing the necessary safeguards.

One of the most important in my view is the retention of the Constabulary in the hands of the Imperial Government. No sane statesman would propose that the Irish Parliament should have the power of raising military forces, and what is the Constabulary in its organization but a military force, armed, drilled, and capable of concentration on any given point? But on the other hand no local Government worthy of the name could be given which would withhold from the local authorities the control of the Police. Both these requirements can be met, however, by introducing into any constitution to be granted for Ireland a provision that as the local authorities supplied at their own cost local police, this general, and at least semi-military, force of Constabulary, maintained at Imperial charge, might be gradually disbanded.

I am astonished that no one seems to have hit upon this solution of this difficulty which appears to me to be a natural and simple one.

In my view there must be no hesitation in dealing liberally with this Force. In fact all the financial arrangements must be conducted on broad and generous lines. Much will depend on this, not only in getting the scheme to be thankfully accepted and cordially worked, but also in getting the necessary safeguards accepted.

In my view it is essential that the Representatives of the Irish people should be taken into consultation in settling how they are to be governed. We have neither the knowledge nor the power to legislate over their heads.

Once they have got legislative independence the less England interferes with Irish legislation the better. There is no fear of separation. Great Britain would keep such troops in Ireland as she sees fit, and would retain the entire control of these and of the Irish militia, and for the life of me I cannot see how the granting of a separate Parliament to Ireland would put her in a better position to take up arms against England, or to harbour an enemy's troops in the country.

The real danger to be apprehended is that, in the present state of exasperation of classes, the rights of property, especially in land, might suffer, but it will only intensify this danger and difficulty if you bring in an appeal to the English Parliament. The propertied classes have too long relied upon English bayonets to protect their rights. In other countries they secure that their interests are attended to by making themselves felt in the councils of the nation, and I see no reason why a constitution should not be devised for Ireland in which a place would be found for the due representation of all classes & interests.

I look upon this question as far beyond one of mere party politics. It is discreditable and dangerous to the Empire that discontent and disaffection should continue and grow in intensity. The crisis is close upon us, and while the risks are tremendous I yet have hope that light will emerge out of the darkness.

This letter, confidential in the highest degree as an expression of my individual views, is confidential in no other sense. I am not saying what any other person thinks or what any other person intends to do, I only try to put you in possession of certain reasons for coming to certain conclusions.

**33.** Lord Spencer to W.E. Gladstone, 22 December 1885; Althorp, Northampton; GP, Add MS 44312, fos 216–221.

I return according to Granville's[133] directions two letters of Jenkinson to you.[134]

I was very glad to read them though they contained nothing new to me as from previous communications I was aware of his views.

His letter put the case for Home Rule ably & well. One question must remain a mere matter of speculation whether the Clan na Gael & Extremists would, if Home Rule which satisfies Parnell & the Parliamentary party were granted, still have a dominating influence in Ireland.

It is a very serious question, the Roman Catholic Clergy form a very important element in the matter, their present inclinations are against separation, but they are not an independent body, they are unduly influenced by public opinion, & we cannot rely on them to maintain opinions which are unpopular among the bulk or most powerful Politicians of their own faith. Jenkinson you will notice takes a strong view as to the interests of property.

I saw Dr. Robert Macdonnell[135] a few days ago, he was in England for a Commission and came here for a night. He is a nephew of old

---

[133] Granville Leveson-Gower (1815–1891), second Earl Granville (1846), Lib. MP for Morpeth (1837–1840) and for Lichfield (1841–1846), Foreign Secretary (1851–1852, 1870–1874, 1880–1885).

[134] See **Documents 27** and **29**. The letters were also circulated to Hartington, Harcourt, and Northbrook: see above, p. 39.

[135] Robert Macdonnell (1838–1889), President of the Royal College of Surgeons of Ireland (1877–1889).

Alexander Macdonnell[136] who so long was at the head of the Irish National Board.

In 1870 Robert Macdonnell wrote a pamphlet on Home Rule under the name of Protestant Celt.[137] He sent it to me the other day and I read it.

When he was here I pressed him as to whether he adhered to his views. He said that the only change he had made was as to the necessity of making terms for the landlords, without this, he said, he would not be in favour of going forward with a scheme of Home Rule.

I send the Pamphlet to you. You will not care to read it all but in the Appendix to the Second Edition on p. 80 you will see what he recommended in 1870.[138]

I was writing to Sir R. Hamilton the other day, and referring to what he said in a letter to me which showed a change of opinion,[139] I said that as we had had so many consultations on this topic I thought it right to tell him that I had changed my opinion in so far that I thought the solution of the difficulty by the old methods which I advocated last May, was now impossible, but that I saw immense difficulties in the alternatives.[140]

I said that I did not write to elicit his views as he might find it impossible to communicate them to me. I got the enclosed from him.[141] It is important. I consider from the last paragraph of his letter that I am justified in showing it to you in strict confidence.

I cannot agree with his views of leaving the landlords to take their chance. His suggestion as to the Constabulary is only a method of getting rid of them, for of course every local authority would speedily create a force of their own. I thought by the way he began the argument that he was going to find some means of keeping the Constabulary as an imperial force which would be difficult. I wrote to him before the *Standard* and *Pall Mall* announcement.[142] Had I foreseen the likelihood of these rumours I should have hesitated about writing to him. I had

---

[136] Sir Alexander Macdonnell (1794–1875), Resident Commissioner of National Education (1839–1871).

[137] *Irish Nationality in 1870: by a Protestant Celt. Second edition, with a commentary on the 'Home-Rule Movement'* (Dublin, 1870). For further letters and articles, see *The Times*, 14 April 1873, p. 8, and 21 April 1873, p. 11; *FJ*, 22 April 1873, pp. 2, 6.

[138] Gladstone read the article on 23 December: *GD*, XI, p. 457.

[139] See **Document 24**.

[140] See **Journal (12 March 1886)**.

[141] See **Document 32**. Matthew mistakes this as referring to Hamilton's memorandum of 21 [31] October 1885 (**Document 20**): see *GD*, XI, p. 447, n. 6.

[142] See **Journal (4 January 1886)**.

in the same way written to Monck[143] a letter fishing for his opinion. I am to hear from him in a day or two.

I will read the debate on the Address in 1882, if I recollect rightly it bore an amendment of the Land Act. You probably have read the Articles in the *Freeman* on your supposed scheme.[144] They are moderate & point to a wish for a settlement: but Gray is less to be depended upon even than the R.C. Hierarchy.

I have not altered the views which I held when at Hawarden,[145] but I see great difficulties in getting the proper guarantees for the landlords without which I do not yet see that a scheme could be proposed.

I wish it were possible for you and Salisbury to agree the heads of a scheme which might be the basis of communication with Mr. Parnell. This would avoid the danger of one party negotiating with Parnell, and laying itself open to the accusation of trying to outbid the other party.

However patriotic those might be who negotiated with Parnell without the knowledge of their opponents, the public would never be got to believe that they were not acting from selfish party motives.[146] This of itself after what has been said at the Elections might wreck a scheme. I presume however that now, unless anything unexpected turns up, everyone must wait for the Government.

I do not write this with a view of asking your opinion or of making you write a letter, but it may be well that after our conversations you should know how my thoughts are running.

Macdonnell who as a Doctor in large practice is in the way of learning Political opinion in Dublin, told me that he had noticed no indication that Conservatives or moderate Liberals in Dublin were leaning to some form of Home Rule.

The new feature which he noticed was that moderate R. Catholics for the first time in his experience openly denounced the line of their Archbishops & Bishops in the recent elections.

Formerly if they felt annoyed with their clergy they never showed it to a Protestant.

[143] Charles Stanley Monck (1819–1894), fourth Viscount Monck (1849), Governor-General of British North America and the Dominion of Canada (1861–1868), commissioner of National Education (1871–1894). For Monck's response, see Gladstone to Spencer, 26 December 1885, repr. *RE*, II, p. 90.

[144] See *FJ*, 18, 19, 21, 22 December 1885, p. 5.

[145] Spencer had long talks with Gladstone during his stay at Hawarden between 8 and 10 December 1885: Spencer to Lady Spencer, 8 and 9 December 1885, repr. *RE*, II, pp. 81–82.

[146] A reference to rumoured negotiations between Gladstone and Parnell: see above, p. 39, and *The Times*, 18 December 1885, p. 6.

I send you a letter from Jenkinson to me.[147]

**34.** W.E. Gladstone to Lord Spencer, 23 December 1885; Hawarden Castle, Chester; AP, Add MS 76863.

I thank you for your very interesting inclosures, most of all for your letter.[148]

The spirit in which you approach the great and difficult question of Irish Government is the only spirit which gives any hope of a tolerable issue. [*Gladstone lists the necessary conditions for progress.*]

I inclose some off hand comments on main points raised by your and by Hamilton's letters.[149]

Jenkinson's first letter struck me as an important fact in the case. His opinions in the letter to you do not rest on his position and opportunities of knowledge, and I do not give them so much weight.[150]

I heartily wish we could exchange ideas and information orally from day to day.

One step in advance I have taken by two letters to Mr. A. Balfour, which I inclose, and which I hope and think you will approve.[151] Please return them.

The relations of the Government to the Nationalists ought to be cleared up between this time and the meeting. This only they can do.

I also enclose a letter from MacColl[152] to Herbert: no I find it is to me.[153] I have spoken freely to him: but was quite unaware that he was going to see Salisbury.[154] I shall take care that he makes it clear that he had no authority, and carried no message, from me, and that his

---

[147] See **Document 31**.

[148] See **Documents 31, 32**, and **33**.

[149] See Gladstone's memorandum, 23 December 1885 (holograph), repr. *GD*, XI, p. 460.

[150] See **Documents 27** and **31**.

[151] Arthur James Balfour (1848–1930), first Earl of Balfour (1922), Con. MP for Hertford (1874–1885) and for Manchester East (1885–1906), President of the Local Government Board (1885–1886), Secretary of State for Scotland (1886–1887), Chief Secretary for Ireland (1887–1891), Prime Minister (1902–1905). See Gladstone to Balfour, 20 and 23 December 1885, repr. *GD*, XI, pp. 455, 459.

[152] Malcolm MacColl (1831–1907), canon of Ripon (1884); amongst his many publications was *Reasons for Home Rule* (London, 1886).

[153] See George W.E. Russell (ed.), *Malcolm MacColl: memories and correspondence* (London, 1914), pp. 122–124.

[154] MacColl met Salisbury on 14 December: Andrew Roberts, *Salisbury: Victorian titan* (London, 1999), p. 364; Roy Jenkins, *Gladstone* (London, 1995), p. 523.

account was his opinion of my opinions and intentions. The account of Salisbury himself is very interesting. A happy Christmas.

**35.** Lord Spencer to W.E. Gladstone, 25 December 1885; Althorp, Northampton; AP, Add MS 44312, fos 230–231.

I thank you very much for your letter,[155] I entirely agree as to the spirit in which every one should approach this extremely difficult subject, if I have acted in that spirit up to this I shall try & continue to do so.

I am very glad that you had some communication with A. Balfour, & think that it is a good thing that Lord Salisbury should be aware of the tendency of your mind, although Mr. McColl spoke & wrote to Salisbury without your authority, it was a bold thing for that little man to do.

I have written some comments on your three headings Separation, Police, Landlords.[156]

I have put some of the difficulties which will be pressed on us if we are to get to a Bill.

I would say something on another matter viz. the judicial establishment in Ireland, but I will not attempt that now: but if you wish it later on I will give you some of the ideas which are pressing through my mind on that very important part of the subject.

I return you the interesting letters which you sent to me.[157] Jenkinson is of course no authority on tactics or mode of procedure, but as his letter to me was a commentary on his to you I thought I had better let you see it.[158]

Thanks for your Xmas greetings. We heartily wish the same to you & yours. I will return your notes & anything I say upon them tomorrow.

**36.** Lord Spencer to W.E. Gladstone, 25 December 1885; GP, Add MS 44312, fos 232–237.

I. Separation

I am inclined to agree that absolute separation is not desired by the large majority of Home Rulers at this moment.

[155] See **Document 34**.
[156] See **Document 36**.
[157] See **Document 34**.
[158] See **Document 31**.

I also agree that no doubts can exist as to the feeling of England and of Scotland on this matter.

No separation would be tolerated; if the Irish tried to get it they would be put down by force.

But a different argument may be used.

If we do not satisfy the Irish, after making a concession on the limitations laid down by Mr. Gladstone, & they still remain hostile to England, we shall have given them a new & better basis for agitation in a Representative Irish Assembly in Dublin, we shall also have given up some of our present means of defending ourselves without having gained anything sufficient to justify the risks we incurred?

We shall have disorganized Irish Gov[ernmen]tal Departments, disbanded the Police, alienated the classes dependent on property etc.

The only defence for taking these risks is that we look to satisfy the reasonable part of the Irish people.

If the Extremists gained the upper hand, separation would be the object of an Irish Parliament, & hostility to England would be as bitter as ever.

This view may be taken by certain people.

It has to be weighed. Other difficulties occur to me if this view were correct but I am rather disposed to think that we should disarm those who now attack us, & raise up a New party of moderate men in Ireland if we could satisfy them with a good scheme.

## II. Police

It must not be overlooked that in Parnell's Central Bd. scheme it was not proposed to withdraw the Police from the hands of the Central & Imperial Govt.

It would be a great risk to give up control of even Dublin Police, but I expect it must be faced for I shd. like to see the responsibility of keeping law & order thrown on the Irish members if a separate Parliament be granted to them for local affairs.

It might be dangerous to leave this armed force for use against the Imperial authority.

Even if the present force were broken up into county & borough forces, they might, under a strong Central National Govt. opposed to England, be used together as Regiments of one force.

Probably that was the view of Sir R. Hamilton, & his proposals would be a method of gradually or even rapidly disbanding this Irish Army.

No doubt liberal terms will have to be given to the force.

There is I fear already great consternation among them at the idea of their being placed under any but Imperial management.

This disturbance has been aggravated by the premature & unauthorized statement of Mr. Gladstone's policy.

## III. The landlords

By far the most difficult part of the question belongs to the 'Protection for the Minority'.

As yet I see no effectual way of meeting it except by some expedient system of purchase.

If this could be carried out we should get rid of most of the difficulties which would arise from minority representation & other grievances. Davitt's proposal in the *Pall Mall* might be a basis for settlement.[159]

What I should like to arrive at would be some plan which would be a check on the Irish Representatives & prevent their continued agitation against Landlords.

If they knew that to come to terms with the best Irish Landlords would save them for 50 years a large amount of Taxation, they might be disposed to be more reasonable.

I agree with Mr. Gladstone that the wholesale emigration of the resident proprietors is not desirable.

Of all people in the world the Irish small farmers & peasants need example & authority over them.

I hope that if a scheme of Home Rule were once started many of the good Resident Landlords (& I always mention that many such are to be found) would fall in with the new state of things: but at first they must be protected from the violence of those who have been persistently attacking their rights of property.

I have several letters from Ireland on the subject of Home Rule.

The working of the Land Act & the appointment of Commissioners & Assistant Commissioners is quoted as a matter where the present Parnellite leaders would not act with impartiality.

Certainly I can remember the grossest speeches from Healy & others on the subject. One of Healy's in Ulster where he said that Judicial Rents were to benefit the Tenants & therefore Tenants' men alone should be appointed to fix the Rents.[160]

The partiality & violence of these leaders in their past action will create some of the most difficult arguments to meet.

The anti Home Rulers say how can the Govt. of Ireland be handed over to such violent & partial men?

As to Protestants I should not on the whole be afraid on their behalf, but in country places they might at first be oppressed.

[159] *PMG*, 23 December 1885, pp. 1–3.
[160] Healy delivered the speech at Dungannon on 27 September 1883: see *FJ*, 28 September 1883, pp. 6–7.

The operation of the Labourers Act[161] is quoted to show this. It is said that the present Boards of Guardians in the South & West select the lands of Protestants as those on which the houses are to [be] built. The answer to this now is, that the Local Govt. Board inquiries & the appeal to the Privy Council practically protect all such persons & prevent injustice: but when all these authorities are in the hands of the Parnellites these safeguards will be gone.

**37.** Sir Robert Hamilton to Lord Spencer, 27 December 1885; Chief Secretary's Office, Dublin Castle; 'Very Confidential'; AP, Add MS 77060.

I was glad to get your letter.[162] I think it bad in the public interest that I should be identified in the public mind with any particular line of policy and that my views should be quoted, but subject to this I do not object to you showing my letter to any one in whom you have confidence.

I have no copy of what I said but I could not have conveyed my views fully if I led you to gather that I thought no safeguards were necessary to protect the landlords' interest beyond securing them a voice in the Government of their country.

The present difficulty is of course much intensified by the fall in the value of land, due to other causes than agitation, and I see a serious difficulty in the fact that Irish landlords and their friends won't admit this. Some great scheme of purchase is I think a necessity, and this would have to be provided in any settlement of the Irish question.

As you know I always opposed to the utmost of my power the advance of the whole of the purchase money to the occupiers. I never did, and never could, understand why if a man pays a fair rent he should be bribed to pay less now, and receive eventually his land for nothing.

But I would give this benefit to the Irish State. The objections to the State being a large landowner disappear, when the state means Ireland and not England. I would give the Irish State the benefit of the provisions of the Land Act of last session, under which the purchase of a farm of say £100 a year can give 20 years' purchase to the landlord, and repay only for principal and interest £80 a year for 49 years, at which time payment would cease.

[161] See **Journal (11 September 1885)**.
[162] Not traced.

The occupier would be out of it altogether. He gets a fair rent and there is an end of him. He is virtually a peasant proprietor subject to a rent charge. If he pays £100 a year as his fair rent, he should continue to pay it, but the state would only have to appropriate £80 of it to the sinking fund – the remainder would go in aid of the state's revenue, and it could be to the interest of the general taxpayer that the state should purchase in any case in which the landlord was willing to sell for such a number of years' purchase as would leave a balance in favour of the state.

I should not mind in such a case the term being extended so as to reduce the annual payment and increase the immediate margin.

The Imperial Govt. should guarantee money raised for this purpose & the landlords should be paid at par in guaranteed bonds carrying 3 per cent. Beyond this the Imperial Government should have nothing to do with the matter.

One result of such a scheme would be that a substantial value would at once attach, as it might to the landlord's interest, and another result would be that the state being themselves landlords would look after their interests as landlords, and that private landlords would benefit in the general support of such rights which it would be in the interests of the state to afford.

What rent the tenant should fairly pay would be of course, as it has been in the past, the great difficulty, but a scheme of this sort would be to make it to the advantage of the state that he should not pay too little. Such a scheme too so far as it operated would to some extent meet the views of those who advocate what is called the naturalization of land. I would give to the state, and not to individuals, the benefit arising from pledging the credit of England, and [sic] would lead to a large eventual reduction in the taxation of the country.[163]

I shall read the paper you have sent me on the participation of England and Ireland respectively in the general revenue and expenditure.[164] I myself tried my hand upon this, & I shall be curious to see whether the results at all agree.[165]

I'm glad you agree with me as regards the Constabulary. I think it would be a good thing, as soon as it can be done, that there should be some authoritative announcement to the Constabulary that, come what may, their interests will be looked after, and that they will in no

---

[163] For Gladstone's comments on this proposal, see Gladstone to Spencer, 14 January 1886, repr. *GD*, XI, pp. 478–479.

[164] See 'Maximum of Irish contribution to imperial charges': AP, Add MS 77329.

[165] See **Journal (28 October 1885)** and **Document 20**.

circumstances be handed over with their present organization to an Irish Parliament.

We may have bad days before us, and if we could not fall back upon the Constabulary we should be [in] a bad way indeed.

The feeling as far as I could gauge it among the people in Ireland having something to lose, was just after the election, that some sort of Home Rule was inevitable and imminent. But I think they are beginning to fancy England will never stand it. The tone of the London press I think has caused this change. A great deal of English money, something like 100 millions I believe, is advanced on land in Ireland, largely by Insurance Companies, & financial people have great weight with the London press.

The Nationalists are I think very confident, and I think I can detect in their writings the sobering effect that responsibility in prospect creates.

Please send a line to acknowledge receipt.

**38.** Lord Spencer to W.E. Gladstone, 28 December 1885; Althorp, Northampton; GP, Add MS 44312, fos 240–241.

I do not like to keep the enclosed back from you.[166] Hamilton's explanations were drawn from him by my criticizing what he said about the landlords finding their own level in any new Assembly.[167]

I reread his letter before I sent my criticism, & I told him that I thought I did perhaps misunderstand his meaning.

The explanation is interesting. It affords a scheme but a very big one. I believe something big will be wanted, there is a lot[168] attractive in his argument.

As to the Constabulary I told him that I did not think any one would propose to hand over an armed force like that to an Irish Executive, & that probably his method of dealing with that part of the question might answer.

As to his present desire that some statement should be made as to considering claims of the Police, I have told him I do not think it possible that any statement such as he wishes can be made now. Everything is too chaotic for that.

---

[166]See **Document 37**.
[167]See **Document 32**.
[168]The word 'something' has been deleted.

I may possibly go up to see Hartington tomorrow, I shall be very guarded in what I say of your plans.[169]

PS. I don't think Hamilton would write to me, even in the confidential way he has done, if the Tories have settled on a big scheme.

**39.** W.E. Gladstone to Lord Spencer, 28 December 1885; Hawarden Castle, Chester; 'Secret'; AP, Add MS 76863.

When you get the memorandum I have sent to Granville you will find that it is confined to considering some alternatives & ways of procedure, and does not touch the difficulties inherent in the question of a separate government for Ireland.[170]

This not because I think them disposed of but they belong to another branch of the case before us.

I have no doubt they are both great and diversified; the chief one of all being that on which we convinced him pretty largely. In principle I think you and I are agreed; but I look at the question rather as one meeting us *in limine* than as arising in ulterior stages.

I have not the smallest fear, for several reasons, of any attempt to employ the Police as a military force against us: what I feel apprehensive about is the preliminary question shall we have a state of legality in Ireland to start from? If we have this, I should feel pretty sanguine as to the future; but I know not that at the present moment we have any warrant for attaining it. By a state of legality I mean a condition not substantially worse than that in which you left the country. Nor do I know how situated as we now are it is possible to get at all the facts, which until Parliament has met will remain at the command of the Government exclusively.

**40.** Sir Robert Hamilton to Lord Spencer, 3 January 1886; Chief Secretary's Office, Dublin Castle; 'Very Confidential'; AP, Add MS 77061.

Sunday is the only day I can find time to write – hence your last letter[171] has remained unanswered till now.

[169]The meeting did not take place: Spencer to Granville, 29 December 1885, repr. *RE*, II, p. 94.
[170]See Gladstone to Granville, 26 December 1885, repr. *GD*, XI, pp. 462–463; and see John Morley, *The Life of William Ewart Gladstone*, 3 vols (London, 1908), III, pp. 269–273.
[171]Not traced.

I think the tide of feeling in Ireland is again setting towards the inevitableness of something like Home Rule. The more the question is discussed the clearer it becomes that the only alternative is disenfranchisement.

It is futile to talk, as many do, of a reform of Dublin Castle as a way out of the difficulty. You may replace men and other officials by others, but unless the new men possess the confidence of the national party, you are certainly no better off, and if you could induce, and this I don't for a moment believe you could, Healy & Sexton & such men to take office, they would be immediately disowned & abused like O'Shaughnessy, for this is not what the party wants.

I quite see the great difficulty as regards yourself. Some two months ago, before the elections in a conversation with Fottrell I said, "I have had no communication with Lord Spencer since he left on Irish matters, but I undertake to say that by & bye you will acknowledge that there is no truer friend to Ireland than Lord Spencer." I have no doubt that this has been repeated to the nationalist leaders, but whatever effect, if any, it may have upon their attitude towards you, of course it does not affect your attitude as regards them.

It is simply hopeless to try to do anything without carrying the Irish members with you, and I believe they would be more reasonable at the present moment than later. The quiet of the past few months is distinctly in favour of a settlement now. There is a marked absence both in the utterances of agitation and of the extreme press of the bitterness against England which was so marked during the last few years. I am quite aware that it is a matter of policy with them at present to refrain from such utterances but making all allowances for this, I believe a real improvement is discernable. It would be a thousand pities to lose the advantage this would give to a settlement now. I don't think it would be desirable that you should come back again as Lord Lieutenant, if the liberals come in, tho' I think it is essential that you should take a leading part in dealing with the matter in the Cabinet. I should have a dummy Lord Lieutenant, and a Chief Secretary in the Cabinet at this crisis, when the important matter is legislation not administration. It is most important that the Chief Secretary should be a person who would be acceptable to the Irish Parliamentary party, and I believe the best man would be John Morley. If you wish to avoid hopeless collapse, don't send Childers or Lefevre.[172]

There is a lurking affection for Mr. Gladstone notwithstanding all the abuse that has been heaped upon him, and a belief, and this I thoroughly share, that he is the man and the only man to settle the question.

---

[172] See **Document 24** and **Journal (3 February 1886)**.

Please excuse me for writing so freely. I am betraying no confidences. I am only putting you as my late chief in possession of my individual views on a matter so vital as to put all mere party considerations absolutely in the shade.

Please send just one line in acknowledgement of this that I may know it has reached you.

**41.** Andrew Reed, 'Inspector General's confidential report regarding the position and progress of the Irish National League', 14 January 1886; Chief Secretary's Office, Dublin Castle; CSO RP 1888/26523.

As will be seen by the reports received from the Divisional Magistrates the Irish National League has made great advance within the past twelve months. By the attached returns, shewing the number of branches of the League by Divisions and also by Counties for the past three years, it will be seen that the number of branches in Ireland for the three years (ending) 1883, 1884, and 1885 respectively are 242; 592; and 1260. The growth of the League during the past twelve months is remarkable. Several causes have advanced the interests of the League. The following are the principal.

(1) For the past four years owing to falling prices for stock the farming class has suffered great loss. The severest year upon them has been 1885. The traders in towns whose business in an agricultural country like Ireland depends upon the condition of the farming class have not been prosperous. (Trade in Dublin and in the small towns in Ireland is at present very bad). Discontent has been produced by this want of prosperity, and the tenant farmers have not been able yet to realise substantially the great benefits conferred upon them by the Land Act of 1881. (I am of opinion if the years 83, 84, and 85 had been prosperous for the farmers the state of the National League would now be quite different). The farmers and small traders are led to believe that further agitation will better their condition, and through the National League they hope for success.

(2) The General Election under the new franchise gave a great impetus to the cause of the National League, many of the branches formed within the past six months were established principally for Election purposes, and many of them will languish and fall away now that the excitement has passed, unless some fresh stimulus is given to them.

(3) Since the R.C. Bishops committed the subject of Education to the charge of the Parnellite party the Bishops have patronised the National League (only a few of them were ardent supporters of it previously). It looks as if a compact was entered into by the Bishops and the League that if the latter pushed in the Education question the Bishops could support the League for other political purposes. The Bishops now give it every support and allow the priests to take office and part in the League. Were it not for the support of the R.C. Bishops and Clergy the League would have had little or no success in the greater part of Ireland. In many Counties it had no success whatever, till the Clergy took part in the movement. Many of the Bishops who previously gave no countenance to the League now recommend it to the people. The great majority of the Irish Roman Catholics are still led by their Bishops and Clergy. I don't agree with the statement that the Irish people drive the Clergy before them in the political movement at the present time. With the exception of a few Counties where Fenianism and Secret Societies exist, the Irish people are still under the influence of the Clergy. A perusal of the reports of the proceedings of the I.N. League will prove this. Three fourths of the active and successful branches would decay were it not for the moral and educational force imparted to their work by the Clerical leaders in those branches. These Clergymen say and do what laymen would not venture upon. They rely upon the protection against the law which their clerical status gives them. Supported as they are by the people their worldly prosperity depends upon the numbers and condition of the farming class, consequently they are opposed to emigration and endeavour by every means to make this class prosperous. Many of the young Clergy are separatists, as regards the Government of Ireland.

The League is now a powerful organisation and capable of instigating the commission of crime if threatened in its objects. It has, embraced within its fold, all the discontented, disaffected, and disloyal classes (including Fenians, Ribbonmen &c.) in the country. The sanction of its law in general is boycotting – and this mode of intimidation can to a large extent be carried on with impunity so long as the proceedings of the branches are held in private and the Police excluded from the meetings. To put down boycotting effectually either the League should be suppressed or its proceedings should be open to the observation of the Police. In this event the Police can themselves furnish evidence to prove the charge if intimidation be ordered by the League.

Should the Parnellites fail in getting what they want the N.L. Branches will become more dangerous to the peace of society as the commission of serious crime will be directed by the League in many Counties in Ireland.

The League has now a great protection and support to all its proceedings by the 86 members they have in the House of Commons – some of whom belong to the Fenian organization. Should the Nationalist movement be checked in Parliament it is not probable the Fenian party will remain connected with the League – they are becoming very active just now but they have little or no money. They would help the cause, indirectly, by the commission of serious outrage, when the time for disturbance arises.

Lord Carnarvon            RGCH    14/1/86

**42.** Andrew Reed, 'Confidential report for the Chief Secretary. Irish National League', 17 January 1886; CSO RP 1886/17972.

Power and influence of the I.N.L. and means by which it exercises that power &c.

Over the greater part of Ireland the Irish National League is now a most powerful organization. Its machinery and operations are reduced to a most perfect system, and under the direction of the Central Authority in Dublin it controls the conduct of the farmers, labourers, and tradesmen in many of the Counties of Ireland. It is a much stronger organization than the Land League was, as its machinery is more perfect and it has now the warm support of the Roman Catholic Bishops and Clergy, which support was only very partially extended to the Land League. It has now the constitutional support of 86 members in the House of Commons. The means by which it exercises that power and influence are two fold

(1) It points the tenant farmers of Ireland to the great benefits to them which, as is alleged, were obtained through the Land League and National League agitation, and which benefits the occupiers of land now enjoy under the Land Act and other Acts of Parliament passed in their favour. It promises further gains to this class and to the agricultural class by the agitation of the National League. It persuades the Fenians and Separatist class that the Parliament in College Green if granted is the final step towards complete separation.

(2) It is paternal in its authority and, as is pretended for the good of the general body, the National League enforces its law by the sanction of fines inflicted on persons transgressing these laws, after a formal inquiry has been held and sentence pronounced; or by expulsion from the body followed by ostracism and boycotting. These Courts are held

with closed doors in the National League branches, from which the Police are excluded. The offender is summoned before these Courts and after hearing if found guilty is fined, admonished, or expelled. The influence of these Courts is confined to the branches in some Counties where the National League is most powerful and has not the same effect in most of the branches. The offences are principally having or caring for an evicted or surrendered farm, evicting a tenant, paying rent contrary to order of the League, aiding a boycotted person by working for him, selling food to or succouring him, aiding the Police, and numerous other offences of a similar character. It should not however be supposed that all these evils exist wherever there is a branch of the League.[173] The working of each branch very much depends upon the character of the President (frequently a clergyman) and the local public opinion. In many of the branches there is little real harm done, as the operations of the Branch are kept within bounds. (Many of the clergy exert themselves to another direction).

Whether there is any means of counteracting such power and influence

At present there are no means for counteracting the influence exercised by some of the branches which hold Courts. The Police are powerless to bring the offenders to justice for the reason that the proceedings of the League are carried on with closed doors[174] – and that the very persons present who relate to the Police afterwards what occurs will if examined by a magistrate on oath profess entire ignorance of what took place. The Police however have been most successful in prosecuting many offenders for boycotting under the Conspiracy Against Property Act 1875,[175] but the persons which this law can reach are the mere tools of the League. The instigators and influential movers in the matter are outside the reach of the law.

Whether any means now at disposal of Government can be exercised as to prevent the exercise of such unconstitutional power or influence

Under the existing law boycotting and intimidation cannot effectually be stopped. I am however of opinion much more might be done under the ordinary law than has been done. I brought under

---

[173] This sentence was subsequently deleted.

[174] In January 1884, the Irish executive stopped the police attending branch meetings without the consent of committee members: see Ball, 'Policing the Land War', pp. 242–243.

[175] See **Journal (28 May, 19 October 1885)**.

notice of Government when I was appointed Inspector General that whenever these N.L. Courts are held – if a magisterial inquiry were instituted upon a charge of intimidation under the Whiteboy Acts[176] – though no prosecution might be the result, still the exposure of the actors in the proceedings of the N.L. Branch by examination by a Court of Magistrates and by their being obliged to perjure themselves in order to save their friends from prosecution would be calculated to check the action of such Courts.

The suppression of the National League if such an act were accompanied by a strong Coercion Act would no doubt stop boycotting. But this is a matter for most serious consideration. The suppression of such a vast organization which has now grown to such a magnitude and which is backed by the Spiritual Leaders of the people is a most serious matter. It must be remembered that the Irish National League has for the past two years done all in its power to prevent the commission of serious outrage. If it be suppressed the consequences likely to flow therefrom for some time are the following. The Irish National League leaders will remove the restraint upon such of its party as are in favour of the commission of outrage – the secret society members of the body will at once instigate the commission of outrage – murders, dynamite outrages, firing into dwellings, and other Whiteboy outrages will follow in the disturbed Counties, attempts on the lives of officials will be tried in Dublin and in the Provinces. The League driven from its secret chambers will hold public meetings (if allowed), these meetings will be conducted by some of the R. Catholic Bishops and Clergy who will probably do all in their power to provoke the Government to prosecute them, and make state martyrs of them. The commission of outrage will be carried on principally in the Counties of Cork, Kerry, Limerick, Clare, Tipperary, Waterford, and Galway East Riding – and as crime is infectious in Ireland it may extend into Counties hitherto tranquil. The Police under the existing law will not in that event be able to cope with a general outbreak of outrage – they will be as helpless as they had been in 1881 and 1882 till the Prevention of Crime Act was passed. To enable the Police to prevent the commission of such extensive outrage, the cardinal provisions of the Prevention of Crime Act of 1882 will have to be re-enacted *pari passa* with the suppression of the League. Without such powers it would be impossible for the Police to protect life and property under the reign of terror which would be attempted upon the suppression of the League. Even if the League is not suppressed the Government

---

[176] A series of statutes from the 1770s for the suppression of 'tumultuous risings' in Ireland. Reed subsequently suggested using them to suppress National League activities: Reed, 'Confidential report for Chief Secretary', 18 January 1886: CSO RP 1886/17972.

must be prepared for the serious increase of outrage following the refusal of the demand for an Irish Parliament. If the Executive be armed with strong powers by fresh legislation (and these must be exceptionally strong), such a crisis can be provided for.

I am of opinion the [*sic*] strengthening the Executive by some fresh legislation to provide for boycotting, and a renewal of some of the Provisions of the P. of C. Act of 82 would be a safer course than the suppression of a League which is now supported by the great majority of the Irish people led by their Bishops and Clergy. That the latter have still sway and power over the people cannot be denied; and that they are taking a greater interest now in the National movement than ever they did before is the case. As I have stated in previous reports in my opinion the land question is at the bottom of this agitation and as the tradesmen and labourers in town and country in Ireland are dependent upon the success of the farmers, it may be said this is the real question about which the great majority of the Irish people are really interested. The other N.L. questions are of secondary importance to the majority.

P.S.  I have not time to read this over having prepared this paper today
    upon a few hours' notice.

**43.** Sir Robert Hamilton to Lord Spencer, 17 January 1886; Chief Secretary's Office, Dublin Castle; 'Private'; AP, Add MS 77061.

I am not afraid that a local Irish Government would be unable to keep the peace against Invincibles and secret organizations generally. What gives such associations the great power they possess is that their machinations are directed against Landlords and their agents, including caretakers of evicted farms and against officials of the English Government. With the land question settled, and a representative Irish Government in power, both the landlords as landlords will have gone, and the English official in Ireland will be a thing of the past. Secret organizations directed against other objects could not, so far as I can see, enlist the same general sympathy (from which they derive their power) as such associations do at present, and I think could be dealt with locally.

We are in a most critical state. I doubt if the forces behind Parnell will allow him to accept, or help to work, anything short of his whole programme. In fact I believe they will require him to oppose anything which may be proposed short of legislative independence for Ireland.

The enclosed extract from Archbishop Walsh's speech at Thurles the other day which you may have read in the *Times* is very significant.[177]

With the land question settled the larger the measure of Home Rule that is granted the better. The millennium will by no means have come then. The difficulties of the Irish Government will always be great. The keen religious differences, and the complications arising therefrom, the different circumstances of the manufacturing industries in the north and the agricultural industry in the richer parts of the middle and south, and the terrible problem of the congested districts would always make the Government of Ireland a very complicated problem. But surely there is more hope of these matters being satisfactorily dealt with by those who know the circumstances and represent the various interests at stake themselves directing the Govt. of the Country than if they are dealt with by a centralized system of Government directed by a Lord Lieutenant and Chief Secy whose tenure of office is seldom sufficiently prolonged to enable them to acquire anything like a thorough knowledge of the complicated local issues involved in the Government of Ireland.

The great difficulty in the way of a purchase scheme is the old one of what is a fair rent. I daresay you may remember I always thought the policy of having the Government valuations of the same holding differing considerably in amount, the one determining the rates and the other the rent, or the rent-charge as it really is, was a great mistake. Griffith's valuation,[178] with or without some general qualification, must I think be the basis of any great transfer scheme, based as it is on the agricultural output of each holding, reduced into money at specified prices of produce.

But the question of a fair rent is also raising immediate and most formidable difficulties. Undoubtedly many tenants cannot pay their judicial rent this year, and where the landlords don't make reductions, the full powers of the law must be used to put starving people on the roadside, or evictions must be suspended by legislation with the effect that the tenants will get more demoralized than they are by being allowed to remain in their holdings without paying for them even so much as they can afford to pay. I look upon this in itself as a more difficult matter to deal with than the question of the future government of the country regarding which there are only two courses open. The

---

[177] Walsh addressed a public meeting during his visit to Archbishop Croke at Thurles on 14 January 1885: *The Times*, 16 January 1886, p. 6.

[178] The Primary Valuation of Land in Ireland was directed by Sir Richard Griffith during 1852–1865. It placed the assessment of poor rates on a uniform basis and, although not representing the true value of land, was widely used as a yardstick for rents prior to the slump of 1878–1879.

country must be allowed to govern itself, and make the power of its non local government felt and respected, or the supremacy of the English Government must be asserted. Desperate risks attend either course. The one might lead to chaos. The other to disenfranchisement, but still one or the other must be taken, but the economic difficulty baffles me. I can see no possible fair solution but a sliding scale, and this would be a gigantic and most difficult change to make.

I feel very much for the position of landlords whatever may have been the failings and shortcomings of their class in former years. The English public mind naturally recoils from the practical extermination of a class of society, more particularly as that class has always been regarded as the loyal class, but it is inevitable if the Country is ever to be at peace, and it must come sooner or later, unless they are prepared to accept the change in the circumstances and make their influence felt as citizens merely and not as landlords.

I fancy however it is the bug bear of separation which is the great obstacle in the English mind to any big scheme at present. Many extreme Liberals appear to think they cannot do wrong in following the example of the United States to the length, if need be, of fighting to prevent a rupture of the Empire. I should like to commend to them the following extract from a leading article in the *New York Evening Post* of 18th Decr.:
"Mr. Chamberlain reminded his audience apropos of this that Americans had shed torrents of blood to prevent the dissolution of the Union, and set it before them as an example to be remembered in dealing with Irish claims. But he ought to have reminded them also that the United States did not conquer the South for the purpose of regulating its local affairs, or holding it by a large military force."[179]

Please send one line of ackt.


**44.** Sir Robert Hamilton to Lord Carnarvon, 17 January 1886; Chief Secretary's Office, Dublin Castle; 'Secret'; CP, Add MS 60822, fos 20–26.

I gathered from my conversation today with the Attorney-General that the question of suppressing the National League is under the consideration of the Government. I have not been asked to express my views on the subject which is one of high state policy, but Your

---

[179] *New York Evening Post*, 18 December 1885.

Excellency has always treated me with such confidence that I am emboldened, even unasked, to lay my views before you.

Although the Irish Government ever since the establishment of the National League have not interfered with its operation, they have been careful never to say in so many words that they regarded it as a legal association. There was always the possibility that it might so conduct its operations that it might have to be broken up. But in my view this is a step the gravity of which it is impossible to overrate.

As I said in my memorandum of the 14[180] the three main evils that arise out of the National League are

(1) Boycotting
(2) Combinations against paying rent without an all round reduction
(3) Informal courts levying fines for breaches of its rules.

These are grave evils indeed, but on the other hand the influence of the League has during the last few months been strongly used against the grosser forms of outrage, and undoubtedly with effect. The first result of the suppression of the League would be that this influence would cease to be operative. Its local organization which is far more perfect than that of the old Land League would be used by the most violent spirits for the concoction of all sorts of horrible outrages. The Bishops and priests who have almost unanimously joined it would say that their religion had been insulted, and the whole body of the nationalist members elected by means of its operations would become your implacable foes.

Secret societies would spring up all over the country out of the ruins of the League. All the Irish in America and the Colonies who have been supporting the League would regard the step as a declaration of war to the death, and assassination and dynamite outrages would certainly follow in England. Even with all the powers of the Prevention of Crime Act which you would require to obtain from Parliament, many lives would be lost before the Country was again subdued into sullen quiet.

Is the present state of Ireland such that it calls for such a measure? And after it is all over, you will only be rather further off from a settlement than you are now.

You have got the whole body of the constitutionally elected members of the Country members of the League. You have also got the whole body of the Catholic priesthood. Are you going to brand them all as belonging to an illegal association? Why not rather take them into council. This would surely be acting in the spirit of constitutional government. With them rests the power of stopping boycotting,

---

[180]'Memo. by Mr. Robert Hamilton, dated 14th January 1886 – addressed to Lord Carnarvon' (copy): RCHL 1/11. 1232.

intimidation against payment of rent, & illegal courts. Make it a condition with them that every thing in reason that they demand will be granted upon their cooperating to check these evils, but don't declare war upon the Country unless you are prepared to carry it out to the bitter end.

I have written hurriedly to catch the post. I should have been glad had I had more time to arrange my ideas, and to give them more force, but I should not have felt that I was discharging my duty to you if I had remained silent at a crisis like this.

**45.** E.G. Jenkinson to Lord Carnarvon, 24 January 1886; 'Private'; CP/TNA, PRO 30/6/62 (59).

I saw Mr Smith yesterday before he left for Dublin,[181] and explained to him as well as I could in the short time I had with him the present situation in Ireland. I told him about the R.I.C., and the necessity of removing the uncertainty from the men's mind. I also told him how necessary it is to have the machinery in good working order, and to have strong men at the head of it, should it be decided to attack the League, and what lies behind it. And I also stated my opinion that whatever may be our policy towards Ireland, the one question which must be dealt with is the Land Question. I spoke of the difficulties before us should we make up our mind to overthrow the National League but I did not I think say enough on the great danger of tackling the League without being prepared to face the consequences, & to hit out vigorously and hard. Your Excellency knows what would be the result of putting down the League. By itself it would be merely scratching the skin. It would be like poking the fire, a blaze would follow which could not be extinguished without very exceptional powers and by vigorous action. If there is any real intention of suppressing the League, the Government should be armed before hand with exceptional powers. It would be foolish to do it otherwise. The safety valve would be shut down, and instead of one open society, we should have several secret societies in their worst form to deal with. Time is precious, and if anything is to be done it should be done without delay, but how long will it take to get them? Your Excellency knows how much I am against a policy of coercion, but if we are to put our foot down, let us be prepared to face the consequences, and do not let us find ourselves face to face with a

---

[181] See **Journal** (**27 January 1886**).

worse state of things than there was in 1882, and with no sufficient
powers to act vigorously & with effect.

**46.** Sir Robert Hamilton to Lord Spencer, 11 April 1886; 'Private';
AP, Add MS 77061.

The way in which Mr. Gladstone's proposals have been received by
the press, both English & Scotch, and apparently by many genuine
Liberals, makes the position a very critical one. It may be that the tide
may set in the other direction as the hopelessness of any alternative
solutions of the question gets impressed on the public mind, but if
this should not occur the question will have to be faced whether
he will stand by the scheme as proposed by him, or whether any
modifications in it are possible which would prevent the falling away
of a large number of his supporters.

Mr. Gladstone has the enormous advantage that the general
outlines of his scheme are cordially accepted by the Irish
Parliamentary party, and no modifications should be introduced into
it which have not their acceptance. This is vital, as without their
concurrence and cooperation no scheme can work. But they are
sensible men, and it is very important to them that a scheme such
as they can accept should be carried, and I believe they will be found
ready to approach the consideration of this matter in a reasonable
spirit.

It is clear that the Scotch Liberal who looks forward to a measure of
Home Rule for Scotland dreads the precedent which the exclusion of
Irish members from the House of Commons would set for Scotland.
This is not entirely an idle fear. I do not think such exclusion could
ever take place against the unanimous wish of the Scotch members
to remain in Westminster, but I have heard Conservatives say that if
they could only get the Scotch as well as the Irish members out of the
House of Commons they would be pretty sure of getting their own
way. Could not this be met? The Irish would not, I believe, seriously
object to a continuance of their representation at Westminster. If some
way could be found out of this difficulty, I believe the most powerful
part of the opposition now offered to Mr. Gladstone's scheme would
be overcome. I don't change my views in the least as to the real merits
of the scheme. I prefer Mr. Gladstone's as it stands but rather than it
should fail and this country be left in the throes of revolution, I would
accept such a modification of it.

I am quite aware of the extreme difficulty of modifying
Mr. Gladstone's scheme in this respect. He himself in his speech

pointed out this in the strongest way, but his fertility of resource is inexhaustible, & I believe he could find some solution.[182] There is no sort of precedent that I can think of that meets the case, but then all the circumstances are unprecedented.

As regards the position of the three parties, Mr. Gladstone's is far the strongest. He says I will do what Ireland wants, reserving only what the interests of the Empire require to be reserved. Lord Hartington and the Tories say, we will do nothing, and are prepared to go to the fullest lengths in coercion.[183] Mr. Chamberlain and those who follow him say, we will have no coercion but we will force Ireland to do what we think she ought.[184]

Mr. Gladstone's lines must eventually be adopted. The Tory position might be successful for a short time, but Mr. Chamberlain's position is simply impossible. Without coercion it must become Mr. Gladstone's. With it, it becomes the scheme of the Tories – i.e. coercion, but coercion after the Irish have got a powerful machinery for upsetting the govt. of the Country in the shape of a representative Council in Dublin, which would greatly aggravate the difficulties of the situation.

All except the most blinded Tories see that Mr. Gladstone's statement has made a wide scheme of self government for Ireland sooner or later inevitable. The whole success of the working of the scheme will depend upon whether it is accepted by the Irish representatives or not. They are with him now, and their cordial cooperation should at all hazards be maintained. Such details in his scheme as he may, with their concurrence, modify to disarm the opposition of timid Liberals, should be modified, & there is no departure from principle in doing this. The only principle underlying the whole scheme is that without sacrificing Imperial interests the Country should be governed in accordance with the views of the people and not against them. In no other way can you escape coercion, & make law and order respected in the Country.

To go on to another point by no means so important. As you know I was always against Mr. Gladstone's plan of taking the revenue paid on dutiable articles in Ireland as the measure of Ireland's income. (1) because it does not accurately represent the amount of taxes paid by the Irish people which it exceeds by about £1,400,000 a year, & (2) because putting it on the income side of the account necessitates an increase *pro tanto* in the amount of contributions Ireland pays to

---

[182] See **Journal (15 April 1886)**.
[183] Spencer's note reads, 'Did Hartington go to this length?'
[184] Spencer: 'Did Chamberlain declare against coercion?'

England.[185] But there is also another reason which had occurred to me, & this is one of principle. I forget if I mentioned it to you, but I was reminded of it by a remark in yesterday's *Scotsman*. It is this. Suppose that the Imperial Govt. in time of war increases the duty on tobacco. The increased duty paid in Ireland in respect of tobacco consumed in England will go to the benefit of the Irish revenue, altho' the Irish Exchequer will share no part of the burden of the war which the extra duty was imposed to meet.

I am quite aware that the adoption of my plan in place of Mr. Gladstone's would necessitate that an account should be kept by each country of all dutiable articles passing from the one to the other on which duty had been paid, but this would not be serious, & the general practice would undoubtedly be that the great bulk of the dutiable articles would pass from one country to the other under permit, in which case no accounts could be involved.

Would you kindly let Mr. Morley see this letter?

**47.** Sir Robert Hamilton to Lord Spencer, 19 July 1886; Chief Secretary's Office, Dublin Castle; AP, Add MS 77061.

I was very glad to get your letter and to find that you had returned benefited by your trip.[186]

The present position is very serious, and much will depend upon the way the result of the election in England is presented to the Irish people.[187]

If it is put to them in this way, that a year ago there were only about 40 Irish members in favour of Home Rule, and that now there are 86 Irish and 190 English in favour of that policy, the matter will be regarded in the light of a triumph, and full of hope for the future.

If on the other hand it is represented that England has given an emphatic "no" to a Home Rule policy for Ireland, and that as Mr. Gladstone has failed to carry the English people with him no one else can in future succeed in doing so, then resort will be had I fear to other than constitutional means.

When Mr. Morley was over here last week he saw all the DMs & some RMs & is in possession of the latest information on the state of the

[185]Spencer: 'Or rather if we consider the present contribution the only fair one it is necessary to add their sum to the receipts to balance account.'

[186]Letter not traced. Spencer had visited Aix-les-Bains: see *The Times*, 13 July 1886, p. 7.

[187]See **Journal (5 December 1886)**.

Country.[188] You will no doubt see him, so I need not attempt to describe it. Much will depend on the composition of the new Government.

As regards my self, whatever may happen I feel I have only done my duty, and have not over stepped its limits.

No one is more strong than I am on the point of the inexpediency of permanent servants of the state taking sides in party politics, & I feel that I am not fairly open to such a charge.

It is my business, under my political chiefs, to carry on the Govt. of the country. Affairs had reached a crisis which it was my business to point out, & this I did when the Conservatives were last in power. I merely repeated my views when a change of Govt. occurred.

It is impossible for a man in my position, unless he is a fool, to have no views one way or the other on the Govt. of the Country which is his business.

If the Conservatives think it is desirable to replace me by some one holding their views, whatever these may be, well & good – they can get rid of me. But this would be an admission on their part that the man holding the office I hold should have the views of the Govt. of the day, and would logically lead to my post being filled by a new man at each change of Government. This might be done by making it a political post, but to keep it a permanent office & to apply this plan to it would be introducing the American system, which is admittedly so bad a one that Americans are at present engaged in doing their best to alter it.

I say so much about the present question because I think at the present moment it has considerable political importance, altho' so far as I am individually concerned, if the Conservatives dealt fairly liberally with me in the way of pension & this I should think they would do, my retirement would not be personally disagreeable to me.

[188]Morley was in Dublin between 12 and 16 July 1886 to co-ordinate the policing of Orange anniversaries: *The Times*, 13 and 16 July 1886, p. 7.

# APPENDIX: BIOGRAPHIES

## George Drevar Fottrell

Fottrell was born on 6 February 1849 and educated at Belvedere College and the Catholic University, where he was president of the Literary and Historical Society.[1] After training as a solicitor at the King's Inn Law School from 1865, he joined his father's firm of George D. Fottrell & Sons at 46 Fleet Street, Dublin. In 1872, he married Mary Watson, with whom he had one son and five daughters. He quickly established himself within Dublin's emerging Catholic professional class at a time when its influence over Irish public affairs was growing. Recent study of the Catholic elite of this period has demonstrated the importance of the university question to its 'cultural and political awakening'. In educational matters, Fottrell was a secularist who wished to develop what he described as 'a free and independent lay Catholic public opinion'. He was critical of reforms that tended to tighten the grip of ecclesiastical schools upon Catholic higher education and argued that sufficient funding for the Catholic University in Dublin was necessary to enable its graduates to compete on an equal footing with the predominately Protestant graduates of Dublin University.[2] Alongside T.D. Sullivan and John Dillon, Fottrell took a leading role in the Catholic University's Bono Club, which aimed to create common ground between the ecclesiastical establishment and the educated laity, and Fottrell was assured by Cardinal Newman that

> You will be doing the greatest possible benefit to the Catholic cause all over the world, if you succeed in making the University a middle station at which clergy and laity can meet, so as to learn to understand and to yield to each other.[3]

[1] See his *Inaugural address delivered before the Literary and Historical Society of the Catholic University of Ireland, at its opening meeting, on Friday, 2nd December, 1870.*

[2] Senia Paseta, *Before the Revolution: nationalism, social change and Ireland's Catholic elite, 1879–1922* (Cork, 1999), p. 22; Fottrell to Gladstone, 21 July 1879, 15 January and 26 February 1873: GP, Add MS 44460, fos 276–277, Add MS 44437, fos 27–28, 246–247.

[3] Emmet Larkin, *The Roman Catholic Church and the Emergence of the Modern Irish Political System, 1874–1878* (Washington, DC, 1996), pp. 167–168, 246; C.S. Dessain (ed.), *The Letters and Diaries of John Henry Cardinal Newman*, XXVI (Oxford, 1974), pp. 393–394.

In 1872, Fottrell tried to formulate reforms that might prove acceptable to both Protestant and Catholic opinion by proposing two universities for Ireland – the Queen's University and an amalgamation of Trinity College, Dublin and the Catholic University.[4] He argued that Gladstone's University Education Bill, which proposed a single university for Ireland, would fatally damage the higher education of Catholics because it would denude the Catholic University of students. In 1879, he advised Gladstone to provide endowments for lay professorships in the Catholic University so as to enable Catholic students to escape the influence of ecclesiastical schools. Fottrell pursued his interest in Irish university education for many years, becoming an organizer of the Catholic Lay Committee of 1903 and publishing an influential tract on the subject two years later.[5]

During his early legal career, Fottrell built up a large practice that specialized in property transactions and developed personal relationships with a number of Irish nationalists, one of his clients being the veteran Fenian Charles Kickham. Having sat on the council of the Irish Home Rule League since 1874, Fottrell joined advanced nationalists such as Patrick Egan, Joseph Biggar, and Charles Stewart Parnell in Charles Russell's stormy but successful parliamentary campaign at Dundalk in 1880. He was a close friend of John Dillon, for whom he acted as solicitor and visited in prison in 1881 and 1888, and was one of a select group who met with Dillon and Parnell upon their release from Kilmainham Jail in May 1882.[6] Fottrell was also acquainted with Michael Davitt, on whose behalf he joined Charles Russell and James Bryce to mitigate the circumstances of his imprisonment and secure his release in 1882. While Fottrell claimed to be 'wholly unconnected with the Land League' and criticized the violent tactics to which some of its supporters resorted, he supported the campaign to improve conditions for tenant farmers. He believed that future peace and stability in Ireland could only be secured if a large class of peasant proprietors was created and argued that effective land purchase measures were therefore essential. In evidence to a select committee of the House of Lords he stated, 'I think so long as the

---

[4] See his *Letter Containing a Scheme of Irish University Reform Addressed to the Most Noble Marquis of Hartington, Chief Secretary of Ireland* (Dublin, 1873), and Paseta, *Before the Revolution*, pp. 33–34.

[5] Fottrell to Gladstone, 4 April 1879; 21 July 1879: GP, Add MS 44460, fos 221–224, 276–277. See also *GD*, IX, p. 427; Thomas J. Morrissey, *Towards a National University: William Delany, SJ (1835–1924): an era of initiative in Irish education* (Dublin, 1983), pp. 224–227; George Fottrell, *What is a National University?* (Dublin, 1905).

[6] R.V. Comerford, *Charles J. Kickham: a study in Irish nationalism and literature* (Portmarnock, 1979), p. 176; *Irish Times*, 5 September 1874, p. 3; *Freeman's Journal*, 29 March 1880, p. 5; F. Hugh O'Donnell, *A History of the Irish Parliamentary Party*, 2 vols (New York, 1910), I, p. 464. T.H. Burke to Fottrell, 17 May 1881; F.W.D. Mitchell to Fottrell, 24 July 1888: TCD, Dillon Papers, MSS 6800/44a, 6800/155a; *Irish Times*, 6 May 1882, p. 4.

relation of landlord and tenant continues to be the almost universal relation in Ireland, you must have a state of unstable equilibrium in politics.[7]

Fottrell came to public prominence in August 1881 when he was appointed solicitor to the Irish Land Commission, which was established to adjudicate rent levels under the Land Act. However, his close connection to the leaders of the Land League made him an object of suspicion in governing circles. After dining at the Chief Secretary's Lodge in November 1881, Florence Arnold Forster, the daughter of the Chief Secretary, commented 'He is said to be "smart", but is certainly not an attractive young man – vulgar, I thought – "a snake in the grass" Father says, but this of course I had no means of judging.'[8] Fottrell's stock at Dublin Castle fell further when a pamphlet he had written and distributed under the auspices of the Land Commission came to the attention of the House of Lords. The pamphlet, *How to be the Owner of Your Own Farm*, consisted of a collection of articles from the *Freeman's Journal* and was reprinted at Fottrell's request for distribution to the sub-commissions. Forster was concerned that an official publication containing what he regarded as a partisan view of the land question would undermine landowners' confidence in the Land Act and it was decided that the pamphlet should be withdrawn.[9]

On 11 February 1882, Fottrell resigned but, in the ensuing parliamentary debate, Lord Randolph Churchill revealed that Fottrell had previously acted on behalf of Parnell in transacting the purchase of the Land League's newspaper *United Ireland*, a publication that was subsequently suppressed by the Government. Fottrell was referred to in a letter written by Richard Pigott, the previous owner of the business, as 'the confidential solicitor of the Land League', a charge that was refuted on Fottrell's behalf by Edmund Dwyer Gray.[10]

[7] Fottrell to Davitt, 10 February 1881, 5 May 1882: TCD, Davitt Papers, MSS 9346/468, 30/2552; *The Times*, 29 April 1882, p. 7; Land Law (Ireland): First Report from the Select Committee of the House of Lords: *PP* 1882, XI, 1, p. 244.

[8] T.W. Moody and R.A.J. Hawkins, with Margaret Moody (eds), *Florence Arnold-Forster's Irish Journal* (Oxford, 1988), p. 314.

[9] Allen Warren, 'Gladstone, land and social reconstruction in Ireland, 1881–1887', *Parliamentary History*, 2 (1983), p. 113; Moody and Hawkins, *Irish Journal*, pp. 368–369, 374–375. Forster to Justice John O'Hagan, 7 February 1882; O'Hagan to Forster, 8 February 1882: Land Commission (Ireland) (Mr. Fottrell): *PP* 1882, LV, 301, pp. 1–2; *The Times*, 15 February 1882, p. 10. Fottrell confirmed that he had written the articles to the Select Committee on Land Law: *PP* 1882, XI, 1, p. 247.

[10] *Hansard*, CCLXVI, cols 440–441, 468–470, 480, 790–794; CCLXVII, cols 1280–1282, 1292–1293. The transaction was later examined during the investigation of *The Times'* allegations against Parnell: *Special Commission Act, 1888: reprint of the shorthand notes of the speeches, proceedings and evidence taken before the Special Commission appointed under the above named Act*, vol. 6, pp. 548–549.

Forster subsequently claimed that he had questioned Fottrell about his connection with the Land League before appointing him but had not been told of this transaction. This provoked a correspondence with Fottrell over the accuracy of this statement and Forster was forced to amend his account of events.[11]

Although this incident was to cause lasting resentment, Fottrell continued to supply information on Irish affairs to leading Liberal politicians and published valuable guidelines on current land and transport legislation.[12] He returned to public service as Clerk of the Crown for the County and City of Dublin in October 1884, which required him to administer the court of assize and grand jury for criminal business and supervise the quarterly commissions of the Court of Queen's Bench. Fottrell held the post on a temporary basis until 1893, when he assumed the additional role of Clerk of the Peace on a permanent basis.[13] Meanwhile, he continued in private practice and transacted the first sale of land under the Land Purchase Act at Cookstown, Co. Tyrone in November 1885, with, as *The Times* commented, 'a rapidity not very usual in legal transactions'.[14] Fottrell subsequently wrote a number of books and articles on the subject of land purchase,[15] provided John Dillon with a penetrating critique of the Land Bill of 1887, and advised on the resettlement of tenants evicted as a consequence of the Plan of Campaign. He also furnished Lord Spencer with valuable advice on the land question by tirelessly canvassing opinion among progressive landowners.[16] When the Liberals returned to power in September 1892, Fottrell was considered for the prestigious position of Judicial

[11] Fottrell to Forster, 11, 14, and 17 February 1882; Henry Jephson to Fottrell, 13 and 16 February 1882: *PP* 1882, LV, 301, pp. 4–6; *Hansard*, CCLXVI, cols 441, 469, 790–794; Moody and Hawkins, *Irish Journal*, pp. 368, 374–375.

[12] **Journal (11 April 1886)**. Fottrell to Spencer, 2 September 1882; Fottrell to Hamilton, 28 September 1883: AP, Add MS 77152; and see his *A.B.C. Guide to the Arrears Act, 1882 . . . for the use of Irish landlords and tenants* (Dublin, 1882) and (with John Fottrell) *Handbook of Law and Practice under the Irish Tramways Acts* (Dublin, 1883).

[13] Fottrell replaced Edward Geale at a salary of £1,500: CSO RP 1884/22365; *Hansard*, CCCIX, col. 297. The office was granted by letters patent and, while usually held for life, could be revoked at the Crown's pleasure. From 1877, clerkships of the Crown and of the Peace were amalgamated on the death or retirement of either official, the holder of the joint office becoming a civil servant appointed by the Lord Lieutenant: CSO RP 1893/769, 1893/8213, 1893/8929.

[14] *The Times*, 11 November 1885, p. 7.

[15] *Land Purchase Tables* (Dublin, 1886); *A Practical Guide to the Land Purchase Acts (Ireland), 1870–1891* (Dublin, 1889); and 'Land purchase in Ireland', *Nineteenth Century*, 40 (November 1896), pp. 829–837.

[16] John Dillon's diary (21 June 1887); Fottrell to Dillon, 22 January 1892: TCD, Dillon Papers, MSS 6587, 6819/10. Fottrell to Lord Spencer, 4 and 9 April and 4 June 1887, 12 July 1889, 26 June and 1 July 1891; Spencer to Fottrell, 28 June 1887: AP, Add MS 77152.

Land Commissioner. However, upon consulting John Redmond, the Chief Secretary discovered that, while the Parnellite leader regarded Fottrell as highly qualified, he did not consider him to be the best candidate for the post. Nevertheless, Fottrell continued to work on behalf of tenant farmers and, after giving evidence before the Evicted Tenants Commission, was appointed to the Royal Commission on Irish Land in 1897.[17]

Fottrell was a valuable source of information on Irish politics for home rule Liberals concerned by the consequences of Unionist government for Ireland, as he continued to 'test the views of men' of different political camps. He was a guest at Althorp House on several occasions and continued to correspond with Lord Spencer for many years.[18] Fottrell remained on terms with both wings of the Irish Parliamentary Party after the Parnell split in 1891 and maintained a keen interest in home rule and the devolution of power within empires.[19] He tried to ensure that home rulers secured places within the Irish administration as, in 1908, when his brother was considered for a post at Dublin Castle, he reminded John Dillon that it would be useful to have such 'a genuine friend of Irish nationality' at the 'centre of the web'. Similarly, in 1914, he warned John Redmond against allowing the recently established National Volunteers to pass 'into the control of selfish, or narrow minded, or mischievous men' who might frustrate the aims of the home rule party.[20]

While Fottrell is unlikely to have welcomed the subsequent ascendance of Sinn Fein in Ireland, it was said that the new government appreciated 'the enormous help which he gave in transforming the work of the [Central Criminal] Court', and he remained prominent within the Irish legal establishment up until his death. He earned the respect of the Irish judiciary for his efficiency as an administrator and was well regarded by members of the legal profession, to whom he gave sound advice based on long experience. In 1919, he was created a KCB in recognition of his services to the Crown. Fottrell was greatly interested in music and closely followed the fortunes of the Feis Ceoil as he campaigned for the provision

---

[17] Lawrence W. MacBride, *The Greening of Dublin Castle: the transformation of bureaucratic and judicial personnel in Ireland, 1892–1922* (Washington, DC, 1991), pp. 43–44; *The Times*, 6 December 1892, p. 6; 13 July 1897, p. 10.

[18] Fottrell to Spencer, 4 December 1887 and memorandum of 25 January 1888; and see Fottrell to Spencer, 31 July 1887, 2 February, 18 and 19 June, and 29 November 1888, 14 January 1890, 31 March and 1 December 1892, 27 August 1894, 7 September and 6 November 1903, 15 October 1904: AP, Add MS 77152.

[19] See his 'Local autonomy and imperial unity: the example of Germany', *Nineteenth Century*, 59 (February 1906), pp. 331–344.

[20] Fottrell to Dillon, 22 August 1908: TCD, Dillon Papers, MS 6775/1147; Fottrell to Redmond, 10 June 1914: NLI, Redmond Papers, MS 22187.

of a concert hall for Dublin. A member of the Reform Club, the St Stephen's Green Club, Dublin, and the Royal Irish Yacht Club, Kingstown, he was sufficiently well known in Dublin society to feature in the 'Cyclops' and 'Circe' episodes of James Joyce's *Ulysses*.[21] Sir George Fottrell died on 1 February 1925.[22]

## Robert George Crookshank Hamilton

Hamilton was born on 30 August 1836 at Bressay in the Shetland Isles, where his father, Rev. Zachary Macaulay Hamilton, was minister.[23] He was educated at University and King's College, Aberdeen. After obtaining an MA in 1855, he joined the War Office and was posted to the Crimea as a clerk in the commissariat department. He subsequently rose through the ranks of the civil service and served in the Office of Works, where he specialized in education and finance, and as accountant of the Board of Trade, where he reorganized the Board's financial department, before being appointed assistant-secretary in 1872. In 1878, Hamilton became Accountant-General of the Navy, where he clarified the process of naval book-keeping and, having served on the Earl of Carnarvon's Royal Commission on Colonial Defence in 1879, was appointed Permanent Secretary of the Admiralty in May 1882.[24] A few days later, he was offered the position of Under-Secretary of State for Ireland, following the assassination of Thomas Burke. Burke, an Irish Catholic who had spent his entire working life in Dublin Castle, had been the lynchpin of the Irish administration and a strong man was required to replace him. Gladstone recommended Hamilton who, as secretary to the Irish Civil Service Enquiry Committee, had investigated schemes for the reorganization of Dublin Castle in 1874. Hamilton was reluctant to go to Dublin and his acceptance of the post was later described by Lord Northbrook as 'as fine an instance of public spirit I know'.[25]

Hamilton's secondment was intended to last for six months, but in August 1882 it was extended at Spencer's request until 1 May 1883. By March, however, Hamilton was eager to return to Whitehall

[21] James Joyce (ed. Danis Rose), *Ulysses* (London, 1999), pp. 328, 430; his character briefly appears in the cinematic version of the book made in 1967.

[22] *Irish Times*, 2 February 1925, p. 8; 4 February 1925, p. 3; *The Times*, 4 February 1925, p. 9; *Who Was Who, 1916–1928*, II (4th edition, London, 1967), p. 372.

[23] His father, a cousin of Lord Macaulay, became an honorary DD of Edinburgh University in 1864.

[24] *Dictionary of National Biography: second supplement* (London, 1912–1913), II, p. 382. With John Ball, he published an influential book entitled *Book-keeping* (Oxford, 1868).

[25] Spencer to Gladstone, 7 and 8 May 1882; Gladstone to Spencer, 8 May 1882 (telegram); Spencer to Northbrook, 7 May 1882: AP, Add MSS 76854, 76918; B. Mallet, *Thomas George, Earl of Northbrook* (London, 1908), p. 165.

and, so it was rumoured, would not remain in Dublin 'at any price'. Spencer was aware of the paucity of administrative talent within Irish government departments and the reluctance of first-class civil servants to leave London. He regarded Hamilton's 'balanced judgment and excellent commonsense' as indispensable and anticipated that his loss would greatly disrupt his administration.[26] Spencer therefore secured Northbrook's agreement for Hamilton to become the permanent head of the civil administration in Ireland, and persuaded the Treasury to substantially improve the under-secretary's salary.[27] Although the position was inferior in rank to Hamilton's previous position, he was in urgent need of funds to educate his seven children and, upon being assured that Spencer would continue to act as Viceroy, he accepted the post.[28]

Over the next two years, Hamilton's services were highly valued by Spencer, who considered him cool and reliable under pressure and believed that his balanced judgment was informed by sound common sense. Hamilton was described by Lord Lingen as 'the most all-round man' he knew, and by Sir Thomas Farrer as 'one of the ablest, if not the ablest, administrator I have met with during a life spent in the public service'. Hamilton was rewarded with a CB in April 1883 and a KCB in January 1884.[29] In spite of being manoeuvred from office in November 1886, at which point he would have preferred retirement, Hamilton threw himself into his new duties as Governor of Tasmania.[30] In the course of his term as governor (11 March 1887– 30 November 1892), he encouraged industrial development, public works, and the investment of British capital in the colony. As President of the Royal Society of Tasmania, he fostered the advancement of science and public education and helped to found the University of Tasmania. An enthusiast of Australian federation, he presided over the

[26] Spencer to Northbrook, 21 August 1882, 22 February 1883; Spencer to Gladstone, 3 and 31 August 1882; Spencer to Hugh Childers, 25 February and 17 April 1883; Spencer to George Trevelyan, 4 March 1883; Spencer to Lord Granville, 14 March 1883: AP, Add MSS 76918, 76855, 76914, 76915, 76952, 76883.

[27] Hamilton received £600 in personal allowances and a salary of £2,000. A proposal to pay Hamilton a gratuity was quashed by the Treasury, as the last Irish civil servant to have been so rewarded was Sir Charles Trevelyan after the Great Famine, a fact that had 'been quoted against the Treasury from that day to this!': Childers to Spencer, 18 April 1883; Sir Ralph Lingen to Childers, 18 April 1883: AP, Add MSS 76914, 76915; Trevelyan to W.H. Smith, 26 April 1883: CSO RP 1883/23763.

[28] Northbrook to Spencer, 23 February 1883; Spencer to Trevelyan, 13 April 1883; Spencer to Gladstone, 22 April 1883; Hamilton to Edward Hamilton, 9 May 1883: AP, Add MSS 76858, 76918, 76954, 76857. Hamilton was married in 1863 to Caroline Jane Ball (d. 1875) and in 1877 to Teresa Felicia Reynolds.

[29] The Times, 31 July 1886, p. 5. Spencer to Childers, 25 February 1883; Spencer to Gladstone, 22 April 1883; Gladstone to Spencer, 30 December 1883: AP, Add MSS 76914, 76857, 76858.

[30] **Document 47**; Hamilton to Spencer, 10 September 1887: AP, Add MS 77061.

Federal Council of Australasia at Hobart in 1887, and even considered entering Australian politics.[31] While abroad, Hamilton maintained his close interest in Irish affairs and remained convinced that Liberal policies would 'ultimately triumph' and that home rule was 'perfectly assured'. In November 1891, he offered to assist in the development of Liberal policy and, if circumstances allowed, to resume his post as Irish Under-Secretary.[32] Upon his return to England, he abandoned a plan to stand for Parliament and placed himself at the disposal of the Liberal ministry. He sat upon commissions of inquiry into the working of the constitution of Dominica and the financial relations between Great Britain and Ireland; and, having been considered for the post of Deputy Master of the Mint, he was appointed as Chairman of the Board of Customs in 1894. Sir Robert Hamilton died in London at the age of 58 on 22 April 1895, and was buried in Richmond, Surrey.[33]

## Edward George Jenkinson

Jenkinson was born in 1836, the eldest son of Rev. J.S. Jenkinson, Vicar of Battersea, and Harriet Grey, daughter of Sir George Grey and sister of the future Home Secretary, to whom, Lord Spencer was to remark, Jenkinson bore a strong resemblance.[34] He was educated at Harrow School and Haileybury College and, in 1856, entered the service of the East India Company and was posted to Benares in northern India as an assistant magistrate. On the outbreak of the Sepoy rebellion in June 1857, Jenkinson raised a force of 150 English and Indian horsemen, which he led into action at Chanda and Amereepur under the direction of Brigadier General Franks. He served on the staff of General Lugard and was awarded the Indian Mutiny medal. In 1865, he married Annabella, daughter of Captain

[31] A.F. Pollard, rev. David Huddleston, 'Hamilton, Sir Robert George Crookshank', in H.G.C. Matthew and Brian Harrison (eds), *Oxford Dictionary of National Biography* (Oxford, 2004), XXIV, pp. 895–896; Douglas Pike (ed.), *Australian Dictionary of Biography*, IV (Melbourne, 1972), pp. 331–332.

[32] Hamilton to Spencer, 2 May and 25 July 1888, 1 November 1891, 13 February and 6 November 1892: AP, Add MS 77061. See his, 'The Irish question from an administrative standpoint', *The Speaker*, 7 (13 May 1893), pp. 536–538.

[33] Hamilton to Spencer, 11 August 1894: AP, Add MS 77061; Dudley W.R. Balhman (ed.), *The Diary of Sir Edward Walter Hamilton, 1885–1906* (Hull, 1993), pp. 269–270; *The Times*, 23 April 1895, p. 13.

[34] Sir George Grey (1799–1882), Chancellor of the Duchy of Lancaster (1841, 1859–1861), Home Secretary (1846–1852, 1855–1858, 1861–1866), Colonial Secretary (1854–1855). Harriet's sister Jane married Francis Thornhill Baring, first Baron Northbrook (1796–1866): Spencer to Gladstone, 3 August 1882: AP, Add MS 76855.

Thomas Monck Mason RN, with whom he had three sons.[35] He subsequently enjoyed success as a magistrate, collector, and settlement officer at Mirzapore, Farukabad, and Serahrunpore where he settled numerous difficult land claims, supervised improvements to sanitary conditions, and suppressed dacoits. He served as Commissioner of Revenue and Circuit in the Jhansi division of Oudh and, in January 1879, was appointed Commissioner of the Fyzabad division.[36]

After returning to England in July 1879, Jenkinson retired from the Indian service due to ill health and took up a position as private secretary to his cousin Lord Northbrook, the First Lord of the Admiralty, with responsibility for non-naval matters. Having followed Irish politics closely, Jenkinson next secured the post of private secretary to the new Irish Viceroy, Lord Spencer, in May 1882. He witnessed the Phoenix Park murders and distinguished himself during the crisis that followed, chairing an important committee of inquiry into police organization.[37] In August 1882, a vacancy for the recently created post of Assistant Under-Secretary for Police and Crime arose. Although Spencer was concerned about the political effect of appointing an 'Indian' to the post, Jenkinson's varied experience as an administrator and his liberal outlook meant that he was preferred to more experienced candidates.[38] He assumed responsibility for the administration of the Irish police and rapidly improved the Constabulary's crime detection and intelligence capabilities by establishing a Crime Special Branch. This enabled the authorities to prosecute suspected members of republican and agrarian secret societies that had been active during the Irish Land War, including the 'Invincibles' who had assassinated the Irish Chief and Under Secretaries in Dublin. Armed with the wide-ranging and severe powers of the Crimes Act, the Irish police had, by mid-1883, suppressed all significant opposition to the law in Ireland.[39] This

---

[35] His youngest son, Harry Grey Jenkinson, a midshipman on HMS Canada, drowned at Bedford Basin on 10 July 1887 (The Times, 21 July 1887, p. 1); and his eldest son, Lt. Edward John Jenkinson, died of typhoid fever in India four months later. Captain John Jenkinson was killed in the attack on the Hohenzollern Redoubt at the Battle of Loos on 13 October 1915: The Times, 27 October 1915, p. 11.

[36] Hansard, CCLXXIII, cols 689–695; The Times, 24 April 1865, 8 January 1870, 31 May 1880, 1 July 1892; The India List, Civil and Military (London, 1877–1880).

[37] Spencer to Jenkinson, 2 May 1882; Jenkinson to Spencer, 3 May 1882; Spencer to Gladstone, 3 August 1882; Spencer to Queen Victoria, 2 August 1882: AP, Add MSS 77031, 76855, 76831. See also Jenkinson's report of 12 May 1882: CSO RP 1882/34096.

[38] Spencer to Trevelyan, 1 and 2 August 1882: AP, Add MS 76948. The Chief Secretary had first to refute allegations from Nationalist MPs that Jenkinson had participated in atrocities committed in suppressing the Indian Mutiny: Hansard, CCLXXIII, cols 686–698.

[39] The number of agrarian outrages fell sharply from 7,872 (including 57 homicides) in 1881–1882 to 1,632 (including two homicides) in 1883–1884. For the development of

has been described as 'one of the most distinct British successes of the later nineteenth century', and Spencer fully acknowledged the role that Jenkinson had played in this, telling him in 1885, 'from the first moment of our landing until the end of my administration, you contributed as much, if not more than anyone to whatever success attended my efforts to make the law respected'.[40]

In March 1883, Jenkinson was seconded to the Home Office to reinforce security measures against Fenian dynamite attacks in Great Britain and to assist in the establishment of a new Irish Bureau within the Metropolitan Police CID, the origin of what later became the Special Branch. On his return to Dublin, he assumed responsibility for all anti-Fenian operations in Ireland, America, and the Continent and became known as 'the soul and centre of what may be called the Spy system of the Empire'.[41] In March 1884, Jenkinson went back to the Home Office to co-ordinate anti-Fenian operations by the Irish and British police and to reorganize the CID at Scotland Yard – tasks for which, as the Home Secretary put it, 'there was no other man living except Jenkinson who could take the responsibility'. Although he was exceptionally well paid, Jenkinson became disillusioned as friction with the London Metropolitan Police and the Home Secretary progressively increased.[42] While he achieved some success against the dynamitards in 1883–1884, he was given neither nominal authority nor a permanent position within the Home Office. In recognition of the 'singular success' of his 'very exceptional' services in Ireland, however, Jenkinson was awarded a CB in January 1884 and a KCB in June 1888.[43]

After leaving government service in January 1887, Jenkinson joined the Board of the Manchester Ship Canal Company and became

police intelligence in Ireland, see Richard Hawkins, 'Government versus secret societies: the Parnell era', in T. Desmond Williams (ed.), *Secret Societies in Ireland* (Dublin, 1973), pp. 100–112; Stephen Ball (ed.), *A Policeman's Ireland: recollections of Samuel Waters, RIC* (Cork, 1999) and 'Policing the Land War: official responses to political protest and agrarian crime in Ireland, 1879–91' (unpublished PhD thesis, University of London, 2000), pp. 287–312.

[40] John Vincent, 'Gladstone and Ireland', *Proceedings of the British Academy*, 63 (Oxford, 1977), p. 206; Spencer to Jenkinson, 1 July 1885: AP, Add MS 77036.

[41] 'Our secret police', *PMG*, 8 January 1887, p. 8.

[42] William Harcourt to Spencer, 4, 6, and 8 March 1884; Spencer to Harcourt, 5, 6, and 7 March 1884: AP, Add MS 76933; *The Times*, 22 May 1884, p. 11. Jenkinson received a total annual payment of £3,000 for his duties as Assistant Under-Secretary in Dublin and 'Government Agent' in London: Godfrey Lushington to Childers, 23 February 1886: TNA, HO 144/721/110757.

[43] Horace Seymour to Spencer, 19 December 1883; Spencer to Gladstone, 27 December 1883; Gladstone to Spencer, 30 December 1883: AP, Add MS 76858; *Belfast Newsletter*, 16 January 1884, p. 7; *The Times*, 4 June 1888, p. 6.

Chairman of its Finance Committee in 1894.[44] During this time he was plagued by controversies arising from his secret service work. In November 1887, the Birmingham Watch Committee investigated charges that he had manufactured evidence against John Daly in 1884.[45] It was also alleged that he had employed *agents provocateurs* in the 'Jubilee Plot' of 1886 and is thought to have been active in collecting evidence in favour of Parnell during the Special Commission investigations of 1888–1890.[46] In the midst of rumours that he was to return to head the secret service, Jenkinson briefly pursued a political career but failed to secure the parliamentary seat of East Grinstead at the general election of 1892.[47] The following year, he was examined as a witness in a court case involving an alleged filibuster plot to annex territory in Baja California during his time as the Chairman of the Mexican Land and Colonization Company.[48] Exonerated of any involvement in the plot, he went on to have a long and successful career as a company director and trustee and ended his career as Chairman of the Daimler Motor Company in April 1906.[49] A veteran swordsman, he was President of the Epee Club of London from 1900 and died on 1 March 1919.[50]

### John Poyntz Spencer, fifth Earl Spencer (1835–1910)

While Earl Spencer served twice as Viceroy of Ireland (1868–1874, 1882–1885) and sat in four Liberal Cabinets as Lord President

[44] *The Times*, 19 November 1887, p. 11; 16 April 1894, p. 4.

[45] See **Document 2**; Harcourt to Spencer, 3 November 1887: AP, Add MS 76934.

[46] William O'Shea to Joseph Chamberlain, 28 December 1888: JC8/8/1/117; Chamberlain to O'Shea, 31 December 1888: NLI, MS 5752, fos 376–379; Harcourt to Spencer, 10 October 1890: AP, Add MS 76935; Bernard Porter, *The Origins of the Vigilant State: the London Metropolitan Police Special Branch before the First World War* (London, 1987), pp. 73–75, 191. For a colourful account of Jenkinson's role in these episodes and other aspects of his career in the secret service, see Christy Campbell, *Fenian Fire: the British Government plot to assassinate Queen Victoria* (London, 2002).

[47] *Glasgow Herald*, 2 December 1893, p. 5; *The Times*, 11 July 1892, p. 6. He did, however, remain an active Gladstonian and a member of the National Liberal Federation: see *The Times*, 21 February 1893, p. 5; *Liverpool Mercury*, 11 March 1893, p. 5.

[48] *The Times*, 16 January 1894, p. 10; Donald Chaput, 'The British are coming! or, the army of India and the founding of Ensenada', *Journal of San Diego History*, 33, no. 4 (Fall 1987), pp. 151–164.

[49] Other companies included Manchester Liners Ltd, North Worcestershire Breweries Ltd, and the Railway Rolling Stock Trust Ltd: *The Times*, 16 April 1894, 16 May 1896, 19 August 1897, 24 April 1898, 3 September 1900, 29 November 1901, 3 February 1902. On his retirement, Jenkinson was presented with a portrait painted by Sir Hubert von Herkomer: *The Times*, 9 November 1906, p. 14.

[50] 'Epee-De-Combat', in *Encyclopedia Britannica* (11th edition, London, 1911); *The Times*, 4 March 1919, p. 12.

(1880–1882, 1886), Viceroy (1882–1885), and First Lord of the Admiralty (1892–1894, 1894–1895), a full biography has not yet been written of this important politician and administrator. Readers are therefore directed to an extensive survey of his career and correspondence in Peter Gordon (ed.), *The Red Earl: the papers of the fifth Earl Spencer 1835–1910*, 2 vols (Northamptonshire Record Society, 1981 and 1986) and Gordon's article in H.G.C. Matthew and Brian Harrison (eds.), *Oxford Dictionary of National Biography* (Oxford, 2004), LI, pp. 871–877.

# INDEX

This index covers people, places, topics, and events. Numbers in **bold** indicate authors and addressees of letters, reports, and memoranda. Numbers in *italics* point to footnotes giving significant (generally biographical) information. Peers are indexed under their title, not their family name, except where the title was conferred after the period covered by the documents in this volume (1884–1887). Women are indexed under the surname that they held at their first appearance in this collection.